Visual Basic

Easy Windows™ Programming

Visual Basic

Easy Windows™ Programming

Namir C. Shammas

Windcrest®/McGraw-Hill

FIRST EDITION
FIRST PRINTING

© 1992 by **Namir C. Shammas**.
Published by Windcrest Books, an imprint of TAB Books.
TAB Books is a division of McGraw-Hill, Inc.
The name "Windcrest" is a registered trademark of TAB Books.

Library of Congress Cataloging-in-Publication Data

Shammas, Namir Clement, 1954-
    Visual Basic : easy Windows programming / by Namir C. Shammas.
        p. cm.
    ISBN 0-8306-3733-8 (p)
    1. Windows (Computer programs)   2. Microsoft Visual BASIC.
    I. Title.
    QA76.76.W56S47   1991
    005.4′3—dc20   91-5123
                                                                CIP

TAB Books offers software for sale. For information and a catalog, please contact
TAB Software Department, Blue Ridge Summit, PA 17294-0850.

Acquisitions Editor: Brad J. Schepp
Book Editor: Mark Vanderslice
Book Design: Jaclyn J. Boone
Managing Editor: Sandra L. Johnson   WT1

To Bobbi and Joseph

Contents

Acknowledgments

This book is the fruit of the support and encouragement from a lot of people. I would like to thank Brad Schepp of TAB Books for his backing, encouragement, and shared vision for the project. I am also grateful to Christy Gersich at Microsoft for using the "Einstein Express" to send me things when I wanted them "yesterday." I also would like to thank Matt Wagner at Waterside Productions, my literary agent, for his support to make this project come to light. I would like to acknowledge managing editor Sandra Johnson and book editor Mark Vanderslice for their efforts in shaping up the book. Finally, I would like to thank the Visual Basic team at Microsoft for making this product *the easiest* tool to program for Windows.

Introduction

Visual Basic is considered a product that has made a significant break-through in programming for Windows. The extremely difficult task of programming in Windows has been simplified by Visual Basic to enable the masses of programmers to quickly write and prototype Windows applications. This book introduces you to programming for Windows using Visual Basic. Because Visual Basic builds on the DOS-based Quick Basic, I assume that you are familiar with Quick Basic, or at least either BASICA or GW-BASIC. Appendix A contains a quick reference for Visual Basic. You should also be familiar with the Windows operating environment.

The book contains 19 chapters that present various topics of programming Visual Basic. The chapters can be divided into three logical groups: introductory, intermediate, and advanced.

CHAPTER 1 offers a technical introduction to the basic notions and concepts behind programming Visual Basic.

CHAPTER 2 explains how to use the built-in help system. This system uses hypertext technology and offers you a lot of information without resorting to the Visual Basic manuals.

CHAPTER 3 summarizes the three basic stages involved in building a

Visual Basic application. The chapter offers three programs that give you a basic idea on how to program Visual Basic applications.

CHAPTERS 4, 5, and 6 detail the steps involved in writing a Visual Basic application. These chapters also introduce you to special program documentation that I use throughout the book.

CHAPTER 7 focuses on the text box object. This is a versatile control that allows you to input and view text. The chapter also discusses how to use the text box control to emulate scrollable screens.

CHAPTER 8 discusses the creation and use of Visual Basic menus. Visual Basic offers a very easy way to design menus, including nested menu options.

CHAPTER 9 deals with multi-form applications. Using multiple forms allows you to extend the interface of your applications by offering special dialog boxes and visual forms.

CHAPTER 10 discusses various ways to obtain input from the user. These include dialog boxes, check boxes, option buttons, and scroll bars.

CHAPTER 11 presents the various ways that a Visual Basic program can provide unformatted and formatted output, and discusses how you can use a visual form to emulate a screen.

CHAPTER 12 focuses on Visual Basic graphics. The chapter discusses topics like user-defined graphics scales and the basic Visual Basic graphics statements. The chapter presents the SHAPES program, which illustrates a nontrivial graphics program that exercises the various aspects of basic graphics drawing.

CHAPTER 13 discusses using the mouse more effectively in Visual Basic applications. Two graphics programs illustrate the various mouse manipulation features offered by Visual Basic.

CHAPTER 14 looks at writing Visual Basic programs that are interactive. This includes using the Windows clipboard, using timer controls, and detecting any key on your keyboard, including function keys and cursor control keys.

CHAPTER 15 focuses on error handling in Visual Basic programs. The chapter presents the built-in error-handling mechanism and discusses the various types of error-handling schemes.

CHAPTER 16 presents the visual controls that make up the Visual Basic file system. These controls allow you to select the current drive, current directory, and a file. The chapter offers a simple text editor to demonstrate the controls of the file system.

CHAPTER 17 discusses using files for input and output, including sequential files, random-access files, and binary files. The chapter also presents program examples that can serve as utilities.

CHAPTER 18 deals with offering context-sensitive on-line help in your Visual Basic applications. The chapter presents an example help form that you can easily use in your own applications.

CHAPTER 19 focuses on extending Visual Basic by using the *Dynamic Link Libraries* (DLL). Such libraries are widely used by Windows and its applications. The chapter also discusses how to tap into the low-level Windows DLL. A section is dedicated to showing you how to translate calls in the C language to Visual Basic DLL declarations.

APPENDIX A provides a quick reference for the Visual Basic language. APPENDIX B briefly discusses installing the accompanying disk.

This book shows you how to write nontrivial programs, such as text file viewers, text file editors, and graphics drawing utilities. Such programs enable you to see how the various controls in Visual Basic work together. I have used icons to highlight various important points.

☠ This icon shows where to find warnings.

☞ These icons point out things you should know

✎ These icons precede programming notes or tips.

✳ The text following the asterisk tells you something specific to Visual Basic.

1

In the beginning

Microsoft Windows is a user interface that is more sophisticated and easier to use than DOS. The price to pay for the sophistication of Windows is that it is much more complex to program. Many programming language vendors are rolling out Windows versions of their popular compilers and interpreters. Programmers used to the DOS versions of these language implementations are finding out that there is a significant learning curve to program for Windows. Visual Basic is a Windows adaptation of the popular Microsoft Quick Basic compiler. In this book, I assume that you are familiar with using Windows (opening, closing, moving, and resizing windows, to name a few basic operations) and at least acquainted with programming in Quick Basic (appendix A contains a quick language reference for Visual Basic). Visual Basic empowers you to develop Windows applications more easily and quickly than with other languages. In this chapter, I discuss the basic notions and components of programming Visual Basic.

Windows and OOP

The computer and software industry goes through cycles of promoting new technology. This is usually accompanied by some media hype and the advent of a new set of buzzwords (just what we all need!). The year 1986 witnessed the boom of *artificial intelligence* (AI). This was short-lived, because the hype over AI promised much more than the state of the art could actually deliver. A few years ago, the software industry promoted *object-oriented programming* (OOP)—again with a new set of buzzwords. Unlike AI, object-oriented programming had a more defined set of objectives and did not promise the moon. Object-oriented programming was billed as superior to structured programming in reusing code and providing more sound program development. This claim was substantiated again with the advent of Microsoft Windows. Using a non-OOP popular language like C did not make programming Windows applications any easier. It took multiple pages of C code just to show a simple window with a "Hello World!" message. The advocates of OOP (such as the Whitewater Group, which developed the OOP Actor language) kept reminding Window programmers (and those who aspired to be) that OOP languages can give the almighty C a run for its money; they were not exaggerating. Software developers started paying more attention to a new successor of C, C++, which offers object-oriented programming features.

The year 1989 saw the advent of OOP language extensions to DOS-based compilers. It was only a matter of time before various languages (such as C++, Pascal, and Modula-2), armed with OOP features, were rolled out for programming Windows applications. So as not to leave BASIC out of the family of Windows-oriented languages, Microsoft offered Visual Basic. While Visual Basic lacks formal OOP language extensions, it does implement a number of essential OOP elements.

Object-oriented programming basics

Object-oriented programming views the world around as one of objects. Each object has a number of characteristics or attributes and a specified set of functionalities. For example, my CASIO Data Bank watch is an object. It is composed of an LCD display, a miniature keyboard, control buttons, a casing, and the internal electronics. The functionality of the watch includes displaying the date and time, telephone numbers, short memos, schedules, a calculator, and an alarm.

The concept of objects can be easily applied to the various visible components of any Windows application, including Visual Basic. For example, each button in a dialog box is an object, with its display characteristics and underlying functionality.

The example of my watch also serves to illustrate another important programming concept used by Visual Basic (and other Windows languages), namely, event-driven programming. Let me explain event-driven programming using my watch. Normally, the watch performs its main function — displaying the current date and time. However, I can press a side button to search for a phone number. Pressing the button sends an electrical signal to the internal logic circuits. The signal is handled by a hardcoded procedure that displays the main menu for selecting phones, memos, and schedules. Thus, event-driven programming involves generating events and handling them. This differs significantly from the linear programming method used in Quick Basic. Visual Basic implements event-handling through a family of procedures, which you write. These procedures are on standby, ready to deal with a specified set of events. Combining the concepts of objects and event-handling makes it even easier to design Visual Basic programs; the visual objects handle the events generated, for example, by clicking on a mouse button or pressing a key. I discuss this topic in more detail later in this chapter.

The Visual Basic features

Visual Basic is designed to work in the versatile Windows graphic interface. With Visual Basic, you can create single and multiple windows, each with visual control objects. These objects include command buttons, option buttons, check boxes, list boxes, combo boxes, text boxes, scroll bars, frames, menu bars, file selection boxes, directory selection boxes, and drive selection boxes. This impressive list of control objects clearly indicates that Visual Basic is by no means a "toy" Windows application. In fact, Visual Basic offers the following features:

- Run-time response to the mouse of the keyboard.
- Showing and hiding control objects during program execution.
- The ability to access the clipboard and the printer directly. Accessing the clipboard enables your Visual Basic applications to transfer data to and from other Windows applications.
- Exchanging data with other Windows applications using the *Dynamic Data Exchange* (DDE).
- Interacting with other Windows applications calling the Dynamic Link Libraries (DLL).
- Making direct system calls to the Windows functions.
- The ability to debug your programs during the development phase.
- The ability to test part of your code in an immediate-mode window.
- A library of clip art and icons, which allows you to enhance the appearance of your Visual Basic applications.

The Visual Basic control panel

Visual Basic offers an interface, shown in FIG. 1-1, that is very different from that of Quick Basic. As the figure shows, the Visual Basic interface is made up of multiple window components, or tools. These windows can be moved around, resized, closed, and opened. The windows are described in the next few paragraphs.

The Properties bar   This is the top window in FIG. 1-1. The Properties bar serves two purposes. First, it contains the pull-down menu options (namely, File, Edit, Code, Run, Window, and Help) that enable you to manage the design your Visual Basic application, manage the Visual Basic interface windows, and obtain on-line help. Second, manages the properties of the control objects (the command button, option button, etc.). This is accomplished using the two combo boxes that are located below the pull-down options. The left and narrower combo box contains a

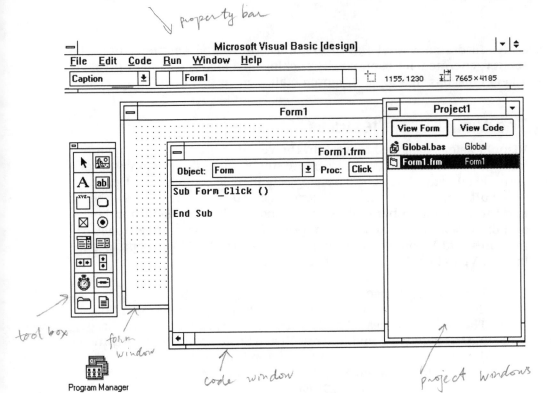

property bar

Microsoft Visual Basic [design]

File Edit Code Run Window Help

Caption   Form1   1155, 1230   7665×4185

Form1   Project1

View Form   View Code

Global.bas   Global
Form1.frm   Form1

Object: Form   Proc: Click

Sub Form_Click ()

End Sub

tool box

form window

Program Manager

code window

project windows

1-1 The Visual Basic interface.

list of the properties of the currently edited control object. The right and wider combo box contains the current setting of the property shown by the left window. The first example, located in chapter 3, should further clarify the role of these combo boxes.

The Project window   This is the window with the title Project1, located on the right side in FIG. 1-1. This window lists all of the files that are part of a single Visual Basic programming project.

The Form window   This is the window with the title Form1, located immediately below the Properties bar in FIG. 1-1. The Form window is the object that contains the control objects. When a Visual Basic application is executed, the form window and its control objects are at center stage. A Visual Basic project must have at least one form.

The Toolbox   This is the tall and narrow window located at the left of FIG. 1-1. The Toolbox contains two columns of tool icons. These icons (except the arrow icons) represent control objects that are inserted in the form object.

The Code window   This is the window with the title Form1.frm that is overlaying the Form window in FIG. 1-1. This window allows you to write and edit the code associated with the various control objects (more about this in the next section).

Not shown in FIG. 1-1 is the *Palette* window. As the name suggests, the Palette window enables you to select the colors for your Visual Basic applications.

Event-driven programming in Visual Basic

Earlier, I used the example of my watch to introduce you to the basic notion of event-driven programming. To explain more fully the dynamics of event-driven programming in Visual Basic, consider a typical company and its employees. Each employee has a title and a job description that defines his or her skills, responsibilities, and role in the company's daily activities. The company interacts with the outside world though a series of events such as phone calls, mail, telexes, faxes, electronic bulletin boards, travels, and meetings. Each event is handled by the appropriate employee(s). For example, the incoming company mail is sorted and distributed by people in the company mailroom. This is not the job of the receptionist or the accountant.

Just like the company's events, Visual Basic responds to the mouse and keyboard events by invoking the appropriate procedures. If none are found, the event is abandoned and ignored. The pseudo-code that describes event-driven programming is typified by the following Do-Loop and Select-Case statements:

```
initialize_application
exit_flag = False
Do
   GetNextEvent(NewEvent)
   Select Case NewEvent
      Case event1
         handle_event1
      Case event2
         handle_event2
      Case event3
         handle_event3
      Case end_application
         handle_exit
         exit_flag = True
      Case Else
         ignore_event
   End Select
Loop Until exit_flag = True
```

This pseudo-code shows that an event-driven application uses a loop to obtain the next event. Once the event is obtained, the Select-Case statement is used to handle the event or ignore it (in the Case Else clause). As this pseudo-code shows, there is usually a Case clause reserved for exiting the Do-Loop and ending the application.

The designers of Visual Basic defined a set of events for the form object and for each control object. An object's response to an event is provided by a specific procedure. Visual Basic derives the name of the procedure from the names of the object and the event handled. The following general syntax is used:

Sub objectName_eventName (<optional list of parameters>)

Thus, the operation of a form or a control object is defined by the associated event-handling procedures.

To give you a general idea about the life cycle of an event in Visual Basic, consider the event generated by clicking on a command button:

1. The event is generated by clicking on a command button, titled Command1.
2. The button (a control object) recognizes the action as an event that must be handled.
3. Visual Basic looks for a procedure that matches the event and the object responding to it. The logic of a Select-Case is used as shown in the pseudo-code here:

```
Select Case NewEvent
    ' click mouse button the Command1 button
    Case Click
        Command1_Click( )
    ' use tab key to select Command1 button
    Case GotFocus
        Command1_GotFocus( )
    ' press any key while Command1 button is selected
    Case KeyPress
        Command1_KeyPress( )
    Case Else
        'ignore
End Select
```

Because the event is a mouse click, the event name is Click. Combining the event name with the button name, Command1, yields the name of the sought procedure, Command1_Click. This procedure is called to handle the click event. If the event is a key being pressed while the Command1 button was in focus (that is, selected), then the event name is KeyPress and the sought procedure is accordingly, Command1_KeyPress.

The properties of an object

I mentioned earlier that objects have characteristics and operations. The objectName_eventName procedures define the operations. What about the characteristics? The designers of Visual Basic have specified a fixed set of properties for each type of object. Thus, the form and control objects resemble user-defined (or factory-defined, if you prefer) types that specify the fields and their data types. Moreover, Visual Basic assigns default values (also called *settings* by the Visual Basic manuals) to each property. A good example is the properties of a text box. The following is a sample of four properties and their settings:

Property	Setting
CtlName	Text1
Text	"Text1"
ForColor	black
BackColor	white

The beauty of Visual Basic is that you can change most settings during the application design time or at run-time. Changing the setting during design time is a manual process that involves clicking on the Combo box in the Properties bar and typing new values. Changing the setting during run-time involves placing statements that assign new setting values and/ or modify the existing ones. When a setting is changed at run-time, Visual Basic updates the appearance of the object to reflect the new setting.

Visual Basic has a control name property, CtlName, for each control object. When a control is created, Visual Basic automatically assigns it a default control name. The default control name takes into consideration the order of creating that control. For example, the first text box has the default name Text1. The second text box has the control name of Text2, and so on. You can and should change these default control names to better reflect the functionality of the control objects. In a similar way, Visual Basic uses a default text or caption for the form object and the control objects.

Starting Visual Basic

You can start Visual Basic by clicking on the Visual Basic icon in Windows. This opens a Visual Basic window with another Visual Basic icon. Click on this icon to bring up the Visual Basic interface.

You can also start Visual Basic from the File Manager. Select the Run option from the File pull-down menu. To run Visual Basic, you need to type:

\vb\vb [/run filename] [/cmd commandLine]

The /run option enables you to start Visual Basic, load a project file, and run that project. The filename should include the full DOS directory path, if the file is not located in the current directory. The /cmd option allows you to include command line arguments. These arguments can be retrieved by the Visual Basic applications.

Also, you can start Visual Basic from DOS. To run Visual Basic you need to type the following:

win \ vb \ vb [/run filename] [/cmd commandLine]

The win command first loads Microsoft Windows. The vb command then loads Visual Basic. The /run and /cmd commands are the same ones that I explained.

To exit from Visual Basic, select the Exit option from the File pull-down menu (in the Properties bar).

2
The Visual Basic
help system

On-line help systems for programming languages have proliferated since 1989. In fact, the Microsoft Quick Basic 4.5 compiler, which offered extensive on-line help, rivaled the product's own manuals. Microsoft has set the industry standard by applying hypertext technology and data compression. With Windows 3.0, Microsoft offers and promotes a "standard" help system that is incorporated in diverse parts of Windows as well as various other Windows applications and programming languages. In this chapter, I present the on-line help system for Visual Basic and discuss the various ways you can use it. It makes sense to get acquainted early with the on-line help system, since you will likely have a lot of questions about different aspects of Visual Basic. In this chapter, you will learn about the following characteristics of the Visual Basic help system:

- It is context-sensitive.
- It uses hypertext technology.
- It supports indexed searching for keywords.
- It offers flexible navigation through the help information.

The Visual Basic help system is a potent tool at your fingertips. Do not shy away from using it. You can obtain information quickly and efficiently, since your computer will do the search for you.

Since the best way to learn about a new application is to use it, I suggest that you start Visual Basic. Experiment with the features that I will be discussing in the upcoming sections.

About hypertext

If you are familiar with hypertext technology, you may skip this section. Hypertext is a technique that links various parts of a long document using *hypertext links*. These links are special words that are part of the text, but are distinguished by having a different display attribute (usually a catchy color). Internally, these links are associated with pointers to other locations in the document. The links guide the hypertext viewer (the utility that permits you to view hypertext documents) in jumping to another part of the document associated with the hypertext link. Often, the hypertext viewer enables you to backtrack to the previous document locations — this is also the case with the Visual Basic help system.

Some hypertext viewers also use *definition links*. They resemble hypertext links, except that they cause a window to pop up and show a brief definition. The Visual Basic help system also implements this technology.

Context-sensitive help

Visual Basic offers context-sensitive help in three main areas:

- Visual Basic windows.
- Words that are elements of the Visual Basic programming language.
- Error messages generated by the Visual Basic compiler.

I'll explain the first two types of context-sensitive help in more detail. When you start Visual Basic, the interface systematically pops up a form window, labeled Form1. Press the F1 function key to invoke context-sensitive help. Figure 2-1 shows what you see on the screen. The help screen presents information about the form object, which includes a scaled-down image of a typical form window and the related explanation. The normal text is displayed in red characters, while the hypertext links and definition keywords are displayed in green. The hypertext links have a green solid underline, while the definition links have a green dotted underline. If you move the mouse to either of the links, the shape of the mouse cursor automatically changes from the pointing arrow to a hand pointing upward. Let's see how these links work.

Move the cursor to the first definition link, controls. The mouse cursor changes shape to indicate that the help system has detected a special link. Holding down the left mouse button causes a small window to pop up, displaying the definition of the word controls, as shown in FIG. 2-2. Release the mouse button and the definition window promptly disappears. Now move the mouse cursor to Project window hypertext link. This time click the left mouse button. The help system now displays help information on the project window. To go back to the previous help

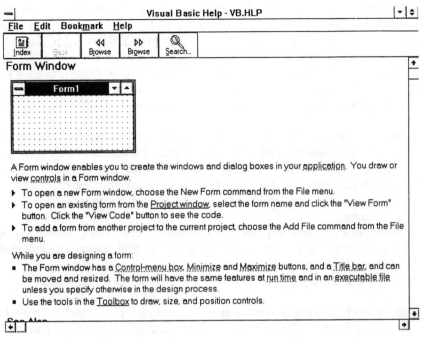

2-1 The Help system displaying information on the form window.

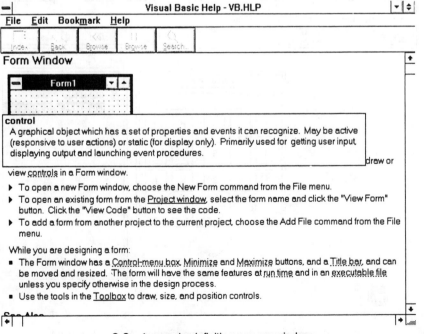

2-2 A sample definition pop-up window.

screen, click on the Back button located below the help system main menus. To end demonstrating context-sensitive help with Visual Basic windows, select the Exit option from the File menu. This brings back the Visual Basic interface.

To use context-sensitive help with a Visual Basic programming keyword, you need to load an existing program (since I have not demonstrated how to write one yet). Follow these steps:

1. Select the Open Project . . . option from the File menu. This brings up a dialog box that enables you to select a file from any directory. The dialog box has a directory list box and a matching files box.
2. Select the samples directory by clicking on the [samples] entry in the directory list. The \VB\SAMPLES path becomes the current directory.
3. Now click on the [calc] directory name to make \VB\SAMPLES\CALC the current path. The matching files box now shows one selection, the CALC.MAK project file.
4. Click on the CALC.MAK file to load the CALC project.

The project window appears on the screen. The window lists two files: Global.bas and CALC.FRM. Clicking on CALC.FRM displays the corresponding form, which looks like a simple calculator (see FIG. 2-3). Move the mouse cursor to the button labeled 8 and double click the mouse. The

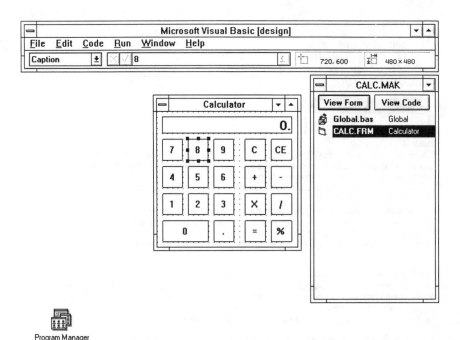

2-3 The project and form windows for the CALC.MAK project.

code attached to that button is displayed. The code shows the procedure Number_Click. Move the cursor to the If keyword on the line below the subroutine heading. To obtain help on the If keyword, press the F1 function key. The help system displays information on the If-Then-Else structure, as shown in FIG. 2-4.

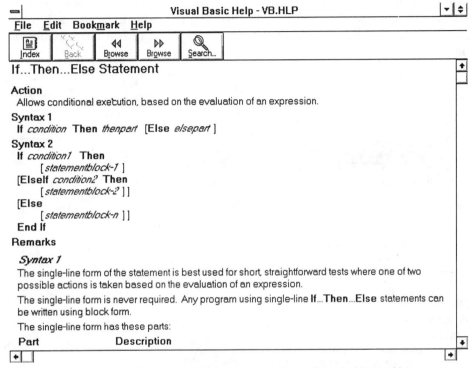

2-4 The Help system displaying information on the If-Then-Else decision-making structure.

Navigating through the help system

The help system offers flexible navigation through the help screens. This includes the use of the Back and Browse (previous and next screen) buttons. To move back to the previous screen, you can either click on the Back button or press the B key. To view the next or previous screens, there are two similar Browse buttons. The first Browse has two left arrow heads and serves to view the previous help screen. You can either click on that button or press the R key. The second Browse button has two right arrows and serves to view the next help screen. You can either click on that button or press the O key.

The Help system also offers the bookmark feature that allows you to mark a number of particular help screens. Later you can zoom in to any of the marked screens without having to repeatedly press the Back button. The help system contains the Bookmark pull-down menu options. When you select the Bookmark menu, the pull-down option shows you the Define . . . option and a list of the current bookmarks (initially the list is empty). When you choose the Define . . . option, the help system will pop up a dialog box, as shown in FIG. 2-5. This dialog box enables you to add, change, and delete bookmarks. The dialog box contains a text box, a bookmark list box, an OK button, a Cancel button, and a Delete button. When the dialog box first appears, the text box contains the text for a new bookmark, supplied by the Help system. You can edit the bookmark text. Click on the OK button to add the new bookmark to the current list of bookmarks.

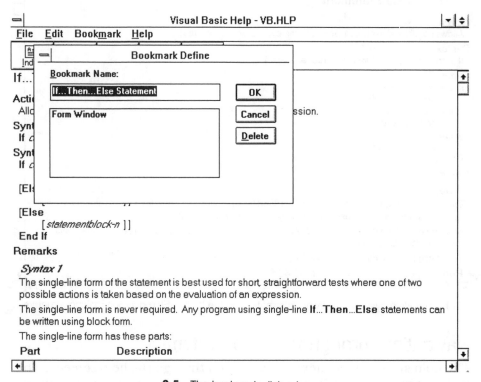

2-5 The bookmark dialog box.

To delete an entry in the bookmark list, locate the sought entry and click on it. Then click on the Delete button, or press the D key.

To edit the text of a current bookmark, locate the bookmark and double click on it. This puts a copy of the selected bookmark in the text box, where you can edit the bookmark text. Once you are finished editing, click on the OK button. Notice that the edited bookmark is added to the list of bookmarks. The original bookmark text is still in the list of bookmarks. This permits you to create alias bookmarks. If this is not what you want, delete the older version of the bookmark.

The list of bookmarks is maintained between sessions by the help system. To remove the entire list, you have to delete each of its members.

Using the index button

The Visual Basic help system has an Index button below the main menu. When you click on the Index button, or press the key I, the help system displays an index of the main help topics, as shown in FIG. 2-6. The help index entries are hypertext text links that direct you towards the subject of interest. The general topics covered are described here.

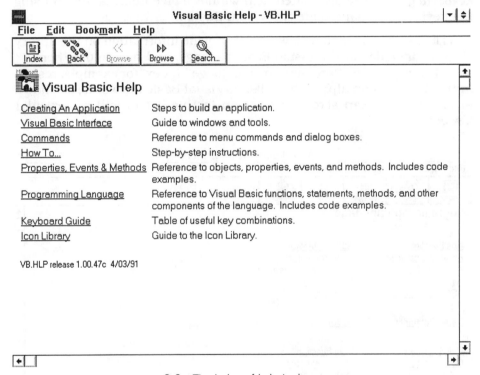

2-6 The index of help topics.

Creating an application The related help windows give information on the steps involved in creating a Visual Basic application.

Visual Basic Interface The associated help windows offer information on the various windows that make up the Visual Basic interface, such as the Project window and the Toolbox.

Commands The related help windows provide more detailed information on the main menu located in the Properties bar. This menu includes the File, Edit, Code, Run, Windows, and Help menus.

How To This hypertext link leads to a long scrollable window that lists how to perform various tasks in Visual Basic. The list of tasks is grouped by topics. Each task name is a hypertext link that leads you to other help windows, which explain how to perform that task in more detail.

Properties, Events & Methods The associated windows offer help on properties, events, and methods. These items are vital ingredients that breathe life into a Visual Basic application.

Programming language The related windows offer help on the Visual Basic keywords with example code.

Keyboard guide The associated help windows give information on using the keyboard to manipulate the Visual Basic interface.

Icon Library The related help windows provide information on the library of icons, included in the Visual Basic package, and how to use them.

Clicking on the "Programming Language" index, for example, results in the display of an alphabetized list of Visual Basic keywords, as shown in FIG. 2-7. You can scroll up or down in this list to find a particular keyword.

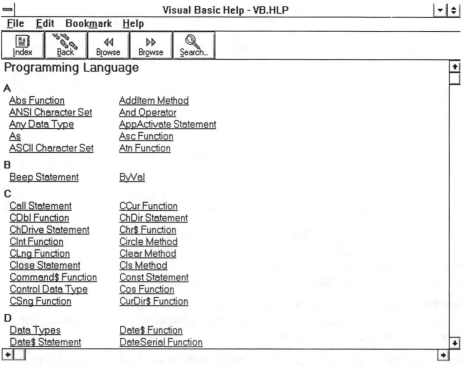

2-7 The help screen showing the leading part of the alphabetized list of Visual Basic keywords.

Using the search button

The Visual Basic help system also provides a quick way to search for a keyword or topic with the Search button, located to the right of the Browse buttons. When you click on the Search button or press the S key, the help system pops up a Search dialog box, shown in FIG. 2-8. The Search dialog box contains a current-selection text box, keywords list box, a matching topics box, a Search button, a Cancel button, and a Go To button. When the Search dialog box appears for the first time, the current-selection box contains a copy of the first entry in the keywords list box displayed as selected text (in this case, the keyword Abs). You can scroll through the keywords list box to select a new topic to search. When you find the topic you want, click on it. This puts a copy of the topic in the current-selection box. You can also directly key in the topic you want to search. In this case, the Search dialog box monitors what you type and scrolls the list accordingly to show the keyword that most closely matches what you have keyed in so far.

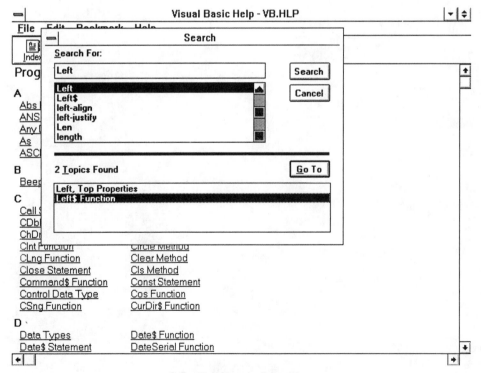

2-8 The Search dialog box.

Once you have selected a keyword, click on the Search button. The matching topics are displayed in the bottom box of the dialog box. Click on a matching topic to obtain the corresponding help windows.

Additional help

If you are somewhat overwhelmed by the help system itself, there is some good news. The help system offers information on itself. This is found in the Help menu option of the help screens. The same menu option also has an on-line tutorial option.

3
Your first applications

In this chapter we start programming in Visual Basic. I will present three simple examples to give you a general idea of the basics of application development. In this chapter you will learn about:

- The basic steps involved in creating a Visual Basic application.
- The Project window.
- The Project files.
- Working with a form and with control objects.
- Setting the properties of the control objects.
- Attaching code to control objects.
- Running and halting a Visual Basic application.
- Saving and loading Visual Basic project files.

☞ In this book, I assume that all of the Visual Basic application files are stored in the directory \VB\EASYVB. A separate directory prevents mixing the Visual Basic files of this book with other Visual Basic files that you might have already developed or obtained from a friend. Please create this directory now.

The programming examples in this chapter expose you to the three basic steps involved in crafting a Visual Basic application. The next three chapters examine in more detail each of these steps. So, buckle your seat belt and on we go!

The first Visual Basic application

The first Visual Basic application performs the following simple task: click on a button to view the current date and time. Simple, but how do we get there? The first step is to load Visual Basic, as explained in Chapter 1. When Visual Basic is loaded it systematically puts an empty form window on the screen. This form is part of a new Visual Basic application project. The form window represents a stripped-down window with minimal functionality. To build a Visual Basic application you need to perform the following basic steps:

1. Construct the interface for your application by drawing the required control objects on the form.
2. Set or fine-tune the properties of the form and controls to influence their appearance and behavior.
3. Attach Basic code to the form and/or control objects.

Visual Basic projects

The steps in building an application are performed in the framework of a project. To better understand a Visual Basic project, bring up the Project window (if it is not already displayed) by selecting the Project window option from the Window menu. The project window lists the files involved in a Visual Basic application. There are three types of such files:

Global module file Each project has exactly one global module file. The default name is GLOBAL.BAS. This is a module that declares global constants, variables, and data types (but no procedures). The declared items are accessed by other parts of the Visual Basic application. The global module can be empty.

Form files A project can have zero, one, or more of these. Form files contain the interface parts of a Visual Basic application, which include the controls drawn on each form, the event-handling procedures attached to the forms and controls, and the general definitions and procedures that are not attached to the forms or control objects. Form files typically have the .FRM extension. Typically, you need at least one form in your Visual Basic applications.

Module files These are .BAS files that contain libraries of auxiliary and supporting procedures that are called by other parts of the application (other modules of the code attached in the forms and controls). Modules are suitable for long applications. A project can have zero, one, or more module files.

The project files are stored with the .MAK extension.

Drawing controls in the form

The control objects are vital components of a Visual Basic application. The designers of Visual Basic have defined a specific set of controls. Each control has its own set of properties, default values assigned to these properties, behavior, and events that it can handle. These predefined items greatly reduce the amount of coding you need to do, and still offer flexible control over your application design.

To draw the controls on the form, you need to invoke the Toolbox window by selecting the Toolbox option in the Window menu. The Toolbox contains a set of icons, representing the various controls. This intentionally resembles the drawing tools of PaintBrush. I say intentionally, because selecting the controls is very similar to selecting the drawing tools in PaintBrush — you click on the icon of the control you need, then move the cursor (which changes from a pointing arrow to a cross hair) to the form window. Holding the mouse button down and dragging the mouse cursor draws the selected control in the form.

Now let's start drawing the controls needed by the application. First, select the Text Box tool (the second icon in the second column of the Toolbox) and draw a wide text box on the form (see FIG. 3-1). Next, select the Command Button tool (the third icon in the second column of the Toolbox) and draw a command button (see FIG. 3-1). The command button is now the currently selected control, as indicated by the black square dots that appear at the edge of the control.

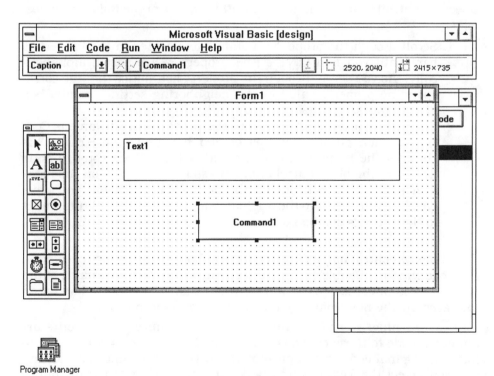

3-1 The form of the first application with the text box and the command button.

Altering the control properties

Visual Basic assigns default values to the properties of the controls you draw. While most of these default values are appropriate, at least for now, there are a few properties that should be changed. These include the control names, the command box caption, and the contents of the text box. Visual Basic assigns default control names, which include the drawing sequence. The text box is named Text1 and the command button is labeled Command1. If you add a second text box, Visual Basic assigns Text2 as the default control name of that box. Similarly, if you draw a second command button, its default caption is Command2. It is recommended that you rename the controls you draw on the form, using names that are more descriptive of what these controls do — maybe even catchy! The control names are used as a reference to their object in the event-handling code. To see a good example of the change, double click on the button. Visual Basic responds by displaying the Code window that handles mouse clicks on the command button. The Code window contains the first and last statement of the subroutine Command1_Click. The subroutine name is derived from the current control name of the button. Close the Code window.

To change the name of the command button (which is the currently selected control) from Command1 to Button, perform the following steps:

1. Scroll though the properties combo box, located in the Properties bar, until you find CtlName (the properties are sorted alphabetically). As you scroll through the property list, notice that the corresponding property value in the neighboring settings combo box also changes.
2. The setting (that is, the value of the property) of CtlName is Command1. Click on the Settings combo box and type Button. This changes the name of the command button. Once you are done keying in the new control name, press Enter or click on the Check icon next to the Settings combo box. To cancel what you have typed in and return to the original value, click on the X button next to the settings combo box.

The new control name of the command button should be reflected in the Code window. Double click on the command button. The name of the subroutine is now Button_Click, an indication that Visual Basic has taken into account the new control name of the command button.

💀 Warning! Always change the control names *before* you start attaching code to these controls. Failing to do so causes Visual Basic to hide the original code and to present you with a new empty procedure!

Now select the Text box and perform a similar operation to change the control name from Text1 to OutputLine. Since control names do not determine the appearance of the control objects, you will not see any changes in the form—the text box still contains the string Text1 and the command button is still labeled Command1. To change these settings you need to repeat the above process, this time altering other properties.

The Text box has the Text property that specifies the initial contents of the box when the Visual Basic application starts running. Select the Properties combo box and find the Text property. The corresponding Settings combo box now shows the string Text1. Click on the Settings combo box and erase the string by using the Backspace key. Notice that as you delete each character from the settings combo box, the content of the text box is immediately updated to reflect the changed setting. When you have deleted the entire string, press the Enter key.

The Command button has the Caption property, which designates the label of the button. To change the current caption from Command1 to The Time is, first select the Command button. Now the contents of the Properties and Settings combo boxes are those of the Command button. Select the Properties combo box and locate the Caption property. The corresponding setting is Command1. Select the Settings combo box and type the text The Time is. Again, notice that as you type in the new caption, the same characters appear on the command button. Press Enter when you finish keying in the new caption. Figure 3-2 shows the updated form.

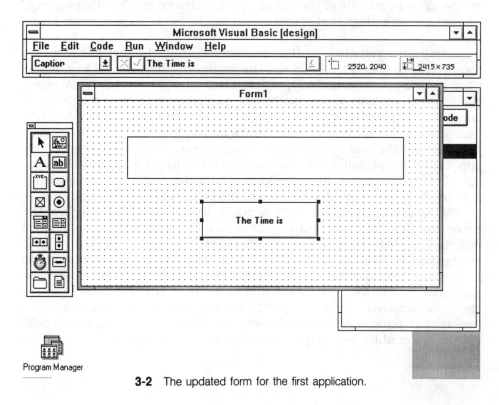

3-2 The updated form for the first application.

Attaching event-handling procedures

So far, the form provides the desired visual appearance, but is otherwise a dud! This is due to the lack of event-handling procedures that define the exact response of the controls to user-generated events. However, Visual Basic offers a predefined set of events for each class of controls. This greatly simplifies things for you, the programmer—it is a matter of selecting which control responds to which event. In the first application, we need to make the Command button respond to mouse clicks.

To attach the needed code, click twice on the The Time is command button. This brings up the Code window with the empty procedure Button-_Click(). Type the following statement inside the procedure:

```
OutputLine.Text = "Date: " + Date$ + "Time: " + Time$
```

The statement you type assigns a string expression that contains the system date and time to the Text property of the OutPutLine text box. The general syntax for assigning a new setting to a property of the form and other control objects is:

```
objectName.propertyName = newSetting
```

Likewise, the general expression objectName.propertyName can appear on the right-hand side of the equal sign to retrieve an object's property. The syntax resembles that of manipulating the fields of user-defined data types.

Every time you click on the command button, the text box displays the current date and time. To run the program, press the F5 key. If you have made a syntax error in typing the Basic statement, the Visual Basic compiler will indicate your mistake using an error window. If the program is correct, it generates a screen image that should resemble FIG. 3-3. You can click on the buttons as many times as you like. To stop the application, choose the End option in the Run menu. You can also stop the application by pressing Ctrl–Break, or by closing the application window. In the third application program of this chapter, I will demonstrate how to use a command button to quit a Visual Basic application.

When you bring up the Code window, Visual Basic first displays the procedure that handles clicking the mouse on the selected form or control object. The Code window (see FIG. 3-4) contains two important combo boxes, labeled Object and Proc. The Object combo box empowers you to inspect the code attached to the other controls in the form, or inspect the general code. The Proc combo box allows you to select the other events for the same selected control. Visual Basic displays in bold characters the events that have corresponding event-handling procedures. Using bold characters enables you to quickly find out which events are handled by an object.

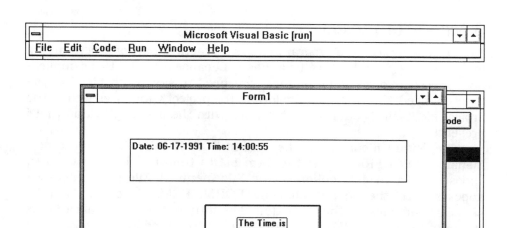

3-3 The first application run time window.

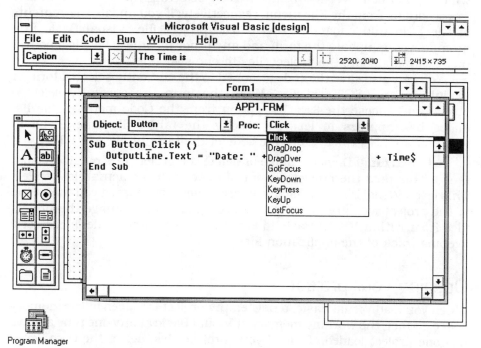

3-4 The Code Window with the Proc combo box showing the various events.

Saving your project

Saving your project and program files is a practical part of programming in any language, including Visual Basic. Because a Visual Basic application project involves multiple files, you need to save each file that you have changed. This includes the files in the project window as well as the project file itself. Look at how this work with the first application that I presented.

The default filename for the form is FORM1.FRM. To use the new filename, APP1.FRM, select the form file in the project window. Then choose the Save File As option in the File menu. A File List dialog box appears with the default filename FORM1.FRM. Type \VB\EASYVB\ APP1.FRM and click on the OK button. The form of the first application is stored in file APP1.FRM. Notice that the Project window now associates the filename APP1.FRM with the form.

The default filename for the project is PROJECT1.MAK. To use the filename APP1.MAK, select the Save Project As option from the File menu. A File List dialog box appears with the default filename PROJECT1.FRM. Type \VB\EASYVB\APP1.MAK. The new filename is the same as the new caption of the Project window, APP1.

Once you have specified new filenames for the form and the Project window, you can save future updates by selecting the Save File and Save Project options from the File menu, respectively. If you update the contents of the form and choose to update the project file, Visual Basic first prompts you to update the form and any other modules. This is a convenient way to update the project files in one swoop!

You can also save the code attached to the currently selected form or module to an ASCII text file. Make the form the currently selected object, and choose the Save Text option from the Code menu. A file list dialog box appears to let you specify the target filename. Type in \VB\EASYVB\APP1.TXT to store the code of the form in file APP1.TXT.

Warning! Do not rename or delete the project files outside Visual Basic. This puts the project file out of sync with the actual list of files. This leads Visual Basic to display an error message to warn you that some of the project files are missing. Always update and manage the project files from within Visual Basic to ensure that the project file is correctly keeping track of the application files.

Opening your project

When you load Visual Basic, a new empty project is placed in the memory space. In fact, the working memory of Visual Basic at any one time always has one project loaded. To load your project files, select the Open Project option from the File menu. A File List dialog box appears to allow you to select the project file as well as move to a new directory. To select the \VB\EASYVB directory, click on the [easyvb] entry in the directory list box. The file list box is updated to show the .MAK files in the currently selected directory. Click on the sought .MAK file to load its project files.

✍ By selecting the \VB\EASYVB directory when you load a project file, that directory becomes the current one. Thus, when you subsequently save a project, form, or module file, you need not specify the \VB\EASYVB\ path with the filename you supply.

The second application

The second Visual Basic program also deals with time. However, unlike the first application, this program implements a simple countdown timer. The application's Text box serves both the input and output. You type in the start-up number of seconds and click the command button. The application has a Text box and a command button (see FIG. 3-5) with the following altered properties:

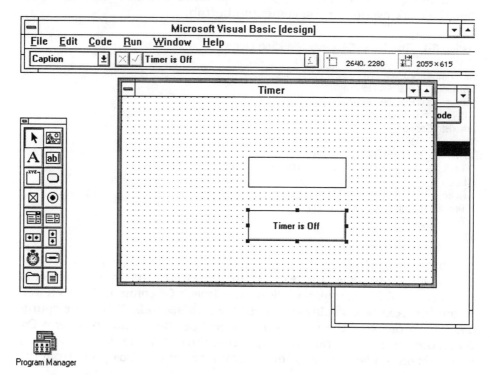

3-5 The updated form for the second Visual Basic application.

Object	Property	Custom setting form	Caption	Countdown timer
Text box	CtlName	TextLine	Text	(empty string)
Command button	CtlName	TimerBtn	Caption	Timer is Off

Draw the Text box and command button, as described earlier, and adjust the settings to the values shown.

The click event is translated into the following series of actions. First, the number of seconds is obtained from the Text box. If the numeric conversion fails (for example, the Text box is empty or contains ordinary text), the conversion yields a zero. In this case, a default of 15 seconds is assumed. Next, the caption of the command button is changed at run time from Timer is Off to Timer is On. A Do-While loop is used to monitor the elapsed time. The body of the loop is used to update the countdown that appears in the text box. When the countdown ends, the application beeps and the caption of the command button is changed back to Timer is Off. Finally, the text line is cleared.

Listing 3-1 contains the code of the procedure TimerBtn_Click that handles the click events for the command button.

Listing 3-1 The Timer_Click event-handling procedure.

```
Sub TimerBtn_Click ()
Dim Count, Total As Double
Total = Val(TextLine.Text)
    If Total = 0 Then Total = 15
TimerBtn.Caption = "Timer is On"
Count = Timer
Do While (Timer — Count) < Total
   TextLine.Text = Str$(Int(Total — (Timer — Count)))
   Loop
   Beep
   TimerBtn.Caption = "Timer is Off"
   TextLine.Text = ""
End Sub
```

Run the application by pressing the F5 function key. To use the countdown timer, select the text box and type in the maximum number of seconds — 10, for example. Click on the Timer is Off command button and watch the Text box display the countdown in seconds. While the countdown is in progress the command button has the caption of Timer is On. When the countdown ends, the caption of the command button becomes Timer is Off once again. To end the program, select the End option from the Run menu.

The second application illustrates the following: using the Text box for input and output and changing the setting of a control object at run time. The expression Val(TextLine.Text) obtains the number that you key in the text Box, the input. The assignments made to TextLine.Text update the caption of the text box to show a new output. The assignments made to TimerBtn.Caption altered the caption of the command button while the Visual Basic application is executing.

Save the form and the project in the files APP2.FRM and APP2.MAK, respectively.

The changes made to the command button can include more profound ones, such as disabling the button. When the code of LISTING 3-1 is running, the caption of the command button changes, but it might not be clear to a user whether or not the button is still active. The answer is that the button is effectively disabled while the attached code is running. To better reflect this fact, you can insert the following statement:

```
TimerBtn.Enabled = 0 ' disable Command button
```

after the statement that assigns Timer is On to the command button caption. You also need to insert the following statement after the Beep command:

```
TimerBtn.Enabled = −1 ' enable Command button
```

Now run the application by pressing the F5 function key. Click on the command button. What do you see when you run the program in Listing 3-2? The button not only changed the caption, but also the appearance of the caption text has changed. It is now a shaded text, indicating that the button is disabled. When the execution of the attached code ends, the button is enabled once more. This is reflected by the change in the appearance of the caption. To end the program, select the End option from the Run menu.

Listing 3-2   The modified TimerBtn__Click event-handling procedure.

```
Sub TimerBtn__Click ()
Dim Count, Total As Double
Total = Val(TextLine.Text)
If Total = 0 Then Total = 15
TimerBtn.Caption = "Timer is On"
TimerBtn.Enabled = 0 ' disable Command button
Count = Timer
Do While (Timer − Count) < Total
   TextLine.Text = Str$(Int(Total − (Timer − Count)))
   Loop
   Beep
   TimerBtn.Enabled = −1 ' enable Command button
   TimerBtn.Caption = "Timer is Off"
   TextLine.Text = ""
End Sub
```

The third application

The third application is a simple window with a text box and three command buttons. One command button toggles the character case of the string in the Text box. Another command button reverses the characters of the string in the Text box. The third button ends the program execution. The following table lists the control objects and indicates the program's custom settings:

Object	Property	Custom setting form	Caption	Text manipulation
Text box	CtlName	TextLine	Text	(empty string)
Command button 1	CtlName	ToggleBtn	Caption	Toggle case
Command button 2	CtlName	ReverseBtn	Caption	Reverse string
Command button 3	CtlName	QuitBtn	Caption	Quit

Figure 3-6 shows the application form with its control objects, after customization.

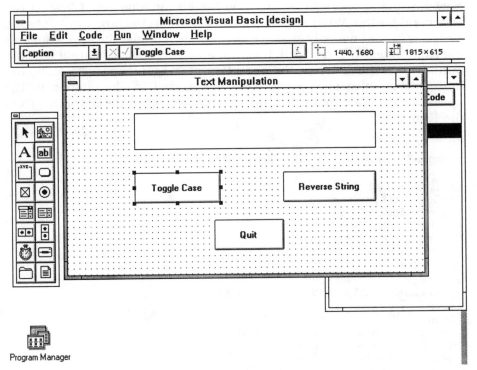

3-6 The updated form of the third Visual Basic application.

The text manipulation program works by having various command buttons perform tasks.

The ToggleBtn command button   The procedure attached to this button toggles the character case of the string in the Text box. If the Text box is empty, the procedure simply assigns Hello World!. If the Text box is not empty, the procedure performs these steps:

1. If the uppercase flag is 0, then
   Assign 1 to the uppercase flag
   Convert the characters of the Text box into uppercase
2. Else
   Assign 0 to the uppercase flag
   Convert the characters of the Text box into lowercase

The ReverseBtn command button   The procedure attached to this button reverses the characters of the Text box. If the Text box is empty, the procedure simply assigns the string Hello World!. Otherwise, it performs the following steps:

1. Assigns the length of the text box string to the local variable L.
2. Assigns a null string to the local variable S.
3. Uses a For-Next loop to copy the characters of the Text box to string S, in reverse.
4. Assigns the string S to the Text box.

The QuitBtn command button   The code attached to this button simply ends the program execution with an End statement.

Listing 3-3 contains the code for the three procedures. Notice that the ToggleBtn_Click() procedure declares the local static variable Is_UCase. When the application starts to execute, this variable is assigned a 0. Consequently, the first time you press the Toggle command button (and the Text box is not empty), the string in the Text box is converted into uppercase. The second time you click on the Toggle button, the text is converted into lowercase, and so on.

Listing 3-3   The code attached to the various controls of the text-manipulating program.

```
Sub ToggleButton_Click ()
Static Is_UCase As Integer
If TextBox.Text = "" Then
   TextBox.Text = "Hello World!"
   Else
   If Is_UCase = 0 Then
      Is_UCase = −1
      TextBox.Text = UCase$(TextBox.Text)
   Else
```

Listing 3-3 Continued.

```
      Is_UCase = 0
      TextBox.Text = LCase$(TextBox.Text)
      End If
   End If
End Sub

Sub ReverseButton_Click ()
Dim S As String
Dim I, L As Integer
If TextBox.Text = "" Then
   TextBox.Text = "Hello World!"
   Else
   L = Len(TextBox.Text)
   S = ""
   For I = 1 To L
      S = S + Mid$(TextBox.Text, L + 1 - I, 1)
   Next I
   TextBox.Text = S
   End If
End Sub

Sub QuitButton_Click ()
End
End Sub
```

Save the form and the project in files APP3.FRM and APP3.MAK, respectively. Run the program by pressing the F5 function key. You can simply click on the Toggle and Reverse command buttons and watch the manipulation of the string Hello World!. Click on the Quit button whenever you wish to end the program execution. This takes you back to the windows that were visible just before you started running the program.

4
Drawing the application form

This chapter focuses on the first step in developing a Visual Basic application — the design of the visual interface. In the last chapter I presented an overview of this step while developing the first application. This chapter digs a bit deeper into the topic.

The design of the visual interface for your Visual Basic application involves drawing the various control objects in the application's form(s). As with coding Quick Basic programs, you should not rush into pasting various controls on the form. Instead, apply the general disciplines of good programming and plan ahead using the following steps:

1. Define the basic operation of your application. What is the main purpose of your program?
2. Define the secondary operations of your application. What additional features you want to implement?
3. Specify how you want your application to interact with the user.
4. Based on the previous steps, draw a rough version of the interface on a piece of paper (or use the PaintBrush application that is included in the Windows 3.0 package). Using the storyboard concept, go over what happens when you interact with the interface that you have just sketched. Change the sketched interface as needed. You may include "bells and whistles" that make your Visual Basic program stand apart from others. Repeat this step as many times as needed to fully envision your application at work.
5. Using the final version of your sketched interface, start Visual Basic and begin to draw the controls on the form. I recommend that you apply the storyboard concept one more time as you view the actual controls in the form. This enables you to make any final changes.

These steps indicate that care should be applied when designing the form of an application. It is easier to redesign on a piece of paper (or using the PaintBrush program) than on the Visual Basic interface, especially if you have a complex application interface. In addition, the nature of Visual Basic applications promotes the use of the storyboard concept to visualize the animated application.

This rough-design process may seem trivial, and so much like common sense advice as not to require mention. However, the easy visual programming style of Visual Basic will likely lure you into jumping ahead and drawing controls—after all, drawing these controls is a fun process, especially when you are new to it.

✍ Programming Tip: Plan the interface of your Visual Basic application before you start to program.

The ToolBox

To make the process of creating the interface of a Visual Basic application a bit clearer, I now introduce you to the set of control objects available through the Toolbox. The Toolbox contains the icons for the various controls, as shown in FIG. 4-1. A brief description of each control is presented in the next several paragraphs.

The Picture box   This control displays graphic images from a bitmap, icon, or other special files. The size of the Picture box determines how much of the graphic image you see. By setting the AutoSize property to True, you are able to resize the image to fit inside the box.

The Text box   This control is used to display text and accept input from the user. The text box can display text in multiple lines when the MultiLine property is set to True. The ScrollBars properties enable you to add vertical and/or horizontal scroll bars to the text box, enabling you to view text from an ASCII file.

The Command button   This button is also known as the *Push button*, and is the control that you click on or push to carry out a task. This is normally done by selecting the button, then pressing Enter.

The Option button   Also called the *Radio button*, this is an on/off button. Normally, you have a group of option buttons that provide you with a set of alternate choices, so that only one choice is made at any time (you could say that each option is antagonistic to all other options). When you turn on an option button, all of the other option buttons in the same group are turned off. This single selection resembles the button of a radio (whence the name Radio button) that allows you to select only one station at a time.

The List box   This is a control that shows a list of items from which you may select one. Items can be added or removed from the list at run time. If the size of the list box is insufficient to display all of the items in the list, a scroll bar is automatically added.

The Vertical scroll bar   This control enables you to quickly scroll through a long list of data. The vertical scroll bar can be used alone or in conjunction with a list box. When used alone, the scroll bar serves to select a numeric value for a setting (such as mouse sensitivity, keyboard speed, or graph scale).

The Drive list box   This list box allows you to display the drives that are on-line and to select a current disk drive. This information is useful in determining the physical, RAM-based, and logical drives that are currently on-line in your system.

The File list box   Using this control, you can locate, display, and select files in the current directory. The File list box also allows you to open files for reading, writing, and random-access I/O. You can select a subset of file-names that appear in the list by specifying file attributes, such as wild-card filenames.

The Label control   This displays fixed text on the form. I use the term "fixed" to stress that you cannot change the text of a label as easily as that of a text box. The label can be altered at run time from within a procedure.

The Frame control   The Frame control serves to group a family of related controls (such as the option buttons or the check boxes). The grouping of controls occurs in two ways—logically and visually. The logical aspect relates to the operation of the code. The visual aspect helps the end-user by giving the form more visual organization, clarity, and ease of use.

The Check box   The operation of this control is similar to the option button. However, unlike the alternate choices offered by a group of option buttons, check boxes allow you to select multiple options. For example, check boxes can be used in searching for text. The typical check box options are search forward, case-sensitive, and whole word. You may select any or all of these options. The combination of your choices defines the behavior of the related task.

The Combo box   This control blends or combines (whence the nickname Combo) the characteristics of a text box and a list box. A combo box allows you to make a selection either by typing it or by choosing an item from the accompanying list box.

The Horizontal scroll bar   This is similar to the vertical scroll bar; the difference between the two is their visual orientation.

The Timer   This control is a special one which runs code at preset regular time intervals. Timer controls are visible at design time, but not at run time.

The Directory list box This list box displays the directory tree hierarchy and allows you to select a new directory at run time.

The Drive, Directory, and File list boxes work together in viewing and accessing files anywhere in your system. Each of these list boxes contributes part of the search path of the sought files.

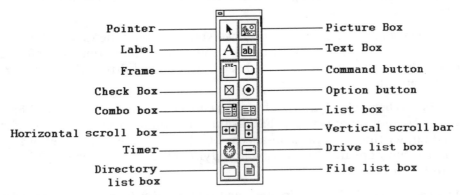

Pointer —————— Picture Box
Label —————— Text Box
Frame —————— Command button
Check Box —————— Option button
Combo box —————— List box
Horizontal scroll box —————— Vertical scroll bar
Timer —————— Drive list box
Directory list box —————— File list box

4-1 The Toolbox.

Figure 4-2 shows a form with each of the above controls (with default settings). The order of the controls in the form is roughly the same order as that of the control icons in the Toolbox.

✍ Programming Note: Each control has a predefined set of properties, events it can handle, and methods. The properties fine-tune the visual appearance and behavior of the control object. The predefined events determine the type of response that can be obtained from the control. The preset methods are special preprogrammed procedures that are used to manipulate the control at run time. The *Microsoft Visual Basic Language Reference* describes in detail the properties, events, and methods for the various controls.

The command-oriented scientific calculator

Let's look at drawing the interface of a new Visual Basic application. Following the steps that I described earlier, I begin by defining the various levels of functionality for the new Command-Oriented Scientific Calculator (COSC). The application's basic operation, or purpose, is mainly a command-oriented scientific calculator. I use the term "command-oriented" to indicate that the interface uses a few text boxes to hold the operands, the operator or math function, and the result. The advantage of this kind of calculator is that you can add more functions and operators without changing the interface.

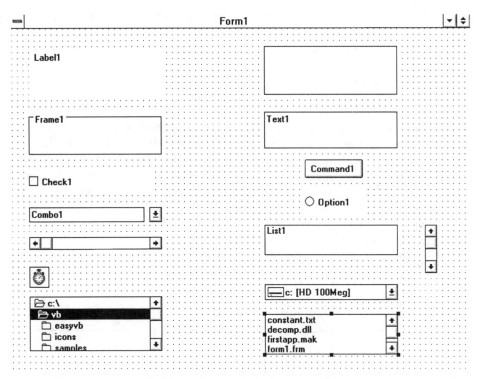

4-2 The various controls drawn on a form.

The secondary level operations include the following features:

- The calculator displays error messages due to division-by-zero errors or because the first operand is not a valid argument for the specified math function.
- The result can be stored in a single-letter variable. The supported variables are A to Z. The variable names are not case-sensitive.
- The operands may be either a numeric constant or a variable.

The third step in creating the interface involves specifying how the application interacts with the user:

- The user keys in the operands and operator (or math function) in their respective Text boxes.
- The specified operation or math function is executed by pressing an Execute command button.
- The result of a valid math operation or function evaluation is placed in the Result text box.

- The name of a variable used to store the current result is typed in a special text box.
- A Store command button allows the user to store the result in the specified variable.
- All error messages are displayed in a dedicated text box.
- A Quit command button enables the user to exit the application.

The fourth step involves sketching the interface of the application. Figure 4-3 shows such a sketch, drawn using PaintBrush. The sketch includes comments that I have enclosed in square brackets. I have also marked some of the labels with the asterisk symbol to indicate that they respond to a click. This is an example of adding "bells and whistles" to the application. To substitute the name of a variable in either the operand or operator box with the value stored in that variable, the user will click on the corresponding label. To clear the contents of the error message box, the user will click on the associated label.

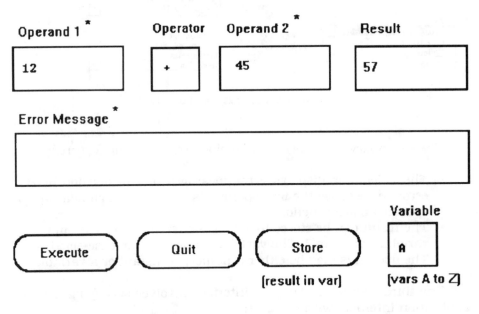

[* label responds to clicks]

4-3 The PaintBrush sketch for the command-oriented scientific calculator.

Drawing the controls

Armed with a stable design of the interface, let's start creating the Visual Basic form for the COSC application. I will carry out the form design process in two phases. In the first phase, presented in this chapter, I will draw the required controls. In the second phase, presented in the next chapter, I will fine-tune the settings of the various controls. The aim of the first phase is to create a form with controls that resemble FIG. 4-4.

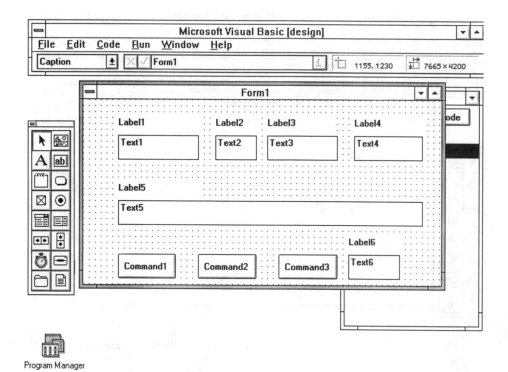

Program Manager

4-4 The form of the command-oriented scientific calculator (COSC) application, showing the default settings.

Drawing a control

There are two methods of drawing a control: the normal method and the shortcut method. To draw the first text box using the normal method, apply these steps:

1. Choose the Toolbox option from the Window menu, if the Toolbox is not already displayed.
2. Click on the desired icon tool (the Text Box icon, in this case).
3. The mouse cursor changes shape and becomes cross hair. Move the cross hair to the form area. To revert to the arrow cursor, without drawing any control, click the Arrow icon.
4. Move the cross hair cursor to the point where you want the upper right corner of the control to be.
5. Drag the cross hair cursor until the text box has the desired dimensions.

6. Release the mouse button. A text box with the string Text1 appears on the form and the arrow mouse cursor is restored. Figure 4-5 shows a snapshot taken while drawing the first text box.

Repeat the above process for the other controls shown in FIG. 4-4.

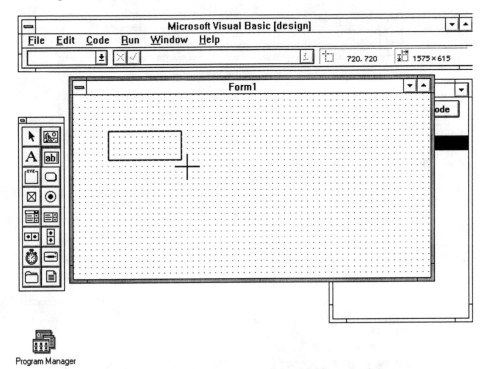

4-5 Drawing the first text box of the COSC application.

☞ The shortcut method works by double clicking the Toolbox icon of the sought control. This causes the chosen control to appear in the middle of the form. You can then move and resize the control. Resizing and moving controls are discussed in the next subsections.

Resizing a control

To resize a control, perform the following steps:

1. Select the control to be resized by clicking on it. This causes a number of small black rectangles, called *sizing handles*, to appear at the edge of the control object. Figure 4-6 shows a selected command button.
2. To simultaneously resize both dimensions of the control, drag one of the corner sizing handles. To resize in one direction only, drag a sizing handle on the side you want to expand or contract.

3. Release the mouse button. This updates the size of the control. The same control remains selected (you still see the sizing handles). To deselect the control, click on an empty location in the form.

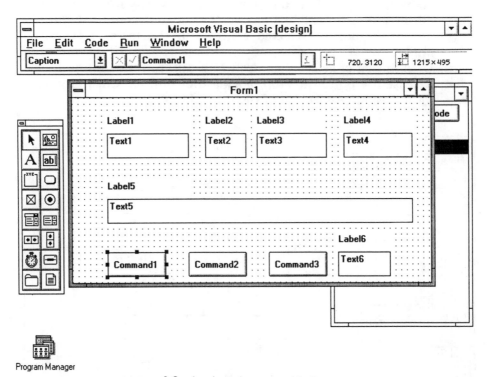

4-6 A selected command button.

Moving a single control

You can move a single control by performing the following steps:

1. Select the control to be moved. The sizing handles appear.
2. Locate the mouse cursor anywhere **inside** the control and hold down the mouse button.
3. Drag the control to its new position on the form.
4. Release the mouse button.

Moving multiple controls

You can also move a group of controls at one time. This causes the controls to be moved the same distance in the same direction. You can move a group of controls by carrying out the following steps:

1. Select the first control by clicking on it.

2. To select additional controls, hold the Ctrl key and click on each of the other target controls. Notice the following two things: first, the sizing handles change color from black to gray; second, the sizing handles appear on all of the selected controls. To deselect any control, click on that control while holding down the Ctrl key. In effect, you are toggling the selection of that control. Figure 4-7 shows a group of selected controls in the form of the COSC application.
3. Drag the set of selected controls to a new position on the form.
4. Release the button to stop moving the controls. Click on a clear form area to deselect all of the controls.

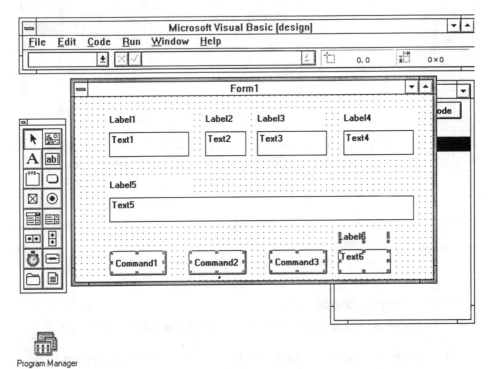

4-7 A group of selected controls in the form of the COSC application.

Deleting a single control

You can delete a single control by performing the following tasks:

1. Select the control you want to delete by clicking on it.
2. Press the Del key (some keyboards spell out "Delete"). You can also remove a control by selecting the Delete option from the Edit menu.

Deleting multiple controls

You can also delete multiple controls in one swoop. Follow these steps:

1. Select the first control you want to delete by clicking on it.
2. To select all subsequent controls, hold the Ctrl key and click on each of the other target controls. To deselect any control, click on that control while holding down the Ctrl key.
3. Press the Del key. You may also remove the group of controls by selecting the Delete option from the Edit menu.

Aligning the controls

The Visual Basic form uses a grid that determines the increments of space by which a control moves. The grid is very helpful in aligning controls. You can make the grid finer or coarser by selecting Grid Settings in the Edit menu. Figure 4-8 shows the Grid Settings dialog box which contains two input lines and two check boxes. The input lines enable you to adjust the vertical and horizontal grid spacing by pixels. The Align to Grid check box determines whether or not the controls are aligned with the grid. When you turn off the align option, the controls can be moved more

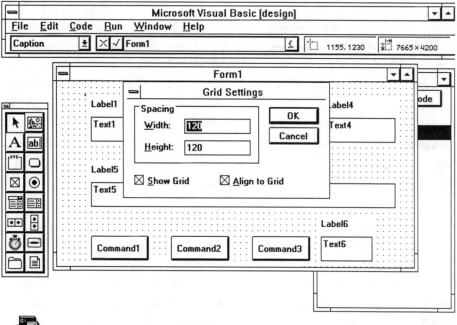

Program Manager

4-8   The Grid Setting dialog box.

smoothly on the form. The Show Grid check box specifies whether or not the grid is visible.

Saving your work

Save the form and project using the SCICALC.FRM and SCICALC.MAK. filenames, respectively. The next chapter looks at altering the properties of the controls in more detail.

Documenting the Visual Basic forms

The new visual programming approach of Visual Basic brings with it new requirements for documenting your applications. This becomes an even more formidable challenge since the Visual Basic code is not linear (as is the case with Quick Basic or GW-BASIC). The nonlinear nature of the Visual Basic code comes from the fact that code is dispersed—it is attached to the various forms and control objects. Therefore, it is a good practice to document the various components of an application.

Figure 4-9 shows a sample for the basic design documentation. The suggested documentation form lists the application name, code name, version number, date of creation, programmers, company, and the list of

Application name: _____

Application code name: _____

Version: _____ Date created: _____

Programmer(s): _____

Company: _____

List of filenames

Storage path: _____

Project _____

Global _____

Form 1 _____ Module 1 _____

Form 2 _____ Module 2 _____

Form 3 _____ Module 3 _____

Form 4 _____ Module 4 _____

Form 5 _____ Module 5 _____

Form 6 _____ Module 6 _____

Form 7 _____ Module 7 _____

Form 8 _____ Module 8 _____

Form 9 _____ Module 9 _____

4-9 A sample for the basic design documentation.

application files—the project file, the global file, the form file(s), and the module file(s).

Figure 4-10 presents a documentation form for the individual Visual Basic visual form. The information includes the form number, form filename, version number, date of creation, and a list of control objects. This list tabulates the type of control, the default control name (as initially assigned by Visual Basic), the purpose of the control, the location of its upper right corner, and the dimensions of the control (length and width). The last two attributes are optional—they are needed only when the location and size of the control are important. In the next two chapters I will present other documentation forms that keep track of the custom settings.

Form # _____   Form filename: _____

Version: _____   Date: _____

Control object type   **Default CtlName**   **Purpose**
(location)
(dimensions)

NOTE: The "location" refers to the coordinates of the upper right corner of the object. The "dimensions" refer to the length and width of the objects. All dimensions are expressed in pixels.

4-10   The documentation for the individual.

Applying the documentation forms of FIGS. 4-9 and 4-10 to the COSC application yields FIGS. 4-11 and 4-12. Notice that FIG. 4-12 does not include the location and size of the controls, because such information is not critical to the application's interface. In other words, you may eyeball the location and size of the controls when you try to reproduce the COSC interface yourself. Had the location and size of the controls been vital, FIG. 4-12 would have surely included them—and you would have been required (for whatever reason) to draw the controls according to the supplied data.

Application name: Command-oriented Scientific Calculator
Application code name: COSC
Version: 1.0   Date created: June 18, 1991
Programmer(s): Namir C. Shammas
Company: N/A

List of Filenames
Storage path: C:\VB\EASYVB
Project SCICALC.MAK
Global GLOBAL.BAS
Form 1 SCICALC.FRM

4-11   A sample for the basic design documentation.

Form #1 Version: 1.0		Form Filename: SCICALC.FRM Date: June 18, 1991
Control object type	**Default CtlName**	**Purpose**
Text Box	Text1	Key in operand 1
	Text2	Key in operator
	Text3	Key in operand 2
	Text4	Display the result
	Text5	Display error message
	Text6	Key in the variable names
Label	Label1	Label of Text1 Replace variable with numeric value
	Label2	Label of Text2
	Label3	Label of Text3 Replace variable with numeric value
	Label4	Label of Text4
	Label5	Label of Text5 Clear error message
	Label6	Label of Text6
Command button	Command1	Execute math operation
	Command2	Quit
	Command3	Store the result in a variable

4-12 The documentation for the individual controls of SCICALC.FRM.

5
Changing control settings

The predefined visual controls that you draw in a form come with a built-in set of properties. These properties determine the appearance and the behavior of the various forms and controls, especially during program execution. Each property has a default setting or *property value* which is provided by Visual Basic. While these "factory-supplied" default settings are suitable for most applications, Visual Basic allows you to alter them to fine-tune your application. This chapter looks more closely at changing the control settings. You will learn about the following:

- Working with the Properties bar.
- Documenting custom settings.
- Viewing and changing settings in general.
- Changing the setting for the Command-Oriented Scientific Calculator.

Table 5-1 lists the properties of the various Visual Basic objects. The table associates each control with a data type and lists the objects that own that property. This table should give you a clear idea of the important role of properties in Visual Basic. The *Microsoft Visual Basic Language Reference* describes each property. Keep in mind that the same property may play a somewhat different role in the various objects that own that property.

Working with the Properties bar

The Properties bar contains two combo boxes that enable you to view and edit the settings for the forms and control objects. Note that some settings

Table 5-1 The Visual Basic properties.

Property	Data type	(Access mode)	Applies to
ActiveControl*		(O)	Screen
ActiveForm*		(O)	Screen
Alignment	Integer 0 to 2	(R)	Label
Archive	True/False	(R)	File
AutoRedraw	True/False	(R)	Form, Picture
AutoSize	True/False	(R)	Label, Picture
BackColor	Long integer	(R)	Check, Clipboard, Command, Dir, Drive, File, Form, Frame, Label, List, Option, Picture, Printer, Text
BorderStyle	Integer	(O)	Form, Picture, Text
		(R)	Label
Cancel	True/False	(R)	Command
Caption	String	(R)	Check, Command, Form, Frame, Label, Menu, Option
Checked	True/False	(R)	Menu
ControlBox	True/False	(O)	Form
CtlName	String	(X)	Check, Combo, Command, Dir, Drive, File, Frame, Label, List, Menu, Option, Picture, Scroll, Text, Timer
CurrentX*	Integer	(R)	Form, Picture, Printer
CurrentY*	Integer	(R)	Form, Picture, Printer
Default	True/False	(R)	Command
DragIcon	Icon	(R)	Check, Combo, Command, Dir, Drive, File, Frame, Label, List, Option, Picture, Scroll, Text
DragMode	Integer 0 to 1	(R)	Check, Combo, Command, Dir, Drive, File, Frame, Label, List, Option, Picture, Scroll, Text
DrawMode	Integer 1 to 16	(R)	Form, Picture, Printer
DrawStyle	Integer 0 to 6	(R)	Form, Picture, Printer
DrawWidth	Integer	(R)	Form, Picture, Printer
Drive*	String	(R)	Drive
Enabled	True/False	(R)	Check, Combo, Command, Dir, Drive, File, Form, Frame, Label, List, Menu, Option, Picture, Scroll, Text, Timer
Filename*	String	(R)	File
FillColor	Long Integer	(R)	Form, Picture, Printer
FillStyle	Integer	(R)	Form, Picture, Printer

Table 5-1   Continued.

Property	Data type	(Access mode)	Applies to
FontBold	True/False	(R)	Check, Combo, Command, Dir, Drive, File, Form, Frame, Label, List, Option, Picture, Printer, Text
FontCount*	Integer	(O)	Printer, Screen
FontItalic	True/False	(R)	Check, Combo, Command, Dir, Drive, File, Form, Frame, Label, List, Option, Picture, Printer, Text
FontName	String	(R)	Check, Combo, Command, Dir, Drive, File, Form, Frame, Label, List, Option, Picture, Printer, Text
Fonts*	Integer	(O)	Printer, Screen
FontSize	Integer	(R)	Check, Combo, Command, Dir, Drive, File, Form, Frame, Label, List, Option, Picture, Printer, Text
FontStikethru	True/False	(R)	Check, Combo, Command, Dir, Drive, File, Form, Frame, Label, List, Option, Picture, Printer, Text
FontTransparent	True/False	(R)	Picture, Printer
FontUnderline	True/False	(R)	Check, Combo, Command, Dir, Drive, File, Form, Frame, Label, List, Option, Picture, Printer, Text
ForeColor	Long integer	(R)	Check, Combo, Dir, Drive, File, Form, Frame, Label, List, Option, Picture, Printer, Text
FormName	String	(X)	Form
hDC*	Integer	(O)	Form, Picture, Printer
Height	Single	(R)	Check, Combo, Command, Dir, Drive, File, Form, Frame, Label, List, Option, Picture, Printer, Screen, Scroll, Text
Hidden	True/False	(R)	File
InWnd*	Integer	(O)	Form
Icon	Icon	(R)	Form
Image*	Integer	(O)	Form
Index	Integer	(O)	Check, Combo, Command, Dir, Drive, File, Frame, Label, List, Menu, Option, Picture, Scroll, Text, Timer
Interval	Integer	(R)	Timer
LargeChange	Integer	(R)	Scroll
Left	Single	(R)	Check, Combo, Command, Dir, Drive, File, Form, Frame, Label, List, Option, Picture, Scroll, Text
LinkItem	String	(R)	Label, Picture, Text
LinkMode	Integer	(R)	Form, Label, Picture, Text

Table 5-1   Continued.

Property	Data type	(Access mode)	Applies to
LinkTimeout	Integer	(R)	Label, Picture, Text
LinkTopic*	String	(R)	Form, Label, Picture, Text
List*	String	(R)	Combo, List
		(O)	Dir, Drive, File
ListCount*	Integer	(O)	Combo, Dir, Drive, File, List
ListIndex*	Integer	(R)	Combo, Dir, Drive, File, List
Max	Integer	(R)	Scroll
MaxButton	True/False	(O)	Form
Min	Integer	(R)	Scroll
MinButton	True/False	(O)	Form
MousePointer	Integer 0 to 12	(R)	Check, Combo, Command, Dir, Drive, File, Form, Frame, Label, List, Option, Picture, Screen, Scroll, Text
MultiLine	True/False	(R)	Text
Normal	True/False	(R)	File
Page	Integer	(R)	Printer
Parent*	Form	(O)	Check, Combo, Command, Dir, Drive, File Frame, Label, List, Menu, Option, Picture, Scroll, Text, Timer
Path*	String	(R)	Dir, File
Pattern	String	(R)	File
Picture	Integer	(R)	Form, Picture
ReadOnly	True/False	(R)	File
ScaleHeight	Single	(R)	Form, Picture, Printer
ScaleLeft	Single	(R)	Form, Picture, Printer
ScaleMode	Integer 0 to 7	(R)	Form, Picture, Printer
ScaleTop	Single	(R)	Form, Picture, Printer
ScaleWidth	Single	(R)	Form, Picture, Printer
ScrollBars	Integer 0 to 3	(O)	Text
SelLength*	Long integer	(R)	Combo, Text
SelStart*	Long integer	(R)	Combo, Text
SelText*	String	(R)	Combo, Text
SmallChange	Integer	(R)	Scroll
Sorted	True/False	(O)	Combo, List
Style	Integer 0 to 2	(O)	Combo
System	True/False	(R)	File
TabIndex	Integer	(R)	Check, Combo, Command, Dir, Drive, File, Frame, Label, List, Option, Picture, Scroll, Text

Table 5-1   Continued.

Property	Data type	(Access mode)	Applies to
TabStop	True/False	(R)	Check, Combo, Command, Dir, Drive, File, List, Option, Picture, Scroll, Text
Tag	String	(R)	Check, Combo, Command, Dir, Drive, File, Frame, Label, List, Menu, Option, Picture, Scroll, Text, Timer
Text	String	(O)	List*
		(R)	Combo, Text
Top	Single	(R)	Check, Combo, Command, Dir, Drive, File, Form, Frame, Label, List, Option, Picture, Scroll, Text
Value	Integer	(R)	Check, Command, Option, Scroll
Visible	True/False	(R)	Check, Combo, Command, Dir, Drive, File, Form, Frame, Label, List, Menu, Option, Picture, Scroll, Text
Width	Single	(R)	Check, Combo, Command, Dir, Drive, File, Form, Frame, Label, List, Option, Picture, Printer*, Scroll, Text
		(O)	Screen*
WindowState	Integer 0 to 2	(R)	Form

Access mode code is:

  R read/write at run time
  O read-only at run time
  X not available at run time

The * symbol indicates that the property (or properties) is not available at design time.

True/False indicates a special enumerated integer, such that:

    True $= -1$
    False $= 0$

are not available during design time. The Properties combo box contains an ordered list of properties. The Settings combo box contains the current settings. Let's first see how you can select properties to view their settings.

Viewing properties and settings

The first step in viewing the properties and settings of an object involves selecting that object. If you need to select the form, click anywhere on the clear area of the form. To select a control object, click on that object. The Properties bar displays the current property and its setting for the currently selected item. It is interesting to note that if you select multiple controls, the combo boxes of the Properties bar go blank. The Properties combo box displays the currently selected property. To select another property click on the down arrow in the combo box. This causes the list of properties to appear. You can scroll through the list using either the mouse or the cursor keys. The current entry is displayed as selected text (in white characters with a black background). You can jump to certain entries by typing the first letter of that entry. For example, if you are inspecting the properties of a text box, you can zoom to the Text property by typing T (either uppercase or lowercase) a few times—every time you press T the combo box selects the next item that starts with that letter. Press Enter to select the current entry from the list. Figure 5-1 shows the Properties combo box with the list of properties. When you select a new property, the corresponding setting is displayed in the Settings combo box.

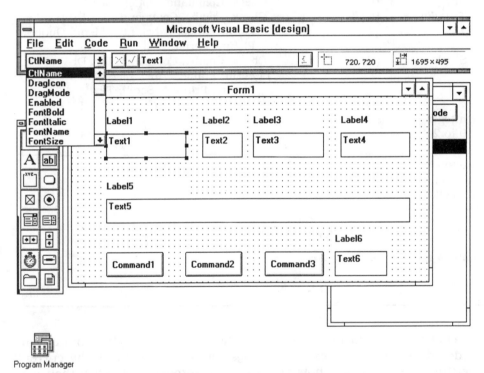

5-1 The Properties bar and the properties combo box.

Changing the current setting

The first steps in changing the current setting of an object are the same as for viewing the object's settings. Since there are two basic types of settings, there are also two basic methods for changing these settings.

The first type of setting contains *discrete* (also called *enumerated*) integer values. The most popular examples are the True (-1) and False (0) values. When you select the Settings combo box, notice if the accompanying Arrow button is active or not. If the button is active, then you are dealing with an enumerated setting. In this case, click on the Arrow button to reveal the available choices. You may select a new value by scrolling through the list of values and then pressing Enter or by clicking on the Check button located to the left of the Settings combo box. You can also zoom in on an enumerated value by typing the first letter of that value. For example, you can select False from a True/False enumerated list by pressing F. To reject the new selection and revert to the previous one, click the X button located just to the left of the Check button. Figure 5-2 shows the Settings combo box displaying an enumerated True/False choice.

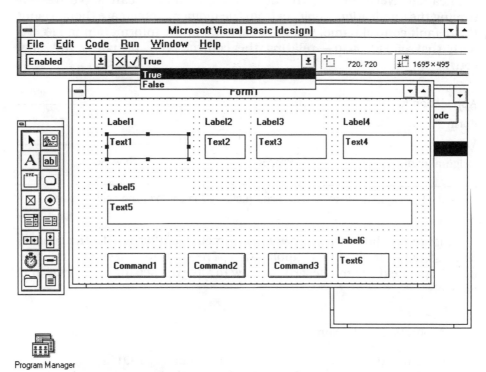

5-2 The Properties bar and the settings combo box.

The second kind of setting contains data of the various basic types, such as integers, long integers, strings, and singles. You may type any value that is within the valid range for the corresponding data type of that setting. To enter a new setting, type in the new value. Press Enter or click on the Check button to accept the new setting. Click on the X button to resort to the previous setting.

Documenting custom settings

It is sound programming practice to keep track of the changes you make to the settings of the form or controls. Documenting these changes permits you (or anyone else) to easily keep track of an application's objects. In the previous chapter I presented two documentation forms that can be used to describe the initial phases of building a Visual Basic application. Now I present FIG. 5-3, which contains a suggested documentation form for keeping track of the setting changes. As the number of such forms increases, you need to establish a link between the information in these forms. Borrowing from the basic notions of relational databases, I recommend the use of the default form and control names as a way to keep track of the various objects. Ironically, though, you invariably change these control names to better describe the function of the control in your application. Nevertheless, the default object names can serve well in tracing the application's objects from the moment you create them. Using the default control name, you are able to tie in the information in FIG. 5-3 with that of FIG. 4-10—relating the control type, purpose, and new setting.

Application (Code) Name: _____

Form # _____

Version: _____   Date: _____

Original control name   Property   New Setting

_____   _____   _____

5-3 The suggested form for documenting changes in the form and control settings.

Figure 5-4 shows the suggested documentation form with the custom settings data for the COSC application. The data for these settings are used in the next section describing how to alter the settings for forms and controls.

Application (Code) Name: COSC
Form #1
Version: 1.0   Date: June 19, 1991

Original control name	**Property**	**New setting**
Form1	Caption	Scientific Calculator
Text1	CtlName Text	Operand1Box (empty string)
Text2	CtlName Text	OperatorBox (empty string)

5-4 The changes in the settings for the COSC application.

Text3	CtlName	Operand2Box
	Text	(empty string)
Text4	CtlName	ResultBox
	Text	(empty string)
Text5	CtlName	ErrorMessageBox
	Text	(empty string)
Text6	CtlName	VariableBox
	Text	(empty string)
Label1	CtlName	Operand1Lbl
	Caption	"Operand1"
Label2	CtlName	OperatorLbl
	Caption	Operator
Label3	CtlName	Operator2Lbl
	Caption	Operand2
Label4	CtlName	ResultLbl
	Caption	Result
Label5	CtlName	ErrorMessageLbl
	Caption	Error Message
Label6	CtlName	VariableLbl
	Caption	Variable
Command1	CtlName	ExecuteBtn
	Caption	Execute
Command2	CtlName	QuitBtn
	Caption	Quit
Command3	CtlName	StoreBtn
	Caption	Store

5-4   Continued.

Changing the scientific calculator's settings

Using the instructions described earlier, change the settings listed in FIG.
5-4 to obtain the form shown in FIG. 5-5. You might need to load the COSC
project again by opening the SCICALC.MAK project (in the \VB\EASYVB
directory). Open the form by double clicking on the form file. To alter the
settings of the Text1 text box, for example, perform the following steps:

1. Select the Text1 text box by clicking on it.
2. Select the Properties combo box. If the current property is not
   CtlName, scroll through the list until you find it. When the CtlName
   property is highlighted, press the Enter key to select it.

3. The corresponding setting is Text1, the default value supplied by Visual Basic. Click on the Settings combo box, type Operand1Box, and press the Enter key.
4. Select the Properties combo box again. Scroll through the list (or press T) until the Text property becomes highlighted. Press Enter to select the Text property.
5. The corresponding setting is Text1, the default contents of the selected text box. Click on the Settings combo box and press the space bar, followed by the Backspace key. This makes the current setting a null string. Press the Enter key to accept the new setting.

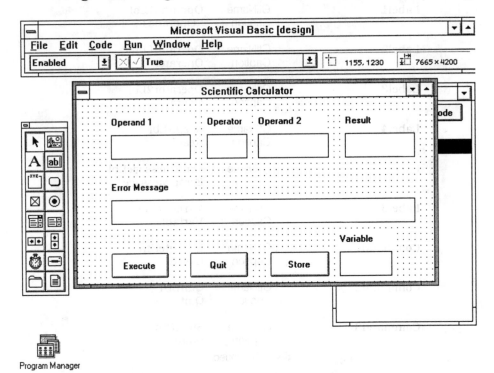

5-5 The modified form for the COSC application.

✍️ You can perform the other changes in a manner similar to the way you changed the settings of the Text1 text box—change all of the settings of the same control before moving on to the next control. There is another approach that is a bit easier and faster. It involves the following steps:

1. Change the settings of similar controls, one category at a time. For example, start by editing all the settings of the Text box, then the Command buttons, then the labels.

2. While working with each group of similar controls, edit the setting of the same property before moving on to the next property. Why? Because when you edit a property of a control, that property remains the selected one when you select the next similar control. This feature reduces the number of searches you need to perform in the Properties combo box. In addition, you can focus on entering or selecting the new setting.

When you have finished changing the settings, save the form and project files, using the Save File and Save Project options in the File menu.

6

Attaching code
to the controls

This chapter looks at the third general step involved in developing a Visual Basic application. In chapter 4, the form and controls were drawn for the COSC application. In chapter 5, the settings for the form and the controls were adjusted. In this chapter we attach the code to the various controls to bring the application to life.

You will learn about the following aspects of Visual Basic in this chapter:

- Coding a Visual Basic application.
- Writing event-handling procedure.
- Working with the Code window.
- The Global module.
- Attaching code to the COSC application.
- Running the COSC application.
- Creating an .EXE file.

Coding a Visual Basic application

Visual Basic is far easier to use than most other implementations of Windows programming languages, like Pascal or C++. The reason is the visual programming approach employed by Visual Basic. Rather than starting from scratch, you are provided with a well-developed set of visual objects. A lot of programming has been done by the designers of Visual Basic to give the various objects their appearance and behavior. This is seen in three major areas: properties, events, and methods. The predefined properties may be regarded as parameters or data fields that set or query the appearance and behavior of the various Visual Basic objects.

The predefined events determine how an object may interact with the application user. Methods are special procedures that manipulate the various objects.

This chapter looks at coding the controls to respond to specific events. While each kind of control is able to respond to an entire fixed set of events, you will rarely program any control to do so. Typically, a control is programmed to respond to a few events. In the case of the COSC application, controls respond to one event—the mouse click. Since clicking on a control is common in Windows applications, the Click event is among the most popular events handled.

In Chapter 4, I began presenting the COSC application by discussing the operation of the program. Here is a review of the command-oriented scientific calculator's basic functions:

1. The user types in the operands and the operator in their respective text boxes. Alternately, the user may type the argument of a function in the text box labeled Operand 1 and enter the name of the math function in the Operator text box. The name of the function is not case-sensitive.
2. The user clicks the Execute button to perform the desired operation or function evaluation. The result is calculated and displayed in the Result text box.
3. The result can be stored in a single-letter variable (A to Z). This is carried out by typing the name of the target variable in the Variable text box and then clicking the Store button.
4. Clicking on the Operand 1 and Operand 2 labels translates the name of a variable (if found) in the Operand 1 and Operand 2 text boxes.
5. Clicking on the Error Message label clears the content of the Error Message text box.
6. Clicking on the Quit button terminates the program.

Writing event-handling procedures

Every control that you draw on the form, as well as the form itself, can respond to a specific set of events. The number and types of events vary for each kind of control. Table 6-1 lists the Visual Basic events and the objects that respond to each type of event. In coding a Visual Basic application, you must associate the different controls to the events they should handle. The number of controls associated varies from one control to all of the controls on the form (if you have a very sophisticated application). The association between a control and an event is called *code attachment*. The procedure that implements an attached code derives its name from the name of the control and the name of the event it handles, using the following general syntax:

Table 6-1   The Visual Basic events.

Event	Applies to
Change	Combo, Dir, Drive, Label, Picture, Scroll, Text, Timer Check, Combo, Command, Dir, File, Form, Label, List, Menu, Option, Picture
DblClick	Combo, File, Form, Label, List, Option, Picture
DragDrop	Check, Combo, Command, Dir, Drive, File, Form, Frame, Label, List, Option, Picture
DragOver	Check, Combo, Command, Dir, Drive, File, Form, Frame, Label, List, Option, Picture
DropDown	Combo
GotFocus	Check, Combo, Command, Dir, Drive, File, Form, List, Option, Picture, Scroll, Text
KeyDown	Check, Combo, Command, Dir, Drive, File, Form, List, Option, Picture, Scroll, Text
KeyPress	Check, Combo, Command, Dir, Drive, File, Form, List, Option, Picture, Scroll, Text
KeyUp	Check, Combo, Command, Dir, Drive, File, Form, List, Option, Picture, Scroll, Text
LinkClose	Form, Label, Picture, Text
LinkError	Form, Label, Picture, Text
LinkExecute	Form
LinkOpen	Form, Label, Picture, Text
Load	Form
LostFocus	Check, Combo, Command, Dir, Drive, File, Form, List, Option, Picture, Scroll, Text
MouseDown	Dir, File, Form, Label, List, Picture
MouseMove	Dir, File, Form, Label, List, Picture
MouseUp	Dir, File, Form, Label, List, Picture
Paint	Form, Picture
PathChange	File
PatternChange	File
Resize	Form
Timer	Timer
UnLoad	Form

```
Sub objectName_eventName(<list of parameters>)
    sequence of Basic statements
End Sub
```

The object name for a control is taken from the setting of the CtlName property. In the case of the form itself, the object name is automatically taken as Form, regardless of the CtlName setting:

```
Sub Form_eventName(<list of parameters>)
    sequence of Basic statements
End Sub
```

The event-handling procedures resemble normal Quick Basic Sub procedures that you have most likely written as a programmer. The difference is that they are automatically invoked by the run time system when the event eventName occurs at the object objectName. For example, consider the following sample code that handles clicking on a command button (with a Command1 control name and Caption property):

```
Sub Command1_Click( )
    C$ = Command1.Caption ' save caption
    Command1.Caption = "You clicked me!"
    Beep
    WaitForWhile 2000 ' wait for 2 seconds
    Command1.Caption = C$ ' restore caption
End Sub
```

When you click on the Command1 command button, it recognizes the event and invokes the Command1_Click procedure to handle the click event. When the Command1_Click procedure ends, the event is declared handled. If there is no matching event-handling procedure, the event is abandoned. In the case of Command1_Click, the procedure displays a new caption for the button, beeps, waits for 2 seconds (the procedure WaitForWhile is assumed to be available in a module), and then restores the original button caption.

Event-handing procedures are similar to those for controls. A sample event-handling procedure for clicking on the form is shown below:

```
Sub Form_Click( )
    Beep
    WaitForWhile 100
    Beep
End Sub
```

When you click on a clear area in the form, the form invokes the Form_Click procedure, which results in two beeps.

Working with the Code window

Developing and attaching code for your Visual Basic application occurs in the Code window. This special window makes it easier to write event-handling procedures. The features of the Code window include providing templates for the event-handling procedures and offering combo boxes that list the various objects and their events. I will talk more about these features later in this section.

To access the Code window you can double click on the form or a control, press the F7 function, or select the View Code option from the Code menu. In any case, the Code window pops up and displays the click event-handling procedure for the currently selected object (the form or one of its controls). When you first view them, these procedures have no statements.

The flexibility of the Code window includes the ability to view the other events that are handled by the currently selected object. This is made possible by the Proc combo box. Click on that box to select it and then click on the Down Arrow button to pop up the list of other events. Figure 6-1 shows the Proc combo box for a command button. The events in the Proc list that appear in bold characters are the ones that have an event handler for the current object. If you select another event from the Proc combo box, the Code window displays the procedure for the selected event.

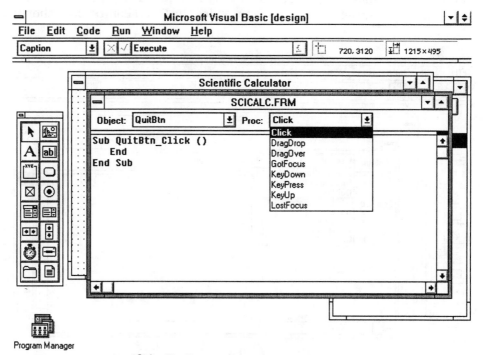

6-1 The Proc combo box in the Code Window.

Once you have selected the event you want to code for the current object, the Code window becomes a text editor. You can then type the

Basic statements that make up the body of the event-handling procedure. As with Quick Basic, the Visual Basic system checks, by default, the syntax of each line you type. This syntax checking occurs either when you press Enter or when you move the editing cursor up or down. While you are on the same edited line, you can move the cursor back and forth without provoking the wrath of the syntax checker. You can turn off syntax checking by selecting the Syntax Check option in the Edit menu. The Edit and Code menus offer the options for finding, replacing, copying, cutting, and pasting text. While editing a procedure, you can split the edit window by moving the mouse cursor to the small black rectangle located just above the vertical scroll bar. Drag that rectangle downward and you will see the edit window split into two views. This enables you to edit one location of a long procedure while viewing another location. When you no longer need the split views, moving the small black rectangle upward to its default position closes the upper view.

When you have finished coding the event-handling procedures for the current object, you may want to move on to the next object. The Code window provides you with an easy way to navigate to the other controls, the form, or to the general code area. This area stores declarations for common constants, variables, and data types. To edit the procedures for the other objects, the Code window provides the Object combo box, shown

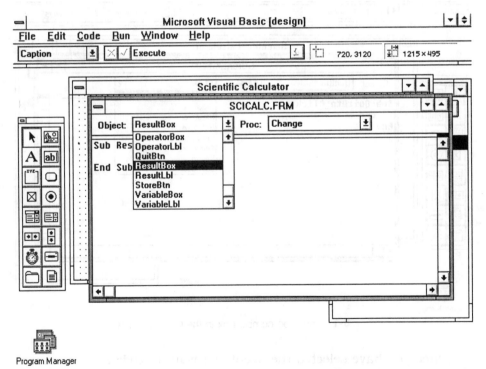

6-2 The Object combo box in the Code Window.

in FIG. 6-2. This combo box alphabetically lists the various objects and includes the general declarations area. Select the object to which you want to attach code.

Inserting code in the GLOBAL.BAS file

Before I discuss attaching the event-handling code to the various controls, I want to focus on the contents of the GLOBAL.BAS module. Initially, the file GLOBAL.BAS is empty. Select the GLOBAL.BAS file in the Project window and click on the View Code button. Select the Load Text option from the Code menu and type \VB\CONSTANT.TXT to load the Basic code lines paritally shown in LISTING 6-1. Save the global file as file \VB\EASYVB\GLOBAL.BAS. Using Save File As ensures that it is stored in the \VB\EASYVB directory with the other files that are related to this book.

Listing 6-1 The first few lines of the GLOBAL.BAS file.

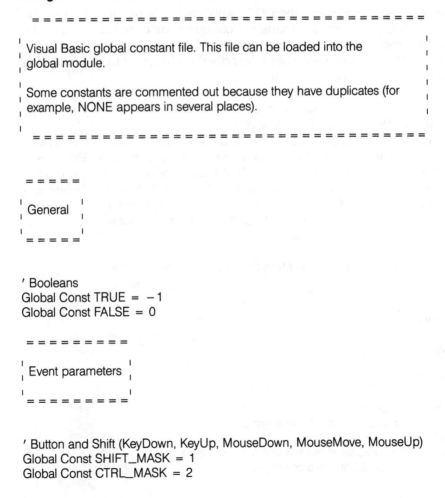

```
= = = = = = = = = = = = = = = = = = = = = = = = = = = = = = = = = = = =

' Visual Basic global constant file. This file can be loaded into the
' global module.

' Some constants are commented out because they have duplicates (for
' example, NONE appears in several places).

'
 = = = = = = = = = = = = = = = = = = = = = = = = = = = = = = = = = = = =


 = = = = =
'       '
' General '
'       '
 = = = = =


' Booleans
Global Const TRUE = −1
Global Const FALSE = 0


 = = = = = = = = =
'             '
' Event parameters '
'             '
 = = = = = = = = =


' Button and Shift (KeyDown, KeyUp, MouseDown, MouseMove, MouseUp)
Global Const SHIFT_MASK = 1
Global Const CTRL_MASK = 2
```

Listing 6-1 Continued.

```
Global Const ALT_MASK = 4
Global Const LEFT_BUTTON = 1
Global Const RIGHT_BUTTON = 2
Global Const MIDDLE_BUTTON = 4
```

The contents of the GLOBAL.BAS file are global declarations that I will use with the various programs in this book. I am including comments that specify a version number and a version date in anticipation of adding more items in GLOBAL.BAS as we go along. The version number and date should prevent confusion about what version is needed. Currently, the module GLOBAL.BAS declares the constants True and False that are used to mimic logical, or *Boolean* data types.

Attaching code to the controls

The next step in developing the COSC application is to code the various event-handling procedures. Listing 6-2 contains the code attached to the various controls, as well as the general declarations section. Following the method of attaching code that I described earlier, key in the following code fragments (in any order you like):

1. Select the general entry from the Object combo box. Type in the declaration for the TheVars array.
2. Select the ExecuteBtn, StoreBtn, and QuitBtn buttons one at a time, and key in the statements for their respective procedures (ExecuteBtn_ Click, StoreBtn_Click, and QuitBtn_Click) that handle the click events.
3. Select the Operand1Lbl, Operand2Lbl, and ErrorMessageLbl labels one at a time, and key in the statements for their respective procedures (Operand1Lbl_Click, Operand2Lbl_Click, and ErrorMessageLbl_Click) that handle the click events.

Listing 6-2 The code attached to the form and various controls.

```
Dim TheVars(65 To 90) As Double

Sub QuitBtn_Click ( )
  End
End Sub

Sub StoreBtn_Click ( )
  Dim C As String
  Dim Index As Integer
  ' process the contents of the Variable text box
  If VariableBox.Text < > " " Then
    ' obtain the uppercase of the first character in the text box
    C = UCase$(Left$(VariableBox.Text, 1))
```

Listing 6-2 Continued.

```
       ' is the character in the range A to Z?
       If (C > = "A") And (C < = "Z") Then
           ' Yes! Get the ASCII code for the character
           Index = Asc(C)
           ' store the value of the Result box in the array TheVars#
           TheVars#(Index) = Val(ResultBox.Text)
           ' clear the error message box
           ErrorMessageBox.Text = " "
       Else
           ' No! The text box has an invalid variable name
           ErrorMessageBox.Text = "Invalid variable name"
           Beep
       End If
   Else
       ' the text box is empty!
       ErrorMessageBox.Text = "Missing variable name"
       Beep
   End If
End Sub

Sub ExecuteBtn_Click ( )
   Dim X, Y, Z As Double
   Dim Xchar As String
   Dim Ychar As String
   ErrorMessageBox.Text = " " ' clear error message box
   ResultBox.Text = " "            ' clear result box
   ' obtain the uppercase of the first character in the
   ' Operand1Box text box
   Xchar = UCase$(Left$(Operand1Box.Text, 1))
   ' obtain the uppercase of the first character in the
   ' Operand2Box text box
   Ychar = UCase$(Left$(Operand2Box.Text, 1))
   ' convert string in Operand1Box text box to its
   ' numeric value. Note that if the conversion fails,
   ' X will be assigned a zero.
   X = Val(Operand1Box.Text)
   ' is X = 0 when Xchar$ is not "0"? This test detects
   ' failed conversions
   If (X = 0) And (Xchar < > = "0") Then
       ' Yes! Is Xchar in the range A to Z
     If (Xchar > = "A") And (Xchar < = "Z") Then
           ' treat the content of Operand1Box as storing
           ' the name of a variable. Assign the value of
           ' the variable to X
           X = TheVars#(Asc(Xchar))
     End If
   End If
   ' convert text in Operand2Box to numeric value
```

Listing 6-2 Continued.

```
Y = Val(Operand2Box.Text)
' check if Operand2Box has a variable
If (Y = 0) And (Ychar < > "0") Then
   If (Ychar > = "A") And (Ychar < = "Z") Then
      ' Yes! there is a variable. Assign its
      ' value to variable Y
      Y = TheVars#(Asc(Ychar))
   End If
End If
' examine the content of the OperatorBox text box
Select Case UCase$(OperatorBox.Text)
   Case " + "
      Z = X + Y
   Case " - "
      Z = X - Y
   Case " * "
      Z = X * Y
   Case "/"
      If Y < > 0 Then
         Z = X / Y
      Else
         ErrorMessageBox.Text = "Division by zero error"
         Beep
      End If
   Case "^"
      Z = X ^ Y
   Case " = " ' simply copy the value of the first
                    ' operand into the result box
   Z = X
Case "LN"
   If X > 0 Then
      Z = Log(X)
   Else
      ErrorMessageBox.Text = "Bad function argument"
      Beep
   End If
   Case "LOG"
      If X > 0 Then
         Z = Log(X) / Log(10)
      Else
         ErrorMessageBox.Text = "Bad function argument"
         Beep
      End If
   Case "EXP"
      Z = Exp(X)
   Case "SQR"
      If X > = 0 Then
```

Listing 6-2 Continued.

```
      Z = Sqr(X)
    Else
      ErrorMessageBox.Text = "Bad function argument"
      Beep
    End If
  Case "SIN"
    Z = Sin(X * Pi / 180)
  Case "COS"
    Z = Sin(X * Pi / 180)
  Case "TAN"
    Z = Tan(X * Pi / 180)
  Case Else
    ErrorMessageBox.Text = "Invalid operator"
    Beep
  End Select
  ' if the error message box is still empty, there is
  ' no error. Therefore, convert the variable Z into
  ' a string and display it in ResultBox
  If ErrorMessageBox.Text = " " Then
    ResultBox.Text = Str$(Z)
  End If
End Sub


Sub Operand1Lbl_Click ( )
  Dim Xchar As String
  ' get the uppercase of the first character in the Operand1Box
  Xchar = UCase$(Left$(Operand1Box.Text, 1))
  ' is the character in the range A to Z?
  If (Xchar > = "A") And (Xchar < "Z") Then
    ' Yes! Obtain the variable from the array and write
    ' its numeric value to the text box
    Operand1Box.Text = Str$(TheVars#(Asc(Xchar)))
  End If
End Sub


Sub Operand2Lbl_Click ( )
  Dim Xchar As String
  ' get the uppercase of the first character in the Operand2Box
  Xchar = UCase$(Left$(Operand2Box.Text, 1))
  ' is the character in the range A to Z?
  If (Xchar > = "A") And (Xchar < = "Z") Then
    ' Yes! Obtain the variable from the array and write
    ' its numeric value to the text box
    Operand2Box.Text = Str$(TheVars#(Asc(Xchar)))
  End If
End Sub
```

Listing 6-2 Continued.

```
Sub ErrorMessageLbl_Click ( )
    ' clear the error message text box
    ErrorMessageBox.Text = " "
End Sub
```

Figure 6-3 shows the code window displaying the code of an event handler for the Execute command button.

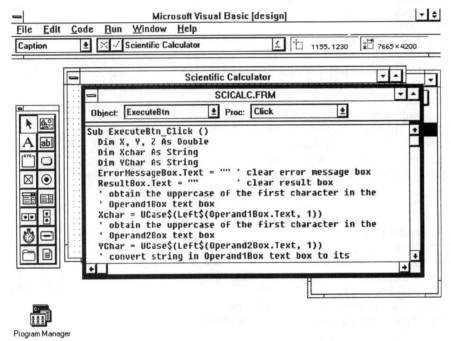

6-3 The Code window displaying procedure Sub ExecuteBtn_Click.

Listing 6-2 should be fairly easy to read. Most of the code is easily recognized as event-handling procedures. The name of each procedure reflects the association between a control and an event it handles. Any code at the beginning of the listing that is not part of an event-handling procedure comes from the general declarations section.

Now that I have presented the code attached to the SCICALC.FRM form, let's see how it works. I will discuss the procedures in the order in which they appear in the listing.

1. The DIM statement declares a double-precision array, TheVars, with indices that range from 65 to 90. These numbers represent the ASCII code for the letters A and Z. Consequently, you can index the elements of array TheVars simply by providing the ASCII code of the single-letter variable name.

2. The QuitBtn_Click procedure uses an END statement to end the program execution.

3. The StoreBtn_Click procedure allows you to store the result of an operation in a variable. If the Variable box is empty, the procedure displays an error message in the Error Message box. Otherwise, the procedure performs the following steps:

   • Obtains the upper case of the first character in the Variable text box.
   • Checks to determine if the extracted character is in the range A to Z.
   • When the above test is positive, the ASCII code of the extracted character is assigned to the local variable Index. The contents of the Result text box are converted into a number and then stored in the array TheVars, using the variable Index as an index to the sought array element.
   • The Error Message box is cleared to signal that the storage process is successful and also to remove any previous error message.

4. The ExecuteBtn_Click procedure is the heart of the command-oriented scientific calculator. In brief, the main purpose of this procedure is to convert the strings in the Operand text boxes into numbers, read the string in the Operator text box, perform the sought operation or function evaluation, and write the result in the Result box.

   Obtaining numeric operands from the Operand text boxes is complicated by the fact that they can contain the following kinds of data:

   • The Operand text box is empty.
   • The string in the Operand text box represents a valid number.
   • The first character of the string in the Operand text box is a letter.
   • The first character of the string in the text box is neither a letter, nor a number, nor the + symbol, nor the − symbol.

   To resolve these complications we start with the conversion of a string into a number as implemented by the Val function. There are two of such conversions that occur at the following statements:

   X = Val(Operand1Box.Text)
   Y = Val(Operand2Box.Text)

   The function returns a zero if it cannot convert at least the leading characters of a string into a number. Thus, when the Val function returns zero in the ExecuteBtn_Click procedure, it could mean one of the following things: the Operand text box has a string with zeros, a variable, an invalid number, or it is empty.

The first case is the least likely one—you don't need a computer to carry out an operation that involves a zero! This means that the code must check for a variable if the Val function returns zero (and the first character in the text box is *not* zero). The event-handling procedure uses a series of If statements to check if the upper case of the first character of an operand text box is a letter. If this test is positive, the value of the variable is retrieved from the array TheVars by using the expressions TheVars (ASC(Xchar)) and The-Vars(ASC(Ychar)).

The procedure uses a Select-Case statement to execute the desired math operation or function evaluation. The list of the math operators and functions include:

Operators: +, −, *, /, ^, and = (assign operand 1 to the result)
Functions: Ln, Log, Exp, Sqr, Sin, Cos, and Tan.

The Case clauses include argument/operand checking when appropriate. When a bad argument of operand is detected, the Error Message box displays an error message. The result of function evaluation is stored in the local variable Z.

The last If statement in the procedure tests if the Error Message text box has remained empty, as initialized earlier in the procedure. An empty Error Message box indicates that there is no error. The statement in the accompanying Then clause converts the value of the variable Z into the new content of the Result text box.

5. The Operand1Lbl_Click and Operand2Lbl_Click procedures perform very similar tasks—replacing the name of a variable with its contents. The code for these procedures examines the upper case of the first character in an operand text box. If that character is a letter, the data for the corresponding variable is retrieved from the TheVars array. The string image of the number obtained is written to the operand text box.

6. The ErrorMessageLbl_Click procedure assigns a null string to the Text property of the Error Message text box.

Running the COSC application

To run the COSC application you can either press the F5 function key or select the Start option in the Run menu. If Visual Basic detects any errors it will display a window and highlight the offending code portion. If this occurs, check the code you typed and make the necessary corrections. Figure 6-4 shows the screen during a sample session with the COSC application.

Experiment with the various program features. If you feel comfortable with programming in Visual Basic, add a few more math functions or operators by expanding on the Select Case statement in the ExecuteBtn_ Click procedure. When you have finished, save the project files by using the Save Project option in the File menu.

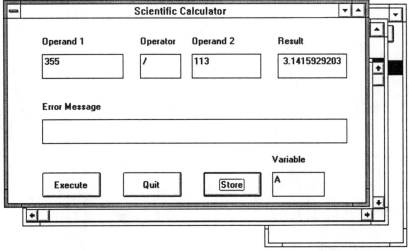

Scientific Calculator

Operand 1   Operator   Operand 2   Result
355   /   113   3.1415929203

Error Message

Variable

Execute   Quit   Store   A

Program Manager

6-4 A sample session with the COSC application.

Creating an .EXE file

Until now, you had to run Visual Basic in order to execute any Visual Basic program. Visual Basic enables you to create stand-alone .EXE files that run under Windows 3.0 (or later). The process of creating executable files is very easy and involves the following steps:

1. Open the project you need to compile into executable code.
2. Select option Make EXE option from the File menu.
3. Enter the name of the executable file in the input box. Visual Basic supplies a default filename, based on the project filename, with an .EXE extension. In the case of the COSC application, Visual Basic supplies you with the SCICALC.EXE filename.
4. Select the OK button to accept either the default filename or the different filename that you just typed. The executable file is written to the current directory, \VB\EASYVB.

    ☞ Under Windows 3.0, your Visual Basic programs can take advantage of running in the background. This feature is very suitable for applications that can run unattended, such as number-crunching and text processing programs. This is an advantage that you do not have with QuickBasic.

7

Text boxes and command buttons

Having covered the three basic steps involved in developing a Visual Basic application, I will begin to focus on the aspects of Visual Basic that involve the various controls, the different non-control objects, and important programming topics. In this chapter, as well as the ones to follow, I will discuss those control properties that are generally relevant to applications. The style of presentation stresses the practical side, rather than that of a reference.

This chapter focuses on text boxes and command buttons. The examples presented in this chapter illustrate how some of the properties of these controls can be manipulated at run time. In this chapter you will learn about:

- The important properties of a text box.
- The important properties of a command button.
- Setting access keys for command buttons.
- Manipulating the tab order of the various controls.
- Simulating a screen using a multi-line scrollable text box.

Text boxes

In the previous chapters, I presented programs that use Text boxes which were used to type in a single-line input or display a single-line output. Among the text box properties are the following, which prove to be interesting (at least for now).

The Multiline **property.**   This Boolean property enables a Text box to display multiple lines of text. The Multiline property should be set to True at design time. The sequence of Chr$(13) and Chr$(10) characters are used to visually separate the lines in a text box. For example, the following Visual Basic code stores an array of strings in a multi-line text box, such that each string element appears on a separate line:

```
Dim F As String
Dim NL As String * 2
Dim I As Integer
Dim A (1 To 10) As String
ReadTheStrings A() ' get the data from somewhere
F = ""
NL = Chr$(13) + Chr$(10)
For I = LBound(A, 1) To UBound(A, 1)
   F = F + A(I) + NL
Next
TextBox.Text = F
F = ""
```

The array A provides you with the strings. The variable NL is a two-character string that stores the Chr$(13) and Chr$(10) character sequence used to delimit text lines.

✍ The variable F is used to sequentially build the large string that contains the members of the string array A, delimited by the NL strings. Once the variable F has been built, it is assigned to the Text property of TextBox. This technique produces a better visual effect, in that all of the lines in the text box appear at the same time.

The ScrollBars **property** This is an enumerated integer type that specifies whether or not a text box has scroll bars. The possible values for this property are:

0 — No scrollable bars appear with the text box.
1 — Horizontal scroll bar.
2 — Vertical scroll bar.
3 — Both scroll bars.

By setting the Multiline property to True and setting the ScrollBars property to a nonzero value, Visual Basic practically turns a text box into a window that views and edits text. The keyboard cursor controls, such as Home and End, are active, and the mouse can be used to select text for copying, deleting, and pasting. The first program in this chapter explores some of these powerful features.

The SelStart, SelLength, **and** SelText **properties** These properties, which are not available at design time, handle the selected text in text boxes.

The SelStart property sets or returns the starting point of the selected text. The valid range of values for SelStart is 0 to the length of the string in the text box. The value of SelStart indicates that the first character of the selected text is (SelStart + 1). If SelStart is assigned a value greater than the length of the text box string, Visual Basic automatically resets SelStart to the length of that string.

The SelLength property assigns or yields the size of the selected text. This is identical to the result of Len(SelText)). The valid range of values for SelLength is from 0 to the length of the string in the text box. When SelStart changes values, SelLength is automatically assigned a 0. A run time error occurs if a negative value is assigned to SelLength.

The SelText property assigns or returns the characters of the currently selected text. The SelText property contains an empty string when there is no selected text.

The general syntax for using the SelStart, SelLength, and SelText properties are:

[form.][textBox.]SelStart [= index&]
[form.][textBox.]SelLength [= length&]
[form.][textBox.]SelText [= stringExpression$]

The Visible **property**   This Boolean property empowers you to show or hide a text box. When the setting of the Visible property is True (−1), the text box is visible. By contrast, if the setting is False (0), the text box is invisible and inaccessible. The general syntax for the Visible property is:

[form.][textBox.]Visible [=boolean%]

The first program in this chapter uses all of the above text box properties.

Command buttons

Command buttons are popular controls used by Windows application in general. All of the programs that I presented earlier in this book use command buttons to perform various tasks. In this section I focus on the following command button properties:

The Visible **property**   Command buttons have the Visible property which works just like with text boxes. The general syntax for using the Visible property with command buttons is:

[form.][commandButton.]Visible [=boolean%]

The Enabled **property**   This Boolean property lets you enable or disable a command button while still showing the button (unlike the Visible property). Setting the Enabled property to False (0) disables a command button. This also affects the visual appearance of the button's caption—the caption of a disabled command button appears in a faint text font to indicate that the button is not in service. Setting the Enabled property to True (−1) activates a command button. The text for the button's caption returns to normal to indicate that the button is active. The general syntax for using the Enabled property is:

[form.][commandButton.]Enabled [=boolean%]

The Default **property**   This Boolean property specifies if a command button is the default button, which is the button that is initially selected when the host form is loaded. Pressing Enter invokes the default button. The general syntax for using the Default property is:

> [form.][commandButton.]Default [=boolean%]

The Cancel **property**   This Boolean property that sets or determines if a command button is the Cancel button, which is the one automatically invoked when you press the Esc key. Each form can have either one or no command button designated as the Cancel button. The Cancel button is selected at design time or run time. The general syntax for using the Cancel property is:

> [form.][commandButton.]Cancel [=boolean%]

The first program that I will present later in this chapter uses all of the above command button properties.

A text file viewer

The text box and command properties that I presented earlier in this chapter are the ingredients of a text file viewer application. The main purpose of the application, named FVIEW1, is to view ASCII text files. The secondary operations of the program include:

- Performing a simple case-sensitive text search,
- Invoking the DOS shell to execute a DOS command or run a DOS program.
- Running a Windows application.
- Searching for a file.

The specifications for the text file viewer application are listed in FIG. 7-1, 7-2, and 7-3. These figures use the documentation forms presented in chapters 4 and 5.

Application Name: Text File Viewer
Application Code Name: FVIEW1
Version: 1.0   Date Created: June 27, 1991
Programmer(s): Namir Clement Shammas
List of filenames
Storage Path: C:\VB\EASYVB
Project FVIEW1.MAK
Global GLOBAL.BAS
Form 1FVIEW1.FRM

7-1 General project specifications for the FVIEW1 project.

```
Form #1                                Form filename: FVIEW1.FRM
Version: 1.0                           Date: June 27, 1991
Command Button      Command1          Reads the file specified in Text1
                    Command2          Finds the file specified in Text1
                    Command3          Toggles the Enabled setting of
                                         Command1
                    Command4          Finds the text in Text2
                    Command5          Executes a DOS command/program
                    Command6          Executes a Windows application
                    Command7          Hides Command5, Command6,
                                         Text3, and Label3
                    Command8          Exits the application

Text Box            Text1             Contains the filename to read
                    Text2             Contains the text search string
                    Text3             Contains the DOS/Windows
                                         command line
                    Text4             Displays the text lines of a file

Label               Label1            Label of Text1
                    Label2            Label of Text2
                    Label3            Label of Text3
```

7-2 List of control objects for the FVIEW1 project.

```
Application (Code) Name: FVIEW1
Form #1
Version: 1.0
   Date: June 27, 1991
```

Control object type	Default CtlName	Purpose
Form	Caption	File Viewer
Command1	CtlName	ReadBtn
	Caption	Read
	Default	True
Command2	CtlName	FindFileBtn
	Caption	Find File
Command3	CtlName	ToggleBtn
	Caption	Toggle Read Button
Command4	CtlName	FindBtn
	Caption	Find
Command5	CtlName	DosBtn
	Caption	DOS Command

7-3 The modified control settings for the FVIEW1 project.

Original control name	Property	New setting
Command6	CtlName	WinBtn
	Caption	Windows Command
Command7	CtlName	ShowOSBtn
	Caption	Show/Hide OS
Command8	CtlName	QuitBtn
	Caption	Quit
	Cancel	True
Text1	CtlName	FilenameBox
	Text	(empty string)
Text2	CtlName	FindBox
	Text	(empty string)
Text3	CtlName	DosBox
	Text	(empty string)
Text4	CtlName	TextBox
	Text	(empty string)
	MultiLine	True
	ScrollBars	3 - both
Label1	CtlName	FilenameLbl
	Caption	Filename Input
Label2	CtlName	FindLbl
	Caption	Find Input
Label3	CtlName	DosLbl
	Caption	DOS/Win Input

7-3 Continued.

Figure 7-4 shows the form for the file viewer application with all of its controls, as specified in FIG. 7-3. Now that you have seen the program interface, let's discuss the operation of the program in more detail.

The program's operations

The main purpose of the program is to view ASCII text files. This is carried out by typing the name of a file (including the full directory path of that file) in the Filename Input text box. When the filename is entered, click on the Read button, and the text lines of the specified file are displayed in the large text box. Use the scroll bars of the text box to view the various

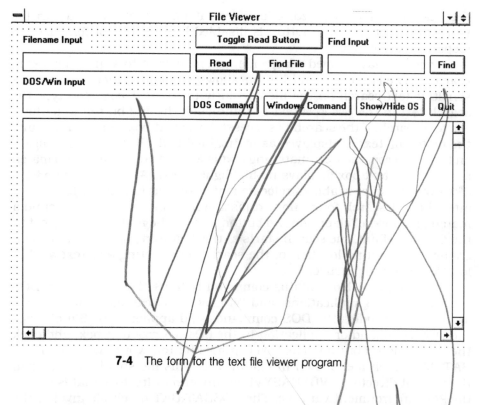

7-4 The form for the text file viewer program.

parts of the file. The text box has its MultiLine and ScrollBars properties set to True and 3, respectively, at design time. The result is a versatile file viewer.

Since the first task that you probably want to perform is reading a file, the Default property of the Read button is set to True. This means that when you start the program, you can type in a filename and press Enter to view the text in that file. As long as you do not select any other command button, the default status of the Read button remains in effect. Once you select another command button, you need to click on the Read button again to read the specified file.

Text boxes are no match for the File List boxes when it comes to locating and selecting a file. Since File List boxes are introduced in a later chapter, we have to work with the text boxes for now. The Find File button performs a simple file search based on the DOS 5.0 dir command. To locate a file, type its name and the starting directory path. If this is omitted, the search begins from the current directory. Press the Find File button. If you are not running Windows 3.0 with DOS 5.0, you need to use an alternate method. I will discuss the technical aspects behind the Find File button in the next subsection.

The Toggle Read button illustrates how to disable and enable a command button in general, and in this case, the Read button. Pressing the Toggle Read button toggles the Enabled property of the Read button. When the Read button is disabled, clicking on it has no effect. You can tell whether or not the Read button is disabled by the style of font used in displaying the caption.

Once you have loaded a large file, you may want to search for text in that file. The Find command button allows you to conduct simple case-sensitive text search on the file currently in the text box. You type the search text in the Find Input text box and click the Find button to perform the text search. If the search is successful, the text box gets the focus and the matching text is displayed as highlighted text. When you click again on the Find button, the next matching text is located, and so on. If no match is found, the text box displays no highlighted text. As coded, the FindBtn_ Click event handler is able to relocate matching text in a cyclic fashion — after the last search found no text (assuming previous searches found a match), the next click on the Find button locates the first matching text in the file. By default, the search starts at the beginning of the file. You can change the starting location of the search by selecting any text at that location using the mouse.

The program also contains command buttons that let you run DOS commands, DOS applications, and Windows applications. The DOS Command button handles the DOS commands and applications. Simply type the DOS command or application in the DOS/Win Input text box, and click the DOS Command button. The DOS Command button works with the DOS-BAT.BAT batch file, shown in Listing 7-1. This file should be either in the current directory \VB\EASYVB or any other directory that is part of the PATH environment variable. The DOSBAT.BAT batch file invokes the COMMAND.COM DOS command processor, assumed to be located in the root directory of the current drive. If this is not the case in your system, you need to edit file DOSBAT.BAT to reflect the correct location of the COMMAND.COM file (or any compatible replacement). The pause statement in the DOSBAT.BAT file allows commands like the DOS DIR command to pause after they finish working. Otherwise, when the DOS command execution is finished, the screen switches back to the Visual Basic program without giving you a chance to view the last DOS screen generated by the DOS command.

Listing 7-1 The DOSBAT.BAT batch file that must be placed at the root directory.

```
@echo off
\command.com /c %1 %2 %3 %4 %5 %6 %7 %8 %9
pause.
```

To run a Windows application, type the required command in the DOS/Win Input text box and click on the Windows Command button.

The Show/Hide OS command button toggles the visibility of the DOS Command button, the Windows Command button, the DOS/Win Input text box, and the label of that box.

To exit the text file viewer application, either press the Esc key or click on the Quit command button. The Esc key actually selects the Quit button, because the Cancel property of that button was set to True at design time.

The program code

Listing 7-2 contains the code for the various event-handling procedures in the program. In this subsection I discuss the code of the various program procedures in the sequence in which they appear in the listing.

1. The QuitBtn_Click procedure that exits the Visual Basic text file view.
2. The ReadBtn_Click procedure that reads the text line of the file specified in the Filename Input text box. The procedure performs the following main tasks:
   - Stores the Text setting of FilenameBox into the local variable F.
   - Exits the procedure if the variable F contains an empty string.
   - Assigns the sequence of Chr$(13) and Chr$(10) to the local variable NL.
   - Sets the error-handler to trap the error that is caused by attempting to open a nonexistent file (as specified by variable F).
   - Opens the file F for input. The file buffer number, or *handler*, is 1.
   - Assigns an empty string to the variable F. This variable is reused in storing the lines of the text files.
   - Reads the file text lines using the Do-While loop. Each line read is stored in the local variable L. The variable F is appended to the L + NL string expression. This ensures that each line read is followed by a carriage return/line feed pair of characters.
   - Assigns the variable F, which now stores the text lines, to the Text property of TextBox.
   - The file buffer closes and the exits procedure.

The remaining statements in the procedure form the error-handling statements. This includes the statement with the predefined MsgBox procedure that displays a "Cannot Open file *filename*" message. I will discuss the MsgBox procedure further in Chapter 10.

The ReadBtn_Click procedure performs file I/O and error-handling. These topics, which should be familiar to Quick Basic and GW-BASIC programmers, are discussed in more detail in later chapters.

Listing 7-2   The listing for the FVIEW1 project.

```
Sub QuitBtn_Click ( )
   End
End Sub

Sub ReadBtn_Click ( )
   Dim F As String
   Dim L As String
   Dim NL As String * 2
   ' obtain filename from the filename text box
   F = FilenameBox.Text
   ' if filename is an empty string, exit
   If F = " " Then Exit Sub
   NL = Chr$(13) + Chr$(10)
   ' set error-handler
   On Error GoTo BadFile
   ' open the file
   Open F For Input As 1
   F = " " ' clear variable to reuse it
   ' loop to read the text lines from the ASCII file
   Do While Not EOF(1)
      Line Input #1; L
      F = F + L + NL ' append a new line
   Loop
   TextBox.Text = F ' copy F into text box
   ' close the file
   Close #1
   ' exit procedure
   Exit Sub
'********** Error-handler **********
BadFile:
   Beep
   MsgBox "Cannot open file " + F, 0, "File I/O Error"
   On Error GoTo 0
   Resume EndOfSub
EndOfSub:
End Sub

Sub FindBtn_Click ( )
   Static CurIndex As Long
   Dim Find As String
   ' update the index to the current character
   CurIndex = TextBox.SelStart + 1
   ' store the text of the Find box in the variable Find
   Find = FindBox.Text
   ' is variable Find empty?
   If Find = " " Then Exit Sub ' nothing to find
   ' locate the index of the next substring Find in the
   ' text box
```

Listing 7-2 Continued.

```
    CurIndex = InStr(CurIndex + 1, TextBox.Text, Find)
    ' found a match?
    If CurIndex > 0 Then
      ' Yes! Display the matching text as selected text
      TextBox.SelStart = CurIndex - 1
      TextBox.SelLength = Len(Find)
      TextBox.SetFocus
    Else
      ' No! Clear any selected text
      TextBox.SelStart = 0
      TextBox.SelLength = 0
    End If
End Sub

Sub DosBtn_Click ( )
    Dim Dummy As Integer
    ' invoke the DOSBAT batch file
    Dummy = Shell("dosbat.bat " + DosBox.Text, 1)
End Sub

Sub FindFileBtn_Click ( )
    Dim Dummy As Integer
    ' invoke the DOS dir command with the /s
    ' subdirectory option and the /p paginated
    ' output option
    Dummy = Shell("dosbat.bat dir " + FilenameBox.Text + " /s/p", 1)
End Sub

Sub ToggleBtn_Click ( )
    ReadBtn.Enabled = Not ReadBtn.Enabled
End Sub

Sub ShowOSBtn_Click ( )
    ' toggle the Visible property of the DosBox text box,
    ' the DosBtn button, the WinBtn button, and the DosLbl
    ' label
    DosBox.Visible = Not DosBox.Visible
    DosBtn.Visible = Not DosBtn.Visible
    WinBtn.Visible = Not WinBtn.Visible
    DosLbl.Visible = Not DosLbl.Visible
End Sub

Sub WinBtn_Click ( )
    Dim Dummy As Integer
    ' invoke a Windows application
    Dummy = Shell(DosBox.Text, 1)
End Sub
```

3. The FindBtn_Click procedure performs simple case-sensitive text search. The procedure employs the local static variable CurIndex to keep track of the character index for the last matching text. The procedure performs the following tasks:

   • Assigns the value of TextBox.SelStart + 1 to the static variable CurIndex. The value of TextBox.SelStart is 0 when you first start the text search or when the last search found no match. Nonzero values for SelStart result from the presence of either the last matching text or user-defined selected text. The 1 is added to the SelStart to prevent the search process from being stuck in the same location of a previous match. Moreover, if SelStart is 0, adding 1 makes the CurIndex variable point to the first character in TextBox.
   • Assigns the string in FindBox to the local string variable Find.
   • Exits the procedure if the Find string is empty.
   • Locates the occurrence of the next matching text using the predefined InStr function. The call to InStr includes the CurIndex argument to start the search at the CurIndex character of TextBox. Omitting the CurIndex argument results in the search always being conducted from the beginning of the file. The result of the InStr function is reassigned to the CurIndex variable.
   • Examines whether the new value of CurIndex is positive. If so, there is a matching string found at character CurIndex. The first two statements in the Then clause make the matching text the new selected text. The last statement in the Then clause sets the focus to TextBox to make the selected text visible. If CurIndex is zero, there is no matching text and the statements in the Else clause are executed to turn off any existing selected text. This action visually signals the absence of any matching text.

4. The DosBtn_Click procedure allows you to execute a DOS command or DOS application. The procedure uses the Shell function to execute the DOSBAT.BAT file. The arguments for that batch file are provided by the DOS/Win Input text box. As shown in Listing 7-1, the DOSBAT.BAT file systematically invokes a copy of COMMAND.COM (the full filename is used). The /c option tells DOS that you want a copy of COMMAND.COM. The arguments you supply in the DOS/Win Input box, such as dir *.exe, specify exactly what you want DOS to do.

5. The FindFileBtn_Click is a special procedure that searches for DOS files. You can say that this procedure is a special version of the DosBtn_Click procedure. The current code for FindFileBtn_Click uses the new /s directive for the DOS 5.0 DIR command. The filename

wildcard, obtained from the Filename Input text box, is inserted between the dir and /s/p arguments.

■ If you are not running Windows under DOS 5.0 or later, you need to change the first argument of the Shell function. If you have access to a file-finding utility, such as WhereIs or Peter Norton's FileFind, you can use either of the following statements:

```
Dummy = Shell("dosbat.bat whereis " + FilenameBox.Text", 1)
Dummy = Shell("dosbat.bat filefind " + FilenameBox.Text", 1)
```

6. The ToggleBtn_Click procedure toggles the Enabled property of the Read command button. The procedure uses the Not operator in a simple assignment.
7. The ShowOSBtn_Click procedure toggles the Visible property of the DOS Command button, the Windows Command button, and the DOS/Win Input text box and its label. This procedure uses a series of simple assignments involving the Not operator to reverse the Boolean value of the Visible property.
8. The WinBtn_Click procedure invokes a Windows application using the Shell function. The arguments for the Shell function should include the application's full name (including path and extension name) and any command-line arguments (this will make a lot of command-line junkies happy!).

Running the file viewer

Once you have typed the code for the file viewer, or loaded it from the disk, press the F5 function key to run the program. A sample session of using the text file viewer is shown in FIG. 7-5.

Setting access keys to command buttons

Access keys enable you to select a command button by pressing the Alt key with the designated character for that button. The designated character is the underlined character that appears as part of the button's caption. If a command button has no character that is underlined, it has no access key associated with it.

To assign an access key to a command button, type an ampersand, (&) before the designated character in the caption. The ampersand itself does not become part of the visible caption—it is merely an access key selector. For example, to make the Alt−R the access key to the Read button in the text file viewer, make the caption of that button &Read. Access keys are not case-sensitive and need not be the first character, but they must be unique.

Figure 7-6 shows the updated settings for the text file viewer that assign access keys to the control buttons. The accompanying disk stores

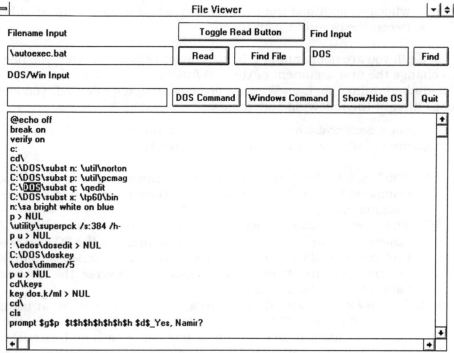

7-5 A sample session with the text file viewer program.

Object	Property	New setting
Form	Caption	File Viewer (1B)
Command1	Caption	&Read
Command2	Caption	F&ind File
Command3	Caption	&Toggle Read Button
Command4	Caption	&Find
Command5	Caption	&DOS Command
Command6	Caption	&Windows Command
Command7	Caption	&Show/Hide OS
Command8	Caption	&Quit

7-6 The updated settings for the text file viewer that introduces access keys to the command buttons.

the updated form and project files under FVIEW1B.FRM and FVIEW1B.MAK, respectively.

Manipulating the tab order of controls

Visual Basic keeps track of the order in which you create the various controls on your form. By default, Visual Basic uses that same order when you press the Tab key to select the next control. This is known as the *tab order*. Thus, a well-planned and well-created form enables you to smoothly navigate between controls which are either visually or logically associated. By contrast, a hastily assembled form causes the Tab key to jump erratically between controls. Fortunately, Visual Basic allows you to override that default tab order.

Many controls possess the TabStop property, which is usually set to True. This value indicates that the control can be selected when you cycle through the controls using the Tab key. Setting TabStop to False makes Visual Basic bypass that control when you Tab through the form controls.

Controls that have the TabStop property also possess the TabIndex property. This is the property that Visual Basic uses in determining the tab order. You can view the TabIndex setting for each control by selecting the TabIndex property in the Properties combo box. The lowest value for the TabIndex is 0. Negative TabIndex values generate an error. The tab order can be changed either at design time or at run time. You can type in a new tab order value for the currently selected control. Visual Basic automatically adjusts the TabIndex setting for the controls that have the same setting or greater—the TabIndex of these controls is incremented by one. If you type in a tab order that is higher than the upper limit, Visual Basic adjusts that value to the upper limit. This upper limit is equal to the total number of controls in the tab order minus one.

Altering the tab order during run time is carried out by assigning a new value to the TabIndex property. The best place to insert the new tab order setting is the Form_Load procedure.

Emulating DOS screens

☞ Programming with Visual Basic is fun and succeeds in building on your prior knowledge of Quick Basic (and to a lesser extent, GW-BASIC and BASICA). No meaningful BASIC program is without the Print statement. Visual Basic supports the Print statement for the form and for the printer (see chapter 11), but not for the text box. This section explores one programming method that allows you to emulate the Print statement in a text box and treat the text box as a pseudo-screen that emulates a DOS screen. Concerning the task of emulating a DOS screen, there is some good news and some bad news. First the bad news: the method presented here causes the emulated screens to show text more slowly than the original DOS screens. The good news is that you can have screens of various sizes (rows and columns) and you can show multiple emulated screens in the same application. An added bonus is that the emulated screens can be scrollable.

The next subsections discuss the programming approach to designing an emulated DOS screen, show two versions of the code, and present a Visual Basic program that tests the simpler code version.

The basic approach

The concept of emulating a DOS screen (which I will call a pseudo-screen from now on) builds on the ability of text boxes to display multiple lines of text. The design of pseudo-screens involves the following components and features:

- The pseudo-screen has a user-defined maximum number of rows and columns. This helps to keep text in check.
- The pseudo-screen has a hidden cursor that keeps track of the location of the text displayed for the next time you want to write to the screen.
- You can move the cursor and query its location. The cursor is bound by the pseudo-screen dimensions.
- You can write a string at the current screen location using a pseudo-PRINT procedure. The text can wrap around to the next line. The pseudo-PRINT emulates a Quick Basic PRINT stringExpression$; statement and thus excludes moving the cursor to the next line (unless the text wraps). A separate procedure is used to move the cursor to next line.

The above specifications describe the general behavior of the pseudo-screens, but shed no light on the basic approach for the implementation. The implementation involves a sequence of design choices. The first choice is whether or not to directly update the text lines in the text box. Directly updating requires you to read and write the substrings that form individual lines in the multi-line text box. Since Visual Basic does not implement methods to perform the above type of substring accesses, the task can be involved and maybe even slow.

Another option is to maintain a copy of the text lines in an array of dynamic strings. The changes to the screen are made in two quick steps: first update the array elements, then copy the array elements to the screen to refresh the display. Whereas this approach uses twice as much memory to display the text, it is easier to code. This is because using arrays permits you to apply the "divide-and-conquer" programming principle, and deal with each line separately. In addition, you can write to several lines on the pseudo-screen before updating the display.

When using an array of strings to maintain a copy of the pseudo-screen, you have two options for manipulating the text in the array elements. The first choice initializes the array elements with spaces; that is, each element has a string of spaces equal to the maximum number of screen columns. Consequently, writing to the pseudo-screen involves overwriting the initial spaces in the array elements. Operations like clearing the screens involve overwriting the array elements with spaces.

The second option in using arrays of strings is more memory conservative than the first, after all, these arrays already duplicate the viewed text lines. The array elements are expanded only as needed. This expansion is due to the use of the pseudo-PRINT command or to moving the cursor. In the latter case, the array element of the sought line is padded with spaces up to the column position of the cursor.

Another design choice for the pseudo-screen involves how general the code should be. At one extreme, the code handles a single pseudo-screen and its associated array of strings. At the other extreme, the code handles any text box associated with at least one array of strings. In the next section I present both extremes.

The code for the first pseudo-screen

Let's start with the simple case where a single pseudo-screen is implemented using a text box and an array of strings. Listing 7-3 contains the code for the procedures that manipulate the pseudo-screen. The code is located in the declarations section and has access to the ScreenBox text box, which is used to emulate a DOS screen. The general section declares the MAX_ROWS and MAX_COLS constants to specify the size of the pseudo-screen. In addition, the same code section declares the ScrLine string array, the CursX variable, and the CursY variable. The last two variables store the current cursor location. There are other variables that are also declared in this section. I will explain these variables later in this subsection.

The procedures that manipulate the pseudo-screen supported by object ScreenBox, array ScrLine, and variables CursX and CursY are:

1. The ClearScreen procedure clears the pseudo-screen. This involves assigning empty strings to the ScreenBox and the elements of array ScrLine. In addition, the cursor location is set to the upper right corner of the pseudo-screen, (1, 1), by assigning 1 to the cursor variables.
2. The GotoXY procedure moves the cursor to the screen location (X, Y). The procedure checks if the provided coordinates are valid. The array element of the Y row is padded with spaces if the specified X coordinate is greater than the length of that array element. The valid arguments for X and Y are assigned to the cursor variables, CursX and CursY.
3. The WhereX function returns the value of the variable CursX.
4. The WhereY function returns the value of the variable CursY.
5. The ScrollUp procedure emulates scrolling the pseudo-screen a specified number of lines. Two For-Next loops are used to shift or copy text among the elements of array ScrLine before the pseudo-screen is updated.
6. The NewLine procedure places the cursor on the next line. If the value of CursY is equal to MAX_ROWS, the pseudo-screen is scrolled up by one line.

7. The PPrint procedure implements the pseudo-PRINT that I mentioned earlier. The current implementation allows PPrint to display text that can wrap only to the next line.

8. The SaveScreen procedure saves the present pseudo-screen and the current cursor position to the parameters Buffer(), X%, and Y%, respectively. Later, you can call LoadScreen to restore the screen. The SaveScreen and LoadScreen procedures allow you to take snapshot images of the pseudo-screen and view these images later. The SaveScreen procedure simply copies the ScrLine array to the Buffer array, variable CursX to X%, and variable CursY to Y%.

9. The LoadScreen procedure loads the pseudo-screen from the data in the arguments for Buffer, X%, and Y%. The LoadScreen procedure first copies the Buffer array to the ScrLine array, X% to variable CursX, and Y% to variable CursY. Once the data is copied, the pseudo-screen is updated.

10. The UpdateScreenText procedure updates the ScreenBox to match the strings of array ScrLine.

The PSCREEN project

Listing 7-3 also contains event-handling procedures for a Visual Basic application that allows you to test the above screen-manipulation procedures. The test application uses the PSCREEN.MAK project file and the PSCREEN.FRM form file.

Listing 7-3 The code for the PSCREEN project.

```
' constants the define the size of the emulated screen
Const MAX_ROWS = 25, MAX_COLS = 80
' the array and variables that maintain the data for
' the emulated screen
Dim ScrLine(1 To MAX_ROWS) As String
Dim CursX As Integer
Dim CursY As Integer
' declarations for the screen buffer
Dim ScreenBuffer(1 To MAX_ROWS) As String
Dim BufX As Integer
Dim BufY As Integer

Sub ClearScreen ()
    ' clear the screen by assigning empty strings to the
    ' ScreenBox and ScrLine array and setting the cursor
    ' variables to 1.
    Dim I As Integer
    ScreenBox.Text = " "
    For I = 1 To MAX_ROWS
      ScrLine(I) = " "
    Next I
```

Listing 7-3 Continued.

```
   CursX = 1
   CursY = 1
End Sub

Sub GotoXY (X As Integer, Y As Integer)
   ' move the hidden cursor to (X,Y)
   Dim L As Integer
   If (X < 1) Or (Y < 1) Then Exit Sub
   If (Y > MAX_ROWS) Or (X > MAX_COLS) Then Exit Sub
   L = Len(ScrLine(Y))
   If X > L Then ' Pad string with spaces
      ScrLine(Y) = ScrLine(Y) + Space$(X − L)
   End If
   CursX = X
   CursY = Y
End Sub

Function WhereX ( ) As Integer
   ' return the value of CursX
   WhereX = CursX
End Function

Function WhereY ( ) As Integer
   ' return the value of CursY
   WhereY = CursY
End Function

Sub ScrollUp (NumLines As Integer)
   ' scroll up a specified number of lines
   Dim I As Integer
   If NumLines < 1 Then Exit Sub
   ' scroll at most MAX_ROWS rows
   If NumLines > MAX_ROWS Then
      NumLines = MAX_ROWS
   End If
   ' copy leading string to emulate scroll
   For I = 1 To MAXROWS − NumLines
      ScrLine(I) = ScrLine(I + NumLines)
   Next I
   ' assign empty string to trailing strings
   For I = MAX_ROWS − NumLines + 1 To MAX_ROWS
      ScrLine(I) = " "
   Next I
   UpdateScreenText
End Sub

Sub NewLine ( )
   ' move the hidden cursor to the first column of
```

Listing 7-3 Continued.

```
' the next line. Scroll screen up if the cursor
' is already at the last allowed screen row
If CursY < MAX_ROWS Then
   CursY = CursY + 1
   CursX = 1
Else
   ScrollUp 1
   CursX = 1
End If
End Sub

Sub PPrint (S As String, UpdateScreenNow As Integer)
   ' Emulate a simple form of the QuickBasic print:
   '
   '               PRINT Astring$;
   '
   ' The second parameter enable you to update the text
   ' on the screen, or keep the changes hidden (for now).
   Dim LenStr As Integer
   Dim LenLine As Integer
   Dim LenDiff As Integer
   Dim S2 As String
   If S = " " Then Exit Sub
   LenStr = Len(S)
   If CursY = MAX_ROWS Then ScrollUp 1
   LenLine = Len(ScrLine(CursY))
   S2 = " "
   ' string cannot fit on the current line?
   If (CursX + LenStr) > MAX_COLS Then
      LenDiff = CursX + LenStr - MAX_COLS - 1
      ' split original string into two strings
      S2 = Right$(S, LenDiff) ' next-line text
      S = Left$(S, LenStr - LenDiff)
   End If
   ' Pad current line
   If (CursX + LenStr) > LenLine Then
      LenDiff = CursX + LenStr - LenLine
      ScrLine(CursY) = ScrLine(CursY) + Space$(LenDiff)
   End If
   ' write S to current line
   Mid$(ScrLine(CursY), CursX, LenStr) = S
   CursX = CursX + LenStr ' update CursX
   If CursX > MAX_COLS Then NewLine
   ' the next-line string is not empty?
   If S2 < > " " Then ' print to the next line
      If CursY < MAX_COLS Then NewLine
      LenDiff = Len(S2) - Len(ScrLine(CursY))
      If LenDiff > 0 Then ' pad the string for the next line
```

Listing 7-3 Continued.

```
        ScrLine(CursY) = ScrLine(CursY) + Space$(LenDiff)
    End If
    ' write the next-line string
    Mid$(ScrLine(CursY), 1, Len(S2)) = S2
        CursX = Len(S2) + 1
        If CursX > MAX_COLS Then NewLine
    End If
    ' update the screen now?
    If UpdateScreenNow Then UpdateScreenText
End Sub

Sub SaveScreen (Buffer( ) As String, X%, Y%)
    ' save screen to Buffer( ) array.
    ' the current position of the hidden cursor is
    ' stored in parameters X% and Y%
    Dim I As Integer
    For I = 1 To MAX_ROWS
        Buffer(I) = ScrLine(I)
    Next I
    X% = CursX
    Y% = CursY
End Sub

Sub LoadScreen (Buffer( ) As String, X%, Y%)
    ' load screen from the Buffer( ) array
    ' the X% and Y% parameters specify new cursor location
    Dim I As Integer
    For I = 1 To MAX_ROWS
        ScrLine(I) = Buffer(I)
    Next I
    CursX = X%
    CursY = Y%
    UpdateScreenText
End Sub

Sub UpdateScreenText ( )
    ' update the text in the ScreenBox
    Dim I As Integer
    Dim S As String
    Dim NL As String * 2
    NL = Chr$(13) + Chr$(10)
    S = " "
    For I = 1 To MAX_ROWS - 1
        S = S + ScrLine(I) + NL
    Next I
    S = S + ScrLine(MAX_ROWS)
    ScreenBox.Text = S
End Sub
```

Listing 7-3 Continued.

```
Sub QuitBtn_Click ( )
  End
End Sub

Sub ClearBtn_Click ( )
  ClearScreen
  LocateBtn_Click
End Sub

Sub MoveBtn_Click ( )
  Dim X As Integer
  Dim Y As Integer
  X = Val(CursorXBox.Text)
  Y = Val(CursorYBox.Text)
  GotoXY X, Y
  LocateBtn_Click
End Sub

Sub LocateBtn_Click ( )
  CursorXBox.Text = Str$(WhereX( ))
  CursorYBox.Text = Str$(WhereY( ))
End Sub

Sub PrintBtn_Click ( )
  Dim S As String
  S = TextBox.Text
  PPrint S, - 1
  LocateBtn_Click
  End Sub

Sub ScrollUpBtn_Click ( )
  ScrollUp 1
  LocateBtn_Click
End Sub

Sub NewLineBtn_Click ( )
  NewLine
  LocateBtn_Click
End Sub

Sub Form_Load ( )
  ClearScreen
End Sub

Sub SaveBtn_Click ( )
  SaveScreen ScreenBuffer( ), BufX, BufY
End Sub
```

Listing 7-3 Continued.

```
Sub LoadBtn_Click ( )
  LoadScreen ScreenBuffer( ), BufX, BufY
  LocateBtn_Click
End Sub
```

Figures 7-7, 7-8, and 7-9 contain the documentation forms that specify the various objects and their customized settings. FIG. 7-10 shows the controls of the test program during design time. The various command buttons enable you to test various aspects of the pseudo-screen, such as

Application Name: Pseudo-Screen Test Program
Application Code Name: PSCREEN
Version: 1.0   Date Created: June 28, 1991
Programmer(s): Namir Clement Shammas

List of filenames
Storage Path: \VB\EASYVB
Project PSCREEN.MAK
Global GLOBAL.BAS
Form 1 PSCREEN.FRM

7-7   General project specifications for the PSCREEN project.

Form #1   Form Filename: PSCREEN.FRM
Version: 1.0   Date: June 28, 1991

Control object type	Default CtlName	Purpose
Command Button	Command1	Exits the test program
	Command2	Clears the pseudo-screen
	Command3	Moves the cursor
	Command4	Locates the cursor
	Command5	Writes the text in Text4 to the pseudo-screen (Text1)
	Command6	Scrolls up the pseudo-screen
	Command7	Moves the cursor to the next line
	Command8	Saves the pseudo-screen
	Command9	Restore the pseudo-screen
Text Box	Text1	The pseudo-screen
	Text2	The cursor column number
	Text3	The cursor row number
	Text4	Text to write on the pseudo-screen
Label	Label1	Label for Text1
	Label2	Label for Text2
	Label3	Label for Text3
	Label4	Label for Text4

7-8   List of control objects for the PSCREEN project.

Application (Code) Name: PSCREEN
Form #1
Version: 1.0   Date: June 28, 1991

Original control name	Property	New Setting
Form	Caption	Pseudo-Screen
Command1	CtlName	QuitBtn
	Caption	Quit
Command2	CtlName	ClearBtn
	Caption	Clear Screen
Command3	CtlName	MoveBtn
	Caption	Move Cursor
Command4	CtlName	LocateBtn
	Caption	Locate Cursor
Command5	CtlName	PrintBtn
	Caption	Print
Command6	CtlName	ScrollBtn
	Caption	Scroll Up
Command7	CtlName	NewLineBtn
	Caption	NewLine
Command8	CtlName	SaveBtn
	Caption	Save
Command9	CtlName	LoadBtn
	Caption	Load
Text1	CtlName	ScreenBox
	Text	(empty string)
	MultiLine	True
	ScrollBars	3 - both
Text2	CtlName	CursorXBox
	Text	(empty string)
Text3	CtlName	CursorYBox
	Text	(empty string)
Text4	CtlName	TextBox
	Text	(empty string)

7-9 The modified control settings for the PSCREEN project.

Label1	CtlName	ScreenLbl
	Caption	The Screen
Label2	CtlName	ColumnLbl
	Caption	Column
Label3	CtlName	RowLbl
	Caption	Row
Label4	CtlName	TextLbl
	Caption	Text

7-9 Continued.

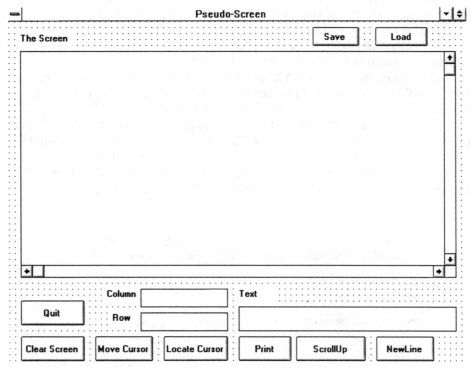

7-10 The control objects of the PSCREEN test application.

clearing the screen, moving the cursor, printing text, scrolling up the screen, saving the screen, and restoring the screen.

Listing 7-3 contains the code for the various event-handling procedures. The Form_Load procedure clears the pseudo-screen when the PSCREEN application starts running.

The Locate Cursor button is actually invoked by the other procedure-handling events to automatically display the updated location of the cursor in the text boxes marked Column and Row. This should compensate for the fact that the cursor is invisible. It is important to point out that the pseudo-screen cursor has nothing to do with the edit cursor that appears when you click in the ScreenBox.

The general declarations section declares the following array and variables that are used in testing the SaveScreen and LoadScreen procedures:

```
' declarations for the screen buffer
Dim ScreenBuffer(1 To MAX_ROWS) As String
Dim BufX As Integer
Dim BufY As Integer
```

The PSCREEN test program uses the above array and variables as its sole buffer that stores the current pseudo-screen. You are welcome to extend the number of buffers used by the program. This requires additional arrays and variables, similar to ScreenBuffer, BufX, and BufY, as well as additional controls to select the target buffer.

After entering the code in LISTING 7-3, or loading it from the disk, run the PSCREEN test program by pressing the F5 function key. Type in some text in the Text text box and then press the Print command button. Try pressing the NewLine button and then press the Print button again. Notice the text on the pseudo-screen. The Row and Column text boxes update the current location of the hidden cursor. Experiment with the various controls to get a feel of pseudo-screen implementation. Figure 7-11 shows the screen image of a sample session with the PSCREEN test program.

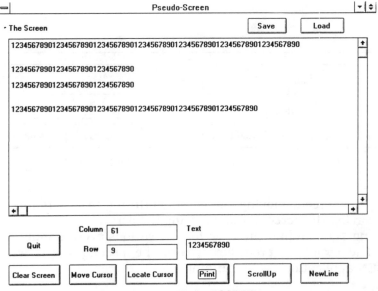

7-11 A sample session with the PSCREEN test program.

The code for the second pseudo-screen

The implementation of the pseudo-screen in LISTING 7-3 may be regarded as a prototype for a more general version of the code. Listings 7-4 and 7-5 contain the more modular version of the pseudo-screen implementation. In LISTING 7-4, the ScreenType user-defined type is declared. This type holds the data fields that manage the screen dimension and cursor location. Listing 7-5 contains the procedures that convert any multiline text box into a pseudo-screen. These procedures should be placed in a module. This enables any Visual Basic form to access the pseudo-screen procedures. Unlike their counterparts in LISTINGS 7-3, the procedures in LISTING 7-5 make no assumptions about the target text box, the supporting array of string, or the cursor variables. All the above information is handled using parameters.

Listing 7-4   The Visual Basic declaration that must be in the global module.

```
Type ScreenType
   MaxRows As Integer
   MaxCols As Integer
   CursX As Integer
   CursY As Integer
End Type
```

Listing 7-5 contains the procedure InitScreen used to initialize the working parameters of a pseudo-screen. Listing 7-3 has no similar procedure. You must use the InitScreen procedure before any other one to ensure that the targeted pseudo-screen works properly.

7-5   The code for the PSCRNLIB.BAS module that supports a general version of the pseudoscreens.

```
Sub InitScreen (MaxRow%, MaxCol%, SD As ScreenType)
   ' initialize screen parameters
   SD.MaxCols = MaxCol%
   SD.MaxRows = MaxRow%
   SD.CursX = 1
   SD.CursY = 1
End Sub

Sub ClearScreen (TBox As Control, SL$( ), SD As ScreenType)
   ' clear the screen by assigning empty strings to the
   ' TBox and SL$ array and setting the cursor variables to 1.
   Dim I As Integer
   If TypeOf TBox Is TextBox Then
      TBox.Text = " "
      For I = 1 To SD.MaxRows
         SL$(I) = " "
```

Listing 7-5 Continued.

```
      Next I
      SD.CursX = 1
      SD.CursY = 1
   End If
End Sub

Sub GotoXY (X%, Y%, SL$( ), SD As ScreenType)
   ' move the hidden cursor to (X%, Y%)
   Dim L As Integer
   If (X% < 1) Or (Y% < 1) Then Exit Sub
   If (Y% > SD.MaxRows) Or (X% > SD.MaxCols) Then Exit Sub
   L = Len(SL$(Y%))
   If X% > L Then
      SL$(Y%) = SL$(Y%) + Space$(X% − L)
   End If
   SD.CursX = X%
   SD.CursY = Y%
End Sub


Function WhereX (SD As ScreenType) As Integer
   ' return the value of SD.CursX
   WhereX = SD.CursX
End Function

Function WhereY (SD As ScreenType) As Integer
   ' return the value of the SD.CursY
   WhereY = SD.CursY
End Function

Sub ScrollUp (NumLines%, TBox As Control, SL$( ), SD As ScreenType)
   ' scroll up a specified number of lines
   Dim I As Integer
   If TypeOf TBox Is TextBox Then
   Else
      Exit Sub
   End If
   If NumLines < 1 Then Exit Sub
   ' scroll at most SD.MaxRows
   If NumLines > SD.MaxRows Then
      NumLines = SD.MaxRows
   End If
   ' copy leading string to emulate scroll
   For I = 1 To SD.MaxRows − NumLines
      SL$(I) = SL$(I + NumLines)
   Next I
   ' assign empty string to trailing strings
   For I = SD.MaxRows − NumLines + 1 To SD.MaxRows
      SL$(I) = " "
```

Listing 7-5 Continued.

```
   Next I
   UpdateScreenText TBox, SL$( ), SD
End Sub

Sub NewLine (TBox As Control, SL$( ), SD As ScreenType)
   ' move the hidden cursor to the first column of
   ' the next line. Scroll screen up if the cursor
   ' is already at the last allowed screen row
   If TypeOf TBox Is TextBox Then
      If SD.CursY < SD.MaxRows Then
         SD.CursY = SD.CursY + 1
         SD.CursX = 1
      Else
         ScrollUp 1, TBox, SL$( ), SD
         SD.CursX = 1
      End If
   End If
End Sub

   Sub PPrint (S$, UpdateScreenNow%, TBox As Control, SL$( ), SD As ScreenType)
      ' Emulate a simple form of the QuickBasic print:
      '
      '               PRINT Astring$;
      '
      ' The second parameter enable you to update the text
      ' on the screen, or keep the changes hidden (for now).
      Dim LenStr As Integer
      Dim LenLine As Integer
      Dim LenDiff As Integer
      Dim S2 As String
      If TypeOf TBox Is TextBox Then
      Else
         Exit Sub
      End If
      If S$ = " " Then Exit Sub
      LenStr = Len(S$)
      If SD.CursY = SD.MaxRows Then ScrollUp 1
      LenLine = Len(SL$(SD.CursY))
      S2 = " "
      ' string cannot fit on the current line?
      If (SD.CursX + LenStr) > SD.MaxCols Then
         LenDiff = SD.CursX + LenStr - SD.MaxCols - 1
         ' split original string into two strings
         S2 = Right$(S$, LenDiff) ' next-line text
         S$ = Left$(S$, LenStr - LenDiff)
      End If
      ' Pad current line
      If (SD.CursX + LenStr) > LenLine Then
```

Listing 7-5 Continued.

```
       LenDiff = SD.CursX + LenStr − LenLine
       SL$(SD.CursY) = SL$(SD.CursY) + Space$(LenDiff)
    End If
    ' write S to current line
    Mid$(SL$(SD.CursY), SD.CursX, LenStr) = S$
    SD.CursX = SD.CursX + LenStr
    ' the next-line string is not empty?
    If SD.CursX > SD.MaxCols Then NewLine TBox, SL$( ), SD
    If S2 < > " " Then ' print to the next line
       If SD.CursY < SD.MaxCols Then NewLine TBox, SL$( ), SD
       LenDiff = Len(S2) − Len(SL$(SD.CursY))
       If LenDiff > 0 Then ' pad the string for the next line
          SL$(SD.CursY) = SL$(SD.CursY) + Space$(LenDiff)
       End If
       ' write the next-line string
       Mid$(SL$(SD.CursY), 1, Len(S2)) = S2
       SD.CursX = Len(S2) + 1
       If SD.CursX > SD.MaxCols Then NewLine TBox, SL$( ), SD
    End If
    ' update the screen now?
    If UpdateScreenNow% Then UpdateScreenText TBox, SL$( ), SD
End Sub

Sub SaveScreen (Buff$( ), BufData As ScreenType, SL$( ), SD As ScreenType)
    ' save screen to Buff$( ) array.
    ' the current position of the hidden cursor is
    ' stored in the fields of the SD parameter
    Dim I As Integer
    For I = 1 To SD.MaxRows
       Buff$(I) = SL$(I)
    Next I
    BufData.MaxRows = SD.MaxRows
    BufData.MaxCols = SD.MaxCols
    BufData.CursX = SD.CursX
    BufData.CursY = SD.CursY
End Sub

Sub LoadScreen (TBox As Control, Buff$( ), BufData As ScreenType, SL$( ), SD As
ScreenType)
    ' load screen from the Buff$( ) array
    ' the fields of the SD parameters specify new cursor location
    Dim I As Integer
    If TypeOf TBox Is TextBox Then
       For I = 1 To SD.MaxRows
          SL$(I) = Buff$(I)
       Next I
       SD.MaxRows = BufData.MaxRows
       SD.MaxCols = BufData.MaxCols
```

Listing 7-5 Continued.

```
      SD.CursX = BufData.CursX
      SD.CursY = BufData.CursY
      UpdateScreenText TBox, SL$( ), SD
   End If
End Sub

Sub UpdateScreenText (TBox As Control, SL$( ), SD As ScreenType)
   ' update the text in the TBox
   Dim I As Integer
   Dim S As String
   Dim NL As String * 2
   If TypeOf TBox Is TextBox Then
      NL = Chr$(13) + Chr$(10)
      S = " "
      For I = 1 To SD.MaxRows − 1
         S = S + SL$(I) + NL
      Next I
      S = S + SL$(SD.MaxRows)
      TBox.Text = S
   End If
End Sub
```

Using the procedures in LISTING 7-5 allows you to have multiple pseudo-screens in the same application. You can even copy text between the pseudo-screens, if their dimensions are compatible.

As an exercise, you are encouraged to create your own Visual Basic program to test the code in LISTING 7-5.

8

Application menus

Menus are an integral part of the Windows graphical user interface. Every Windows application uses menus, and Visual Basic is no exception. Up until now, the Visual Basic programs did not build any custom menus. Instead, they only had the "application" menu that is automatically attached to every Visual Basic program. Incorporating custom menus in your Visual Basic applications is a very easy process. Visual Basic offers you a powerful menu builder that makes it easy to build and modify custom menus. In this chapter you will learn about the following aspects of menus:

- Using the Menu Design Window.
- Incorporating custom menus in an application.
- Controlling menus at run time.
- Assigning shortcut and access keys to the various menu selections and options.
- Creating dynamically-modifying menus using control arrays.

☞ **Definition**   This book uses the following terms to identify menu components:

- A *menu selection* is a member of the main menu.
- A *menu option* is a member of the choices offered by a menu selection, or a parent menu option (in the case of nested menus).
- A *menu item* is a collective name for both a menu selection and a menu option.

The menu design window

Creating a custom application menu is made easy by the Menu Design Window. Visual Basic treats the menu selections and options as controls that recognize the Click event. Due to the nature of menus, the designers of Visual Basic have elected to use a specialized window in building the menus instead of using the Toolbox. Figure 8-1 shows the Menu Design Window while building a sample application menu. The Menu Design Window contains the controls described in the following paragraphs.

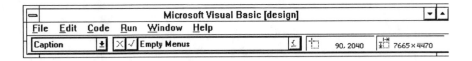

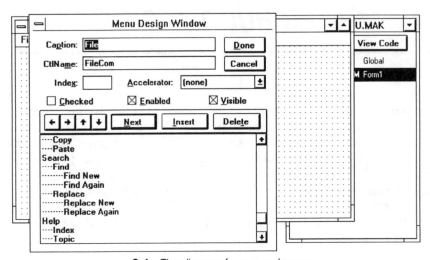

8-1 The diagram for a sample menu.

The Caption **text box**   This stores the caption for a menu option or selection. The hyphen character, –, is a special caption. When a menu item is assigned the hyphen caption it appears as a horizontal separator bar that divides the list of menu options into logical groups.

The CtlName **text box**   This contains the control name of a menu option or selection.

The Index **text box**   This stores the index number for a menu option that is a control array.

The Accelerator **combo box**   This combo box enables you to assign shortcut keys for the various menu options.

The Checked, Enabled, **and** Visible **check boxes** These boxes represent Boolean properties for menu selections and options, and allow you to establish the initial Boolean values for these properties. The Checked property determines whether or not a check mark appears to the left of a menu selection or option, to inform the user of the Boolean state associated with that menu item. The Enabled property allows you to enable or disable a menu item. Disabling a menu selection disables all of its options. Disabled menu items are displayed in lighter, shaded fonts. The Visible property permits you to show or hide a menu item. Setting the Visible property of a menu item to True both disables that item and hides it.

The Done command button Click on this button when you are finished designing the menu. You can return to the Menu Design Window and update the menu design at any time.

The Cancel command button This button cancels the updates you have made in the current session with the Menu Design Window.

The Menu structure text box This is a scrollable text box that displays the various menu items. The vertical scroll bar appears when the text box cannot display all of the menu items. The current menu item is displayed in reverse video.

The Menu-building command buttons These are the command buttons located above the menu structure text box. The Delete button removes the current menu item. The Insert button inserts a new menu item just before the current menu item. The Next button enables you to select the next menu item. The up and down arrow buttons allow you to move the current selection up or down the list of menu items, respectively. The left and right arrow buttons play an important role in creating the menu structure. (More about these important buttons later in this section.)

The process of creating a menu structure is essentially the same as creating an outline in your word processor. In a text outline, you structure your thoughts by reducing the indentation level of more important items and increasing the indentation level of "detailed" items. The Visual Basic menus work the same way—menu selections are not indented, while menu options are. The menu options that are attached to menu selections are indented once by pressing the right arrow button (the left arrow button un-indents the current entry). Visual Basic allows nested options of up to five levels of indentation. Each time you indent a menu option, four dots appear to its left.

Figure 8-2 shows the diagram of a sample menu structure that has menu options nested to two levels. Figure 8-1 shows the menu entries under the Search selection. Notice how the menu options are indented and observe the number of dots that lead the menu options.

You can create the menu structure one level at a time or in a sequence that observes the levels of indentations. Either approach is fine.

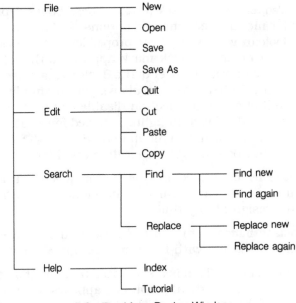

8-2 The Menu Design Window.

Building a bare-bones menu

Let's build the menu structure of FIG. 8-1. Load Visual Basic and work with the new project blank form. Select the Menu Design Window option from the Window menu. When the window appears, perform the following steps to create the menu selections:

1. Click on the Caption text box and type File.
2. Press the Tab key to move to the CtlName text box. Type FileCom.
3. Click the Next command button to move to the end of the menu outline.
4. Click the Insert command button to insert a new menu selection.
5. Repeat steps 1 to 4 for the Edit, Search, and Help menu selections. Use the EditCom, SearchCom, HelpCom names as the control names for their respective selections.

To create the menu options that are indented once, repeat the following steps for each menu option:

1. Click on the menu selection or menu option that comes after the one you wish to insert.
2. Click on the Insert command button to insert a new menu item.
3. Click on the Caption text box and type in the name of the menu option. Use the names that appear in FIG. 8-1 as the captions.
4. Press the Tab key to move to the CtlName text box.

5. Type in the control name for the current menu item; append the letters Com to the caption name and remove any spaces within the caption name. For example, the caption, Save As should have the control name SaveAsCom.
6. Press the right arrow button to indent the menu option. Nested menus require that you press the right arrow button twice. Press the left arrow button to un-indent any entry that you may erroneously over-indent.

Insert a hyphen menu item between the Save As and the Quit menu options to display a separator bar between these two entries. Use the Sep1 control name for the separator bar.

☞ The above steps are by no means the only way to build a menu structure. For example, you can insert a new menu item and then move it to the proper location.

Once you have finished designing the menu, click on the Done key. Now you are back to the form. Notice that the menu selections appear on the form. Press the F7 function key and select the QuitCom control. Insert an End statement inside the QuitCom_Click event-handling procedure. Run the program by pressing the F5 function key and experiment with the menu structure. Figure 8-3 shows one of the nested menu options.

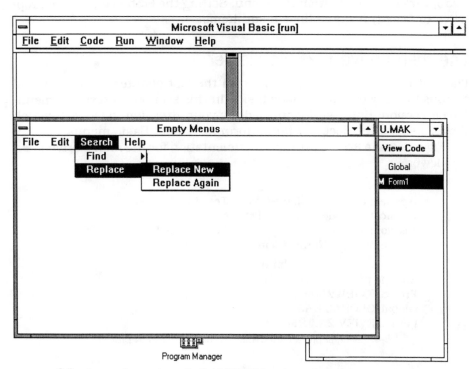

8-3 A sample session with the MTMENU project, showing nested menus.

Clicking on any menu selection or option, except the Quit menu option, accomplishes nothing. When you are finished with the program, select the Quit option from the File menu.

Save the form and project files using the MTMENU.FRM and MTMENU.MAK filenames in directory \VB\EASYVB.

Controlling menus at run time

The Checked, Enabled, and Visible properties can be set and retrieved at run time in a manner very similar to the Toolbox control properties. The general syntax for accessing the menu properties are shown next:

menuItem.Checked *[=Boolean%]*
menuItem.Enabled *[=Boolean%]*
menuItem.Visible *[=Boolean%]*

When the Checked property is assigned a True (−1), a check mark appears before the caption of that menu item. The check mark is a visual flag that indicates the on/off state of a related condition.

Setting the Enabled and Visible properties to False (0) disables that menu item and all of the menu items to which it is connected. The effect on the Enabled property is that the caption of the menu item appears in shaded fonts. By contrast, the effect on the Visible property is that the menu item disappears completely from the menu. Setting the Enabled and Visible properties to True (-1) restores their menu items.

The menu-drive text file viewer

The text file viewer that I presented in the last chapter used command buttons to carry out the various tasks. In this section, I present a menu-driven version. But first, I want to draw your attention to FIG. 8-7, which shows a suggested documentation form for Visual Basic menus.

Figures 8-4 to 8-7 contain the documentation for the menu-driven text file viewer.

Application name: Menu-Driven Text File Viewer
Application code name: FVIEW2A
Version: 1.0   Date created: July 2, 1991
Programmer(s): Namir Clement Shammas

List of filenames
Storage path: C:\VB\EASYVB
Project FVIEW2A.MAK
Global GLOBAL.BAS
Form 1 FVIEW2A.FRM

8-4 General project specifications for the FVIEW2A project.

Form #1   Form Filename: FVIEW2A.FRM
Version: 1.0   Date: July 2, 1991

Control object type	Default CtlName	Purpose
Text Box	Text1	Contains the filename to read
	Text2	Contains the text search string
	Text3	Contains the DOS/Windows command line
	Text4	Displays the text lines of a file
Label	Label1	Label of Text1
	Label2	Label of Text2
	Label3	Label of Text3

8-5 List of control objects for the FVIEW2A project.

Application (code) name: FVIEW2A
Form #1
Version: 1.0   Date: June 27, 1991

Original control name	Property	New Setting
Form	Caption	File Viewer (ver. 2A)
Text1	CtlName	FilenameBox
	Text	(empty string)
Text2	CtlName	FindBox
	Text	(empty string)
Text3	CtlName	DosBox
	Text	(empty string)
Text4	CtlName	TextBox
	Text	(empty string)
	MultiLine	True
	ScrollBars	3 - both
Label1	CtlName	FilenameLbl
	Caption	Filename Input
Label2	CtlName	FindLbl
	Caption	Find Input
Label3	CtlName	DosLbl
	Caption	DOS/Win Input

8-6 The modified control settings for the FVIEW2A project.

Form #1   Form filename: FVIEW2A.FRM
Version: 1.0   Date: July 2, 1991

Caption	Property	Setting	Purpose
File	CtlName	FileCom	
Read	CtlName indented	ReadCom once	Reads a file in Text1
Toggle Read	CtlName indented	ToggleReadCom once	Toggles Read menu option
Find File	CtlName indented	FindFileCom once	Finds a file
—	CtlName indented	Sep1 once	
Quit	CtlName indented	QuitCom once	Exits the application
Search	CtlName	SearchCom	
Find	CtlName indented	FindCom once	Finds text in Text1
Command	CtlName	CommandCom	
DOS Command	CtlName	DosCom	Executes a DOS command
Windows Command	CtlName indented	WinCom once	Runs a Windows application
Toggle OS	CtlName indented	ToggleOsCom once	Shows/hides command options

8-7 The menu structure for FVIEW2A.

Listing 8-1 contains the code for the menu-drive file viewer. Attaching code to the menu items is easy and involves using the Object combo list box in the Code window. The event-handling procedures greatly resemble their counterparts in the FVIEW1 project. The main difference is that the command button names are replaced with menu item control names. Secondary program aspects to look at are:

- The Toggle Read menu option toggles the Enabled property of the Read menu option.
- The Toggle OS menu option toggles the Visible property of the DOS Command menu option, Windows Command menu option, DOS/Win Input text box, and the label for the latter box.
- The Find menu option uses its Checked property to inform you of the status of the last find. If the last text search was successful, the Checked property is set to True to display the check mark.
- If you change the text in the Find Input text box, the FindCom.Checked property is set to False. The procedure FindBox_Change handles the event of changing text in the Find Input text box.

Listing 8-1   The code for the FVIEW2A project.

```
Sub QuitCom_Click ( )
  End
End Sub

Sub DosCom_Click ( )
  Dim Dummy As Integer
  ' invoke the DOSBAT batch file
  Dummy = Shell("dosbat.bat " + DosBox.Text, 1)
End Sub

Sub FindCom_Click ( )
  Static CurIndex As Long
  Dim Find As String
  ' update the index to the current character
  CurIndex = TextBox.SelStart + 1
  ' store the text of the Find box in the variable Find
  Find = FindBox.Text
  ' is variable Find empty?
  If Find = " " Then Exit Sub ' nothing to find
  ' locate the index of the next substring Find in the
  ' text box
  CurIndex = InStr(CurIndex + 1, TextBox.Text, Find)
  ' found a match?
  If CurIndex > 0 Then
    ' Yes! Display the matching text as selected text
    TextBox.SelStart = CurIndex − 1
    TextBox.SelLength = Len(Find)
    TextBox.SetFocus
    FindCom.Checked = True
  Else
    ' No! Clear any selected text
    TextBox.SelStart = 0
    TextBox.SelLength = 0
    FindCom.Checked = False
  End If
End Sub

Sub ToggleReadCom_Click ( )
  ReadCom.Enabled = Not ReadCom.Enabled
End Sub

Sub ReadCom_Click ( )
  Dim F As String
  Dim L As String
  Dim NL As String * 2
  ' obtain filename from the filename text box
  F = FilenameBox.Text
  ' if filename is an empty string, exit
  If F = " " Then Exit Sub
  NL = Chr$(13) + Chr$(10)
  ' set error-handler
  On Error GoTo BadFile
  ' open the file
```

Listing 8-1 Continued.

```
Open F For Input As 1
F = " " ' clear variable to reuse it
' loop to read the text lines from the ASCII file
Do While Not EOF(1)
   Line Input #1, L
   F = F + L + NL ' append a new line
Loop
TextBox.Text = F ' copy F into text box
' close the file
Close #1
' exit procedure
Exit Sub
' ********** Error-handler *********
BadFile:
   Beep
   MsgBox "Cannot open file " + F, 0, "File I/O Error"
   On Error GoTo 0
   Resume End OfSub
EndOfSub:
End Sub

Sub FindFileCom_Click ( )
   Dim Dummy As Integer
   ' invoke the DOS dir command with the /s
   ' subdirectory option and the /p paginated
   ' output option
   Dummy = Shell("dosbat.bat dir " + FilenameBox.Text + " /s/p", 1)
End Sub

Sub WinCom_Click ( )
   Dim Dummy As Integer
   ' invoke a Windows application
   Dummy = Shell(DosBox.Text, 1)
End Sub

Sub ToggleOSCom_Click ( )
   ' toggle the Visible property of the DosBox text box,
   ' the DosBtn button, the WinBtn button, and the DosLbl
   ' label
   DosBox.Visible = Not DosBox.Visible
   DosCom.Visible = Not DosCom.Visible
   WinCom.Visible = Not WinCom.Visible
   DosLbl.Visible = Not DosLbl.Visible
End Sub

Sub FindBox_Change ( )
   FindCom.Checked = False
End Sub
```

Run the program and experiment with the various menu options. Notice that the options of a pull-down menu are available either by clicking on them or by pressing the first letter of the option. In the next section

I will discuss how to control the keys that invoke the various menu options. Figure 8-8 shows a sample session with the menu-driven text file viewer.

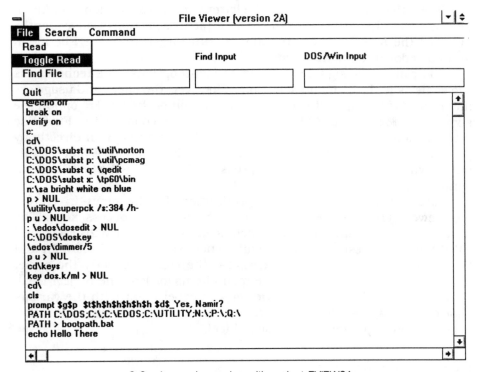

8-8 A sample session with project FVIEW2A.

Assigning shortcut and access keys to menus

The problem with programs like the above menu-driven file viewer is the lack of any quick keys to help you rapidly perform frequent tasks. Such quick keys are really helpful when you become proficient in using certain programs and develop a reflex for performing a sequence of tasks.

Visual Basic allows menus to use both shortcut and access keys. Shortcut keys are Ctrl key combinations (Ctrl−A to Ctrl−Z) that quickly execute specific menu options. Access keys are Alt keys that quickly choose specific menu selections.

☞ You can assign shortcut keys to menu options only (the indented menu items in the Menu Design Window). Use the Accelerator combo box to select the Ctrl key as the shortcut key for the current menu option. Shortcut keys must be unique; in fact, Visual Basic will not allow duplicate shortcut keys when you press the Done command button. By default, a menu option has no shortcut key assigned to it. The shortcut key also appears with the menu option to remind you of that shortcut key.

Assigning access keys for menu selections is similar to assigning access keys to command buttons — place an ampersand in front of the caption character you want to use with the Alt key at run time. The ampersand itself is not displayed as part of the caption. For example, if you insert the ampersand before the letter F in the File caption, the Alt–F key becomes the access key to the File menu selection. Consequently, pressing the Alt–F key combination at run time selects the File menu and pulls down its menu options.

You can also assign access keys to menu options. The technique is the same as with the menu selections. However, the effect and usage are different. For example, if you make the caption of the Find File option the string Find Fil&e, the letter E becomes the access code for the Find File menu option. However, you cannot access that menu option directly by pressing Alt–E. You still have to choose the File selection. When the File pull-down menu appears, you can press the E to invoke the Find File menu option.

Figure 8-9 shows the updated specifications for the menu-driven text file viewer. The new settings include shortcut and access keys. The form and project files for this modification are FVIEW2B.FRM and FVIEW2B.MAK, respectively. The difference between the FVIEW2A and FVIEW2B is only in the menu design — the code is exactly the same. Make the required changes for the menu items (or load the project files). Run the modified menu-driven viewer and experiment with the various shortcut and access keys. This version of the Visual Basic application begins to develop a more professional feel.

Control arrays

Visual Basic supports a new kind of array structure that is applied to controls. While control arrays share a number of properties with standard arrays, they also have their differences.

Control arrays represent a group of controls that offer very similar functions. For example, consider an array of options boxes used in a text search dialog box. The control array is used to determine the search direction — forward, backward, or global.

Since control arrays contain similar individual controls, they can share the same event-handling procedures. For example, the array of the text-search option buttons can share the same SearchDirBtn_Click procedure, as shown:

```
Sub SearchDirBtn_Click(Index As Integer)
```

The Index parameter is required to select the proper control element in the array. Inside the event-handling procedure you can access the sought control using the index parameter. Thus, the controlArrayName(Index) terms accessed the Indexth control for the SearchDirBtn(Index) procedure.

Control arrays have the following features and rules:

Form #1   Form filename: FVIEW2B.FRM
Version: 1.0   Date: July 2, 1991

Caption	Property	Setting	Purpose
&File	CtlName	FileCom	
Read	CtlName	ReadCom	Reads a file in Text1
	Accelerator	CTRL-R	
	indented	once	
Toggle Read	CtlName	ToggleReadCom	Toggles Read menu
	indented	once	option
Find File	CtlName	FindFileCom	Finds a file
	Accelerator	CTRL-F	
	indented	once	
—	CtlName	Sep1	
	indented	once	
Quit	CtlName	QuitCom	Exits the application
	Accelerator	CTRL-Q	
	indented	once	
&Search	CtlName	SearchCom	
Find	CtlName	FindCom	Finds text in Text1
	Accelerator	CTRL-I	
	indented	once	
&Command	CtlName	CommandCom	
DOS Command	CtlName	DosCom	Executes a DOS
	Accelerator	CTRL-D	command
	indented	once	
Windows Command	CtlName	WinCom	Runs a Windows
	Accelerator	CTRL-W	application
	indented	once	
Toggle OS	CtlName	ToggleOsCom	Shows/hides command
	indented	once	options

8-9 The menu structure for FVIEW2B.

- The control array can only be one-dimensional.
- The lowest array index is 0.
- Control arrays do not have preset upper bounds.
- The Visual Basic program can expand the control array at run time. The expansion is non-destructive, unlike the ReDim statement used with dynamic arrays.
- Unlike standard arrays, control arrays can be sparse. This means that you can create a control array with an arbitrary sequence of indices. For example, you can have the SearchDirBtn option button array have elements that are indexed by 0, 1, 5, 9, 10, 11, and 21—the indices need not be in perfect sequence.
- Control arrays are *not* declared in the application code.
- Control arrays are created at design time by using either one of the

two following methods: in the first method, you assign the same name to the CtlName property of two similar controls. The second method creates a control array by assigning a value to the Index property (which is blank for controls that are members of a control array).

- You can change the setting of the Index property of a control at design time only.
- Control arrays cannot be passed as arguments to a procedure or function. However, you can pass an individual element of the control array as an argument.

Control arrays in menus

A good place to start applying control arrays is menus. To add a control array as a menu option you need to perform the following steps:

1. Define the first element of the control array menus as a menu option. That menu option should have the following special settings:

    - The caption is an empty string.
    - The Visible property should be turned off.
    - The Index check box should have a 0.

The menu option should be properly indented and, of course, have a control name (in fact, Visual Basic won't allow blank control names).

2. Create accompanying menu options that add and, where appropriate, delete control array menus. These menu options are declared just like any ordinary menu options and do not have any special settings.
3. Declare a variable in the general declarations section to keep track of the current number of additional control array menus. The menu counter variable should be assigned a 0 in the Form_Load procedure.
4. Insert BASIC statements in the procedure that handles adding control array menus. The code for this procedure should perform the following steps:

    - Obtain the caption of the new menu option.
    - Increment the menu counter variable.
    - Load a new menu option using the Load command. The general syntax for this command is:

        Load ctlName(menuCounter)

    - Assign the new menu option its caption.
    - Set the Visible property of the new menu option to True.

5. Insert BASIC statements in the procedure that handles deleting control array menus. The code for this procedure should perform the following steps:

- Obtain index of the menu option you want to delete.
- Validate the obtain index.
- Reassign the captions of the menu options to override the delete one.
- Unload the targeted menu option using the Unload command. The general syntax for this command is:

   Unload ctlName(menuCounter)

- Decrement the menu counter variable.

6. Insert BASIC code in the event-handling procedure for the control array menus. That procedure must have an integer index parameter, such as Index As Integer. The selection control array menu option is accessed using ctlName(Index).Caption.

Control array menus for the file viewer

The menu-driven file viewer can use control array menus to maintain the names of important files that you want to view at least twice during a program session. During run time you can specify the names of these important files and make them menu options. From then on, selecting these menu options automatically displays these files.

Following the steps that I mentioned in the last section, I begin by updating the menu structure that appears in the Menu Design Window. Figure 8-10 shows the new structure of the new menu and reveals the following new menu items:

- The Add File menu option that adds filenames as new control array menu options.
- The Delete File menu option that deletes an existing control array menu option.
- The first control array menu option with the control name of Quick-Filename and the index of 0.
- Additional hyphen menu options to divide the File pull-down menu into four logical groups.

Listing 8-2 shows the code for the new version of the file viewer (named the FVIEW2C project). The general declaration section contains a declaration for the integer-typed variable NumFiles that maintains the current number of additional control array menu options. Notice that the Form_Load procedure initializes NumFiles to 0. While this assignment is optional since Visual Basic initializes NumFiles to 0 anyway, it is a safer programming practice that produces clearer code.

Listing 8-2 contains the following procedures that manage the control array menus.

The AddFileCom_Click **procedure** This procedure handles adding new control array menu options:

```
Sub AddFileCom_Click ()
    Dim TheFilename As String
    TheFilename = InputBox$("Enter full file name: ")
    NumFiles = NumFiles + 1 ' increment the menu count
    Load QuickFilename(NumFiles) ' load a new menu command
    QuickFilename(NumFiles).Caption = TheFilename
    QuickFilename(NumFiles).Visible = True
End Sub
```

The procedure uses the InputBox$ function to prompt the application user for a filename (stored in the variable TheFilename), and increments the variable NumFiles. It then loads a new control array menu and associates the NumFiles index with that array member. The variable TheFilename is

Listing 8-2 The code for the FVIEW2C project.

```
Dim NumFiles As Integer

Sub QuitCom_Click ()
    End
End Sub

Sub DosCom_Click ()
    Dim Dummy As Integer
    ' invoke the DOSBAT batch file
    Dummy = Shell("dosbat.bat " + DosBox.Text, 1)
End Sub

Sub FindCom_Click ()
    Static CurIndex As Long
    Dim Find As String
    ' update the index to the current character
    CurIndex = TextBox.SelStart + 1
    ' store the text of the Find box in the variable Find
    Find = FindBox.Text
    ' is variable Find empty?
    If Find = " " Then Exit Sub ' nothing to find
    ' locate the index of the next substring Find in the
    ' text box
    CurIndex = InStr(CurIndex + 1, TextBox.Text, Find)
    ' found a match?
    If CurIndex > 0 Then
        ' Yes! Display the matching text as selected text
        TextBox.SelStart = CurIndex - 1
        TextBox.SelLength = Len(Find)
        TextBox.SetFocus
        FindCom.Checked = True
```

Listing 8-2 Continued.

```
  Else
    ' No! Clear any selected text
    TextBox.SelStart = 0
    TextBox.SelLength = 0
    FindCom.Checked = False
  End If
End Sub

Sub ToggleReadCom_Click ( )
  ReadCom.Enabled = Not ReadCom.Enabled
End Sub

Sub ReadCom_Click ( )
  Dim F As String
  Dim L As String
  Dim NL As String * 2
  ' obtain filename from the filename text box
  F = FilenameBox.Text
  ' if filename is an empty string, exit
  If F = " " Then Exit Sub
  NL = Chr$(13) + Chr$(10)
  ' set error-handler
  On Error GoTo BadFile
  ' open the file
  Open F For Input As 1
  F = " " ' clear variable to reuse it
  ' loop to read the text lines from the ASCII file
  Do While Not EOF(1)
    Line Input #1, L
    F = F + L + NL ' append a new line
  Loop
  TextBox.Text = F ' copy F into text box
  ' close the file
  Close #1
  ' exit procedure
  Exit Sub
' ********** Error-handler **********
BadFile:
  Beep
  MsgBox "Cannot open file " + F, 0, "File I/O Error"
  On Error GoTo 0
  Resume EndOfSub
EndOfSub:
End Sub

Sub FindFileCom_Click ( )
  Dim Dummy As Integer
  ' invoke the DOS dir command with the /s
  ' subdirectory option and the /p paginated
  ' output option
  Dummy = Shell("dosbat.bat dir " + FilenameBox.Text + " /s/p", 1)
End Sub
```

Listing 8-2 Continued.

```
Sub WinCom_Click ( )
   Dim Dummy As Integer
   ' invoke a Windows application
   Dummy = Shell(DosBox.Text, 1)
End Sub

Sub ToggleOSCom_Click ( )
   ' toggle the Visible property of the DosBox text box,
   ' the DosBtn button, the WinBtn button, and the DosLbl
   ' label
   DosBox.Visible = Not DosBox.Visible
   DosCom.Visible = Not DosCom.Visible
   WinCom.Visible = Not WinCom.Visible
   DosLbl.Visible = Not DosLbl.Visible
End Sub

Sub FindBox_Change ( )
   FindCom.Checked = False
End Sub

Sub AddFileCom_Click ( )
   Dim TheFilename As String
   TheFilename = InputBox$("Enter full file name: ")
   NumFiles = NumFiles + 1 ' increment the menu count
   Load QuickFilename(NumFiles) ' load a new menu command
   QuickFilename(NumFiles).Caption = TheFilename
   QuickFilename(NumFiles).Visible = True
End Sub

Sub QuickFilename_Click (Index As Integer)
   FilenameBox.Text = QuickFilename(Index).Caption
   ReadCom_Click
End Sub

Sub DeleteFileCom_Click ( )
   Dim N As Integer, I As Integer
   N = Val(InputBox$("Enter number to delete: "))
   If (N > 0) And (N < = NumFiles) Then
      For I = N To NumFiles - 1
         QuickFilename(I).Caption = QuickFilename(I + 1).Caption
      Next I
      Unload QuickFilename(NumFiles)
      NumFiles = NumFiles - 1
   Else
      MsgBox "The number is out-of-range", 0, "Input Error"
   End If
End Sub

Sub Form_Load ( )
   NumFiles = 0
End Sub
```

assigned to the caption of the new control array menu option, and the Visible property of the new array member is set to True.

The DeleteFileCom_Click procedure   In this procedure control array menu options are removed.

```
Sub DeleteFileCom_Click ()
    Dim N As Integer, I As Integer
    N = Val(InputBox$("Enter number to delete: "))
    If (N > 0) And (N <= NumFiles) Then
        For I = N To NumFiles - 1
            QuickFilename(I).Caption = QuickFilename(I + 1).Caption
        Next I
        Unload QuickFilename(NumFiles)
        NumFiles = NumFiles - 1
    Else
        MsgBox "The number is out-of-range", 0, "Input Error"
    End If
End Sub
```

The procedure prompts the user to enter the index of the menu option to be deleted. If the input is within the valid range, it reassigns the captions, unloads the target menu option, and decreases the NumFiles variable. If the input is outside the valid range, the procedure displays an error message box.

The QuickFilename_Click **procedure**   This procedure quickly loads the selected filename.

```
Sub QuickFilename_Click (Index As Integer)
    FilenameBox.Text = QuickFilename(Index).Caption
    ReadCom_Click
End Sub
```

The procedure copies the caption of the selected control array menu option into the Text property of the Filename Input text box, then calls the ReadCom_Click procedure. Notice that the expression QuickFllename(Index).Caption is used to access the desired menu option.

Run the FVIEW2C program (see FIG. 8-10) and use the Add File menu options to add a few text files. Once you build this list, select these menu options to quickly load the text files (see FIG. 8-11).

Caption	Property	Setting	Purpose
&File	CtlName	FileCom	
Read	CtlName	ReadCom	Reads a file in Text1
	Accelerator	CTRL-R	
	indented	once	
Toggle Read	CtlName	ToggleReadCom	Toggles Read menu
	indented	once	option
Find File	CtlName	FindFileCom	Finds a file
	Accelerator	CTRL-F	
	indented	once	
—	CtlName	Sep1	
	indented	once	
Add File	CtlName	AddFileCom	Adds a filename
	indented	once	
Delete File	CtlName	DeleteFileCom	Deletes a filename
	indented	once	
–	CtlName	Sep2	
	indented	once	
(noname)	CtlName	QuickFilename	
	Index	0	
	Visible	off	
	indented	once	
–	CtlName	Sep3	
	indented	once	
Quit	CtlName	QuitCom	Exits the application
	Accelerator	CTRL-Q	
	indented	once	
&Search	CtlName	SearchCom	
Find	CtlName	FindCom	Finds text in Text1
	Accelerator	CTRL-Q	
	indented	once	
&Command	CtlName	CommandCom	
DOS Command	CtlName	DosCom	Executes a DOS
	Accelerator	CTRL-D	command
	indented	once	
Windows Command	CtlName	WinCom	Runs a Windows
	Accelerator	CTRL-W	application
	indented	once	
Toggle OS	CtlName	ToggleOsCom	Shows/hides command
	indented	once	options

8-10 The menu structure for the FVIEW2C project.

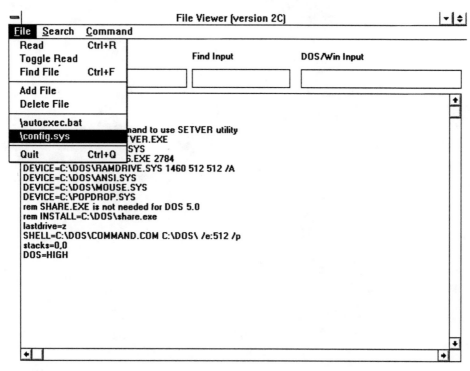

8-11 A sample session with project FVIEW2C.

9
Working with multiple forms

The Visual Basic examples presented so far use a single form. As you become more proficient in programming with Visual Basic, you will find that using a single form is very limiting—there are so many controls that you can draw on a form. This chapter looks at using multiple forms in a Visual Basic application. You will learn about the following topics:

- Dialog boxes and modal forms.
- Methods for managing forms.
- Setting the form properties.
- Selecting the startup form.
- Loading and displaying forms.
- Hiding forms.
- Unloading forms.

Using multiple forms serves two essential purposes: it gives you more form space, and allows you to create forms that logically group a family of controls to perform a specific task. In a manner of speaking, the additional forms are to an application what a Sub procedure is to a Visual Basic program.

Dialog boxes and modal forms

A Visual Basic application that uses multiple forms designates a primary form. This is the form that is automatically loaded into memory and displayed. All other forms are secondary and must be explicitly loaded into memory and displayed. These secondary forms can be *modal*. A modal form is one that does not allow you to switch focus to another window until that form is closed. Dialog boxes are invariably modal windows, since they require you to input data before moving on. Typically, modal windows cannot be minimized or maximized, and have a border style that is different from modeless windows.

Methods and statements that manage forms

New forms are created using the New Form option in the File menu. Visual Basic offers the following statements and methods to manage the forms at run time:

The Load **statement**   This statement loads a form into the working memory enabling other in-memory forms to access the controls and properties of that form. However, the Load statement does not automatically show the form. The general syntax for the Load statement is:

    Load formName

The Unload **statement**   Unload removes a form from memory and from the screen and loses the data in that form. The controls and properties of the removed form are no longer accessible to other in-memory forms. The general syntax for the Unload statement is:

    Unload formName

✐ Programming Tip: Accumulating forms in memory drains the memory. Unload infrequently-used forms when you have finished with them. Keep only those forms that are frequently used to maintain good program speed.

The Show **method**   In this method, a form is first loaded (if it is not already in memory) and then it is displayed. If the specified modal state is 1, the loaded form is modal. A 0 modal state, which is the default if the modal argument is omitted, makes the form modeless. The general syntax for the Show method is:

    [form.]Show [modalState%]

✐ Programming Tip: When a form is loaded by either the Load statement or the Show method, the Form_Load procedure of that method is automatically invoked. This feature enables you to include additional or special form initialization in the Form_Load procedure.

The Hide **method**   Hide makes the form invisible by setting the Visible property of that form to False, while maintaining its data. Other in-memory forms can still access the controls and properties of a hidden form. The general syntax for the Hide method is:

    [form.]Hide

The general syntax for accessing a property in another form is:

    formName.propertyName

The general syntax for accessing the property of a control in another form is:

formNamecontrolName.propertyName

☞ If you try to access the property or controls of a form that is currently not in memory, the run time system will automatically load that form. This interesting feature prevents you from having to set error trapping procedures to protect against accessing a form that is not loaded in memory.

Setting the form properties

The preceding discussions made an important distinction between modal and modeless forms, and the windows they produce at run time. Moreover, modal forms were associated with dialog boxes. In this section I discuss the form properties that fine-tune the appearance and behavior of general forms and dialog boxes. During run time general forms can be resized, minimized, and maximized, and may give the focus to other windows. By contrast, dialog boxes are more self-centered, so to speak. You can only move a typical dialog box. You are not allowed to resize, minimize, or maximize it, or switch to another window, until you are finished with the dialog box.

Table 9-1 lists the properties for the general forms and the dialog boxes that are relevant in their display and behavior at run time. The table also includes the recommended settings, indicating which settings are defaults. The settings for the general forms and the dialog boxes reflect the typical behavior that I described above.

By default, when a Visual Basic window is minimized the standard Visual Basic icon appears. You can customize that icon by changing the setting of the Icon property in the Properties bar. When you select the Icon property, click on the three-dot button that appears to the right of the settings combo box. This action results in the appearance of a dialog box that enables you to select an icon from a .ICO file. You can navigate through different directories to locate and select the .ICO file you want. Visual Basic supplies you with a family of .ICO files located in the \VB\ICONS directory.

Selecting the startup form or module

A quick quiz question: where does a multi-form Visual Basic program start executing? If your answer is "in the main form," you are right! The main form is the default form that is automatically loaded and executed. However, Visual Basic offers two other routes for starting up a multi-form Visual Basic program:

Selecting a secondary form as the startup form This selection enables Visual Basic to start running a secondary form instead of the main form. Such a

Table 9-1   The properties of general forms and dialog boxes.

Form property	Form type	Setting	Default	Comments
BorderStyle	General	2-sizeable	Yes	Window is resizable.
	Dialog	3-fixed double	No	Window is fixed.
MinButton	General	True	Yes	Window can be minimized.
	Dialog	False	No	Window cannot be minimized.
MaxButton	General	True	Yes	Window can be maximized.
	Dialog	False	No	Window cannot be maximized.
ControlBox	General	True	Yes	Adds a fully functional Control menu.
	Dialog	True	Yes	Adds a Control menu and only enables the Move option.
Caption	General	(custom)	No	Assigns custom caption.
	Dialog	(custom)	No	Assigns custom caption.
FormName	General	(custom)	No	Assigns custom form name.
	Dialog	(custom)	No	Assigns custom form name.
Icon	General	(custom)	No	Selects an icon for the minimized window.

selection is made possible by choosing the Set Startup Form option from the Run menu. Visual Basic displays a dialog box with a list of current forms to choose from.

Selecting a startup module   Rather than choosing any one particular form as the startup point, you can begin execution in a module. The rule to follow is that the startup module must contain a procedure called Main. This procedure does not load any form.

☞   Keep in mind the following for loading forms. The default form or your selected startup form is automatically loaded and displayed. All other forms must be explicitly loaded and displayed when needed. If you start up with a BASIC module, then you must explicitly load all of the forms (when each is needed).

An example

Having discussed the various aspects of a multi-form Visual Basic application, let's see an example. The program that I present in this section basically converts among length measurements, temperatures, and numeric bases. The program consists of a main control center form, or main form, that contains buttons that invoke the secondary forms. Each of the three secondary forms is a simple dialog box that converts among the following:

- Meters and feet
- Celsius and Fahrenheit temperatures
- Decimal, hexadecimal, and octal numbers

The main form acts as a focal point. You invoke a conversion form, perform the related calculations, and then return to the focal point.

Figures 9-1 though 9-9 describe the specifications for the four forms involved. The form files and control names are FORMS1.FRM (Form), LENGTHFO.FRM (LengthForm), TEMPFORM.FRM (TempForm), and BASEFORM.FRM (BaseForm). The specifications indicate the custom form settings needed to make dialog boxes out of the secondary forms, in addition to specifying a modal state of 1 when showing these forms. The project filename is FORMS1.MAK. Figures 9-10 through 9-13 show screen images of the four forms.

Application Name: Conversions Application
Application Code Name: FORMS1
Version: 1.0   Date Created: July 3, 1991
Programmer(s): Namir Clement Shammas

List of filenames

Storage path: \VB\EASYVB
Project FORMS1.MAK
Global GLOBAL.BAS
Form 1 FORMS1.FRM
Form 2 LENGTHFO.FRM
Form 3 TEMPFORM.FRM
Form 4 BASEFORM.FRM

9-1   The general specifications for the FORMS1.MAK project.

Form #1   Form filename: FORMS1.FRM
Version: 1.0   Date: July 3, 1991

Control object type	Default CtlName	Purpose
Command Button	Command1	Invokes the LengthForm
	Command2	Invokes the TempForm
	Command3	Invokes the BaseForm
	Command4	Exits the application

9-2   Basic specifications for the main form.

Application (code) name: FORMS1
Form #1
Version: 1.0   Date: July 3, 1991

Original control name	Property	New setting
Form	Caption	Control Center
Command1	CtlName	LengthBtn
	Caption	Convert Length
Command2	CtlName	TempBtn
	Caption	Convert Temp.
Command3	CtlName	BaseBtn
	Caption	Convert Base
Command4	CtlName	QuitBtn
	Caption	Quit

9-3 Updated settings for the main form.

Form #2   Form filename: LENGTHFO.FRM
Version: 1.0   Date: July 3, 1991

Control object type	Default CtlName	Purpose
Text Box	Text1	Stores meters
	Text2	Stores inches
Label	Label1	Label for meter box
	Label2	Label for inch box
Command Button	Command1	Returns to the main form

9-4 Basic specifications for the LENGTHFO.FRM form.

Application (code) name: FORMS1
Form #2
Version: 1.0   Date: July 3, 1991

Control object type	Property	New setting
Form	Caption	Length Conversion
	BorderStyle	3 - Fixed Double
	MinButton	False
	MaxButton	False
	FormName	LengthForm
Text1	CtlName	MeterBox
	Text	(empty string)

9-5 Updated settings for the LENGTHFO.FRM form.

Control object type	Property	New setting
Text2	CtlName	FeetBox
	Text	(empty string)
Label1	CtlName	MeterLbl
	Caption	Meters
Label2	CtlName	FeetLbl
	Caption	Feet
Command1	CtlName	ReturnBtn
	Caption	Return To Main

9-5 Continued.

Form #3
Version: 1.0

Form filename: TEMPFORM.FRM
Date: July 3, 1991

Control object type	Default CtlName	Purpose
Text Box	Text1	Stores Celsius degrees
	Text2	Stores Fahrenheit degrees
Label	Label1	Label for Celsius box
	Label2	Label for Fahrenheit box
Command Button	Command1	Returns to the main form

9-6 Basic specifications for the TEMPFORM.FRM form.

Application (code) name: FORMS1
Form #3
Version: 1.0　　　　　　　　　　　　　　　　Date: July 3, 1991

Original control name	Property	New setting
Form	Caption	Temperature Conversion
	BorderStyle	3 - Fixed Double
	MinButton	False
	MaxButton	False
	FormName	TempForm
Text1	CtlName	CBox
	Text	(empty string)
Text2	CtlName	FBox
	Text	(empty string)
Label1	CtlName	CLbl
	Caption	Celsius

9-7 Updated settings for the TEMPFROM.FRM form.

Original control name	Property	New setting
Label2	CtlName	FLbl
	Caption	Fahrenheit
Command1	CtlName	ReturnBtn
	Caption	Return To Main

9-7 Continued.

Form #4
Version: 1.0

Form filename: BASEFORM.FRM
Date: July 3, 1991

Control object type	Default CtlName	Purpose
Text Box	Text1	Stores a decimal number
	Text2	Stores a hexadecimal number
	Text3	Stores a octal number
Label	Label1	Label for the decimal number
	Label2	Label for the hexadecimal number
	Label3	Label for the octal number
Command Button	Command1	Returns to the main form

9-8 Basic specifications for the BASEFORM.FRM form.

Application (code) name: FORMS1
Form #4
Version: 1.0 Date: July 3, 1991

Control object type	Property	New setting
Form	Caption	Base Conversion
	BorderStyle	3 - Fixed Double
	MinButton	False
	MaxButton	False
	FormName	BaseForm
Text1	CtlName	DecBox
	Text	(empty string)
Text2	CtlName	HexBox
	Text	(empty string)
Text3	CtlName	OctBox
	Text	(empty string)

9-9 Updated settings for the TEMPFORM.FRM form.

Control object type	Property	New setting
Label1	CtlName	DecLbl
	Caption	Decimal
Label2	CtlName	HexLbl
	Caption	Hexadecimal
Label3	CtlName	OctLbl
	Caption	Octal
Command1	CtlName	ReturnBtn
	Caption	Return To Main

9-9 Continued.

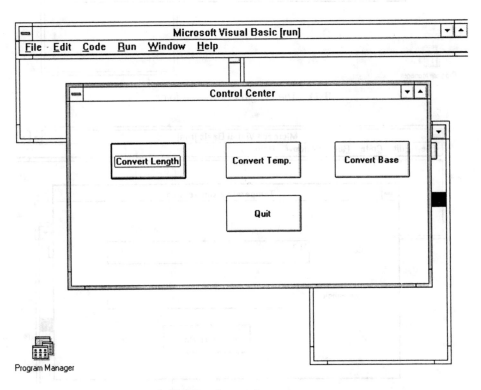

9-10 The Control Center form.

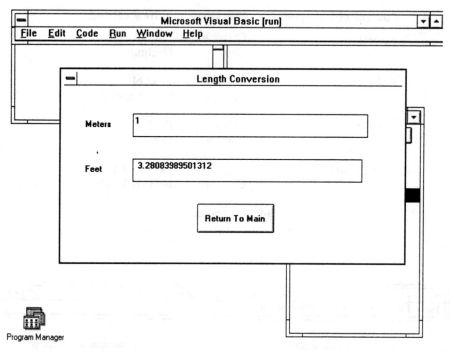

9-11 The Length Conversion form.

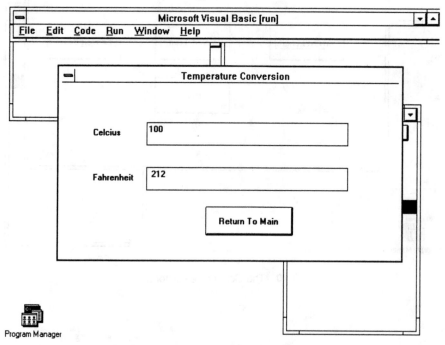

9-12 The Temperature Conversion form.

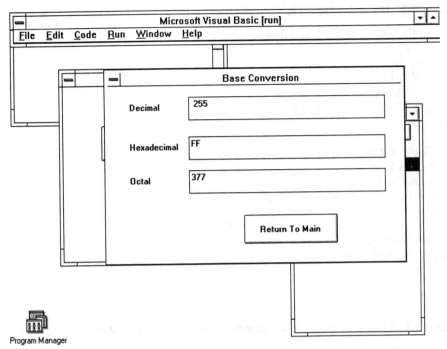

9-13 The Base Conversion form.

Listings 9-1 through 9-4 contain the attached code for each form. The procedures handling the Click event for the command buttons in the main form invoke the Show method on the different secondary forms. In each case, a modal of 1 is specified. This value, combined with the custom form settings, produces dialog boxes. Also notice that the QuitBtn_Click procedure contains the End statement that is needed to exit this multi-form application.

Listing 9-1 The code attached to the controls of the main form.

```
Sub QuitBtn_Click ( )
  End
End Sub

Sub LengthBtn_Click ( )
  LengthForm.Show 1
End Sub

Sub TempBtn_Click ( )
  TempForm.Show 1
End Sub

Sub BaseBtn_Click ( )
  BaseForm.Show 1
End Sub
```

Listing 9-2 The code attached to the controls of the LENGTHFO.FRM form.

```
Const FEET_PER_METER = .3048

Sub MeterBox_LostFocus ( )
  Dim X As Double
  X = Val(MeterBox.Text)
  FeetBox.Text = Str$(X / FEET_PER_METER)
End Sub

Sub FeetBox_LostFocus ( )
  Dim X As Double
  X = Val(FeetBox.Text)
  MeterBox.Text = Str$(X * FEET_PER_METER)
End Sub

Sub ReturnBtn_Click ( )
  Unload LengthForm
End Sub
```

Listing 9-3 The code attached to the controls of the TEMPFORM.FRM form.

```
Sub ReturnBtn_Click ( )
  Unload TempForm
End Sub

Sub CBox_LostFocus ( )
  Dim X As Double
  X = Val(CBox.Text)
  FBox.Text = Str$(32 + 1.8 * X)
End Sub

Sub FBox_LostFocus ( )
  Dim X As Double
  X = Val(FBox.Text)
  CBox.Text = Str$((X - 32) / 1.8)
End Sub
```

Listing 9-4 The code attached to the controls of the BASEFORM.FRM form.

```
Sub DecBox_LostFocus ( )
  Dim N As Long
  N = Val(DecBox.Text)
  HexBox.Text = Hex$(N)
  OctBox.Text = Oct$(N)
End Sub
```

Listing 9-4 Continued.

```
Sub HexBox_LostFocus ( )
    Dim N As Long
    N = Val("&H" + HexBox.Text + "&")
    DecBox.Text = Str$(N)
    OctBox.Text = Oct$(N)
End Sub

Sub OctBox_LostFocus ( )
    Dim N As Long
    N = Val("&O" + DecBox.Text + "&")
    HexBox.Text = Hex$(N)
    DecBox.Text = Str$(N)
End Sub

Sub ReturnBtn_Click ( )
    Unload BaseForm
End Sub
```

The code attached to secondary forms contains the event-handling procedures for the text boxes and the Return-to-Main command button. The text boxes trap the LostFocus event, which is generated when you Tab out of that text box or click on another control. This event signals to the event handler that you have finished keying in a new number or editing the one currently in the selected text box. Consequently, the numbers in the other text boxes (in the same form) are also updated. Using this technique enables the program to work without additional command buttons that trigger the numeric conversions.

The ReturnBtn_Click event handler implemented in the secondary forms unload their respective form. This action results in hiding the form, removing it from memory, and returning to the main form.

Run the program and select the length conversion. Select the Meters text box and type 1. Press the Tab key to switch to another control, and watch the equivalent of 1 meter in feet appear in the Feet text box. Select the Feet text box and overwrite the current contents with 10. Press the Tab key and watch the equivalent of 10 feet appear in the Meters text box. Click on the Return To Main command button to go back to the main form. Experiment further with the program by selecting the other conversions.

As an exercise, change the Unload statements in the ReturnBtn_Click procedures into formName.Hide. Run the program and use any one of the conversion forms twice. What do you see? The results from the previous visit are still there, since the form was hidden.

10
Form input

The programs that I have presented so far relied mostly on text boxes to obtain input from the user. In this chapter I discuss other controls that you can draw on the form to obtain different types of input. Here, you will learn about the following:

- Monitoring text box input.
- Option buttons.
- Check boxes.
- List boxes and combo boxes.
- Scroll bars.
- The InputBox$ input dialog box.

I will present short examples for each of the topics listed above, and then show you a new version of the scientific calculator that uses option buttons, check boxes, and a combo box.

Monitoring text box input

All of the programs that I have presented so far have made no attempt to monitor your keystrokes while you typed in a text box. Visual Basic allows you to regulate what is typed in a text box through the KeyPress event. This event is only generated when a standard ASCII character is typed—this includes control characters, the Enter (ASCII 13) character, the Backspace (ASCII 8) character, the alphanumeric characters, and the punctuation characters.

The KeyPress procedure handlers have one parameter, the integer-typed KeyAscii. The KeyPress event allows you to intercept standard ASCII characters that you type *before* they appear in the text box (see FIG. 10-1). This enables the KeyPress event handler to perform one of three tasks:

- Alter the input character.
- Remove the input character.
- Echo the input character without changing it.

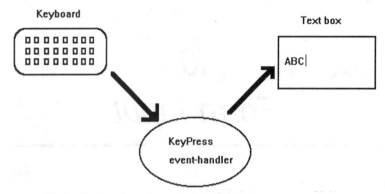

10-1 The keystroke interception of KeyPress event-handlers.

The KeyPress event handler works by examining and manipulating the argument for the KeyAscii parameter which is passed by reference. This parameter represents the ASCII code for the input character. A typical KeyPress event handler performs the following steps:

1. Converts the KeyAscii argument to a single-letter string using the Chr$ function. The result can be assigned to either a dynamic string or a single-character string (i.e., a local variable declared with As String * 1).
2. Examines the string using a variety of relational and logical operators. Examples are given below, assuming that the local variable C has already been assigned Chr$(KeyAscii):

    IF C >= "0" And C <= "9" Then ' is character a digit?
    IF (C < "0" And C > "9") Then ' is character not a digit?
    IF C >= "A" And C <= "Z" Then ' is character an uppercase letter?
    IF C >= "a" And C <= "z" Then ' is character a lowercase letter?
    IF (C >= "a" And C <= "z") Or (C >= "A" AND C <= "Z") Then ' a letter?

3. Takes the appropriate action. If the examined character is satisfactory, the KeyAscii argument is not assigned any new value; rather, it maintains the original value.

If the examined character must be changed to conform to a certain criteria, the string variable is first altered, then its ASCII code is reassigned to the argument KeyAscii. Examples are shown below:

```
' make uppercase
C = UCase$(C)
KeyAscii = ASC(C)
```

```
' Make lowercase
C = LCase$(C)
KeyAscii = ASC(C)
```

☞ If the input character is rejected, the event-handling procedure assigns a 0 to the argument of KeyAscii. As a result, the rejected character that you just typed does not appear in the text box. An example of rejecting an input character is a text box that accepts positive integers (in the decimal base)—any non-digit character is rejected.

Alternate techniques for the above steps may compare the value of KeyAscii with the ASCII code of a character. Examples are shown next:

```
' is character a digit?
IF KeyAscii >= Asc("0") And KeyAscii <= Asc("9") Then
```

```
' is character not a digit?
IF KeyAscii < Asc("0") Or KeyAscii > Asc("9") Then
```

✍ Programming Note: The KeyPress event is available for other controls. You can alter the input character only for the text box and combo box controls. Other controls can use the KeyPress event to examine the input character and then decide how to respond to that character.

Let's look at an example of an application that monitors the input of text boxes. Here I will introduce the integer calculator program, which is a scaled-down version of the scientific calculator program that I presented earlier in this book. This modified program version has the following features:

- Handles positive integers only.
- Supports the four basic math operations and the modulo operator. The list of valid operator symbols and names are:
    ~ Addition: +, Add, and Addition
    ~ Subtraction: −, Sub, and Subtract
    ~ Multiplication: *, Mul, and Multiply
    ~ Divide: /, \, Div, and Divide
    ~ Modulo: Mod and Modulo
- The Execute button executes the specified operator and places the result in the Result text box. Error messages appear in the Error Message text box.

The integer calculator does not support variables. All of the simplifications of the integer calculators (compared to the scientific calculator) enable me to implement typical KeyPress event-handlers. The code detail for these is presented later in this section.

Figures 10-2 to 10-4 contain the specifications for the integer calculator application. The integer calculator contains four text boxes, four labels, and two command buttons. Figure 10-5 shows the visual interface of the integer calculator program.

Application name: Integer Calculator
Application code name: INTCALC
Version: 1.0   Date created: July 5, 1991
Programmer(s): Namir Clement Shammas

List of Filenames

Storage path: \VB\EASYVB
Project INTCALC.MAK
Global GLOBAL.BAS
Form 1 INTCALC.FRM

10-2 The basic specifications for the integer calculator program.

Form #1   Form filename: INTCALC.FRM
Version: 1.0   Date: July 5, 1991

Control object type	Default CtlName	Purpose
Text Box	Text1	Key in operand 1
	Text2	Key in operator
	Text3	Key in operand 2
	Text4	Display the result
	Text5	Display error message
Label	Label1	Label of Text1
	Label2	Label of Text2
	Label3	Label of Text3
	Label4	Label of Text4
	Label5	Label of Text5
Command Button	Command1	Execute math operation
	Command2	Quit

10-3 The basic specifications for the INTCALC.FRM form.

Application (code) name: INTCALC
Form #1
Version: 1.0   Date: July 5, 1991

Original control name	Property	New setting
Form1	Caption	Integer Calculator
Text1	CtlName	Operand1Box
	Text	(empty string)

10-4 Custom settings for form INTCALC.FRM.

Original control name	Property	New setting
Text2	CtlName	OperatorBox
	Text	(empty string)
Text3	CtlName	Operand2Box
	Text	(empty string)
Text4	CtlName	ResultBox
	Text	(empty string)
Text5	CtlName	ErrorMessageBox
	Text	(empty string)
Label1	CtlName	Operand1Lbl
	Caption	Operand 1
Label2	CtlName	OperatorLbl
	Caption	Operator
Label3	CtlName	Operator2Lbl
	Caption	Operand 2
Label4	CtlName	ResultLbl
	Caption	Result
Label5	CtlName	ErrorMessageLbl
	Caption	Error Message
Command1	CtlName	ExecuteBtn
	Caption	Execute
Command2	CtlName	QuitBtn
	Caption	Quit

10-4 Continued.

Listing 10-1 contains the code attached to the various controls of the INTCALC.FRM form. The following paragraphs cover event-handling procedures of particular interest.

Operand1Box_KeyPress **and** Operand2Box_KeyPress **procedures** These procedures reject any character that is neither a digit nor the backspace character. The first If statement checks to see whether the argument for KeyAscii is 8 (the ASCII code for the Backspace character). If the test is positive, the procedure is exited, leaving the argument for KeyAscii unchanged. Removing the first If statement in these procedures causes the backspace character to be rejected as an invalid character. The second If statement examines whether the value of KeyAscii is outside the range for the digit ASCII codes. If the test is positive, the procedure invokes the Beep

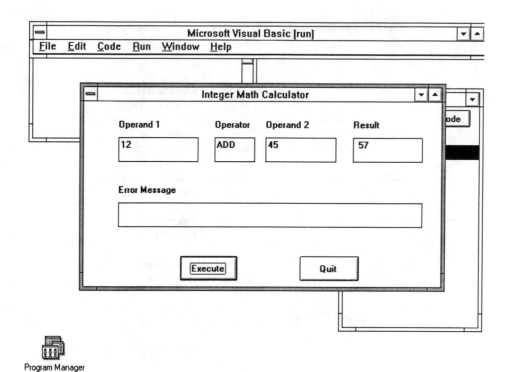

10-5 A sample session with the integer calculator program.

Listing 10-1 The code attached to the INTCALC.FRM.

```
Sub QuitBtn_Click ( )
  End
End Sub

Sub ExecuteBtn_Click ( )
  Dim X As Long, Y As Long, Z As Long
  ErrorMessageBox.Text = " " ' clear error message box
  ResultBox.Text = " " ' clear result box
  X = Val(Operand1Box.Text)
  Y = Val(Operand2Box.Text)
  ' examine the content of the OperatorBox text box
  Select Case UCase$(OperatorBox.Text)
    Case " + ", "ADD"
     Z = X + Y
    Case " - ", "SUB", "SUBTRACT"
     Z = X - Y
    Case " * ", "MUL", "MULTIPLY"
     Z = X * Y
    Case "/", " \ ", "DIV", "DIVIDE"
```

Listing 10-1 Continued.

```
        If Y < > 0 Then
          Z = X \ Y
        Else
          ErrorMessageBox.Text = "Division by zero error"
          Beep
        End If
      Case "MOD", "MODULO"
        If Y < > 0 Then
          Z = X Mod Y
        Else
          ErrorMessageBox.Text = "Modulo of zero error"
          Beep
        End If
      Case Else
        ErrorMessageBox.Text = "Invalid operator"
        Beep
    End Select
    ' if the error message box is still empty, there is
    ' no error. Therefore, convert the variable Z into
    ' a string and display it in ResultBox
    If ErrorMessageBox.Text = " " Then
      ResultBox.Text = Str$(Z)
    End If
End Sub

Sub ErrorMessageLbl_Click ( )
  ErrorMessageBox.Text = " "
End Sub

Sub Operand1Box_KeyPress (KeyAscii As Integer)
    ' is the KeyAscii the ASCII code for
    ' the Backspace character?
    If KeyAscii = 8 Then Exit Sub
    If (KeyAscii < Asc("0")) Or (KeyAscii > Asc("9")) Then
      Beep
      KeyAscii = 0
    End If
End Sub

Sub Operand2Box_KeyPress (KeyAscii As Integer)
    ' is the KeyAscii the ASCII code for
    ' the Backspace character?
    If KeyAscii = 8 Then Exit Sub
    If (KeyAscii < Asc("0")) Or (KeyAscii > Asc("9")) Then
      Beep
      KeyAscii = 0
    End If
End Sub
```

Listing 10-1 Continued.

```
Sub OperatorBox_KeyPress (KeyAscii As Integer)
    Dim C As String * 1
    C = Chr$(KeyAscii) ' convert ASCII code to character
    C = UCase$(C) ' convert to uppercase
    KeyAscii = Asc(C) ' convert character to ASCII code
End Sub
```

statement and then assigns a 0 to the KeyAscii argument. This assignment causes the character that you keyed to be rejected.

OperatorBox_KeyPress **procedure** This procedure converts the letters that you type into upper case. The statements in the procedure represent the typical code, which I described earlier, to alter the user input.

Run the integer application by pressing the F5 function key. Type the operands in their respective text boxes. While typing an operand, press a non-digit key, such as the space bar or a letter. What happens? The corresponding KeyPress procedure beeps at you and rejects your input. Or type the name of an operation, such as add. Notice that the uppercase letters ADD appear in the next box even though you are typing them in lower case.

Option buttons

Option buttons, or radio buttons, are special controls that enable you to provide input by selecting a logical state. Option buttons usually work in groups of two or more. You can only select one option button in a group. When you select one option button, the others in the same group are automatically deselected. The option buttons represent logically Ored states; each state is a mutually exclusive alternative.

Option buttons should be grouped in a form. This grouping is carried out in one of two ways:

Draw a control array in the form Each group of option buttons shares the same name but has a distinct setting for the Index property. The Visual Basic interface allows you to draw an option button control array in two ways: explicit or implicit. In the explicit method, you draw the first member of the option button array and assign a value to the Index property. This tells the Visual Basic interface system that you started a new control array. When you draw the rest of the control arrays, type in the same control name; the Index setting is automatically assigned by the Visual Basic interface. In the second method, you draw the first control as a non-array object. So far the Visual Basic interface thinks you are drawing a single control. When you draw the second option button, type in the same control name. This duplicate name causes the Visual Basic interface to ask you whether or not you want to create a control array. Select the Yes button from the inquiring dialog box. The rest of the buttons are created with the same name; the Index setting is automatically assigned by the Visual Basic interface. In either method, enter an Index setting if you wish to bypass the incremented control array numbers that are provided by the Visual Basic interface.

✍ Programming Note: You can use different control names for option buttons in a frame or a picture box and still have the single-alternative feature enforced by Visual Basic. Visual Basic treats such option buttons as a group, since they are located in a grouping control.

Draw a frame or a picture box, then draw the option buttons inside the frame   The option buttons are drawn as control arrays, since the Visual Basic interface understands that these option buttons are related.

Option buttons possess a number of properties that define their visual appearance and behavior. Some properties, such as Caption, CtlName, Enabled, and Visible, resemble those of command buttons. The most relevant option button property is Value. This is a logical property that determines whether or not an option button is selected. The general syntax for the Value property is shown here:

*[form.][optionButton.]*Value *[=Boolean%]*

When the Value property of an option button is True (−1), the button is selected and the Value of all the other option buttons in the same group are set to False (0). The Value property can be set and queried both at design and run time.

Option buttons can be selected by either clicking the mouse on them or by tabbing to the desired option and then pressing the space bar.

Let me present an example of a Visual Basic program that uses option buttons. The program is an enhanced version of the APP1.MAK project that displays the current date and time. In the new version I include two groups of option buttons. Each group is located inside a frame. These option button groups enable you to select the date and time display formats. The date format options are DD-MM-YYYY, MM-DD-YYYY, and YYYY-MM-DD. The time formats are AM/PM and 24 hours.

Figures 10-6 to 10-8 contain the specifications for the OPTION.FRM form. The date-format and time-format option buttons have the array

Application name: Option Button Demonstration
Application code name: OPTION
Version: 1.0   Date created: July 5, 1991
Programmer(s): Namir Clement Shammas

List of Filenames

Storage path: \VB\EASYVB
Project OPTION.MAK
Global GLOBAL.BAS
Form 1 OPTION.FRM

10-6   The general specifications of the OPTION.MAK project file.

Form #1   Form filename: OPTION.FRM
Version: 1.0   Date: July 5, 1991

Control object type	Default CtlName	Purpose
Command Button	Command1	Displays the date and time
	Command2	Exits the test program
Text Box	Text1	Displays the date and time
Frame	Frame1	Contains the date format option buttons
	Frame2	Contains the time format option buttons
Option Button	Option1	0 - DD-MM-YYYY date format
		1 - MM-DD-YYYY date format
		2 - YYYY-MM-DD date format
	Option2	0 - AM/PM time format
		1 - 24 hour time format

10-7 The list of controls in the OPTION.FRM form file.

Application (code) name: OPTION
Form #1
Version: 1.0   Date: July 5, 1991

Original control name	Property	New setting
Form	Caption	Option Button Demo
Command1	CtlName	NowBtn
	Caption	Now
Command2	CtlName	QuitBtn
	Caption	Quit
Text1	CtlName	TextBox
	Caption	(empty string)
Frame1	CtlName	DateFormatFrm
	Caption	Date Format
Frame2	CtlName	TimeFormatFrm
	Caption	Time Format
Option1	CtlName	DateFormatOpt
	Index	0
	Caption	DD-MM-YYYY
	CtlName	DateFormatOpt
	Index	1
	Caption	MM-DD-YYYY

10-8 The custom settings for the controls in the OPTION.FRM form.

Original control name	Property	New setting
	CtlName	DateFormatOpt
	Index	2
	Caption	YYYY-MM-DD
Option2	CtlName	TimeFormatOpt
	Index	0
	Caption	AM/PM
	CtlName	TimeFormatOpt
	Index	1
	Caption	24 Hr

10-8 Continued.

control name of DateFormatOpt and TimeFormatOpt, respectively. Figure 10-9 shows a sample session with the OPTION.MAK project.

Listing 10-2 contains the code attached to the OPTION.FRM form. There are three event-handling procedures:

The Form_load **procedure** This procedure initializes the form by selecting the second date-format option button and the second time-format option button.

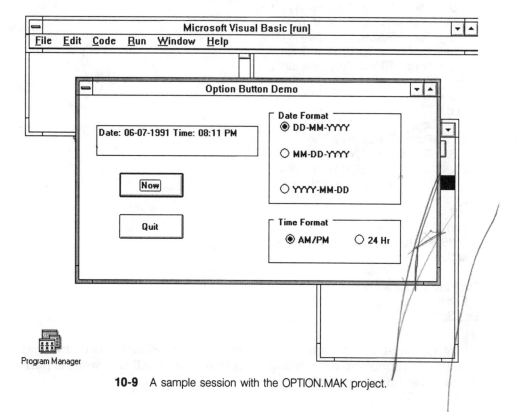

10-9 A sample session with the OPTION.MAK project.

Check boxes   153

The NowBtn_Click **procedure** This displays the current date and time. The procedure uses the local string-typed variable S to build the date and time image. Two extended If-Then-ElseIf statements are used to examine the Value property of the DateFormatOpt and TimeFormatOpt option button arrays. The predefined Now and Format$ functions produce a string that contains the properly formatted date or time. Both If statements have Else clauses that read the date and time from the Date$ and Time$ functions, respectively, when all of the option buttons are turned off in either group. The last procedure statement assigns the local string S to the Text property of TextBox.

The QuitBtn **procedure** QuitBtn exits the test program.

Listing 10-2 The code attached to the OPTION.FRM form.

```
Sub Form_Load ( )
  DateFormatOpt(1).Value = True
  TimeFormatOpt(1).Value = True
End Sub

Sub NowBtn_Click ( )
  Dim S As String
  If DateFormatOpt(0).Value Then
    S = Format$(Now, "dd-mm-yyyy")
  Elself DateFormatOpt(1).Value Then
    S = Format$(Now, "mm-dd-yyyy")
  Elself DateFormatOpt(2).Value Then
    S = Format$(Now, "yyyy-mm-dd")
  Else
    S = Date$
  End If
  S = "Date: " + S + " Time: "
  If TimeFormatOpt(0).Value Then
    S = S + Format$(Now, "hh:mm AM/PM")
  Elself TimeFormatOpt(1).Value Then
    S = S + Format$(Now, "hh:mm")
  Else
    S = S + Time$
  End If
  TextBox.Text = S ' assign new text
End Sub

Sub QuitBtn_Click ( )
  End
End Sub
```

Notice that the attached code has no user-defined procedure that handles selecting and deselecting an option button. All this work is handled by the run time system.

Run the program and select the various date and time format option buttons. After each combination of time and date option buttons, press the Now command button to view the date and time as specified. When you finish examining the option buttons, click on the Quit button to exit.

Check boxes

Check boxes are controls that can be switched on or off. Check boxes can be used individually or in a group to manipulate a series of conditions. The on/off state of each check box is independent of that of other check boxes. You may substitute a group of two option buttons with a single check box, when the alternate choices are clear; otherwise, it may be better to use the option buttons.

The check box control possesses a number of properties, such as Caption, CtlName, Enabled, and Visible, that resemble those of other controls. Like the option button, the check box has the Value property. However, unlike the option button, the Value property of a check box takes one of three values. The general syntax for using the Value property of a check box is:

[form.][checkBox.]Value [=enumeratedSetting%]

The possible settings of the Value property are 0, 1, and 2. When the Value property is set to 0, the check box is cleared. Assigning 1 to the Value property selects the check box, placing an X inside the box. When the Value property is assigned 2, the box is shaded. The value of 2 can be used to implement a semi-disabled state, since the check box is neither checked nor unchecked.

The following short example demonstrates how check boxes are used to alter the display of the date and time. This demonstration program resembles the last one that I presented. The main difference is the use of two check boxes instead of two option button groups. The first check box enables you to toggle between the AM/PM and the 24-hour time formats. The second check box specifies whether or not the current date is included in the TextBox when you click on the Now command button.

Figures 10-10 through 10-12 list the specifications for this demonstration program. The check boxes have the default values of 0—they are

Application name: Check Box Demonstration
Application code name: CHECKBOX
Version: 1.0   Date created: July 5, 1991
Programmer(s): Namir Clement Shammas

List of filenames
Storage path: \VB\EASYVB
Project CHECKBOX.MAK
Global GLOBAL.BAS
Form 1 CHECKBOX.FRM

10-10   The general specifications for the CHECKBOX.MAK project.

Form #1   Form filename: CHECKBOX.FRM
Version: 1.0   Date: July 5, 1991

Control object type	Default CtlName	Purpose
Command Button	Command1	Displays the date and time
	Command2	Exits the test program
Text Box	Text1	Displays the date and time
Check Box	Check1	Displays 24 hour time format
	Check2	Displays the date

10-11 The general specifications for the CHECKBOX.FRM form.

Application (code) name: CHECKBOX
Form #1
Version: 1.0   Date: July 5, 1991

Original control name	Property	New setting
Form	Caption	Check Box Demo
Command1	CtlName	NowBtn
	Caption	Now
Command2	CtlName	QuitBtn
	Caption	Quit
Text1	CtlName	TextBox
	Caption	(empty string)
Check1	CtlName	TimeFormatChk
	Caption	24 Hour
Check2	CtlName	ShowDateChk
	Caption	Show Date

10-12 The new settings for the CHECKBOX.FRM form.

clear when the program starts running. Figure 10-13 shows a sample session with the test program.

Listing 10-3 shows the two procedures attached to the controls in CHECKBOX.FRM. The NowBtn_Click procedure builds the date and time string using a local string variable S. The procedure uses an If-Then statement to compare the Value property of the Show Date check box with 1. If the Show Date check box is selected, the test is positive and the date

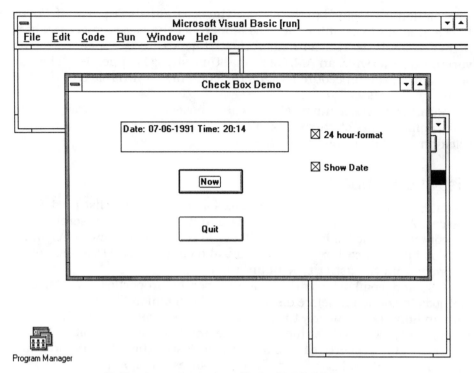

10-13 A sample session with the CHECKBOX program.

Listing 10-3 The code attached to the objects in CHECKBOX.FRM.

```
Sub NowBtn_Click ( )
  Dim S As String
  S = " "
  If ShowDateChk.Value = 1 Then
    S = "Date: " + Date$ + " "
  End If
  S = S + "Time: "
  If TimeFormatChk.Value = 1 Then
    S = S + Format$(Now, "hh:mm")
  Else
    S = S + Format$(Now, "hh:mm AM/PM")
  End If
  TextBox.Text = S ' assign new text
End Sub

Sub QuitBtn_Click ( )
  End
End Sub
```

information is assigned to the string. The program also uses an If-Then-Else statement to examine the Value property of the Time Format check box. If that property is 1, a 24-hour format time string is appended to the variable S; otherwise, an AM/PM format time string is appended. The last statement in the procedure assigns the contents of variable S to the Text property of TextBox.

Run the program and toggle the check boxes. For each of the possible four combinations of check box states, press the Now command button. Click on the Quit button to exit the test program.

List and combo boxes

Visual Basic offers list and combo boxes as controls that list predefined choices. A list box displays a set of data and uses a vertical scroll bar if the contents of the list box cannot all be simultaneously viewed. A combo box combines a text box and a list box, allowing the user to either select an entry from the list or type in an input.

List and combo boxes have a number of properties, events, and methods in common. Before discussing these common traits, let me start with an important property that is unique to the combo boxes. This is the Style property, which determines the type and behavior of a combo box at run time. This property can be set only at design time. During program execution the Visual Basic code can only access this property. The general syntax for the Style property is:

[form.]comboBox.Style

The Style property has one of three values: 0, 1, or 2. The default setting for the Style property is 0. This setting makes the combo box a *dropdown* combo box. When you click on the down arrow button, the associated list appears; you can then either select a list entry or type in the edit area (the text box portion of the combo box). The list is closed after you make a selection.

When you set the Style property to 1, you have a *simple* combo box. This type of box always displays the list and the edit area. The default size of a simple combo box is such that it hides the list. You can alter the Height property to show more of the list.

Setting the Style property to 2 gives you a dropdown list which includes the list but no edit area. This type of combo box forces you to select an item in the list.

When the Style property is set to 0 or 2, you can open the list either by clicking on the down arrow button or by pressing Alt-down arrow when the combo box has the focus.

The list and combo boxes share a number of properties that enable you to maintain and select items from their lists. These items are stored as an array of strings with the lower index of 0. The properties that manage list selections are:

The Sorted **property** This determines whether or not the list items are alphabetically sorted. The Sorted property can be set only during design time. The general syntax for this run time read-only property is:

[form.]{comboBox ¦ listBox}.Sorted

The Sorted property returns a Boolean True (−1) or False (0). If the Sorted property is set to True at design time, the list items are maintained in ascending order.

The Text **property** This property specifies the currently selected text. The general syntax for the Text property is:

[form.]{comboBox ¦ listBox}.Text = *stringExpression$]*

Visual Basic limits the content of the Text property during design time to the following:

- A list box has an empty string in the Text property.
- A combo box can have either an empty string or the default control name supplied by Visual Basic.

You can assign values to the Text property of the combo box when the Style setting is either 0 or 1. Assigning a string to the Text property when the Style setting is 2 results in a run time error, since you can only obtain a selection from the list.

The List **property** List represents an array of strings that contains the list data. The general syntax for the List property is:

[form.]{comboBox ¦ *listBox}*.List(*index%*) *[=stringExpression$]*

Using the List property, you can overwrite a current list item.

⚠ Warning! Overwriting list items when the Sorted property is True may very well corrupt the order in the list. Consequently, you need to have sorting procedures that reorder the items in the list before you add new data items.

The ListIndex **property** This property indicates the index of the currently selected item. The value of the ListIndex for a list box ranges from −1 to the number of data items minus one (that is, ListCount −1). The range of the ListIndex for combo boxes is from −1 to the number of data items minus one. The −1 setting accounts for selections that do not have a matching list member. The general syntax for this run time read-only property is:

[form.]{comboBox ¦ listBox}.ListIndex *[=index%]*

The ListCount **property** This maintains the current number of items in the list. The general syntax for this run time read-only property is:

[form.]{comboBox ¦ listBox}.ListCount

The list box recognizes the Click and DblClick events. Clicking on an item in a list box selects that item. Microsoft recommends the following guidelines on using the single and double click events:

- Each list should be accompanied by a command button. Thus, a single click in the list box selects an item, and a click on the associated command button performs a task using the selected list item.
- Double clicking on a list item should have the same effect as single clicking a list item followed by clicking on the associated command button. Thus, double clicking is a shortcut action.

The combo box recognizes the Click, DblClick, Change, and DropDown events, among others. The Click event is generated when you select a list item. The Change event is recognized (when the Style property is set to 0 or 1) when you edit the contents of the text box. The DropDown event is recognized when the Style property is 0 or 2.

The list and combo boxes have the following methods that are used to add and remove items from the lists.

The AddItem **method**   This method inserts new data items in the list. The general syntax for the AddItem method is:

   [form.]{controlBox ¦ listBox}.AddItem *item$ [,index%]*

The index% is optional. If it is omitted and the Sorted property is False, the new item is appended to the list. If the Sorted property is True, the new item is inserted in its proper place.

▓   When the Sorted property is True, you must omit the index% value, or you will corrupt the order of the items in the list.

When the Sorted property is False, the value of index% can be in the range from 0 to ListCount. If the value of index% is less than ListCount, the list items are shifted upwards from the index% location.

The RemoveItem **method**   This method removes an item from the list. The general syntax for the RemoveItem method is:

   [form.]{controlBox ¦ listBox}.RemoveItem *index%*

The values for the index% range from 0 to ListCount − 1.

Let's look at a simple application that uses the combo box. I have modified the option box demonstration program so that the date format is selected by country. The time format option buttons have been dropped from the combo box demonstration program.

Figures 10-14 to 10-16 show the specifications for the combo box demonstration program. Notice the new settings of the combo box in FIG. 10-16. The Sorted property is set to True and the Style is set to 2 (dropdown list box). Figure 10-17 shows a sample session with the combo box demonstration program.

Application name: Combo Box Demonstration
Application code name: COMBOBOX
Version: 1.0   Date created: July 5, 1991
Programmer(s): Namir Clement Shammas

List of Filenames

Storage path: \VB\EASYVB
Project COMBOBOX.MAK
Global GLOBAL.BAS
Form 1 COMBOBOX.FRM

10-14 The general specifications for the COMBOBOX.MAK project.

Form #1   Form filename: COMBOBOX.FRM
Version: 1.0   Date: July 5, 1991

Control object type	Default CtlName	Purpose
Command Button	Command1	Displays the date and time
	Command2	Exits the test program
Text Box	Text1	Displays the date and time
Combo Box	Combo1	Displays date format by country

10-15 The general specifications for the COMBOBOX.FRM form.

Application (code) name: COMBOBOX
Form #1
Version: 1.0   Date: July 5, 1991

Original control name	Property	New setting
Form	Caption	Combo Box Demo
Command1	CtlName	NowBtn
	Caption	Now
Command2	CtlName	QuitBtn
	Caption	Quit
Text1	CtlName	TextBox
	Caption	(empty string)
Combo1	CtlName	CountryCmb
	Caption	(empty string)
	Sorted	True
	Style	2

10-16 The new settings for the COMBOBOX.FRM form.

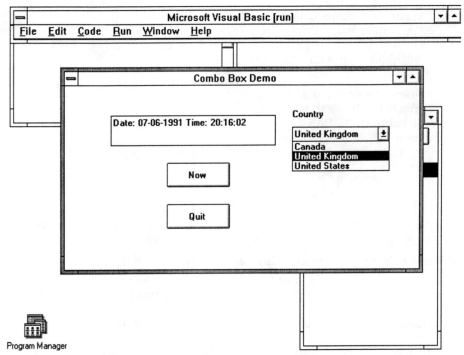

10-17 A sample session with the COMBOBOX program.

Listing 10-4 contains the code attached to the controls of the COMBO-BOX.FRM form. The procedures are:

The Form_Load **procedures**   These procedures add the data to the combo list box using the AddItem method. Since the Sorted property is set to True, no insertion index is specified.

Listing 10-4   The code attached to the controls of the COMBOBOX.FRM form.

```
Sub Form_Load ( )
  ' add items into combo box
  CountryCmb.AddItem "United States"
  CountryCmb.AddItem "United Kingdom"
  CountryCmb.AddItem "Canada"
End Sub

Sub NowBtn_Click ( )
  Dim S As String
  Select Case CountryCmb.Text
    Case CountryCmb.List(2) ' UNITED STATES
      S = Format$(Now, "mm-dd-yyyy")
    Case CountryCmb.List(1) ' CANADA
      S = Format$(Now, "yyyy-mm-dd")
```

Listing 10-4 Continued.

```
    Case CountryCmb.List(0) ' UNITED KINGDOM
      S = Format$(Now, "dd-mm-yyyy")
    Case Else
      S = Date$
  End Select
  TextBox.Text = "Date: " + S + " Time: " + Time$
End Sub

Sub QuitBtn_Click ( )
  End
End Sub
```

The NowBtn_Click **procedure**   With this procedure, the date and time are displayed in control TextBox. The date format is selected based on the country you specify. The CountryCmb.Text returns the selected text. This value is used in a Select-Case statement to compare the selected text with the list items. These items are retrieved using the List property. When the selected text matches a list item, the corresponding date format is used to yield a date string. The time is appended to the date/time string by simply calling the Time$ function.

The QuitBtn_Click **procedure**   This exits the demonstration program.

Vertical and horizontal scroll bars

The vertical and horizontal scroll bars are controls that enable you to quickly go through a list of data. Using scroll bars is typical of Windows applications and utilities. The vertical and horizontal scroll bars are very similar, differing only in their visual orientation. Each scroll bar has two arrow boxes, one at each end. The minimum and maximum ends of a vertical scroll bar are located at the top and bottom ends, respectively. The minimum and maximum ends of a horizontal scroll bar are located at the left and right ends, respectively.

Scroll bars represent integer values. The following properties specify the range of values, the current scroll bar value, and the degree of change in the latter value.

The Min **property**   Min determines the lower range of values for a scroll bar. This property can be set during design and run times, and can be accessed during run time. The general syntax for the Min property is:

  [form.]{hscrollBar ¦ vscrollBar}.Min *[=limit%]*

The values for the Min property range between -32768 and 32767. The default value is 0.

The Max **property** This property determines the upper range of values for a scroll bar. This property can be set during design or run times, and can be accessed during run time. The general syntax for the Max property is:

[form.]{hscrollBar ¦ vscrollBar}.Max *[=limit%]*

The values for the Max property range between -32768 and 32767. The default value is 32767.

The Value **property** This sets or determines the current scroll bar value or reading. This property can be set during design or run times, and can be accessed during run time. The general syntax for the scroll bar Value property is:

[form.]{hscrollBar ¦ vscrollBar}.Value *[=setting%]*

The values for the Value property range are defined by the Min and Max properties, and determine the location of the scroll box.

The SmallChange **property** SmallChange sets and determines the change in the Value property when you click the arrows at either end of the scroll bar. The general syntax for the SmallChange property is:

[form.]{hscrollBar ¦ vscrollBar}.SmallChange *[=change%]*

The values for the SmallChange property range from 1 to 32767, with a default setting of 1.

The LargeChange **property sets and determines the change in the** Value property when you click above or below the scroll box. The general syntax for the LargeChange property is:

[form.]{hscrollBar ¦ vscrollBar}.LargeChange *[=change%]*

The values for the LargeChange property range from 1 to 32767, with a default setting of 1.

The Change event is very important in detecting movement of the scroll box. By retrieving the Value property, you are able to update the information in a related control.

Let's see a simple example for a scroll bar. The next Visual Basic program is a modification of the APP2.MAK project that offered a countdown timer. This new version contains a countdown display text box, a vertical scroll bar, a Count Down command button, and a Quit button. The vertical scroll bar allows you to specify the starting countdown time. The scroll bar values range from 0 to 100. When you click on the countdown button, the text box displays the countdown time. At the same time, the scroll box is updated to reflect the current time—the scroll box slowly creeps upward until it reaches the upper end of the scroll bar. While the program is counting down, the command buttons are disabled. When the countdown is finished, the command buttons are enabled.

Figures 10-18 to 10-20 contain the specifications for the SCROLLBA.MAK project file and the SCROLLBA.FRM form file. Notice

Application name: Scroll Bar Demonstration
Application code name: SCROLLBA
Version: 1.0   Date created: July 5, 1991
Programmer(s): Namir Clement Shammas

List of filenames

Storage path: \VB\EASYVB
Project SCROLLBA.MAK
Global GLOBAL.BAS
Form 1 SCROLLBA.FRM

10-18   The general specifications for the SCROLLBA.MAK project.

Form #1   Form filename: SCROLLBA.FRM
Version: 1.0   Date: July 5, 1991

Control object type	Default CtlName	Purpose
Command Button	Command1	Activates the count-down timer
	Command2	Exits the test program
Text Box	Text1	Displays the date and time
Vertical Scroll Bar	VScroll1	Sets the timer
Label	Label1	Scroll bar label
	Label2	Minimum scroll bar value label
	Label3	Maximum scroll bar value label

10-19   The general specifications for the SCROLLBA.FRM form.

Application (code) name: SCROLLBA
Form #1
Version: 1.0   Date: July 5, 1991

Original control name	Property	New setting
Form	Caption	Scroll Bar Demo
Command1	CtlName	TimerBtn
	Caption	Count Down
Command2	CtlName	QuitBtn
	Caption	Quit
Text1	CtlName	TextBox
	Caption	(empty string)
VScroll1	CtlName	TimeScl
Label1	CtlName	TimerLbl
	Caption	Timer Setting

10-20   The new settings for the SCROLLBA.FRM form.

Original control name	Property	New setting
Label2	CtlName	MinLbl
	Caption	N sec
Label3	CtlName	MaxLbl
	Caption	M sec

10-20 Continued.

that there is only one new setting for the scroll bar — a new control name. The new settings for the Min, Max, Value, SmallChange, and LargeChange properties are made in the Form_Load procedure; this will be discussed later. Also notice the MinLbl and MaxLbl captions — they are N Sec and M sec, respectively. These are dummy captions. The Form_Load procedure sets new captions that reflect the actual settings for the Min and Max properties. Figure 10-21 shows a sample session with the scroll bar demonstration program.

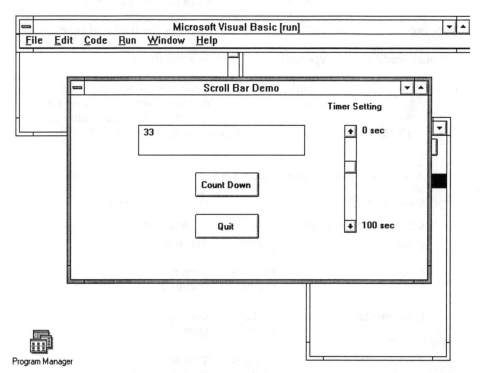

10-21 A sample session with the SCROLLBA program.

Listing 10-5 shows the code attached to the SCROLLBA.FRM and its controls. The general declarations section declares two constants, MIN_VALUE and MAX_VALUE, which define the range of scroll bar values. Also notice the following event-handling procedures:

Listing 10-5 The code attached to the SCROLLBA.FRM form and its controls.

```
Const MIN_VALUE = 0, MAX_VALUE = 100

Sub QuitBtn_Click ( )
  End
End Sub

Sub TimeScl_Change ( )
  TextBox.Text = Str$(TimeScl.Value)
End Sub

Sub Form_Load ( )
  ' set the Min, Max, Value, SmallChange, and
  ' LargeChange properties of the scroll bar
  TimeScl.Min = MIN_VALUE
  TimeScl.Max = MAX_VALUE
  TimeScl.Value = MAX_VALUE \ 10
  TimeScl.SmallChange = 1 ' same as default
  TimeScl.LargeChange = MAX_VALUE \ 10
  ' set the Text property of TextBox
  TextBox.Text = Str$(TimeScl.Value)
  ' Assign captions to the scroll bar labels to
  ' match the program's settings
  MinLbl.Caption = Format$(MIN_VALUE) + " sec"
  MaxLbl.Caption = Format$(MAX_VALUE) + " sec"
End Sub

Sub TimerBtn_Click ( )
  Dim Count As Double, Total As Double, Diff As Double
  Total = TimeScl.Value
  If Total = 0 Then Exit Sub
  QuitBtn.Enabled = False
  TimerBtn.Enabled = False
  Count = Timer
  Do While (Timer - Count) < = Total
    Diff = Int(Total - (Timer - Count))
    ' update the scroll box location
    If Diff > = 0 Then TimeScl.Value = Diff
  Loop
  Beep
  TimerBtn.Enabled = True
  QuitBtn.Enabled = True
End Sub
```

The TimeScl_Change **procedure** This procedure updates the content of the text box when the scroll box moves.

The Form_load **procedure** performs a good amount of initialization. This includes assigning new settings to the Min, Max, Value, SmallChange, and

LargeChange properties. The SmallChange property is reassigned the default setting—I place the assignment so as to include all of the scroll bar properties that I mentioned earlier. The new settings for most of the above scroll bar properties are based on the MIN_VALUE and MAX_VALUE constants. The Form_Load procedure also initializes the contents of the text box. Finally, the procedure assigns new captions for the MinLbl and MaxLbl labels. These captions reflect the values of the MIN_VALUE and MAX_VALUE constants.

☞ **The** TimerBtn_Click **procedure** This handles the countdown process. The total number of seconds to countdown is taken from the Value property of the scroll bar. Notice that the procedure does not explicitly update the contents of the text box, even though the text box shows the decreasing number of seconds during the countdown. What makes the text box update the time automatically? The answer is procedure TimeScl_ Change. Whenever the TimeScl.Value property changes, the contents of the text box are updated accordingly.

Run the scroll bar demo program and experiment with the scroll bar. Press the Count Down button and watch the countdown process. You can alter the MAX_VALUE constant and rerun the program. Notice the new maximum value scroll bar label. It reflects the new value of constant MAX_VALUE.

The InputBox$ and MsgBox dialog boxes

Input boxes are very common types of modal dialog boxes that prompt you to enter a value as a string. The input box contains an edit text box, an OK button, and a Cancel button. If you click the OK button or press the Enter key, you confirm the content of the edit text box. By contrast, if you click the Cancel button you exit the dialog box and disregard the content of the edit box.

Visual Basic offers the InputBox$ function that implements a modal input dialog box. The InputBox$ function returns the content of the edit box if you click the OK button or press the Enter key. It returns an empty string if you click the Cancel button. As a modal dialog box, the InputBox$ does not allow you to switch to another window until you first close it. The general syntax for the InputBox$ functions is:

InputBox$ *(prompt$ [, title$ [, default$ [, xpos%, ypos%]]])*

The prompt$ is the prompting message string. This string can be up to 255 characters long and may contain Chr$(13) + Char$(10) substrings to create line breaks.

The optional title$ parameter is a title string. When title$ is omitted, the input box appears with no title.

The default$ parameter supplies the default content of the edit text box.

The xpos% and ypos% parameters specify the location of the upper right hand corner of the dialog box from the upper right hand screen corner. If these parameters are omitted, the dialog box appears horizontally centered and vertically positioned at about one third the way down the screen.

Visual Basic implements the MsgBox function and the MsgBox statement. The function differs from the statement in that it returns an integer value. However, the MsgBox function is identical to the MsgBox statement in every other aspect. As the name suggests, both forms of MsgBox display a message box, containing a message to the user, and display one or more buttons. The MsgBox function returns a value that indicates the button you clicked as a response to the message, which is a type of input. The general syntax for the MsgBox function and statement is:

MsgBox *(msg$ [, type% [, title$]])*

The msg$ parameter specifies the message text displayed by MsgBox. The msg$ string may be up to 1024 characters (the extra characters are truncated), assuming that the first 255 characters contain at least one space. If not, only the first 255 characters are displayed and the rest of the msg$ string is truncated. MsgBox automatically wraps the text of string msg$. You can make new lines by inserting the Chr$(13) + Chr$(10) substrings in the string msg$.

The type% parameter specifies the number and type of buttons, the accompanying icons, and the default button. Table 10-1 shows the basic values for the type% parameter, grouped by purpose. The argument for the type% parameter can combine one value from each group. For example, to have MsgBox display the following:

- The OK and Cancel buttons (value of 1)
- The Information Message icon (value of 64)
- The second button as the default (value of 256)

You need to supply the value of 321 (equal to 1 + 64 + 256) to the type% argument.

The title$ string enables you to specify a title for the MsgBox. When omitted, the Microsoft Visual Basic title appears instead.

Table 10-2 shows the integer results returned by the MsgBox function. These values are used as a form of input utilizing the MsgBox function.

Next, I present a short example for the InputBox$ and MsgBox statements. The next program is a modified version of the last one—the countdown timer. The new version uses InputBox$ to obtain the countdown time when you press the Count Down button. If you enter a zero or a negative value, a message box appears to tell you that your input value is replaced with 15 (seconds).

Table 10-1 **The basic values for the** type% **parameter in the** MsgBox.

Group	Value	Purpose
Buttons	0	Displays OK button.
	1	Displays OK and Cancel buttons.
	2	Displays Abort, Retry, and Ignore buttons.
	3	Displays Yes, No, and Cancel buttons.
	4	Displays Yes and No buttons.
	5	Displays Retry and Cancel buttons.
Icons	16	Displays Critical Message icon.
	32	Displays Warning Query icon.
	48	Displays Warning Message icon.
	64	Displays Information Message icon.
Default	0	First button is default.
	256	Second button is default.
	512	Third button is default.

Table 10-2 **The integer results returned by the** MsgBox **function.**

Value	Meaning
1	OK pressed.
2	Cancel pressed.
3	Abort pressed.
4	Retry pressed.
5	Ignore pressed.
6	Yes pressed.
7	No pressed.

Figures 10-22 to 10-24 show the specifications for the project file IN-PUTBOX.MAK and the form file INPUTBOX.FRM. Figure 10-25 shows a sample session with the test program.

Application name: InputBox$ and MsgBox Demonstration
Application code name: INPUTBOX
Version: 1.0   Date created: July 5, 1991
Programmer(s): Namir Clement Shammas
List of filenames
Storage path: \VB\EASYVB
Project INPUTBOX.MAK
Global GLOBAL.BAS
Form 1 INPUTBOX.FRM
  10-22 The general specifications for the INPUTBOX.MAK project.

Form #1
Version: 1.0

Form filename: INPUTBOX.FRM
Date: July 5, 1991

Control object type	Default CtlName	Purpose
Command Button	Command1	Activates the count-down timer
	Command2	Exits the test program
Text Box	Text1	Displays the date and time

10-23 The general specifications for the INPUTBOX.FRM form.

Application (code) name: INPUTBOX
Form #1
Version: 1.0

Date: July 5, 1991

Original control name	Property	New setting
Form	Caption	InputBox$ and MsgBox Demo
Command1	CtlName	TimerBtn
	Caption	Count Down
Command2	ClName	QuitBtn
	Caption	Quit
Text1	CtlName	TextBox
	Caption	(empty string)

10-24 The new settings for the INPUTBOX.FRM form.

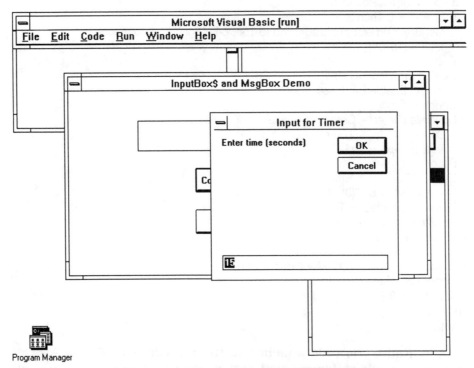

10-25 A sample session with the INPUTBOX program.

Listing 10-6 shows the code attached to the INPUTBOX.FRM. The Timer_Click procedure contains the InputBox$ and MsgBox statements. The InputBox$ statement displays a dialog box titled Input for Timer with an Enter time (seconds) prompt. The default time of 15 (seconds) appears in the edit text box. If you enter a zero or a negative value, the MsgBox statement appears to inform you that your input was replaced with 15. The MsgBox appears with the message Timer input is adjusted to 15, and the title For Your Information. The Information Message icon also appears to the left of the message text.

Listing 10-6   The code attached to the INPUTBOX.FRM.

```
Sub QuitBtn_Click ( )
  End
End Sub

Sub TimerBtn_Click ( )
  Dim Count As Double, Total As Double, Diff As Double
  Dim Prompt As String, Title As String, Default As String
  Prompt = "Enter time (seconds) "
  Title = "Input for Timer"
  Default$ = "15"
  TextBox.Text = InputBox$(Prompt, Title, Default)
  Total = Val(TextBox.Text)
  If Total < = 0 Then
    MsgBox "Timer input is adjusted to 15", 64, "For Your Information"
    Total = 15
  End If
  QuitBtn.Enabled = False
  TimerBtn.Enabled = False
  Count = Timer
  Do While (Timer − Count) < = Total
    Diff = Int(Total − (Timer − Count))
    TextBox.Text = Str$(Diff)
  Loop
  Beep
  TextBox.Text = Str$(0)
  TimerBtn.Enabled = True
  QuitBtn.Enabled = True
End Sub

Sub TextBox_KeyPress (KeyAscii As Integer)
  ' ignore all input
  KeyAscii = 0
End Sub
```

☞ Notice the code attached to the procedure TextBox_KeyPress. It contains a single statement that assigns zero to the KeyAscii argument.

This statement prevents you from keying anything in the text box, making the text box an output-only control.

Run the above program and experiment with positive and negative timer input values. Observe the For Your Information message window appearance when you do not enter positive timer values.

Updating the scientific calculator

The Visual Basic test programs that I presented earlier were small programs that focused on a specific control object. Now that we have seen how these controls work, let me present an updated version of the scientific calculator, which uses option buttons, check boxes, and combo boxes.

The new version of the command-oriented scientific calculator has the following new features:

- A drop-down list box replaces the Operator text box to offer you a list of the available operators and functions. Using this combo box you need not remember whether or not a function or operator is available.
- A check box is used to indicate whether or not you want the variable names in the operand text boxes to be replaced with their values when you click on the Execute command button.
- A check box assists you in automatically selecting the next variable name when you click on the Store button.
- A frame with three option buttons enables you to select the angle mode: radians, degrees, and gradients (grad for short). To convert from gradients to degrees, multiply the gradient angle by 0.9.

Figures 10-26 to 10-28 show the specifications for the SCICALC2.MAK project file and the SCICALC2.FRM form file. Figure 10-29 shows a sample session with this Visual Basic program.

Application name: Command-oriented Scientific Calculator
Application code name: COSC2
Version: 1.0

Date created: July 6, 1991
Programmer(s): Namir C. Shammas
Company: N/A

Lists of filenames
Storage path: C:\VB\EASYVB
Project SCICALC2.MAK
Global GLOBAL.BAS
Form 1 SCICALC2.FRM

10-26 The basic specifications for the SCICALC2.MAK project.

| Form #1 | | Form filename: SCICALC2.FRM |
| Version: 1.0 | | Date: July 6, 1991 |

Control object type	Default CtlName	Purpose
Text Box	Text1	Key in operand 1
	Text2	Key in operand 2
	Text3	Display the result
	Text4	Display error message
	Text5	Key in the variable names
Label	Label1	Label of Text1
		Replace variable with numeric value
	Label2	Label for Combo1 box
	Label3	Label of Text2
		Replace variable with numeric value
	Label4	Label of Text3
	Label5	Label of Text4
		Clear error message
	Label6	Label of Text5
Command button	Command1	Executes math operation
	Command2	Exit the application
	Command3	Stores the result in a variable
Combo Box	Combo1	Offers the list of operators and Functions
Check Box	Check1	Automatically substitutes the variables in the operand boxes with their values
	Check2	Automatically selects the next variable name when the Command3 button is clicked.
Frame Box	Frame1	Contains the angle option button
Option Button	Option1	0 - Radians angle mode
	Option2	1 - Degrees angle mode
	Option3	2 - Gradient angle mode

10-27 The list of controls in the SCICALC2.FRM form.

Application (code) name: COSC2
Form #1
Version: 1.0   Date: July 6, 1991

Original control name	Property	New setting
Form1	Caption	Scientific Calculator (Ver. 2)
Text1	CtlName	Operand1Box
	Text	(empty string)

10-28 The changes in the settings for the COSC2 application.

Original control name	Property	New setting
Text3	CtlName	Operand2Box
	Text	(empty string)
Text4	CtlName	ResultBox
	Text	(empty string)
Text5	CtlName	ErrorMessageBox
	Text	(empty string)
Text6	CtlName	VariableBox
	Text	(empty string)
Label1	CtlName	Operand1Lbl
	Caption	Operand 1
Label2	CtlName	OperatorLbl
	Caption	Operator
Label3	CtlName	Operator2Lbl
	Caption	Operand 2
Label4	CtlName	ResultLbl
	Caption	Result
Label5	CtlName	ErrorMessageLbl
	Caption	Error Message
Label6	CtlName	VariableLbl
	Caption	Variable
Command1	CtlName	ExecuteBtn
	Caption	Execute
Command2	CtlName	QuitBtn
	Caption	Quit
Command2	CtlName	StoreBtn
	Caption	Store
Combo1	CtlName	OperatorCmb
	Sorted	True
	Style	2
Check1	CtlName	SubstitueChk
	Caption	Auto Substitute
Check2	CtlName	SelectChk
	Caption	Auto Select New Variable Name

10-28 Continued.

Original control name	Property	New setting
Frame1	CtlName	AngleModeFrm
	Caption	Angle Mode
Option1	CtlName	RadianOpt
	Caption	Radian
Option1	CtlName	DegreeOpt
	Caption	Degree
Option1	CtlName	GradOpt
	Caption	Grad

10-28 Continued.

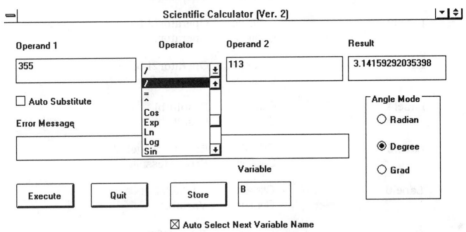

10-29 A sample session with the COSC2 project.

Listing 10-7 contains the code attached to the SCICALC2.FRM and its controls. The listing shows event-handling procedures that are either new to this version or that have been modified from the previous version. The modified procedures follow.

The StoreBtn_Click **procedure** This procedure stores the result in the designated variable. The procedure adds statements that deal with selecting the next variable name. An If statement compares the SelectChk. Value property with 1. If the test is positive, the statements in the Then clause change the value of the local variable Index (which stores the ASCII code for the current single-letter variable name) to select the next variable. These statements take into consideration the case when the current variable is Z. In this case, the value of Index is set to the function Asc("A"), the ASCII code for A.

The ExecuteBtn_Click **procedure** With this procedure, the specified operation or function is executed. The new version of this procedure obtains the

Listing 10-7 Listing The code attached to the SCICALC2.FRM form and its controls.

```
Dim TheVars(65 To 90) As Double
Dim Pi As Double

Sub QuitBtn_Click ( )
  End
End Sub

Sub StoreBtn_Click ( )
  Dim C As String
  Dim Index As Integer
  ' process the contents of the Variable text box
  If VariableBox.Text < > " " Then
    ' obtain the uppercase of the first character in the text box
    C = UCase$(Left$(VariableBox.Text, 1))
    ' is the character in the range A to Z?
    If (C > = "A") And (C < = "Z") Then
      ' Yes! Get the ASCII code for the character
      Index = Asc(C)
      ' store the value of the Result box in the array TheVars#
      TheVars#(Index) = Val(ResultBox.Text)
      ' clear the error message box
      ErrorMessageBox.Text = " "
      ' select the next variable
      If SelectChk.Value = 1 Then
        If Index = Asc("Z") Then
          Index = Asc("A")
        Else
          Index = Index + 1
        End If
        VariableBox.Text = Chr$(Index)
      End If
    Else
      ' No! The text box has an invalid variable name
      ErrorMessageBox.Text = "Invalid variable name"
      Beep
    End If
  Else
    ' the text box is empty!
    ErrorMessageBox.Text = "Missing variable name"
    Beep
  End If
End Sub

Sub ExecuteBtn_Click ( )
  Dim X As Double, Y As Double, Z As Double
  Dim Xchar As String
  Dim YChar As String
  ErrorMessageBox.Text = " " ' clear error message box
```

Listing 10-7 Continued.

```
ResultBox.Text = " " ' clear result box
' is the Auto Substitute check box marked
If SubstituteChk.Value = 1 Then
   Operand1Lbl_Click
   Operand2Lbl_Click
End If
' obtain the first character in the
' Operand1Box text box
Xchar = Left$(Operand1Box.Text, 1)
' obtain the first character in the
' Operand2Box text box
Ychar = Left$(Operand2Box.Text, 1)
' convert string in Operand1Box text box to its
' numeric value. Note that if the conversion fails,
' X will be assigned a zero.
X = Val(Operand1Box.Text)
' is X = 0 when Xchar is not "0"? This test detects
' failed conversions
If (X = 0) And (Xchar < > "0") Then
    ' Yes! Is Xchar in the range A to Z
   If (Xchar > = "A") And (Xchar < = "Z") Then
       ' treat the content of Operand1Box as storing
       ' the name of a variable. Assign the value of
       ' the variable to X
       X = TheVars#(Asc(Xchar))
   End If
End If
' convert text in Operand2Box to numeric value
Y = Val(Operand2Box.Text)
' check if Operand2Box has a variable
If (Y = 0) And (Ychar < > "0") Then
   If (Ychar > = "A") And (Ychar < = "Z") Then
       ' Yes! there is a variable. Assign its
       ' value to variable Y
       Y = TheVars#(Asc(Ychar))
   End If
End If
' examine the content of the OperatorBox text box
Select Case UCase$(OperatorCmb.Text)
   Case " + "
      Z = X + Y
   Case " – "
      Z = X – Y
   Case " * "
      Z = X * Y
   Case "/"
      If Y < > 0 Then
```

Listing 10-7 Continued.

```
      Z = X / Y
   Else
      ErrorMessageBox.Text = "Division by zero error"
      Beep
   End If
Case "^"
   Z = X ^ Y
Case "=" ' simply copy the value of the first
          ' operand into the result box
   Z = X
Case "LN"
   If X > 0 Then
      Z = Log(X)
   Else
      ErrorMessageBox.Text = "Bad function argument"
      Beep
   End If
Case "LOG"
   If X > 0 Then
      Z = Log(X) / Log(10)
   Else
      ErrorMessageBox.Text = "Bad function argument"
      Beep
   End If
Case "EXP"
   Z = Exp(X)
Case "SQR"
   If X > = 0 Then
      Z = Sqr(X)
   Else
      ErrorMessageBox.Text = "Bad function argument"
      Beep
   End If
Case "SIN"
   If RadianOpt.Value Then
      Z = Sin(X)
   ElseIf DegreeOpt.Value Then
      Z = Sin(X * Pi / 180)
   ElseIf GradOpt.Value Then
      Z = Sin(X * .9 * Pi / 180)
   Else
      Z = Sin(X)
   End If
Case "COS"
   If RadianOpt.Value Then
      Z = Cos(X)
   ElseIf DegreeOpt.Value Then
```

Listing 10-7 Continued.

```
            Z = Cos(X * Pi / 180)
        Elself GradOpt.Value Then
            Z = Cos(X * .9 * Pi / 180)
        Else
            Z = Cos(X)
        End If
    Case "TAN"
        If RadianOpt.Value Then
            Z = Tan(X)
        Elself DegreeOpt.Value Then
            Z = Tan(X * Pi / 180)
        Elself GradOpt.Value Then
            Z = Tan(X * .9 * Pi / 180)
        Else
            Z = Tan(X)
        End If
    Case Else
        ErrorMessageBox.Text = "Invalid operator"
        Beep
    End Select
    ' if the error message box is still empty, there is
    ' no error. Therefore, convert the variable Z into
    ' a string and display it in ResultBox
    If ErrorMessageBox.Text = " " Then
        ResultBox.Text = Str$(Z)
    End If
End Sub

Sub Operand1Lbl_Click ( )
    Dim Xchar As String
    ' get the first character in the Operand1Box
    Xchar = Left$(Operand1Box.Text, 1)
    ' is the character in the range A to Z?
    If (Xchar > = "A") And (Xchar < = "Z") Then
        ' Yes! Obtain the variable from the array and write
        ' its numeric value to the text box
        Operand1Box.Text = Str$(TheVars#(Asc(Xchar)))
    End If
End Sub

Sub Operand2Lbl_Click ( )
    Dim Xchar As String
    ' get the first character in the
    ' Operand2Box
    Xchar = Left$(Operand2Box.Text, 1)
    ' is the character in the range A to Z?
    If (Xchar > = "A") And (Xchar < = "Z") Then
```

Listing 10-7 Continued.

```
        ' Yes! Obtain the variable from the array and write
        ' its numeric value to the text box
        Operand2Box.Text = Str$(TheVars#(Asc(Xchar)))
    End If
End Sub

Sub ErrorMessageLbl_Click ( )
    ErrorMessageBox.Text = " "
End Sub

Sub Form_Load ( )
    WindowState = 2 ' set window to maximized state
    ' insert list of operators and functions in the
    ' Operator combo box
    OperatorCmb.AddItem " + "
    OperatorCmb.AddItem "-"
    OperatorCmb.AddItem " * "
    OperatorCmb.AddItem "/"
    OperatorCmb.AddItem "^"
    OperatorCmb.AddItem " = "
    OperatorCmb.AddItem "Sqr"
    OperatorCmb.AddItem "Tan"
    OperatorCmb.AddItem "Cos"
    OperatorCmb.AddItem "Exp"
    OperatorCmb.AddItem "Ln"
    OperatorCmb.AddItem "Log"
    OperatorCmb.AddItem "Sin"
    ' select the Degree option box
    DegreeOpt.Value = True
    ' insert the variable A into the variable box
    VariableBox.Text = "A"
    ' calculate Pi
    Pi = 4 * Atn(1)
End Sub

Sub Operand1Box_KeyPress (KeyAscii As Integer)
    KeyAscii = Asc(UCase$(Chr$(KeyAscii)))
End Sub

Sub Operand2Box_KeyPress (KeyAscii As Integer)
    KeyAscii = Asc(UCase$(Chr$(KeyAscii)))
End Sub

Sub VariableBox_KeyPress (KeyAscii As Integer)
    KeyAscii = Asc(UCase$(Chr$(KeyAscii)))
End Sub
```

name of the operation or function by examining the Text property of the OperatorCmb combo box. Another change is made in the procedure to deal with the various angle modes. The Case clauses for the sine, cosine, and tangent functions employ extended If-Then-ElseIf statements to examine the Value property of the Radian, Degree, and Grad option buttons.

New procedures attached to the form and its controls are:

The Form_Load **procedure** Form_Load performs various initializations. They include the following:

- Setting the WindowState property to 2 (maximized). This causes the form to occupy the entire screen when the program starts running.
- Adding the operator and function names to the combo list. Notice that the items are added in unordered fashion. Since the Sorted property is set to True, the list displays its items in alphabetical order.
- Setting the Value property of the Degree option button to True.
- Inserting the variable name A in the Variable text box.
- Calculating Pi.

The Operand1Box_KeyPress, **The** Operand2Box_KeyPress, **and** VariableBox_KeyPress **procedures** These procedures automatically change all the letters you type into upper case.

Run the program and experiment with the various features of this application.

11
Output

The last chapter discussed various Visual Basic input controls. This chapter looks at the various ways to output both formatted and unformatted information. A few of these methods have already been discussed. Using the text box for output was presented in chapter 7, with emphasis on using text boxes to simulate pseudo-screens. In the last chapter I also presented the MsgBox statement (while discussing the very similar MsgBox function) that displays information. In this chapter you will learn about the following:

- Setting the text characteristics.
- Using the Visual Basic Print statement.
- Formatting output.
- Sending output to the printer.

Setting the text characteristics

Visual Basic allows all of the objects that display characters to support the following font properties, which determine the visual appearance of the text:

- Font (character style)
- Font size
- Font appearance (bold, italic, strikethrough, or underline)

Changing a font characteristic of a Text or Caption property results in the prompt update of the appearance of that property. Consequently, the characters in a Text or Caption property cannot contain mixed fonts.

The properties that control the fonts and their appearances are:

The FontName **property**   selects the font by name. The general syntax for the FontName property is:

*[form.][control.]*FontName *[=name$]*

The standard font names for the Text and Caption properties are Courier, Helv, Modern, Roman, Script, Symbol, System, Terminal, and Tms Roman. The Helv and Tms Roman names are abbreviations for Helvetica and Times Roman, respectively.

The FontSize **property**   sets the font size in points (72 points to an inch). The general syntax for the FontSize property is:

*[form.][control.]*FontSize *[=points%]*

☞   Keep in mind that there is a limited set of font sizes for each font. This means that not every setting for FontSize is accommodated.

The FontBold, FontItalic, FontStrikethru, **and** FontUnderline **properties**   Turn on or off the bold, italic, strikethrough, and underline appearance of a character, respectively. The general syntax for these properties is:

*[form.][control.]*FontBold *[=Boolean%]*
*[form.][control.]*FontItalic *[=Boolean%]*
*[form.][control.]*FontStrikethru *[=Boolean%]*
*[form.][control.]*FontUnderline *[=Boolean%]*

To illustrate how the above font-related properties work, let me present a new version of the menu-driven file viewer, based on the FVIEW2C.MAK project files. This new version adds two new menu selections: Font and Font Size.

The Font menu allows you to select one of three fonts (Courier, System, and Terminal) and permits you to toggle the bold, italic, strikethrough, and underline features. The program places a check mark to the left of the currently selected font name and font appearance options. The Font menu uses a separator line to put the font name in one group and the font appearances in another. It is important to mention that the font name options behave like option buttons—only one font name is allowed. By contrast, the font appearance options act like check boxes—you can turn on any option combination. This type of pull-down menu is common in applications that display text, with or without graphics.

The Font Size menu offers a pop-up menu of font sizes: 9, 10, 12, 14, and 18 points. Naturally, there can be only one selected font size. The program places a check mark to the left of the selected size.

Figures 11-1 to 11-4 show the specifications of the FVIEW3.MAK project file, the FVIEW3.FRM form file, and the updated menu structure. The updated menu structure shows the controls for the font style, font appearance, and font size. Figure 11-5 displays a sample session with the FVIEW3 program.

Application name: Menu-Driven Text File Viewer
Application code name: FVIEW3
Version: 1.0   Date created: July 8, 1991
Programmer(s): Namir Clement Shammas

List of filenames

Storage path: C:\VB\EASYVB
Project FVIEW3.MAK
Global GLOBAL.BAS
Form 1 FVIEW 3.FRM

11-1   General project specifications for the FVIEW3 project.

Form #1   Form filename: FVIEW3.FRM
Version: 1.0   Date: July 8, 1991

Control object type	Default CtlName	Purpose
Text Box	Text1	Contains the filename to read
	Text2	Contains the text search string
	Text3	Contains the DOS/Windows command line
	Text4	Displays the text lines of a file
Label	Label1	Label of Text1
	Label2	Label of Text2
	Label3	Label of Text3

11-2   List of control objects for the FVIEW3 project.

Application (code) name: FVIEW3
Form #1
Version: 1.0   Date: June 27, 1991

Original control name	Property	New setting
Form	Caption	File Viewer (ver. 3)
Text1	CtlName	FilenameBox
	Text	(empty string)
Text2	CtlName	FindBox
	Text	(empty string)
Text3	CtlName	DosBox
	Text	(empty string)
Text4	CtlName	TextBox
	Text	(empty string)
	MultiLine	True
	ScrollBars	3 - both
Label1	CtlName	FilenameLbl
	Caption	Filename Input

11-3   The modified control settings for the FVIEW3 project.

Original control name	Property	New setting
Label2	CtlName	FindLbl
	Caption	Find Input
Label3	CtlName	DosLbl
	Caption	DOS/Win Input

11-3 Continued.

Form #1   Form filename: FVIEW3.FRM
Version: 1.0   Date: July 8, 1991

Caption	Property	Setting	Purpose
&File	CtlName	FileCom	
Read	CtlName	ReadCom	Reads a file in Text1
	Accelerator	CTRL-R	
	indented	once	
Toggle Read	CtlName	ToggleReadCom	Toggles Read menu
	indented	once	option
Find File	CtlName	FindFileCom	Finds a file
	Accelerator	CTRL-F	
	indented	once	
		Sep1	
–	CtlName	Sep1	
	indented	once	
Add File	CtlName	AddFileCom	Adds a filename
	indented	once	
Delete File	CtlName	DeleteFileCom	Deletes a filename
	indented	once	
–	CtlName	Sep2	
	indented	once	
(noname)	CtlName	QuickFilename	
	Index	0	
	Visible	off	
	indented	once	
–	CtlName	Sep3	
	indented	once	
Quit	CtlName	QuitCom	Exits the application
	Accelerator	CTRL-Q	
	indented	once	
&Search	CtlName	SearchCom	
Find	CtlName	FindCom	Finds text in Text1
	Accelerator	CTRL-Q	
	indented	once	
&Command	CtlName	CommandCom	
DOS Command	CtlName	DOSCom	Executes a DOS
	Accelerator	CTRL-D	command
	indented	once	

11-4 The menu structure for the FVIEW2C project.

Caption	Property	Setting	Purpose
Windows Command	CtlName	WinCom	Runs a Windows
	Accelerator	CTRL-W	application
	indented	once	
Toggle OS	CtlName	ToggleOsCom	shows/hides command
	indented	once	options.
Font	CtName	FontCom	Shows fonts
Courier	CtlName	CourierCom	selects Courier font
System	CtlName	SystemCom	selects System font
Terminal	CtlName	TerminalCom	selects Terminal font
–	CtlName	Sep4	
Bold	CtlName	BoldCom	toggles bold characters
Italic	CtlName	ItalicCom	toggles italic characters
Strikethru	CtlName	StrikethrouCom	toggles strikethru characters
Underline	CtlName	UnderlineCom	toggles underlined characters
Font Size			
9	CtlName	Size9Com	selects font size 9
10	CtlName	Size10Com	selects font size 10
12	CtlName	Size12Com	selects font size 12
14	CtlName	Size14Com	selects font size 14
18	CtlName	Size18Com	selects font size 18

11-4 Continued.

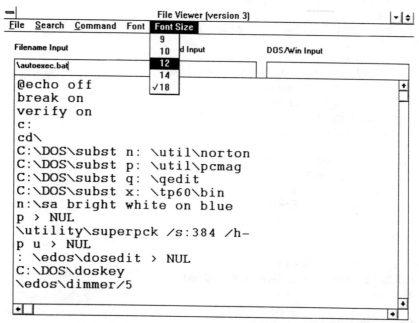

11-5 A sample session with the FVIEW3.MAK project.

Listing 11-1 contains the code attached to the FVIEW3.FRM form. Several auxiliary and event-handling procedures are of interest.

Listing 11-1 The code attached to the FVIEW3.FRM form.

```
Dim NumFiles As Integer

Sub QuitCom_Click ( )
   End
End Sub

Sub DosCom_Click ( )
   Dim Dummy As Integer
   ' invoke the DOSBAT batch file
   Dummy = Shell("dosbat.bat " + DosBox.Text, 1)
End Sub

Sub FindCom_Click ( )
   Static CurIndex As Long
   Dim Find As String
   ' update the index to the current character
   CurIndex = TextBox.SelStart + 1
   ' store the text of the Find box in the variable Find
   Find = FindBox.Text
   ' is variable Find empty?
   If Find = " " Then Exit Sub ' nothing to find
   ' locate the index of the next substring Find in the
   ' text box
   CurIndex = InStr(CurIndex + 1, TextBox.Text, Find)
   ' found a match?
   If CurIndex > 0 Then
      ' Yes! Display the matching text as selected text
      TextBox.SelStart = CurIndex - 1
      TextBox.SelLength = Len(Find)
      TextBox.SetFocus
      FindCom.Checked = True
   Else
      ' No! Clear any selected text
      TextBox.SelStart = 0
      TextBox.SelLength = 0
      FindCom.Checked = False
   End If
End Sub

Sub ToggleReadCom_Click ( )
   ReadCom.Enabled = Not ReadCom.Enabled
End Sub

Sub ReadCom_Click ( )
```

Listing 11-1 Continued.

```
    Dim F As String
    Dim L As String
    Dim NL As String * 2
    ' obtain filename from the filename text box
    F = FilenameBox.Text
    ' if filename is an empty string, exit
    If F = " " Then Exit Sub
    NL = Chr$(13) + Chr$(10)
    ' set error-handler
    On Error GoTo BadFile
    ' open the file
    Open F For Input As 1
    F = " " ' clear variable to reuse it
    ' loop to read the text lines from the ASCII file
    Do While Not EOF(1)
       Line Input #1, L
        F = F + L + NL ' append a new line
    Loop
    TextBox.Text = F ' copy F into text box
    ' close the file
    Close #1
    ' exit procedure
    Exit Sub
' *********** Error-handler **********
BadFile:
   Beep
   MsgBox "Cannot open file " + F, 0, "File I/O Error"
   On Error GoTo 0
   Resume EndOfSub
EndOfSub:
End Sub

Sub FindFileCom_Click ( )
   Dim Dummy As Integer
   ' invoke the DOS dir command with the /s
   ' subdirectory option and the /p paginated
   ' output option
   Dummy = Shell("dosbat.bat dir " + FilenameBox.Text + " /s/p", 1)
End Sub

Sub WinCom_Click ( )
   Dim Dummy As Integer
   ' invoke a Windows application
   Dummy = Shell(DosBox.Text, 1)
End Sub

Sub ToggleOSCom_Click ( )
   ' toggle the Visible property of the DosBox text box,
```

Listing 11-1 Continued.

```
' the DosBtn button, the WinBtn button, and the DosLbl
' label
DosBox.Visible = Not DosBox.Visible
DosCom.Visible = Not DosCom.Visible
WinCom.Visible = Not WinCom.Visible
DosLbl.Visible = Not DosLbl.Visible
End Sub

Sub FindLbl_Change ( )
  FindCom.Checked = False
End Sub

Sub FindBox_Change ( )
  FindCom.Checked = 0
End Sub

Sub AddFileCom_Click ( )
  Dim TheFilename As String
  TheFilename = InputBox$("Enter full file name: ")
  NumFiles = NumFiles + 1 ' increment the menu count
  Load QuickFilename(NumFiles) ' load a new menu command
  QuickFilename(NumFiles).Caption = TheFilename
  QuickFilename(NumFiles).Visible = True
End Sub

Sub QuickFilename_Click (Index As Integer)
  FilenameBox.Text = QuickFilename(Index).Caption
  ReadComClick
End Sub

Sub DeleteFileCom_Click ( )
  Dim N As Integer, I As Integer
  N = Val(InputBox$("Enter number to delete: "))
  If (N > 0) And (N < = NumFiles) Then
    For I = N To NumFiles - 1
      QuickFilename(I).Caption = QuickFilename(I + 1).Caption
    Next I
    Unload QuickFilename(NumFiles)
    NumFiles = NumFiles - 1
  Else
    MsgBox "The number is out-of-range", 0, "Input Error"
  End If
End Sub

Sub Form_Load ( )
  NumFiles = 0
  WindowState = 2
  ' get the font name
```

Listing 11-1   Continued.

```
If SystemCom.Checked Then
   TextBox.FontName = "System"
   CourierCom.Checked = False
   TerminalCom.Checked = False
Elself CourierCom.Checked Then
   TextBox.FontName = "Courier"
   TerminalCom.Checked = False
Elself TerminalCom.Checked Then
   TextBox.FontName = "Terminal"
Else
   TextBox.FontName = "Courier"
End If
' get the fond appearance
TextBox.FontBold = BoldCom.Checked
TextBox.FontItalic = ItalicCom.Checked
TextBox.FontStrikethru = StrikethruCom.Checked
TextBox.FontUnderline = UnderlineCom.Checked
' get the font size
If Size9Com.Checked Then
   TextBox.FontSize = 9
   Size10Com.Checked = False
   Size12Com.Checked = False
   Size14Com.Checked = False
   Size18Com.Checked = False
Elself Size10Com.Checked Then
   TextBox.FontSize = 10
   Size12Com.Checked = False
   Size14Com.Checked = False
   Size18Com.Checked = False
Elself Size12Com.Checked Then
   TextBox.FontSize = 12
   Size14Com.Checked = False
   Size18Com.Checked = False
Elself Size14Com.Checked Then
   TextBox.FontSize = 14
   Size18Com.Checked = False
Elself Size18Com.Checked Then
   TextBox.FontSize = 18
Else
   TextBox.FontSize = 10
End If
End Sub

Sub ClearFontCom ( )
   SystemCom.Checked = False
   CourierCom.Checked = False
   TerminalCom.Checked = False
End Sub
```

Listing 11-1 Continued.

```
Sub ClearSizeCom ( )
    Size9Com.Checked = False
    Size10Com.Checked = False
    Size12Com.Checked = False
    Size14Com.Checked = False
    Size18Com.Checked = False
End Sub

Sub BoldCom_Click ( )
    BoldCom.Checked = Not BoldCom.Checked
    TextBox.FontBold = BoldCom.Checked
End Sub

Sub CourierCom_Click ( )
    ClearFontCom
    CourierCom.Checked = True
    TextBox.FontName = "Courier"
End Sub

Sub ItalicCom_Click ( )
    ItalicCom.Checked = Not ItalicCom.Checked
    TextBox.FontItalic = ItalicCom.Checked
End Sub

Sub Size10Com_Click ( )
    ClearSizeCom
    Size10Com.Checked = True
    TextBox.FontSize = 10
End Sub

Sub Size12Com_Click ( )
    ClearSizeCom
    Size12Com.Checked = True
    TextBox.FontSize = 12
End Sub

Sub Size14Com_Click ( )
    ClearSizeCom
    Size12Com.Checked = True
    TextBox.FontSize = 14
End Sub

Sub Size18Com_Click ( )
    ClearSizeCom
    Size18Com.Checked = True
    TextBox.FontSize = 18
End Sub
```

Listing 11-1 Continued.

```
Sub Size9Com_Click ( )
  ClearSizeCom
  Size9Com.Checked = True
  TextBox.FontSize = 9
End Sub

Sub StrikethruCom_Click ( )
  StrikethruCom.Checked = Not StrikethruCom.Checked
  TextBox.FontStrikethru = StrikethruCom.Checked
End Sub

Sub UnderlineCom_Click ( )
  UnderlineCom.Checked = Not UnderlineCom.Checked
  TextBox.FontUnderline = UnderlineCom.Checked
End Sub

Sub SystemCom_Click ( )
  ClearFontCom
  SystemCom.Checked = True
  TextBox.FontName = "System"
End Sub

Sub TerminalCom_Click ( )
  ClearFontCom
  TerminalCom.Checked = True
  TextBox.FontName = "Terminal"
End Sub
```

The ClearFontCom **procedure**   This procedure sets the Checked properties of the Courier, System, and Terminal options to False. This procedure is called before making assigning True to the Checked property of a font name option.

The ClearSizeCom **procedure**   In this procedure, the Checked properties of the SizeXXCom properties are set to False. This procedure is called before making assigning True to the Checked property of a font size option.

The Form_Load **procedure**   This new version of Form_Load includes many statements that select the startup font name, font appearance, and font size. The first extended If-Then-ElseIf statement examines the settings of the Checked properties of the System, Courier, and Terminal menu options (in that sequence). The If statements selects the font name that you checked in the Menu Design Window. If you checked more than one font name, the first font name checked is the selected one. The priority sequence is System, Courier, and Terminal. If no font name is checked in the Menu Design

Window, which is the case for the current settings, the Courier option is selected by default.

The procedure also contains a group of statements that turn on the font appearance properties according to the Checked settings you made in the Menu Design Window.

The procedure uses a second extended If-Then-ElseIf statement to select the font size according the Checked property that you set in the Menu Design Window. The font size priority sequence is 9, 10, 12, 14, and 18 points. The default font size is 10 points.

The BoldCom_Click **procedure**   This toggles the Checked property of the Bold option. The FontBold property of TextBox is assigned the current Bold-Com.Check setting.

The ItalicCom_Click **procedure**   Here the procedure toggles the Checked property of the Italic option. The FontItalic property of TextBox is assigned the current ItalicCom.Check setting.

The StrikethruCom_Click **procedure**   Here the procedure toggles the Checked property of the Strikethru option. The FontStrikethru property of TextBox is assigned the current StrikethruCom.Check setting.

The UnderlineCom_Click **procedure**   This procedure toggles the Checked property of the Underline option. The FontUnderline property of TextBox is assigned the current UnderlineCom.Check setting.

The CourierCom_Click **procedure**   With this procedure, the Courier font option is selected. The procedure first calls the ClearFontCom to clear all of the Checked properties for the font name options, then sets the CourierCom.Checked to True, and then assigns the Courier font name to TextBox.FontName.

The SystemCom_Click **procedure**   This selects the System font option. The procedure first calls the ClearFontCom to clear all of the Checked properties for the font name options, then sets the SystemCom.Checked to True, and then assigns the System font name to TextBox.FontName.

The TerminalCom_Click **procedure**   This procedure selects the Terminal font. The procedure first calls the ClearFontCom to clear all of the Checked properties for the font name options, then sets the TerminalCom.Checked to True, and then assigns the Terminal font name to TextBox.FontName.

The SizeXXCom **procedures**   This group of procedures selects a font size. Each procedure calls the ClearFontCom to clear all of the Checked properties of the font size options. Then, the Checked property of the appropriate font size control is assigned True and the TextBox.FontSize property is assigned the appropriate font size.

To sum up the action of the above procedures, one could say that the program in Listing 11-1 manipulates the font-related properties of TextBox, based on the current Checked settings of the font-related menu options, to produce a specific text appearance.

Run the above program. First load a text file into the viewing text box and then experiment with the various fonts, font appearances, and font sizes. What do you notice? Not all font sizes are available—the run time system tries its best to accommodate your requests.

Output to a form, a picture box, and the printer

Visual Basic supports the Print statement to display text in a form or in a picture box. In addition, the Print statement can send output to the line printer connected to your system. There are properties common to all three objects (that is, the form, the picture box, and the printer) and there are properties common to the form and picture box; and form and printer. Before I discuss the Print statement, let's briefly look at these output-related properties.

The font related properties FontName, FontSize, FontBold, FontItalic, Font-Strikethru, and FontUnderline are common to all three output objects. Keep in mind that you might be using a printer that is incapable of producing some of the fonts, font size, and font appearances.

The Printer object has the FontCount and Fonts properties. The FontCount is a read-only property that reports the number of fonts that are available to your printer. The Fonts property returns the name of a font specified by index—the first font is Fonts(0), the second Fonts(1), and so on. The general syntax for using the FontCount and Fonts properties is:

```
Printer.FountCount
Printer.Fonts(index%)
```

The FountCount and Fonts properties are also available to the Screen object. This is an object that can represent the current form or a control.

The main difference between the output to the printer and the other two forms is that the print position of a printer is always advancing. By contrast, the print position of a form or picture box is more flexible. In fact, you can reposition that print position to overwrite previous lines. This means that the form and the picture forms act as unscrollable screens. Several properties and methods, described next, can be used to manipulate the text location in a form or picture box:

The Cls **method**   This clears the text emitted by a Print statement in form or picture box. The general syntax is:

```
[form ¦ pictureBox].Cls
```

The controls drawn on a form are not affected.

The CurrentX **and** CurrentY **properties** These properties return the (X, Y) location of the current print position. The general syntax for using these properties is:

> {*[form.][pictureBox.]* Printer.} CurrentX *[=X!]*
> {*[form.][pictureBox.]* Printer.} CurrentY *[=Y!]*

I have included the Printer object in the above syntax to indicate that the CurrentX and CurrentY properties are also available to the printer.

☞ When the Cls method is used, the CurrentX and CurrentY properties are both set to 0. This means that the upper left corner of a form or picture box is (0, 0), *not* (1, 1).

The TextHeight **method** Using this method returns the text height. The general syntax for the TextHeight method is:

> {*[form.][pictureBox.]* Printer.} TextHeight(*stringExpression$*)

The TextHeight is expressed in terms of the Scale coordinate system. The value returned by the TextHeight includes the spacing above the text that separates two consecutive lines. The TextHeight method can be used to translate the user screen row number, for example Yworld, into the actual Y coordinate using the following equation:

> *[object.]* CurrentY = *[object.]* TextHeight("A") ∗ (Yworld − 1)

If the argument of TextHeight contains imbedded Chr$(13) + Chr$(10) strings, the method returns the height of the multi-line string.

The TextWidth **method** TextWidth returns the width of a specified text. The general syntax for this method is shown next:

> {*[form.][pictureBox.]* Printer.} TextWidth(*stringExpression$*)

The TextWidth method can be used to translate the column number, call it Xworld, into the actual X coordinate using the following equation:

> *[object.]* CurrentX = *[object.]* TextHeight("A") ∗ (Xworld − 1)

If the argument of TextWidth contains imbedded Chr$(13) + Chr$(10) strings, the method returns the width of the longest line.

The Visual Basic print statement

The Visual Basic Print statement and syntax is basically the same as is implemented in Quick Basic, BASICA, and GW-BASIC. The general syntax for the Print statement is:

> {*[form.][pictureBox.]* Printer.} Print *[expressionList]*[{; ¦ ,}]

The Print statement can print blank lines (in the absence of an expression list), the value of single expression, or a list of values. The comma enables you to use standard tabbing, while the colon suppresses the carriage return after a value is emitted. As with Quick Basic and the other BASICS, you can use the Tab function to set your own tabbing. Moreover, you can use the Spc function to specify the spacing between two printed items. Examples of using the Print statement are shown below:

```
MyPicture.Print
Printer.Print
Printer 355 / 113 ' prints the value of pi
Print X, Y, Z
MyPicture "X = "; X, "Y = "; Y
Printer Date$; Tab(65); Time$
```

☞ You must remember that the output of a Print statement *does not* wrap around. Instead it is truncated at the right. In the case of the form and picture box, the output is also truncated beyond the bottom edge.

The Format$ function

One of the advantages of Quick Basic and the other BASIC interpreters is formatted output with the Print Using statement. The designers of Visual Basic offer the Format$ function instead of the Print Using statement to provide more flexible formatted output. The Format$ function returns a string that represents formatted numeric data. The general syntax of the Format$ function is:

Format$(numericExpression [,formatString$])

The numeric expression can be any predefined numeric data type. The formatString$ contains symbols that form a template of how the data should look like. Table 11-1 shows the basic formatting symbols. Examples of using the Format$ function are shown in TABLE 11-2.

Table 11-1   The basic formatting symbols in Visual Basic.

Symbol	Purpose
0	Digit placeholder that displays a leading or trailing zeros when appropriate
#	Digit placeholder that does not display leading or trailing zeros
.	Decimal placeholder
,	Thousand separator
—+$()space	Literal characters

**Table 11-2   Examples of using
the Format$ function.**

Example	Result
Format$(23.12, "000.000")	023.120
Format$(23.12, "###.###")	23.12
Format$(23.12, "##0.000")	23.120
Format$(23.12, "$##.##")	$23.12
Format$(2222.2, "$##,###.00")	$2,222.20

The country specified in the Windows Control Panel influences the display of the actual decimal-point and thousands-separator characters. For example, if the country is Germany, the last result of TABLE 11-2 appears as $2.222,00 instead of $2,222.20, despite the $##,###.00 format.

Printer output

The printer object has the following properties and methods that assist in managing the printer output.

The Page **property** This property keeps track of the number of pages printed since the printer was first used or since the last call to EndDoc method. You can use this read-only property to print the current page number being printed.

The NewPage **method**   NewPage performs an explicit form feed. The printer object automatically sends a form feed when you have printed enough lines to fill a page.

The EndDoc **method**   This releases the print device or print spooler and resets the Page property. If the EndDoc is called right after a NewPage, no additional form feed occurs. Otherwise, the printer advances the current page that contains the last part of the document or output you are printing.

You can print a form by using the form.PrintForm method. This method prints the entire form, regardless of how visible the form is. To print the graphics in a form you must set the AutoRedraw property to True. The quality of the graphics output on your printer depends on the printer.

A pseudo-screen in a picture box

In chapter 7, I presented the PSCREEN.MAK project that uses a multi-line text to emulate a pseudo-screen. In this section I present another version of the pseudo-screen that uses the Print statement (the real McCoy!) in a picture box. Using the Print statement in concert with the CurrentX and

CurrentY properties allows the program to display text anywhere in the picture box. This output method makes using an array of strings less critical. In fact, the code implementation in LISTING 11-2 uses no string arrays to store a copy of the screen text. As a result, the features of scrolling, storing and recalling a screen are missing from this new version. I leave it as an exercise for you to implement such a version. Without using string arrays, the picture-based pseudo-screen uses less memory than the text box version.

Figures 11-6 to 11-8 show the specifications for the project and form files. Figure 11-9 shows a sample session with the PSCREEN2.MAK project.

Application name: Pseudo-Screen Test Program
Application code name: PSCREEN2
Version: 1.0   Date created: July 8, 1991
Programmer(s): Namir Clement Shammas

List of filenames

Storage path: \VB\EASYVB
Project PSCREEN2.MAK
Global GLOBAL.BAS
Form 1 PSCREEN2.FRM

11-6 General project specifications for the PSCREEN2 project.

Form #1   Form Filename: PSCREEN2.FRM
Version: 1.0   Date: July 8, 1991

Control object type	Default CtlName	Purpose
Command Button	Command1	Exits the test program
	Command2	Clears the pseudo-screen
	Command3	Moves the cursor
	Command4	Locates the cursor
	Command5	Writes the text in Text4 to the pseudo-screen (Text1)
	Command6	Moves the cursor to the next line
Text Box	Text1	The cursor column number
	Text2	The cursor row number
	Text3	Text to write on the pseudo-screen
Label	Label1	Label for Text1
	Label2	Label for Text2
	Label3	Label for Text3
Picture Box	Picture1	The pseudo-screen

11-7 List of control objects for the PSCREEN2 project.

Application (code) name: PSCREEN
Form #1
Version: 1.0   Date: June 28, 1991

Original control name	Property	New setting
Form	Caption	Pseudo-Screen (Ver. 2)
Command1	CtlName	QuitBtn
	Caption	Quit
Command2	CtlName	ClearBtn
	Caption	Clear Screen
Command3	CtlName	MoveBtn
	Caption	Move Cursor
Command4	CtlName	LocateBtn
	Caption	Locate Cursor
Command5	CtlName	PrintBtn
	Caption	Print
Command6	CtlName	NewLineBtn
	Caption	NewLine
Text1	CtlName	CursorXBox
	Text	(empty string)
Text2	CtlName	CursorYBox
	Text	(empty string)
Text3	CtlName	TextBox
	Text	(empty string)
Label1	CtlName	ColumnLbl
	Caption	Column
Label2	CtlName	RowLbl
	Caption	Row
Label3	CtlName	TextLbl
	Caption	Text
Picture1	CtlName	ScreenPct

11-8 The modified control settings for the PSCREEN project.

The Picture-based Screen   07-08-1991   21:25:12

```
12345678901234567890

1234567890123456789012345678901234567890123456789 0

123456789012345678901234567890123456789012345678901234567890
```

Column   56   Text

Row   7   1234567890

| Clear Screen | Move Cursor | Locate Cursor | Print | NewLine | Quit |

11-9   A sample session with the PSCREEN2 program.

LISTING 11-2 shows the code attached to the PSCREEN2.FRM form. The new version of the pseudo-screen program differs from the first one in the following ways:

1. The general declarations section has fewer declarations. While the constants MAX_ROWS and MAX_COLS are still declared, they have smaller values than their counterparts in PSCREEN.FRM. These values accommodate the Courier 10 fonts used to display the text in the picture box. The string arrays and the cursor management variables are replaced with the ScaleX and ScaleY variables that store the values for TextHeight("X") and TextWidth("X"). These variables are used in translating between the pseudo-screen coordinates and the twips coordinates.

2. The event-handling procedures for scrolling, saving, and recalling a screen are no longer implemented, since their respective features are not offered by the new program version.

3. The auxiliary procedures ClearScreen, GotoXY, NewLine, WhereX, and WhereY are still present, but with a much simpler and shorter code. Cursor management now uses the properties CurrentX and CurrentY and the ScaleX and ScaleY variables.

4. The PPrint procedure in PSCREEN.FRM has been completely removed and its calls are substituted with the Visual Basic Print statement.
5. The LocateBtn_Click procedure now includes statements to clear the form's own text and print a pseudo-label for the pseudo-screen that includes the current date and time.
6. The new program version has the Form_Load procedure, which initializes the application. This includes the following:

- Maximizing the window at run time.
- Selecting the Courier 10 fonts for the picture box.
- Assigning values to the ScaleX and ScaleY variables.
- Clearing the pseudo-screen by calling ClearBtn_Click.
- Assigning the string 1234567890 to the Text property of TextBox.

Listing 11-2   The code attached to the PSCREEN2.FRM form.

```
' constants the define the size of the emulated screen
Const MAX_ROWS = 26, MAX_COLS = 60

Dim ScaleX As Single, ScaleY As Single

Sub ClearScreen ( )
  ScreenPct.Cls
End Sub

Sub GotoXY (X As Integer, Y As Integer)
  ' move the hidden cursor to (X,Y)
  If (X < 1) Or (Y < 1) Then Exit Sub
  If (Y > MAX_ROWS) Or (X > MAX_COLS) Then Exit Sub
  ScreenPct.CurrentX = ScaleX * (X − 1) + .5
  ScreenPct.CurrentY = ScaleY * (Y − 1) + .5
End Sub

Function WhereX ( ) As Integer
  Dim X As Double
  ' return the value of CurrentX
  X = 1 + ScreenPct.CurrentX / ScaleX
  If X < 1 Then X = X + 1
  WhereX = X
End Function

Function WhereY ( ) As Integer
  Dim Y As Double
  ' return the value of CurrentY
  Y = 1 + ScreenPct.CurrentY / ScaleY
  If Y < 1 Then Y = Y + 1
  WhereY = Y
End Function
```

Listing 11-2   Continued.

```
Sub NewLine ( )
  If WhereY( ) < MAX_ROWS Then
    ScreenPct.CurrentY = ScreenPct.CurrentY + ScaleY
    ScreenPct.CurrentX = 0
  End If
End Sub

Sub QuitBtn_Click ( )
  End
End Sub

Sub ClearBtn_Click ( )
  ClearScreen
  LocateBtn_Click
End Sub

Sub MoveBtn_Click ( )
  Dim X As Integer
  Dim Y As Integer
  X = Val(CursorXBox.Text)
  Y = Val(CursorYBox.Text)
  GotoXY X, Y
  LocateBtn_Click
End Sub

Sub LocateBtn_Click ( )
  CursorXBox.Text = Str$(WhereX( ))
  CursorYBox.Text = Str$(WhereY( ))
  Cls
  Print : Print
  Print Spc(10); "The Picture-based Screen";
  Print Tab(50); Date$, Time$
End Sub

Sub PrintBtn_Click ( )
  If (WhereX( ) + Len(TextBox.Text)) < MAX_COLS Then
    ScreenPct.Print TextBox.Text;
    LocateBtn_Click
  End If
End Sub

Sub NewLineBtn_Click ( )
  NewLine
  LocateBtn_Click
End Sub

Sub Form_Load ( )
  WindowState = 2
```

Listing 11-2 Continued.

```
ScreenPct.FontName = "Courier"
ScreenPct.FontSize = 10
ScaleX = ScreenPct.TextWidth("X")
ScaleY = ScreenPct.TextHeight("X")
ClearBtn_Click
' set initial test string
TextBox.Text = "1234567890"
End Sub
```

Run the program in Listing 11-2. Click on the Print and New Line command buttons and watch the text being displayed in various parts of the pseudo-screen. As you click the Print and New Line buttons, observe the cursor text boxes. Experiment with assigning new cursor location and then press the Print button. When you are done with the program, click on the Quit command button.

The calendar form

This section illustrates the use of an additional form that specializes in displayed Print statement output data. Printing to the main form, which normally contains various controls, is cumbersome. By contrast, using a blank form (I will call it the output form) makes the job of sending output to a form much easier, since there is little or nothing in the way. You will need at least one control in the output form. This control may be either a command button or, better yet, a menu, since menus stay out of the way.

The example that I present in this section is a simple calendar maker. You specify the year and month number in text boxes located in the main form and then click a command button to view the calendar in an output form. The output form has a menu with Print and Exit options. There are no other menu options. Simply click the Print menu selection to print the current form. Click on the Exit selection to return to the main form.

Figures 11-10 to 11-14 contain the specifications for the project file

Application name: Simple Calendar Maker
Application code name: CALEND1
Version: 1.0   Date created: July 8, 1991
Programmer(S): Namir Clement Shammas
List of filenames
Storage path: \VB\EASYVB
Project CALEND1.MAK
Global GLOBAL.BAS
Form 1 CALEND1.FRM
Form 2 CAL1FRM.FRM

11-10 The basic specifications for the CALEND1.MAK project.

Form #1   Form filename: CALEND1.FRM
Version: 1.0   Date: July 8, 1991

Control object type	Default CtlName	Purpose
Command Button	Command1	Makes and displays a calendar
	Command2	Exits the application
Text Box	Text1	Stores the year number
	Text2	Stores the month number
Label	Label1	Label for the year number
	Label2	Label for the month number

11-11 The default controls for the CALEND1.FRM form.

Form #2   Form filename: CAL1FRM.FRM
Version: 1.0   Date: July 8, 1991

Caption	Property	Setting	Purpose
&Print	CtlName	PrintCom	Prints form
E&xit	CtlName	ExitCom	Returns to the main form

11-12 The menu structure for the CAL1FRM.FRM form.

Application (code) name: CALEND1
Form #1
Version: 1.0   Date: July 8, 1991

Original control name	Property	New setting
Form	Caption	Calendar Maker
	FormName	CalendarMakerFrm
Command1	CtlName	MakeCalendarBtn
	Caption	MakeCalendar
	Default	True
Command2	CtlName	QuitBtn
	Caption	Quit
	Cancel	True
Text1	CtlName	YearBox
	Text	(empty string)
Text2	CtlName	MonthBox
	Caption	(empty string)
Label1	CtlName	YearLbl
	Caption	Year Number
Label2	CtlName	MonthLbl
	Caption	Month Number

11-13 The updated settings of the CALEND1.FRM form.

Application (code) name: CALEND1
Form #2
Version: 1.0   Date: July 8, 1991

Original control name	**Property**	**New setting**
Form	Caption	Calendar Form
	FormName	CalendarFrm

11-14 The updated settings of the CAL1FRM.FRM form.

CALEND1.MAK and the form files CALEND1.FRM and CAL1FRM.FRM.
Figure 11-15 shows a sample session with the calendar maker application.

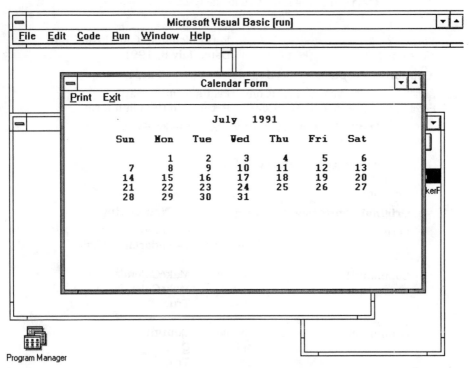

11-15 A sample calendar.

Listing 11-3 shows the following procedures attached to the
CALEND1.FRM.

Listing 11-3 The code attached to the CALEND1.FRM.

```
Sub YearBox_KeyPress (KeyAscii As Integer)
   If KeyAscii = 8 Then Exit Sub
   If KeyAscii < Asc("0") Or KeyAscii > Asc("9") Then
      KeyAscii = 0
```

Listing 11-3 Continued.

```
    End If
End Sub

Sub MonthBox_KeyPress (KeyAscii As Integer)
    If KeyAscii = 8 Then Exit Sub
    If KeyAscii < Asc("0") Or KeyAscii > Asc("9") Then
        KeyAscii = 0
    End If
End Sub

Sub QuitBtn_Click ( )
    End
End Sub

Sub MakeBtn_Click ( )
    Const DAY_SPACE = 2
    Const LEFT_MARGIN = 8
    Dim YearNumber As Integer
    Dim MonthNumber As Integer
    Dim NumberOfDays As Integer
    Dim DayIndex As Integer
    Dim SerialDayNum As Double
    Dim TheWeekDay As Integer
    Dim Frmt As String
    CalendarFrm.AutoRedraw = True
    Frmt = "##" ' set page format
    ' if Year text box is empty use the current year
    If YearBox.Text = " " Then
        YearBox.Text = Format$(Year(Now))
    End If
    ' if the Month text box is empty use the current month
    If MonthBox.Text = " " Then
        MonthBox.Text = Format$(Month(Now))
    End If
    YearNumber = Val(YearBox.Text) ' get the year number
    MonthNumber = Val(MonthBox.Text) ' get the month number
    ' is the year number invalid?
    If YearNumber < 1980 Or YearNumber > 2099 Then
        MsgBox "Invalid Year number", 0, "Input Error"
        Exit Sub
    End If
    ' is the month number invalid?
    If MonthNumber < 1 Or MonthNumber > 12 Then
        MsgBox "Invalid Month number", 0, "Input Error"
        Exit Sub
    End If
    ' show output form
    CalendarFrm.Show
```

Listing 11-3   Continued.

```
' select font name and size
CalendarFrm.FontName = "Courier"
CalendarFrm.FontSize = 10
' clear the form and build a new calendar
CalendarFrm.Cls
CalendarFrm.Print
CalendarFrm.Print Spc(LEFT_MARGIN);
CalendarFrm.Print "    "; MonthName(MonthNumber);
CalendarFrm.Print " "; YearNumber
CalendarFrm.Print
CalendarFrm.Print Spc(LEFT_MARGIN); "Sun";
CalendarFrm.Print Spc(DAY_SPACE); "Mon";
CalendarFrm.Print Spc(DAY_SPACE); "Tue";
CalendarFrm.Print Spc(DAY_SPACE); "Wed";
CalendarFrm.Print Spc(DAY_SPACE); "Thu";
CalendarFrm.Print Spc(DAY_SPACE); "Fri";
CalendarFrm.Print Spc(DAY_SPACE); "Sat"
CalendarFrm.Print
NumberOfDays = DaysInMonth(MonthNumber, YearNumber)
SerialDayNum = DateSerial(YearNumber, MonthNumber, 1)
' write the first day of the month
CalendarFrm.Print Spc(LEFT_MARGIN);
CalendarFrm.Print Spc(2 + (Weekday(SerialDayNum) - 1) * (DAY_SPACE + 4));
CalendarFrm.Print Format$(1, Frmt);
' write every other day
For DayIndex = 2 To NumberOfDays
  SerialDayNum = DateSerial(YearNumber, MonthNumber, DayIndex)
  If Weekday(SerialDayNum) = 1 Then ' Sunday?
    CalendarFrm.Print
    CalendarFrm.Print Spc(LEFT_MARGIN + DAY_SPACE - 1);
    If DayIndex < 10 Then
      CalendarFrm.Print Spc(1);
    End If
    CalendarFrm.Print Format$(DayIndex, Frmt);
  Else ' a day other than Sunday
    CalendarFrm.Print Spc(DAY_SPACE + 1);
    If DayIndex < 10 Then
      CalendarFrm.Print Spc(1);
  End If
  CalendarFrm.Print Format$(DayIndex, Frmt);
  End If
Next DayIndex
End Sub

Function MonthName (MonthNumber As Integer) As String
  Select Case MonthNumber
    Case 1: MonthName = "January"
    Case 2: MonthName = "February"
```

Listing 11-3 Continued.

```
        Case 3: MonthName  =  "March"
        Case 4: MonthName  =  "April"
        Case 5: MonthName  =  "May"
        Case 6: MonthName  =  "June"
        Case 7: MonthName  =  "July"
        Case 8: MonthName  =  "August"
        Case 9: MonthName  =  "September"
        Case 10: MonthName  =  "October"
        Case 11: MonthName  =  "November"
        Case 12: MonthName  =  "December"
    End Select
End Function

Function DaysInMonth (MonthNum As Integer, YearNum As Integer) As Integer
    Select Case MonthNum
        Case 1: DaysInMonth  =  31
        Case 2
            If ((YearNum  −  1988) Mod 4)  =  0 Then
            IfDaysInMonth  =  29
            Else
            IfDaysInMonth  =  28
            End If
        Case 3: DaysInMonth  =  31
        Case 4: DaysInMonth  =  30
        Case 5: DaysInMonth  =  31
        Case 6: DaysInMonth  =  30
        Case 7: DaysInMonth  =  31
        Case 8: DaysInMonth  =  31
        Case 9: DaysInMonth  =  30
        Case 10: DaysInMonth  =  31
        Case 11: DaysInMonth  =  30
        Case 12: DaysInMonth  =  31
    End Select
End Function
```

The YearBox_KeyPress **and** MonthBox_KeyPress **procedures**   These allow only the digits and the backspace character. All other characters are filtered out.

The QuitBtn_Click **procedure**   This procedure exits the application using an End statement.

The MakeBtn_Click **procedure**   is the workhorse of the calendar maker. The procedure performs the following tasks:

- Declares local constants for the left margin and spacing between days.

- Sets the AutoRedraw property of the output form to True. This enables you to minimize the output form and then maximize it without losing the form contents.
- Sets the format for the day number.
- Selects the current year if the Year text box is empty.
- Selects the current month if the Month text box is empty.
- Obtains the year and month numbers.
- Checks if either the year or the month numbers are invalid. If either one is not valid, a message box displays an error message and the procedure exits.
- Shows the output calendar and sets the output font to Courier 10 point.
- Applies a series of Print statements to write the calendar month name, year, weekdays, and the location of the month days. The Spc function is used to place the day numbers in their proper location. The Format$ function is utilized to obtain a formatted day number. A For-Next loop writes the days of the month under the appropriate week day, starting with the 2nd of the month—the first day of the month requires slightly different code.

The procedure uses date/time procedures and functions, such as the Now, DateSerial, and WeekDay functions.

The MonthName **procedure**   This procedure returns the name of a month.

The DaysInMonth **procedure**   This returns the number of days in a month, taking into consideration leap years.

Listing 11-4 shows the two event-handling procedures attached to the menu selections of the output form.

Listing 11-4   The code attached to the output form CAL1FRM.FRM.

```
Sub ExitCom_Click ( )
  Hide
End Sub

Sub PrintCom_Click ( )
  PrintForm
End Sub
```

Run the program by pressing the F5 function key. To view the calendar of the current month, click the Make Calendar command button. Experiment with minimizing and then maximizing the output form. The calendar data are preserved during this resizing test. Click the Print menu option or press the Alt–P keys to print the output form. Click the Exit menu option or press the Alt–X keys to exit the output form. Experiment by typing in other months and years.

The text file printer

The last example in this chapter deals with sending text to the printer. The application is a simple text file printer. The program has a text box that stores the name of the single text file you want to print. A Print command button produces a paginated printer output that includes the page number, the current date, and the current time.

Figures 11-16 to 11-18 show the specifications for the project file PRINTFL1.MAK and the form file PRINTFL1.FRM. Figure 11-19 shows a sample session with the text file printing program.

Application name: Text File Printer (Version 1)
Application code name: PRINTFL1
Version: 1.0   Date created: July 8, 1991
Programmer(s): Namir Clement Shammas

List of filenames

Storage path: \VB\EASYVB
Project PRINTFL1.MAK
Global GLOBAL.BAS
Form 1 PRINTFL1.FRM

11-16   The basic specifications for the PRINTFL1.MAK project.

Form #1   Form filename: PRINTFL1.FRM
Version: 1.0   Date: July 8, 1991

Control object type	Default CtlName	Purpose
Command Button	Command1	Prints a text file specified in Text1
	Command2	Exits the application
Text Box	Text1	Stores the filename
Label	Label	Label of Text1

11-17   The list of controls in the PRINTFL1.FRM form.

Application (code) name: PRINTFL1
Form #1
Version: 1.0   Date: July 8, 1991

Original control name	Property	New setting
Command1	CtlName	PrintBtn
	Caption	Print
	Default	True
Command2	CtlName	QuitBtn
	Caption	Quit
	Cancel	True

11-18   The updated settings for the controls of form PRINTFL1.FRM.

Original control name	Property	New setting
Text1	CtlName	TextBox
	Text	(empty string)
Label1	CtlName	FilenameLbl
	Caption	Filename

11-18 Continued.

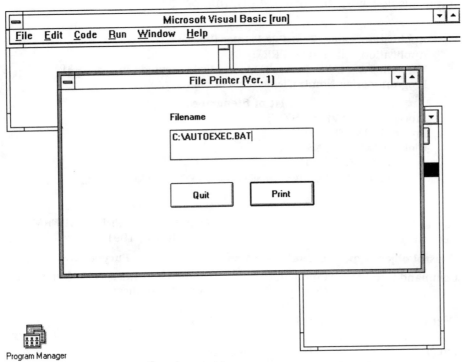

11-19 A sample session with the text file printing program.

Listing 11-5 contains the code attached to the PRINTFL1.FRM form. The general declarations section declares the constant MAX_LINES to specify the maximum number of lines per page, (including the heading). The variables Filename and CurrentLineNumber store the name of the printed file and the current line number, respectively. These variables are used in multiple procedures.

The relevant procedures in the PRINTFL1.FRM form are described next.

Listing 11-5 The code attached to the PRINTFL1.FRM form.

```
Const MAX_LINES = 60

Dim Filename As String
Dim CurrentLineNumber As Integer

Sub QuitBtn_Click ( )
  End
End Sub

Sub PrintBtn_Click ( )
  Dim TextLine As String
  Dim I As Integer
  ' exit sub if text box is empty
  If TextBox.Text = " " Then Exit Sub
  ' find the first internal space
  I = InStr(TextBox.Text, " ")
  ' truncate from the first space location and beyond
  If I > 0 Then
    TextBox.Text = Left$(TextBox.Text, I - 1)
  End If
  ' get the filename from the text box
  Filename = TextBox.Text
  On Error GoTo BadFile ' set error-handling trap
  Open Filename For Input As #1 ' open file for input
  On Error GoTo 0 ' disable error-handling trap
  PrintHeading ' print the heading of the first page
  ' read lines from the text file
  Do While Not EOF(1)
    Line Input #1, TextLine
    ' update line counter
    CurrentLineNumber = CurrentLineNumber + 1
    ' line counter exceed page size?
    If CurrentLineNumber > MAX_LINES Then
      Printer.NewPage ' new page
      PrintHeading        ' print heading
    End If
    Printer.Print TextLine ' print the current line
  Loop
  Printer.EndDoc ' release print device
  Close #1 ' close the file buffer
  Beep
  Exit Sub
'**************** Error-Handling Statements **************
BadFile:
  Beep
```

Listing 11-5 Continued.

```
    MsgBox "Cannot open file " + Filename, 0, "File I/O Error"
    On Error GoTo 0
    Resume ExitSub
ExitSub:
End Sub

Sub PrintHeading ( )
    Const TAB_SIZE = 65
    Printer.Print Filename; Tab(TAB_SIZE);
    Printer.Print "Page "; Format$(Printer.Page, "###")
    Printer.Print Format$(Now, "hh:mm");
    Printer.Print Tab(TAB_SIZE);
    Printer.Print Format$(Now, "MM-DD-YYYY")
    Printer.Print
    Printer.Print
    CurrentLineNumber = 4
End Sub

Sub TextBox_KeyPress (KeyAscii As Integer)
    KeyAscii = Asc(UCase$(Chr$(KeyAscii)))
End Sub
```

The PrintHeading **procedure**   that prints the filename, page number, and the current date and time. The procedure resets the value of the CurrentLine-Number variable to 4, the number of lines printed by the procedure itself. The procedure obtains the current page number using the Printer.Page property.

The PrintBtn_Click **procedure**   prints the text file specified in TextBox.Text. The procedure performs the following steps:

- Searches for a first inner space in the TextBox.Text property. If found, the Text property is truncated starting with that inner space.
- Obtains the filename and sets up the proper error-handling trap before opening the text file.
- Opens the text file. If the file is not found, the error-handling routine is triggered.
- Uses a Do-While loop to read the lines of the text file. The current number of lines is monitored for proper form feed operations. The Printer.Print TextLine statement sends the current text line to the printer.
- Uses the Printer.EndDoc statement to eject the last page.
- Closes the file buffer and exits the procedure.

The TextBox_KeyPress **procedure**   converts all the letters you type into uppercase characters.

12
Fundamental graphics

Under Windows, graphics have become more important than in DOS. Windows applications are partially appealing because they can easily integrate text and images. Visual Basic offers graphics-related methods and properties that enable you to build your own graphics routines. In this chapter you will learn about the following topics:

- Setting the graphics scale.
- Working with the graphics methods and properties to draw various shapes.
- Using the different fill styles.
- Using colors.
- Using different line styles and line widths.
- Using the AutoRedraw property.
- Working with icons.

In this chapter I present a scaled-down graphics drawing program that demonstrates the various aspects of generating various geometric shapes.

Setting the graphics scale

Visual Basic supports a flexible graphics coordinate system, or *scale*, that allows you to customize it or to select between different standard scales. Table 12-1 shows the settings of the ScaleMode property that sets and determines the current scale mode.

Visual Basic offers two ways to customize the scale. The first method uses the ScaleWidth, ScaleHeight, ScaleLeft, and ScaleTop properties. The second

Table 12-1   The settings for the ScaleMode property.

Setting	Meaning
0	User-defined scale. The ScaleMode property is automatically assigned 0 when you directly set the ScaleWidth or ScaleHeight properties.
1	The default twips scale. One inch has 1440 twips.
2	Points. One inch has 72 points.
3	Pixels (the smallest unit of monitor resolution).
4	Characters. A character is 1/6 of an inch in height and is 1/12 of an inch in width.
5	Inches.
6	Millimeters.
7	Centimeters.

method uses the Scale method to set the values of the above four properties in one swoop.

☞ Before I discuss the family of scale-related properties, let me explain the basic orientation in customizing the scale. Visual Basic sets up a scale system by defining the upper left corner coordinates and the height and width of the object.

The ScaleLeft and ScaleTop properties define and access the vertical and horizontal coordinates that define the upper left corner of the form, picture box, or printer. The general syntax for the ScaleLeft and ScaleTop properties is:

[object.]ScaleLeft [=scale!]
[object.]ScaleTop [=scale!]

The default values for the above properties is zero. You can assign positive or negative values to the ScaleLeft and ScaleTop properties.

The ScaleWidth and ScaleHeight properties determine and access the width and the height of the drawing area. The general syntax for the ScaleWidth and ScaleHeight properties is:

[object.]ScaleWidth [=scale!]
[object.]ScaleHeight [=scale!]

The default values for the above properties is zero. You can assign positive or negative values to the ScaleWidth and ScaleHeight properties.

☞ Assigning negative values to the ScaleWidth and ScaleHeight properties alters the orientation of the scale and the graphics images drawn. Thus, you can create a custom scale system that has the same orientation as the mathematical axes — the value of the Y coordinates increases as you move upward. The following equations help you calculate the coordinates of the four corners in the drawing area:

Top left
   X = ScaleLeft
   Y = ScaleTop

Top right
   X = ScaleLeft + ScaleWidth
   Y = ScaleTop

Lower left
   X = ScaleLeft
   Y = ScaleTop + ScaleHeight

Lower right
   X = ScaleLeft + ScaleWidth
   Y = ScaleTop + ScaleHeight

As an example, if you want to define a scale system that has the upper left corner coordinates (0,0) and has 1000 units in width and 500 in height, use the following statements:

ScaleLeft = 0
ScaleTop = 0
ScaleWidth = 1000
ScaleHeight = 500

If you wish to locate the (0,0) at the lower left corner of the drawing area and maintain the same width and height, then you need the following statements:

ScaleLeft = 0
ScaleTop = 500
ScaleWidth = 1000
ScaleHeight = −500

Visual Basic allows you to define a custom scale using the Scale method. The general syntax for the Scale method is:

*[object.]*Scale [(x1!, y1!) − (x2!, y2!)]

The (x1!, y1!) coordinates define the upper left corner of the drawing area. The (x2!, y2!) coordinates define the lower right corner of the drawing area. Using the Scale method automatically sets the ScaleMode property to 0 and sets the scale-related properties to the following values:

```
ScaleLeft = x1!
ScaleTop = y1!
ScaleHeight = y2! − y1!
ScaleWidth = x2! − x1!
```

As an example, if you want to define a scale system that has the upper left corner coordinates (100, 200) and has 1000 units in width and 500 in height, use the following Scale statement:

```
Scale (100, 200) − (1100, 700)
```

The lower right corner has the coordinates (1100, 700). If you wish to reverse the orientation of the scale and locate the (100, 700) at the lower left corner of the drawing area while maintaining the same width and height, you can use the following Scale statement:

```
Scale (100, 700) − (1100, 200)
```

Of course, in this case, the ScaleHeight property becomes −500.

If the pair of coordinates is omitted from the Scale method, the default scale system is restored.

Working with graphics methods and properties

Visual Basic provides you with the tools to draw a number of basic geometrical shapes and fine-tune their appearance. The graphics methods are described in the next several paragraphs.

The Cls **method**   Cls clears both the graphics and the output of Print statements from the form or from a picture box. The general syntax for using the Cls method is:

```
[form.][pictureBox.]Cls
```

By default, the Cls method clears the current form.

The PSet **method**   This method draws a point in a form, picture box, or printer object. The general syntax for the PSet method is:

```
[object.]Pset [Step] (x!, y!) [,color&]
```

The Step keyword specifies that the (x!, y!) coordinates are relative displacements to the current drawing position given by (CurrentX, CurrentY).

The (x!, y!) point specifies the coordinates of the plotted point when the Step keyword is omitted. Otherwise, (x!, y!) is the relative displacement in the X- and Y-axis from the current point. After the PSet plots a point, the CurrentX and CurrentY properties refer to the coordinates of the plotted point.

The color& parameter specifies the color of the plotted point. Using the background color property BackColor as the argument for color& clears a point at the specified coordinates.

An example of drawing and erasing a point is shown next:

```
Scale (100, 100) — (200, 200)
Cls ' clear the screen
BackColor = QBColor(15) ' background is bright white
DrawWidth = 3 ' make the point clearly visible
PSet (150, 150), QBColor(0) ' draw a black point
WaitForAMoment 2000 ' user-declare routine
Pset (150, 150), BackColor ' erase the point
```

The Point **method**   Point returns the color of the point at specified coordinates. The general syntax for the Point method is:

```
[form.][pictureBox.]Point (x!, y!)
```

The Point method returns a long integer that represents the color code of the specified point.

The Line **method**   This method draws a line or a rectangle on a form, a picture box, or the printer. The general syntax for the Line statement is:

```
[object.]Line [[Step] (x1!, y1!)] — [Step](x2!, y2!) [,[color&], B[F]]]
```

The Line method is a versatile command that allows you to draw lines and rectangles in various ways. The (x1!, y1!) represents the start point for the line or the rectangle. If the starting point is preceded by the Step keyword, the (x1!, y1!) coordinates are interpreted as relative displacements from the CurrentX and CurrentY properties.

The (x2!, y2!) coordinates represent the end point for the line or the rectangle. If the end point is preceded by the Step keyword, the (x2!, y2!) coordinates are interpreted as relative displacements from the start point.

If the (x1!, y1!) coordinates are omitted, the current values of the CurrentX and CurrentY properties are used as the start point.

The color& parameter specifies the color of the line or the rectangle. If a Line statement has no argument for color&, the foreground color property, ForeColor, is used.

The B parameter draws a box using the start and end coordinates as the diagonal corners of the box. The F parameter fills the box with the same color used in drawing its edges. The F parameter must be used with the B parameter. If only the B parameter is specified, the box is filled with the FillColor color and FillStyle pattern, which will be covered later in this section.

Examples of drawing and erasing lines are shown here:

```
Scale (100, 100) — (200, 200)
Cls ' clear the screen
BackColor = QBColor(15) ' background is bright white
ForeColor = QBColor(0) ' black foreground
```

```
' draw a triangle
Line (110, 110) — (150, 150) ' draw a line
Line — (130, 150) ' connect new line with first line
Line — (110, 110) ' complete the triangle
WaitForAMoment 2000 ' user-declare routine
Line (110, 110) — (150, 150), BackColor ' erase the first line
Line — (130, 150), BackColor ' erase the second line
Line — (110, 110), BackColor ' erase the third line
```

Examples for drawing boxes are given next:

```
Scale (100, 100) — (200, 200)
Cls ' clear the screen
BackColor = QBColor(15) ' background is bright white
ForeColor = QBColor(0) ' black foreground
Line (125, 125) — (135, 135), ,B ' empty box
Line (110, 110) — (120, 120), ,BF ' box filled with black color
Line — (125, 125), QBColor(1), BF ' box filled with blue color
```

The Circle **method** Using Circle enables you to draw circles, arcs, and ellipses in a form, a picture box, or the printer. The general syntax for the Circle method is:

[object.]Circle [Step](x!, y!), radius! [,color&][,[start!][,end!][,aspect!]]]]

The (x!, y!) coordinates specify the center of the circle, ellipse, or arc. If the Step keyword is included, the above coordinates become relative to the current coordinates given by the CurrentX and CurrentY properties.

The radius! parameter is the radius of the circle, ellipse, or arc. The units of measuring the radius! is given by the Scale property of the object to which the Circle method is applied.

The color& parameter specifies the color of the circle, ellipse, or arc. If a Circle statement has no argument for color&, the foreground color property ForeColor is used.

The start! and end! parameters specify the starting and ending angles (in radians) for drawing an arc or a partial ellipse. The default values for the start! and end! parameters are 0 and 2 * Pi radians (a full 360 degree circle). The two parameters can have arguments that range between −2 * Pi and +2 * Pi radians.

The aspect! parameter specifies the aspect ratio. The default value of aspect! is 1.0, which produces a perfect circle.

Examples for drawing circles, ellipses, and arcs are shown below:

```
Scale (100, 100) — (1000, 1000)
Pi = 4 * Atn(1)
Cls ' clear the screen
BackColor = QBColor(15) ' background is bright white
ForeColor = QBColor(0) ' black foreground
' draw circles
```

```
Circle (500, 500), 100,
Circle (200, 200), 50, RGB(45, 76, 44)
' draw ellipses
Circle (700, 700), 100, , , , 2 ' aspect ratio of 2
Circle (300, 300), 50, RGB(45, 76, 44), , , 1.5 ' aspect ratio of 1.5
' draw arcs
Circle (500, 500), 50, , 0, Pi / 2
Circle (200, 200), 10, RGB(45, 76, 44), Pi / 2, Pi
```

Visual Basic offers the following properties to fine-tune the visual appearance of the graphics:

The BackColor, ForeColor, **and** FillColor **properties**   These properties set and determine the color of the background, the color of the foreground, and the color used to fill a box or a circle. The general syntax for these properties is:

*[form.][pictureBox.]*BackColor *[=color&]*
*[form.][pictureBox.]*ForeColor *[=color&]*
*[form.][pictureBox.]*FillColor *[=color&]*

The color& parameter represents the color code. Visual Basic offers four methods for specifying the color. These methods are:

Using the global constants in file GLOBAL.BAS. Listing 12-1 shows these constants and their equivalent long integer hexadecimal codes.

Listing 12-1   Partial contents of GLOBAL.BAS that show the constants for the colors. DrawMode, DrawStyle, and FillStyle properties.

```
' BackColor, ForeColor, FillColor (standard RGB colors: form, controls)
Global Const BLACK = &H0&
Global Const RED = &HFF&
Global Const GREEN = &HFF00&
Global Const YELLOW = &HFFFF&
Global Const BLUE = &HFF0000
Global Const MAGENTA = &HFF00FF
Global Const CYAN = &HFFFF00
Global Const WHITE = &HFFFFFF


' DrawMode (form, picture box, Printer)
Global Const BLACKNESS = 1          ' 1 - Blackness
Global Const NOT_MERGE_PEN = 2      ' 2 - Not Merge Pen
Global Const MASK_NOT_PEN = 3       ' 3 - Mask Not Pen
Global Const NOT_COPY_PEN = 4       ' 4 - Not Copy Pen
Global Const MASK_PEN_NOT = 5       ' 5 - Mask Pen Not
Global Const INVERT = 6             ' 6 - Invert
Global Const XOR_PEN = 7            ' 7 - Xor Pen
Global Const NOT_MASK_PEN = 8       ' 8 - Not Mask Pen
Global Const MASK_PEN = 9           ' 9 - Mask Pen
Global Const NOT_XOR_PEN = 10       ' 10 - Not Xor Pen
```

Listing 12-1 Continued.

```
Global Const NOP = 11                    ' 11 - Nop
Global Const MERGE_NOT_PEN = 12          ' 12 - Merge Not Pen
Global Const COPY_PEN = 13               ' 13 - Copy Pen
Global Const MERGE_PEN_NOT = 14          ' 14 - Merge Pen Not
Global Const MERGE_PEN = 15              ' 15 - Merge Pen
Global Const WHITENESS = 16              ' 16 - Whiteness

' DrawStyle (form, picture box, Printer)
Global Const SOLID = 0                   ' 0 - Solid
Global Const DASH = 1                    ' 1 - Dash
Global Const DOT = 2                     ' 2 - Dot
Global Const DASH_DOT = 3                ' 3 - Dash-Dot
Global Const DASH_DOT_DOT = 4            ' 4 - Dash-Dot-Dot
Global Const INVISIBLE = 5               ' 5 - Invisible
Global Const INSIDESOLID = 6             ' 6 - Inside Solid

' FillStyle (form, picture box, Printer)
' Global Const SOLID = 0                 ' 0 - Solid
Global Const TRANSPARENT = 1             ' 1 - Transparent
Global Const HORIZONTAL_LINE = 2         ' 2 - Horizontal Line
Global Const VERTICAL_LINE = 3           ' 3 - Vertical Line
Global Const UPWARD_DIAGONAL = 4         ' 4 - Upward Diagonal
Global Const DOWNWARD_DIAGONAL = 5       ' 5 - Downward Diagonal
Global Const CROSS = 6                   ' 6 - Cross
Global Const DIAGONAL_CROSS = 7          ' 7 - Diagonal Cross
```

Using the RGB function to return the color value. The general syntax for the RGB function is:

```
RGB(red%, green%, blue%)
```

The parameters red%, green%, and blue% are integers in the range of 0 to 255 that represents the red, green, and blue components of a color, respectively.

Using the QBColor function to return a color value. This uses Quick Basic color codes, shown in TABLE 12-2. The general syntax for the QBColor function is:

```
QBColor(qbcolor%)
```

Directly setting the color value. This method requires you to create a long integer hexadecimal constants of the following format:

```
&HBBGGRR
```

BB is a two-digit hexadecimal constant that represents the amount of blue in the specified color. The values for BB range from 00 to FF (255 in

Table 12-2 The Quick Basic color codes.

Number	Color
0	Black
1	Blue
2	Green
3	Cyan
4	Red
5	Magenta
6	Yellow
7	White
8	Gray
9	Light Blue
10	Light Green
11	Light Cyan
12	Light Red
13	Light Magenta
14	Light Yellow
15	Light White

decimal). Similarly, GG and RR represent the two-digit hexadecimal code for the green and red colors, respectively. Examples of the direct setting are:

```
BackColor = &HFF0000 ' blue background color
ForeColor = &H00FF00 ' green foreground color
BackColor = &H0000FF ' red background color
```

The CurrentX and CurrentY properties These properties determine the current location for graphics drawing and for output of Print statements. These properties were covered in chapter 11.

The DrawMode property DrawMode determines or returns the graphics output appearance on a form, a picture box, and the printer. The general syntax for the DrawMode property is:

*[object.]*DrawMode [=*mode%*]

Table 12-3 shows the enumerated settings for the DrawMode property. The default setting is 13. Listing 12-1 contains global constants that represent the settings in TABLE 12-3. The most common settings are 4, 7, 11, and 13. The DrawMode property allows you to combine, in various ways, the color of the imaginary drawing pen with the colors of the pixels already on the display.

Let me explain the effect of the DrawMode property on producing a pixel in the display area. I use a few DrawMode settings as examples. When

Table 12-3   The DrawMode property settings.

Setting	Meaning
1	Blackness: the output is black.
2	Not Merge Pen: the output is the inverse of Merge Pen (setting 15).
3	Mask Not Pen: the output combines the colors that are common to both the display and the inverse of the pen.
4	Not Copy Pen: the output is the inverse of the pen.
5	Mask Pen Not: the output combines the colors that are common to both the inverse of the display and the pen.
6	Invert: the output is the inverse of the display color.
7	Xor Pen: the output performs an Xor on the pen and display color.
8	Not Mask Pen: the output is the inverse of the MaskPen color.
9	Mask Pen: the output combines the colors common to the pen and the display.
10	Not Xor Pen: the output is the inverse of the Xor Pen colors.
11	Nop: the colors are not changed.
12	Merge Not Pen: the output combines the colors common to the display and the inverse of the pen.
13	Copy Pen: the output is the pen color specified with the ForeColor property.
14	Merge Pen Not: the output combines the colors common to the pen and the inverse of the display.
15	Merge Pen: the output combines the pen and display colors.
16	Whiteness: the output is white.

DrawMode is set to 4, the display pixels are replaced with the inverse of the pen color. This is shown by the following:

	Pixel value		Pixel value	
Pen color	1100	Not pen color	0011	
Display	0100	Display	0100	<—ignore
		New display pixel	0011	

Thus, the inverse bitwise value of the pen pixel overwrites the target display pixel.

When DrawMode is 7, the new pixel is obtained as the expression (Pen pixel Xor current Display pixel), as shown below:

Pixel value

Pen color	1100
Display	0100 Xor

New display	1000

When DrawMode is 15, the new pixel combines the bits of the pen and display pixels—the pixels are Anded. This is shown below:

Pixel value

Pen color	1100
Display	0101

New display pixel	1101

The DrawStyle **property** This property sets and determines the current line pattern for a form, a picture box, and the printer. The general syntax for the DrawStyle property is:

*[object.]*DrawStyle *[=style%]*

Table 12-4 shows the valid enumerated settings for DrawStyle. Listing 12-1 also contains the global constants for the DrawStyle settings. The default DrawStyle setting is 0, the solid line pattern.

Table 12-4 The DrawStyle
property settings.

Setting	Line pattern
0	Solid (default)
1	Dashes
2	Dots
3	Dash-dot
4	Dash-dot-dot
5	Dash-dot-dot
5	Invisible
6	Inside solid

The DrawWidth **property** Using this procedure sets and determines the line width for graphics output on a form, a picture box, and the printer. The general syntax for the DrawWidth property is:

*[object.]*DrawWidth *[=lineWidth%]*

The default DrawWidth setting is 1. Increasing the line width creates shapes with coarser edges. Increasing the DrawWidth setting is recommended when plotting points — this makes the points more visible than the faint dots that appear with the default setting of 1.

The FillStyle **property** FillStyle sets and determines the pattern used in filling circles and boxes generated by the Circle and Line methods, respectively. The general syntax for the FillStyle property is:

> [form.][pictureBox.]FillStyle [=style%]

The default FillStyle setting is 1, the transparent pattern. Table 12-5 shows the various settings for FillStyle. Listing 12-1 also shows the global constants representing the settings in TABLE 12-5.

Table 12-5   The FillStyle property settings.

Setting	Fill Pattern
0	Solid
1	Transparent (default)
2	Horizontal lines
3	Vertical lines
4	Upward diagonal lines
5	Downward diagonal lines
6	Cross
7	Diagonal cross

Using the AutoRedraw property

One of the features of Windows applications is the ability to minimize them and then maximize them later. Minimizing a window enables you to put it out of the way for later retrieval. When you maximize a window you expect to see its contents intact — something we all take for granted. In fact, the contrary effect of losing the window's contents after maximizing would swiftly generate a bulk of angry phone calls and letters to the application's vendor! Now that it's your turn to write Windows applications, you need to be aware that minimizing a window can result in losing some or all of its contents, unless certain steps are taken. Before the last statement sends chills down your spine, you need to relax and know that the potential loss of the windows contents excludes, by default, the controls that you draw on a form and their contents. What can be lost is the graphics or Print statement output in a form or a picture box. Why? The answer lies in the fact that these items are *not* stored in memory.

Visual Basic offers two ways to maintain these output items. The first method uses the AutoRedraw property. By default, this logical property is set to False, making graphics and Print statement output vulnerable to being lost when the window is minimized. Setting the AutoRedraw property to True tells the Visual Basic run time system to reserve memory for storing any subsequent graphics or Print statement output. If the Auto-Redraw of a form is set to True, then the entire image of the form is saved. If the AutoRedraw property of a picture box is set to True, the run time system saves the image of the graphics belonging to that box.

The second route for redrawing the content of a maximized window is more memory-conserving. The default False value of the AutoRedraw property is maintained, while the graphics and Print statement output is redrawn by code attached to your form. This method works well when you have a finite number of graphics and Print statement output. The work is done by the Paint event-handling procedure attached to the manipulated form. This event is generated when the form is maximized *and* the Auto-Redraw property is False.

The SHAPES program

The SHAPES program is one of those programs that I wrote over several programming sessions — the kind of program that always challenges you to add more features. This program enables you to experiment with drawing different shapes, colors, fill styles, line widths, and line styles. Unlike the other programs presented so far, you need to read about the features of this program and then spend a good part of a late night toying with the program. The SHAPES program not only demonstrates the various individual graphics-related properties and methods, it also shows how they are integrated in a nontrivial fashion (and this is the tip of the iceberg!). In the following subsection, I describe what the program does. In the second subsection, I give some examples of the graphics you can draw with the SHAPES program. These two sections should familiarize you with the program before I discuss its code. This is the opposite of the way I have presented most programs thus far.

Program operation

The SHAPES program is menu driven. Figure 12-1 shows the structure of the program's menu selections and options. The menu selections are:

Quit **(access key is Alt+Q)**   This selection exits the program.

☞   Screen **(Alt+S)**   This selection that enables you to clear the form, save the form into a .BMP file, or load a .BMP file. It is important to point out that the bitmapped image that is loaded from a .BMP file is not affected by the Clear option.

✍   Programming Tip: Use the Save As option to save the current image of the form into a file before attempting to draw graphics shapes

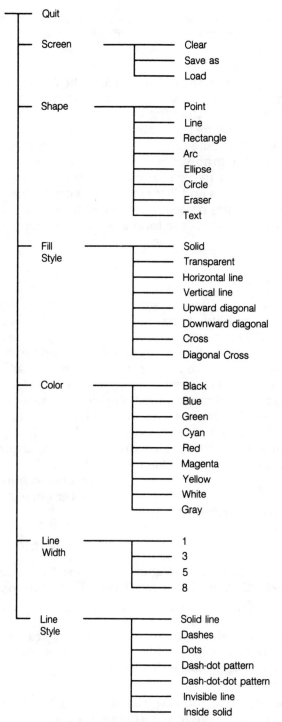

12-1 The menu structure of the SHAPES program.

that you may want to erase. If you are indeed not satisfied with the shapes you just drew, use the Load option to recall the prior image. Once you load the image from file, the next attempts at drawing the same or other "erasable" shapes can be easily undone by selecting the Clear option. Only the shapes you drew since you loaded the .BMP file are erased!

Shape **(Alt+H)**   This selection allows you to select a shape to draw. The shapes include points, lines, rectangles, arcs, ellipses, and circles. The Shape menu selection also contains the eraser option that allows you to erase part of the current drawing. The Text option permits you to type text on the form. A check mark is placed to the left of the current selection.

Fill Style **(Alt+F)**   This selection offers the various graphics fill styles in TABLE 12-5. A check mark is placed to the left of the current selection.

Color **(Alt+C)**   This selection allows you to choose from the first seven Quick Basic colors. A check mark is placed to the left of the current selection.

Line Width **(Alt+W)**   This selection offers line widths of 1, 3, 5, and 8 for the Line and Eraser options in the Shape menu selection. The Line Width selection is disabled for all other shapes. A check mark is placed to the left of the current selection.

Line Style **(Alt+L)**   This selection allows you to select the drawing style for the lines you draw. The options of the Line Style correspond to the various settings of the DrawMode property found in TABLE 12-4. A check mark is placed to the left of the current selection.

Sample program tour

In this subsection I present a few sample screens of graphics produced by the SHAPES program and discuss the dynamic operation of the program.

The program offers various menu selections, of which the Shape selection is pivotal in drawing the various graphics shapes. Run the program and click on the Shape menu or press the Alt+H access keys. The default selection is the Line. A check mark is placed to the left of the current selection. The default Line Width selection is 1. When a line with a line width of 1 is selected, the line style menu is enabled. Increasing the line width, or selecting another shape, disables the line style. When I first wrote the program I made the options of the line style menu available for various line widths. The program output was always a solid line for line widths greater than 1. Therefore, I decided to disable the Line Style menu, because the menu options were practically disabled anyway!

The program uses a cross hair cursor to draw the various shapes. This kind of cursor is very suitable for drawing graphics shapes. The cursor maintains the cross hair shape for all options of the Shape menu, except when erasing pixels. This will be discussed later in this subsection.

Figure 12-2 shows the various types of line styles, drawn for a line width of 1. You can produce a similar image by selecting each option in the Fill Style menu and drawing a line. You don't have to make your lines horizontal.

12-2 The different line styles.

To draw a line, you need to perform the following steps:

1. Move the mouse to the location that represents the start point.
2. Click the mouse. A small dot appears at the mouse location.
3. Move the mouse to the location that represents the end point. The mouse coordinates shown in the text box help you draw perfect vertical or horizontal lines.
4. Click the mouse. The program draws a line connecting the start and end points.

Marking the start point with a dot provides a visual indication for that point. This dot is erased by the program if you make a selection from the Shape, Fill Style, Color, Line Width, or Line Style menus.

The text that you see in FIG. 12-2 is generated by selecting the Text option from the Shape menu, clicking at the intended location, and then typing in the desired text in the input dialog box that appears on the screen.

Now select the Rectangle option from the Shape menu. The first thing you notice is that the Line Width and Line Style menus are disabled. The same thing occurs when you select the Arc, Ellipse, or Circle option. Drawing a rectangle is similar to drawing a line:

1. Move the mouse to the location that represents the start point.
2. Click the mouse. A small dot appears at the mouse location.
3. Move the mouse to the location that represents the end point. The mouse coordinates displayed in the text box enable you to align the box you are drawing with other shapes that are already on the form.
4. Click the mouse. The program draws a rectangle connecting the start and end points, using the current color and fill style options.

Marking the start point with a dot provides a visual indication for that point. This dot is erased by the program if you make a selection from the Shape, Fill Style, or Color menus.

I drew FIG. 12-3 by selecting the Black color option and the various Fill Style options.

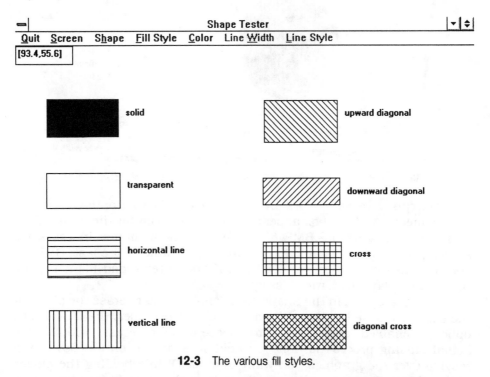

12-3 The various fill styles.

Drawing an arc, an ellipse, and a circle is similar to drawing a rectangle. The start point marks the center of the arc, ellipse, or circle. The end point marks a point on the circumference. The program calculates the radius of the circle as the distance between the start and end points. Arcs are drawn with the start and end angles taken as $-Pi/2$ and $-Pi/3$. Ellipses are drawn with an aspect ratio equal to one plus a random number between 0 and 5. Figure 12-4 shows an arc, an ellipse, and a circle, each with a different fill style. The same figure also shows points and lines. The lines are drawn in various widths.

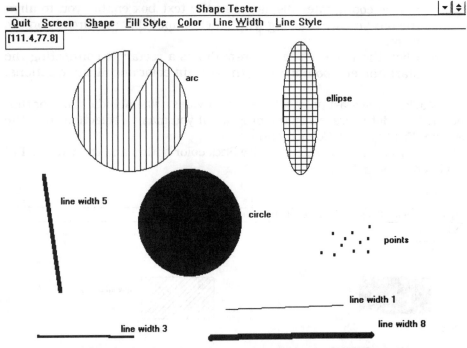

12-4 The family of graphics shapes supported by the SHAPES program.

You can save your work by selecting the Save As option from the Screen menu. A dialog box appears and prompts you for the name of the .BMP file. The SHAPES.BMP file is the default filename. In the same session, the program is able to remember the name of the last .BMP file you used to store or load a .BMP file. If you enter a bad filename, the program displays an error message.

The Eraser option in the Shape menu enables you to erase the pixels at the current mouse location. When you select the eraser, the Line Width option is enabled, allowing you to choose different eraser widths. The actual erasing process is done by holding a mouse button down and moving over the graphics you want to erase. While holding the mouse button down, the cursor changes shape from the cross hair to the small-box icon shape. When you release the mouse button the cursor shape changes back to the cross hair and you can move the mouse around without erasing pixels. The default line width for the eraser is 1. This line width provides you with a very small eraser (you will most likely resort to larger line widths to erase pixels more quickly). I chose to make 1 the default line width for the eraser for safety reasons, especially because the SHAPES program lacks an undo feature. The small line width setting prevents you from accidentally wiping off a lot of pixels in one swoop.

You can save your image any time and retrieve it in a different session by using the Load option in the Screen menu. The Load option also displays a dialog box to obtain the name of the .BMP. If you enter a bad filename, or the file you specify does not store an image in the BMP format, the program will display an error message.

Basic program analysis

The SHAPES program is made up of a number of subsystems that interact with each other. These subsystems are behind the Shape, Fill Style, Color, Line Width, and Line Style menus, as well as the mouse event-handling procedures attached to the form. Figure 12-5 shows a diagram for the interaction among the various program subsystems. All of the menu subsystems interact with the form subsystem. The Shape menu subsystem affects the Line Width and Line Style subsystems. The Line Width menu subsystem affects the Line Style subsystem.

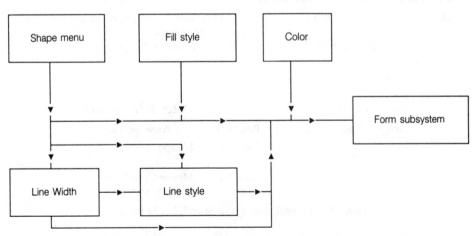

12-5 The interacting sybsystems of the SHAPES program.

The menu subsystems share the task of updating their selections. This is carried out by changing a property setting and updating the visual check mark for the selected menu option. The form subsystem has the task of drawing the selected shapes using the selected fill style, color, and possibly the selected line width and line style.

Program spejcifications

Figures 12-6 to 12-9 contain the specifications for various components of the SHAPES program. The specifications indicate the following:

- The program uses a single text box to display the current mouse coordinates.
- The program has a nontrivial menu structure that enables it to carry out the various program tasks.

Application name: Graphics Demo
Application code name: SHAPES
Version: 1.0   Date created: July 10, 1991
Programmer(s): Namir Clement Shammas
List of filenames
Storage path: \VB\EASYVB
Project SHAPES.MAK
Global GLOBAL.BAS
Form 1 SHAPES.FRM

12-6 The basic specifications for the SHAPES.MAK project file.

Form #1   Form filename: SHAPES.FRM
Version: 1.0   Date: July 10, 1991

Control object type	Default CtlName	Purpose
Text Box	Text1	Displays the current coordinates of the mouse

12-7 List of control objects for the SHAPES.FRM form.

Application (code) name: SHAPES
Form #1
Version: 1.0   Date: July 10, 1991

Original control name	Property	New setting
Form	Caption	Shape Tested
Text1	CtlName	MouseCoordBox
	Text	(empty string)

12-8 The updated settings of SHAPES.FRM form.

Program Code

Listing 12-2 shows the code attached to the various controls of the SHAPES.FRM form. The code for the declarations and the event-handling procedures can be grouped as follows:

The general declarations section This section has the declaration of one constant and a number of variables. The constant Frmt and variables Xstr

Form #1   Form Filename: SHAPES.FRM
Version: 1.0   Date: July 10, 1991

Caption	Property	Setting	Purpose
&Quit	CtlName	QuitCom	Exits application
&Screen	CtlName	ScreenCom	Screen functions
Clear	CtlName	ClearCom	Clears form
	indented	once	
Save As	CtlName	SaveAsCom	Saves screen to a .BMP file
	indented	once	
Load	CtlName	LoadCom	Loads a .BMP file
	indented	once	
S&hapes	CtlName	ShapesCOM	
Point	CtlName	PointCom	Draws a point
	Accelerator	CTRL-P	
	indented	once	
Line	CtlName	LineCom	Draws a line
	Accelerator	CTRL-L	
	indented	once	
Rectangle	CtlName	RectangleCom	Draws a box
	Accelerator	CTRL-R	
	indented	once	
Arc	CtlName	ArcCom	Draws an arc
	Accelerator	CTRL-A	
	indented	once	
Ellipse	CtlName	EllipseCom	Draws an ellipse
	Accelerator	CTRL-E	
	indented	once	
Circle	CtlName	CircleCom	Draws a point
	Accelerator	CTRL-C	
	indented	once	
Eraser	CtlName	EraserCom	Erases a point
	Accelerator	CTRL-X	
	indented	once	
Text	CtlName	TextCom	Writes text
	Accelerator	CTRL-T	
	indented	once	
&Fill Style	CtlName	FillStyleCom	
Solid	CtlName	SolidCom	Selects solid
	indented	once	
Transparent	CtlName	TransparentCom	Selects solid
	indented	once	
Horizontal Line	CtlName	HLineCom	Selects horizontal line
	indented	once	
Vertical Line	CtlName	VLineCom	Selects vertical line
	indented	once	

12-9 The controls and structure for the menu of form SHAPES.FRM.

Caption	Property	Setting	Purpose
Upward Diagonal	CtlName indented	UpDiagCom once	Selects upward diagonal
Downward Diagonal	CtlName indented	HLineCom once	Selects downward diagonal
Cross	CtlName indented	CrossCom once	Selects diagonal cross
Diagonal Cross	CtlName indented	DiagCrossCom once	Selects diagonal cross
&Color	CtlName	ColorCom	
Black	CtlName indented	BlackCom once	Selects black color
Blue	CtlName indented	BlueCom once	Selects blue color
Cyan	CtlName indented	CyanCom once	Selects cyan color
Red	CtlName indented	RedCom once	Selects red color
Magenta	CtlName indented	MagentaCom once	Selects magenta color
Yellow	CtlName indented	YellowCom once	Selects yellow color
White	CtlName indented	WhiteCom once	Selects white color
Gray	CtlName indented	GrayCom once	Selects gray color
Line &Width	CtlName	LineWidthCom	
1	CtlName indented	Size1Com once	Selects line width of 1
2	CtlName indented	Size3Com once	Selects line width of 3
5	CtlName indented	Size5Com once	Selects line width of 5
8	CtlName indented	Size8Com once	Selects line width of 8
&Line Style	CtlName	LineStyleCom	
Solid line	CtlName indented	SolidLineCom once	Selects solid line
Dashes	CtlName indented	DashesCom once	Selects Dashes
Dots	CtlName indented	DotsCom once	Selects dots
Dash-Dot	CtlName indented	DashDotCom once	Selects dash-dot

12-9 Continued.

Caption	Property	Setting	Purpose
Dash-Dot-Dot	CtlName indented	DashDotDotCom once	Selects dash-dot-dot
Invisible	CtlName indented	InvisibleCom once	Selects invisible
Inside solid	CtlName indented	InsideSolidCom once	Selects inside solid

12-9 Continued.

Listing 12-2 The code attached to the form and menu controls of the SHAPES.FRM form.

```
Const Frmt = "##0.0"
Dim IsFirst As Integer
Dim QBColorNum As Integer
Dim MouseIsDown As Integer
Dim X1 As Single, Y1 As Single
Dim BMPfile As String
Dim Xstr As String, Ystr As String

Sub QuitCom_Click ( )
   End
End Sub

Sub ClearCom_Click ( )
   Cls
   Is First = True
End Sub

Sub Form_Load ( )
   IsFirst = True
   BMPfile = "SHAPES.BMP"
   WindowState = 2
   MousePointer = 2 ' Cross
   AutoRedraw = True
   BackColor = WHITE
   ForeColor = RED
   Scale (0, 0)-(100, 100)
   ' select defaults
   LineCom_Click
   TransparentCom_Click
   BlackCom_Click
End Sub

Sub Form_MouseDown (Button As Integer, Shift As Integer, X As Single, Y As Single)
   Dim Radius As Single
   Dim TheColor As Long
```

Listing 12-2 Continued.

```
Dim Pi As Double
Dim TextStr As String
Pi = 4 * Atn(1) ' calculate pie
' get the color using the QuickBasic color code
TheColor = QBColor(QBColorNum)
FillColor = TheColor
' ************** Eraser *************
If EraserCom.Checked Then
   MouseIsDown = True
   MousePointer = 4 ' change mouse cursor
' ************** Text *************
ElseIf TextCom.Checked Then
   IsFirst = True
   CurrentX = X
   CurrentY = Y
   TextStr = InputBox$("Enter text", "Text Input")
   Print TextStr
' ************** Point *************
ElseIf PointCom.Checked Then
   IsFirst = True
   PSet (X, Y), TheColor
' ************** Line *************
ElseIf LineCom.Checked Then
   If IsFirst Then
      X1 = X
      Y1 = Y
      PSet (X, Y), TheColor
   Else
      Line (X1, Y1)-(X, Y), TheColor
   End If
   IsFirst = Not IsFirst
' ************** Rectangle *************
ElseIf RectangleCom.Checked Then
   If IsFirst Then
      X1 = X
      Y1 = Y
      PSet (X, Y), TheColor
   Else
      Line (X1, Y1)-Step(X - X1, Y - Y1), TheColor, B
   End If
   IsFirst = Not IsFirst
' ************** Arc *************
ElseIf ArcCom.Checked Then
   If IsFirst Then
      X1 = X
      Y1 = Y
      PSet (X, Y), TheColor
```

Listing 12-2 Continued.

```
      Else
        Radius = Sqr((X - X1) ^ 2 + (Y - Y1) ^ 2)
        Circle (X1, Y1), Radius, TheColor, -Pi / 2, -Pi / 3
      End If
      IsFirst = Not IsFirst
    ' ************** Circle **************
    ElseIf CircleCom.Checked Then
      If IsFirst Then
        X1 = X
        Y1 = Y
        PSet (X, Y), TheColor
      Else
        Radius = Sqr((X - X1) ^ 2 + (Y - Y1) ^ 2)
        Circle (X1, Y1), Radius, TheColor
      End If
      IsFirst = Not IsFirst
    ' ************* Ellipse **************
    ElseIf EllipseCom.Checked Then
      If IsFirst Then
        X1 = X
        Y1 = Y
        PSet (X, Y), TheColor
      Else
        Radius = Sqr((X - X1) ^ 2 + (Y - Y1) ^ 2)
        Circle (X1, Y1), Radius, TheColor, , , 1 + 5 * Rnd
      End If
      IsFirst = Not IsFirst
    End If
End Sub

Sub ClearShapes ( )
  ' clear pending point?
  If Not IsFirst Then
    PSet (X1, Y1), BackColor
  End If
    IsFirst = True
    DrawWidth = 1
    PointCom.Checked = False
    LineCom.Checked = False
    RectangleCom.Checked = False
    ArcCom.Checked = False
    EllipseCom.Checked = False
    CircleCom.Checked = False
    EraserCom.Checked = False
    TextCom.Checked = False
    Size1Com_Click
    SolidLineComClick
```

Listing 12-2   Continued.

```
        LineWidthCom.Enabled = False
        LineStyleCom.Enabled = False
End Sub

Sub ArcCom_Click ( )
   ClearShapes
   ArcCom.Checked = True
End Sub

Sub CircleCom_Click ( )
   ClearShapes
   CircleCom.Checked = True
End Sub

Sub EllipseCom_Click ( )
   ClearShapes
   EllipseCom.Checked = True
End Sub

Sub LineCom_Click ( )
   ClearShapes
   LineCom.Checked = True
   LineStyleCom.Enabled = True
   LineWidthCom.Enabled = True
End Sub

Sub PointCom_Click ( )
   ClearShapes
   PointCom.Checked = True
   DrawWidth = 3 ' make the points noticeable!
End Sub

Sub RectangleCom_Click ( )
   ClearShapes
   RectangleCom.Checked = True
End Sub

Sub TextCom_Click ( )
   ClearShapes
   TextCom.Checked = True
End Sub

Sub ClearFillStyle ( )
   ' clear pending point?
   If Not IsFirst Then
      PSet (X1, Y1), BackColor
   End If
   IsFirst = True
```

Listing 12-2 Continued.

```
    SolidCom.Checked = False
    TransparentCom.Checked = False
    HLineCom.Checked = False
    VLineCom.Checked = False
    UpDiagCom.Checked = False
    DownDiagCom.Checked = False
    CrossCom.Checked = False
    DiagCrossCom.Checked = False
End Sub

Sub ClearColors ( )
    ' clear pending point?
    If Not IsFirst Then
        PSet (X1, Y1), BackColor
    End If
    IsFirst = True
    BlackCom.Checked = False
    BlueCom.Checked = False
    GreenCom.Checked = False
    CyanCom.Checked = False
    RedCom.Checked = False
    MagentaCom.Checked = False
    YellowCom.Checked = False
    WhiteCom.Checked = False
    GrayCom.Checked = False
End Sub

Sub BlackCom_Click ( )
    ClearColors
    BlackCom.Checked = True
    QBColorNum = 0
End Sub

Sub BlueCom_Click ( )
    ClearColors
    BlueCom.Checked = True
    QBColorNum = 1
End Sub

Sub CyanCom_Click ( )
    ClearColors
    CyanCom.Checked = True
    QBColorNum = 3
End Sub

Sub DiagCrossCom_Click ( )
    ClearFillStyle
    DiagCrossCom.Checked = True
```

Listing 12-2 Continued.

```
  FillStyle = DIAGONAL_CROSS
End Sub

Sub DownDiagCom_Click ( )
  ClearFillStyle
  DownDiagCom.Checked = True
  FillStyle = DOWNWARD_DIAGONAL
End Sub

Sub GrayCom_Click ( )
  ClearColors
  GrayCom.Checked = True
  QBColorNum = 8
End Sub

Sub GreenCom_Click ( )
  ClearColors
  GreenCom.Checked = True
  QBColorNum = 2
End Sub

Sub HLineCom_Click ( )
  ClearFillStyle
  HLineCom.Checked = True
  FillStyle = HORIZONTAL_LINE
End Sub

Sub MagentaCom_Click ( )
  ClearColors
  MagentaCom.Checked = True
  QBColorNum = 5
End Sub

Sub RedCom_Click ( )
  ClearColors
  RedCom.Checked = True
  QBColorNum = 4
End Sub

Sub SolidCom_Click ( )
  ClearFillStyle
  SolidCom.Checked = True
  FillStyle = SOLID
End Sub

Sub TransparentCom_Click ( )
  ClearFillStyle
  TransparentCom.Checked = True
```

Listing 12-2   Continued.

```
  FillStyle = TRANSPARENT
End Sub

Sub UpDiagCom_Click ( )
  ClearFillStyle
  UpDiagCom.Checked = True
  FillStyle = UPWARD_DIAGONAL
End Sub

Sub VLineCom_Click ( )
  ClearFillStyle
  VLineCom.Checked = True
  FillStyle = VERTICAL_LINE
End Sub

Sub WhiteCom_Click ( )
  ClearColors
  WhiteCom.Checked = True
  QBColorNum = 7
End Sub

Sub YellowCom_Click ( )
  ClearColors
  YellowCom.Checked = True
  QBColorNum = 6
End Sub

Sub CrossCom_Click ( )
  ClearFillStyle
  CrossCom.Checked = True
  FillStyle = CROSS
End Sub

Sub ClearSize ( )
  ' clear pending point?
  If Not IsFirst Then
    PSet (X1, Y1), BackColor
  End If
  IsFirst = True
  LineStyleCom.Enabled = False
  Size1Com.Checked = False
  Size3Com.Checked = False
  Size5Com.Checked = False
  Size8Com.Checked = False
End Sub

Sub Size1Com_Click ( )
  ClearSize Size1Com.Checked = True
```

Listing 12-2 Continued.

```
      LineStyleCom.Enabled = True
      DrawWidth = 1
End Sub

Sub Size3Com_Click ( )
   ClearSize Size
   3Com.Checked = True
   DrawWidth = 3
End Sub

Sub Size5Com_Click ( )
   ClearSize
   Size5Com.Checked = True
   DrawWidth = 5
End Sub

Sub Size8Com_Click ( )
   ClearSize
   Size8Com.Checked = True
   DrawWidth = 8
End Sub

Sub ClearDrawStyle ( )
   ' clear pending point?
   If Not IsFirst Then
      PSet (X1, Y1), BackColor
   End If
   IsFirst = True
   SolidLineCom.Checked = False
   DashesCom.Checked = False
   DotsCom.Checked = False
   DashDotCom.Checked = False
   DashDotDotCom.Checked = False
   InvisibleCom.Checked = False
   InsideSolidCom.Checked = False
End Sub

Sub SolidLineCom_Click ( )
   ClearDrawStyle
   SolidLineCom.Checked = True
   DrawStyle = SOLID
End Sub

Sub DashesCom_Click ( )
   ClearDrawStyle
   DashesCom.Checked = True
   DrawStyle = DASH
End Sub
```

Listing 12-2   Continued.

```
Sub DotsCom_Click ( )
   ClearDrawStyle
   DotsCom.Checked = True
   DrawStyle = DOT
End Sub

Sub DashDotCom_Click ( )
   ClearDrawStyle
   DashDotCom.Checked = True
   DrawStyle = DASH_DOT
End Sub

Sub DashDotDotCom_Click ( )
   ClearDrawStyle
   DashDotDotCom.Checked = True
   DrawStyle = DASH_DOT_DOT
End Sub

Sub InsideSolidCom_Click ( )
   ClearDrawStyle
   InsideSolidCom.Checked = True
   DrawStyle = INSIDE_SOLID
End Sub

Sub InvisibleCom_Click ( )
   ClearDrawStyle
   InvisibleCom.Checked = True
   DrawStyle = INVISIBLE
End Sub

Sub EraserCom_Click ( )
   ClearShapes
   EraserCom.Checked = True
   LineWidthCom.Enabled = True
End Sub

Sub Form_MouseMove (Button As Integer, Shift As Integer, X As Single, Y As Single)
   Xstr = Format$(X, Frmt)
   Ystr = Format$(Y, Frmt)
   MouseCoordBox.Text = "[" + Xstr + "," + Ystr + "]"
   ' if mouse is still down and the Eraser is selected
   ' erase the graphics at the current coordinates
   If MouseIsDown And EraserCom.Checked Then
      PSet (X, Y), BackColor
   End If
End Sub

Sub Form_MouseUp (Button As Integer, Shift As Integer, X As Single, Y As Single)
```

Listing 12-2   Continued.

```
    MouseIsDown = False
    MousePointer = 2 ' restore mouse cursor
End Sub

Sub SaveAsCom_Click ( )
    BMPfile = InputBox$("Enter filename", "Save As", BMPfile)
    On Error GoTo BadBMPoutput
    SavePicture Image, BMPfile
    IsFirst = True
    On Error GoTo 0
    IsFirst = True
    Exit Sub
BadBMPoutput:
    MsgBox "Cannot write to file " + BMPfile, 0, "File I/O Error"
    Resume ExitBMPoutput
ExitBMPoutput:
End Sub

Sub LoadCom_Click ( )
    BMPfile = InputBox$("Enter filename", "LOAD", BMPfile)
    On Error GoTo BadBMPinput
    Picture = LoadPicture(BMPfile)
    On Error GoTo 0
    IsFirst = True
    Exit Sub
BadBMPinput:
    MsgBox "Cannot read file " + BMPfile, 0, "File I/O Error"
    Resume ExitBMPinput
ExitBMPinput:
End Sub
```

and Ystr are used by the Form_MouseMove event-handler. I declared these identifiers in the general section to gain some speed, since the Form_Mouse-Move is called every time you move the mouse! Making these identifiers global (with the form) instead of local eliminates the time needed to create and dispose of them. The other variables are used to exchange data between two or more procedures.

IsFirst   is used as a Boolean flag to indicate whether the mouse is click-ing the start or the end point when drawing a line, a rectangle, or circular shapes.

QBColorNum   is assigned the Quick Basic color code by the procedures of the Color menu subsystem.

MouseIsDown   is used with the Eraser option (in the Shape menu). The MouseIsDown variable tracks whether or not you are still holding the mouse down to erase the pixels at the current mouse location.

X1 and Y1   mark the coordinates for the start point. These variables are used in drawing lines, arcs, ellipses, and circles. In addition, the X1 and

Y1 variables are utilized in deleting the dot that marks the start point if you make a selection from a menu option before defining the end point of the shape you are drawing.

BMPfile stores the name of the current .BMPfile.

The Form_Load **procedure**   This procedure initializes the form by performing the following tasks:

- Assigns True to the variable IsFirst.
- Assigns the default .BMP file, SHAPES.BMP, to the BMPfile variable.
- Sets the WindowState property to 2 (maximized).
- Sets the MousePointer to 2 (cross hair).
- Sets the AutoReDraw property to True.
- Sets the BackColor and ForeColor properties to the global constants WHITE and BLACK, respectively.
- Sets the user-defined scale, such that the upper left corner of the window is (0, 0) and the ScaleHeight and ScaleWidth are 100.
- Selects the line as the initial shape by calling the LineCom_Click procedure.
- Selects the transparent fill style as the initial setting for the FillStyle property, by calling the TransparentCom_Click procedure.
- Selects black as the initial color, by calling the BlackCom_Click procedure.

By invoking the above xxxCom_Click procedures, the Form_Load procedure lets these procedures perform their initialization of the shape, color, and fill style menu subsystems.

The Line Style menu subsystem procedures   These procedures include Clear-DrawStyle and the family of related xxxCom_Click routines. The ClearDrawStyle clears the start point if IsFirst is False, sets IsFirst to True, and then clears the Checked properties of all the options of the Line Style menu. A typical member of the family of xxxCom_Click procedures that set the DrawStyle properties is shown below:

```
Sub SolidLineCom_Click ()
   ClearDrawStyle
   SolidLineCom.Checked = True
   DrawStyle = SOLID
End Sub
```

The procedure calls ClearDrawStyle, sets the Checked property of the related option, and then assigns the proper value (using a GLOBAL.BAS constant) to the DrawStyle property.

The Line Width menu subsystem procedures   These procedures include Clear-Size and the family of related xxxCom_Click routines. The ClearSize clears the start point if IsFirst is False, sets IsFirst to True, and then clears the Checked properties of all the options of the Line Width menu. A representative member of the category of xxxCom_Click procedures that set the DrawWidth properties is shown below:

```
Sub Size3Com_Click ()
  ClearSize
  Size3Com.Checked = True
  DrawWidth = 3
End Sub
```

The procedure calls ClearSize, sets the Checked property of the related option, and then assigns the proper setting to the DrawStyle property. The Size1Com_Click procedure includes an additional statement that sets the LineStyleCom.Enabled property to True to enable the Line Style menu.

The Color menu subsystem procedures   These procedures include ClearColors and the related xxxCom_Click routines. The ClearColors clears the start point if IsFirst is False, sets IsFirst to True, then clears the Checked properties of all the options of the Color menu. A typical member of the family of xxxCom_ Click procedures that set the QBColorNum variable is shown below:

```
Sub BlackCom_Click ()
  ClearColors
  BlackCom.Checked = True
  QBColorNum = 0
End Sub
```

The procedure calls ClearColors, sets the Checked property of the related option, and then assigns the proper value to the QBColorNum variable.

The Fill Style menu subsystem procedures   include ClearFillStyle and the family of related xxxCom_Click routines. The ClearFillStyle clears the start point if IsFirst is False, sets IsFirst to True, and then clears the Checked properties of all the options of the Color menu. A representative member of the group of xxxCom_Click procedures that sets the FillStyle property is shown below:

```
Sub SolidCom_Click ()
  ClearFillStyle
  SolidCom.Checked = True
  FillStyle = SOLID
End Sub
```

The procedure calls ClearFillStyle, sets the Checked property of the related option, and then assigns the proper value to the FillStyle property using a GLOBAL.BAS constant.

The Shape menu subsystem procedures   These include ClearShapes and the group of related xxxCom_Click routines. ClearShapes clears the start point if IsFirst is False, sets IsFirst to True, sets the DrawWidth property to 1, and clears the Checked properties of all the options of the Shape menu. The Clear

Shapes procedure also sets the Enabled properties of the Line Width and Line Style menus to False to disable these menu selections. A representative member of the group of xxxCom_Click procedures is shown below:

```
Sub CircleCom_Click ()
  ClearShapes
  CircleCom.Checked = True
End Sub
```

The procedure calls ClearShapes and then sets the Checked property of the related option. The following procedures include some extra statements:

The PointCom_Click procedure. assigns 3 to the DrawWidth property to make the points drawn more visible.

The LineCom_Click procedure. enables the Line Style and Line Width menus by assigning True to their *Enabled* properties.

The EraserCom_Click *procedure.* enables the Line Width menu by assigning True to the LineWidthCom.Enabled property.

The Form subsystem procedures   These are Form_MouseDown, Form_Mouse Move, and Form_MouseUp. In the next chapter I will discuss the mouse-related events in more detail. I am including such event handlers in this chapter because they are vital to the program.

The Form_MouseDown procedure is invoked every time you press a mouse button while pointing to the form. The parameters X and Y represent the coordinates of the mouse when the MouseDown event occurs. The procedure uses an If-Then-Elself statement to draw the proper shape. The various Then clauses perform the following:

- The statements in the first Then clause are executed when the Checked property of the eraser is True. The statements assign True to the variable MouseIsDown, and set the MousePointer property to 4 (the icon).
- The statements in the second Then clause are executed when the Checked property of the text is True. The statements assign True to the variable IsFirst, and the mouse coordinates to the CurrentX and CurrentY properties; prompt you for text; and print your input to the current cursor coordinates.
- The statements in the third Then clause are executed when the Checked property of the point is True. The statements assign True to the variable IsFirst and plot a point at the current mouse coordinates.
- The statements in the remaining Then clauses draw their shapes using a somewhat common set of statements. Each Then clause contains an If statement that examines the variable IsFirst. If that variable is True, the parameters X and Y are stored in the variables X1 and Y1. In addition, a dot is plotted at the current mouse location. On the other hand, if the IsFirst variable is False, the Else clause

is executed to draw the intended shape. The value of the IsFirst variable is toggled right after the End If clause.

The Form_MouseMove procedure performs two simple tasks. First, it updates the text box with the current mouse coordinates. Then, the procedure erases the pixel(s) at the current mouse location if the MouseIs Down variable and the TextCom.Checked property are both True. The pixels are erased by using the PSet method and the background color. The Draw-Width property determines the width of the eraser.

The Form_MouseUp procedure performs two assignments. It assigns False to the MouseIsDown variable, and assigns 2 to the MousePointer property. The first assignment causes the eraser to stop erasing when you move the mouse. The second assignment changes the cursor shape back to the cross hair.

In addition to the procedures of the program's subsystems, there are the procedures attached to the Screen menu selections. These procedures are ClearCom_Click, which clears the screen; SaveAsCom_Click, which saves the form in a .BMP file; and LoadCom_Click, which loads a .BMP file into the form. The last two procedures are similar in that they use input dialog boxes to prompt you for the .BMP file name. Both routines use the BMPfile variable to store the updated .BMP filename. In addition, the two procedures use a similar error-handling mechanism. It is worth pointing out that the error handler of LoadCom_Click also traps errors generated when the supplied file does not contain the expected bitmapped data.

Working with icons

Working with icons in Visual Basic is as easy as spelling the word "icon." The Picture property of a picture box is linked to an icon. Visual Basic provides you with a rich number of icons. These icons are stored in .ICO files and grouped in subdirectories attached to the \VB\ICONS directory. Appendix B of the *Microsoft Visual Basic Programmer's Guide* lists these icons.

Icons can be loaded from .ICO files, .BMP bitmap files, or .WMF Windows metafiles. An icon is loaded into a picture box either at design time or at run time. When you load an icon at design time, you can then compile the program into an .EXE file without worrying about the .ICO file loaded into the picture box. Visual Basic takes care of that for you — the .ICO file is integrated in the .EXE. There are no problems associated with missing .ICO files. By contrast, loading icons at run time means that the .ICO files must be supplied and located where the program expects them to be. The .EXE files for programs that load .ICO files at run time are smaller than their counterparts that have the icons loaded at design time.

Loading an icon at design time is an easy process that requires the following steps:

1. Select the target picture box.
2. Select the Picture property from the Properties combo box.
3. Click the Three-dot button located to the right of the Settings combo box. Visual Basic responds with a file selection dialog box.
4. Select the proper .ICO file.

Loading an icon at run time is also an easy process which requires you to use the LoadPicture function. The general syntax for this function is:

*[form.][pictureBox.]*Picture = LoadPicture(*[stringExpression$]*)

The LoadPicture function loads a picture in a picture box or a form. The stringExpression$ specifies the name of the .ICO file, the .BMP bitmap file, or the .WMF Windows metafile. The stringExpression$ must also contain the full directory path of the target file. If stringExpression$ is omitted, the icon is removed from the recipient picture box.

☞ Loading icons from disk involves disk accesses. If the disk access is too slow for your liking, there is a solution. It is based on the ability to assign the Picture setting of one object to another. The general syntax for assigning graphics is:

*[object1.]*Picture = *[object2.]*Picture

Using this technique you can draw special "buffer" picture boxes in your forms.

You can make these buffer picture boxes invisible at run time by setting their Visible properties to False at design time. Also at design time, you can load the extra icons into these buffer picture boxes.

When the application runs, it copies icons from the invisible picture boxes to the visible ones. You can also have the program swap icons between the two kinds of picture boxes.

The counterpart of the LoadPicture function is SavePicture, which allows you to save the contents of the Picture property of a form or a picture box into a .BMP file. The general syntax for the SavePicture is:

SavePicture *[form.][pictureBox.]*{Picture ¦ Image}, *stringExpression$*

The first parameter for SavePicture is either a Picture or an Image property of a form or a picture box. The stringExpression$ parameter specifies the .BMP filename, including the full path name.

✍ Programming Tip: Using the SavePicture statement with the Load-Picture function enables you to use .BMP files to save and restore the graphics and Print statement output when the AutoRedraw property is set to False. While this method may be a bit slower due to disk access, it is very easy to program. Moreover, this method enables you to save and restore complex graphics drawings without keeping track of their count, size, shape, color, and other attributes.

Using the SavePicture and LoadPicture enables you to take snapshots of the form for later playback.

Icon-based text file viewer

In this section I present a version of the text file viewer that is based on the FVIEW1.FRM form. This new version, stored in FVIEW4.FRM, replaces command buttons with picture boxes that contain icons. Some of the icons are changed when you click on their picture boxes to indicate their update state. These changing icons are:

- The previous Toggle Read command button is replaced with a picture box containing an open-book icon, BOOK01B. When you click on that picture box, the icon is replaced with the closed-book icon, BOOK01A.
- The previous Show/Hide OS command button is replaced with a picture box containing the icon KEY03 (a key with a question mark). When you click on that picture box, the icon is replaced with the icon KEY02 (the key without a question mark).
- The previous Find command button is replaced with a picture box containing the CRDFLE11 icon (a hand searching a Rolodex file). If the text search finds a match, the icon becomes CRDFLE12 (a hand picking a document out of the Rolodex file).

The differences between this version and the first one are mainly visual. The operations of both versions are identical.

Figures 12-10 to 12-12 show the new specifications for the FVIEW4.MAK project file and the FVIEW4.FRM form file. Figure 12-13 contains a sample session with the FVIEW4 program.

Applicataion name: Text File Viewer
Application code name: FVIEW4
Version: 1.0   Date created: July 10, 1991
Programmer(s): Namir Clement Shammas
List of filenames
Storage path: C:\VB\EASYVB
Project FVIEW4.MAK
Global GLOBAL.BAS
Form 1 FVIEW4.FRM

12-10 General project specifications for the FVIEW4 project.

Form #1   Form filename: FVIEW4.FRM
Version: 1.0   Date: July 10, 1991

Control object type	Default CtlName	Purpose
Picture Box	Picture1	Reads the file specified in Text1
	Picture2	Finds the file specified in Text1
	Picture3	Toggles the Enabled setting of Picture1
	Picture4	Finds the text in Text2
	Picture5	Executes a DOS command/program
	Picture6	Executes a Windows application
	Picture7	Hides Picture5, Picture6, Text3, and Label3
	Picture 8	Exits the application
Text Box	Text1	Contains the filename to read
	Text2	Contains the text search string
	Text3	Contains the DOS/Windows command line
	Text4	Displays the text lines of a file
Label	Label1	Label of Text1
	Label2	Label of Text2
	Label3	Label of Text3

12-11 List of control objects for the FVIEW4 project.

Application (code) name: FVIEW4
Form #1
Version: 1.0   Date: June 27, 1991

Original control name	Property	New setting
Form	Caption	File Viewer
Picture1	CtlName	ReadPct
	Picture	\VB\ICONS\OFFICE\FILES04.ICO
Picture2	CtlName	FindFilePct
	Picture	\VB\ICONS\OFFICE\FOLDER05.ICO
Picture3	CtlName	TogglePct
	Picture	\VB\ICONS\WRITING\BOOK01B.ICO
Picture4	CtlName	FindPct
	Picture	\VB\ICONS\OFFICE\CRDFLE11.ICO

12-12 The modified control settings for the FVIEW4 project.

Picture5	CtlName	DosPct
	Picture	\VB\ICONS\COMPUTER\DRIVE01.ICO
Picture6	CtlName	WinPct
	Picture	\VB\ICONS\COMPUTER\MAC03.ICO
Picture7	CtlName	ShowOSPct
	Picture	\VB\ICONS\COMPUTER\KEY03.ICO
Picture8	CtlName	QuitPct
	Picture	\VB\ICONS\COMM\NET11.ICO
Text1	CtlName	FilenameBox
	Text	(empty string)
Text2	CtlName	FindBox
	Text	(empty string)
Text3	CtlName	DosBox
	Text	(empty string)
Text4	CtlName	TextBox
	Text	(empty string)
	MultiLine	True
	ScrollBars	3 - both
Label1	CtlName	FilenameLbl
	Caption	Filename Input
Label2	CtlName	FindLbl
	Caption	Find Input
Label3	CtlName	DosLbl
	Caption	DOS/Win Input

12-12 Continued

Listing 12-3 shows the code attached to the FVIEW4.FRM form and its controls. The code resembles that of the previous version with the following difference: the LoadPicture function loads the icons to display different icons. The following procedures use the LoadPicture function:

The FindPct_Click **procedure** uses the LoadPicture function in the If statement shown:

```
If CurIndex > 0 Then
    ' Yes! Display the matching text as selected text
    . . .
    FindPct.Picture = LoadPicture("\vb\icons\office\crdfle12.ico")
```

```
Else
    ' No! Clear any selected text
    . . .
    FindPct.Picture = LoadPicture("\vb\icons\office\crdfle11.ico")
End If
```

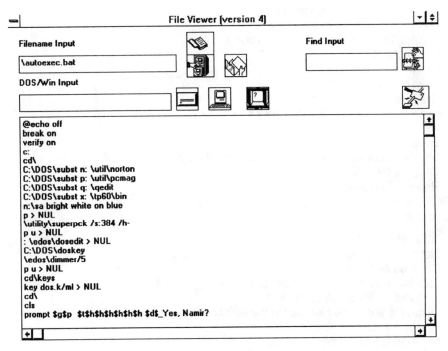

12-13   A sample session with the FVIEW4 program.

Listing 12-3   The code attached to the form and controls of FVIEW4.FRM.

```
Sub QuitBtn_Click ( )
    End
End Sub

Sub ReadPct_Click ( )
    Dim F As String
    Dim L As String
    Dim NL As String * 2
    ' obtain filename from the filename text box
    F = FilenameBox.Text
    ' if filename is an empty string, exit
    If F = " " Then Exit Sub
    NL = Chr$(13) + Chr$(10)
    ' set error-handler
    On Error GoTo BadFile
    ' open the file
    Open F For Input As 1
```

Listing 12-3 Continued.

```
    F = " " ' clear variable to reuse it
    ' loop to read the text lines from the ASCII file
    Do While Not EOF(1)
      Line Input #1, L
      F = F + L + NL ' append a new line
    Loop
    TextBox.Text = F ' copy F into text box
    ' close the file
    Close #1
    ' exit procedure
    Exit Sub
' ********** Error-handler **********
BadFile:
    Beep
    MsgBox "Cannot open file " + F, 0, "File I/O Error"
    On Error GoTo 0
    Resume EndOfSub
EndOfSub:
End Sub

Sub FindPct_Click ( )
    Static CurIndex As Long
    Dim Find As String
    ' update the index to the current character
    CurIndex = TextBox.SelStart + 1
    ' store the text of the Find box in the variable Find
    Find = FindBox.Text
    ' is variable Find empty?
    If Find = " " Then Exit Sub ' nothing to find
    ' locate the index of the next substring Find in the
    ' text box
    CurIndex = InStr(CurIndex + 1, TextBox.Text, Find)
    ' found a match?
    If CurIndex > 0 Then
      ' Yes! Display the matching text as selected text
      TextBox.SelStart = CurIndex − 1
      TextBox.SelLength = Len(Find)
      TextBox.SetFocus
      FindPct.Picture = LoadPicture(" \ vb \ icons \ office \ crdfle12.ico")
    Else
      ' No! Clear any selected text
      TextBox.SelStart = 0
      TextBox.SelLength = 0
      FindPct.Picture = LoadPicture(" \ vb \ icons \ office \ crdfle11.ico")
    End If
End Sub

Sub FindFilePct_Click ( )
    Dim Dummy As Integer
```

Listing 12-3 Continued.

```
   ' invoke the DOS dir command with the /s
   ' subdirectory option and the /p paginated
   ' output option
   Dummy = Shell("dosbat.bat dir " + FilenameBox.Text + " /s/p", 1)
End Sub

Sub DosPct_Click ( )
   Dim Dummy As Integer
   ' invoke the DOSBAT batch file
   Dummy = Shell("dosbat.bat " + DosBox.Text, 1)
End Sub

Sub WinPct_Click ( )
   Dim Dummy As Integer
   ' invoke a Windows application
   Dummy = Shell(DosBox.Text, 1)
End Sub

Sub QuitPct_Click ( )
   End
End Sub

Sub TogglePct_Click ( )
   ReadPct.Visible = Not ReadPct.Visible
   If ReadPct.Visible Then
      TogglePct.Picture = LoadPicture(" \ vb \ icons \ writing \ book01b.ico")
   Else
      TogglePct.Picture = LoadPicture(" \ vb \ icons \ writing \ book01a.ico")
   End If
End Sub

Sub Form_Load ( )
   WindowState = 2
End Sub

Sub ShowOSPct_Click ( )
   ' toggle the Visible property of the DosBox text box,
   ' the DosBtn button, the WinBtn button, and the DosLbl
   ' label
   DosBox.Visible = Not DosBox.Visible
   DosPct.Visible = Not DosPct.Visible
   WinPct.Visible = Not WinPct.Visible
   DosLbl.Visible = Not DosLbl.Visible
   If DosPct.Visible Then
      ShowOSPct.Picture = LoadPicture(" \ vb \ icons \ computer \ key03.ico")
   Else
      ShowOSPct.Picture = LoadPicture(" \ vb \ icons \ computer \ key02.ico")
   End If
End Sub
```

If a match is found, the value of CurIndex is positive and the CRDFLE12 icon is loaded. Otherwise, the CRDFLE11 icon is loaded to indicate that the last text search found no match.

The TogglePct_Click **procedure,** which toggles the read file picture box, uses the LoadPicture function in the following If statement:

```
If ReadPct.Visible Then
    TogglePct.Picture = LoadPicture("\vb\icons\writing\book01b.ico")
Else
    TogglePct.Picture = LoadPicture("\vb\icons\writing\book01a.ico")
End If
```

The BOOK01B icon is loaded if the Visible property of the ReadPct picture box is True; otherwise, the BOOK01A icon is loaded.

The ShowOSPct_Click **procedure** uses the LoadPicture function in this If statement:

```
If DosPct.Visible Then
    ShowOSPct.Picture = LoadPicture("\vb\icons\computer\key03.ico")
Else
    ShowOSPct.Picture = LoadPicture("\vb\icons\computer\key02.ico")
End If
```

The KEY03 icon is loaded if the Visible property of DosPct picture box is True; otherwise, the KEY02 icon is loaded.

13
Managing mouse events

The Click event is perhaps the most frequently used mouse-related event. However, it is by no means the only one. This chapter looks at the other mouse events and how you can use them in your Visual Basic applications. You will learn about the following topics:

- The events that reflect the mouse status.
- Using the Shift, Ctrl, and Alt keys with mouse events.
- Dragging and dropping controls.

The mouse events

Visual Basic offers the following mouse events that are related to the mouse status:

The MouseDown **event**   This event occurs when you press on any mouse button. A typical event-handling procedure for the MouseDown event is shown here:

```
object_MouseDown(Button As Integer, Shift As Integer, X As Single,
    Y As Single)
```

The Button parameter is bit-oriented. The three least-significant bits give the status of the mouse button. The other bits of the integer-typed parameter are not used. Table 13-1 shows the arguments for the Button parameter. Keep in mind that the convention for numbering the bits of an integer calls the least significant bit bit number 0 and the most significant bit bit number 7.

The Shift parameter indicates whether or not the Shift, Ctrl, and Alt

Table 13-1   The arguments for the Button parameter.

Bit number	Value when on	Meaning
(none)	0	No button is pressed
0	1	The left button generated the MouseDown event
1	2	The right button generated the MouseDown event
0 and 1	3	The left and right buttons generated the MouseDown event
2	4	The middle button generated the MouseDown event
0, 1, and 2	7	All three buttons generated the MouseDown event

Table 13-2   The arguments for the Shift parameter.

Bit number	Value when on	Meaning
(none)	0	No key was pressed
0	1	The Shift key is pressed
1	2	The Ctrl key is pressed
2	4	The Alt key is pressed
0 and 1	3	The Shift and Ctrl keys are pressed
0 and 2	5	The Shift and Alt keys are pressed
1 and 2	6	The Ctrl and Alt keys are pressed
0, 1, and 2	7	All three keys are pressed

keys were held down when the MouseDown event occurred. Table 13-2 shows the arguments for the Shift parameter.

The X and Y parameters report the coordinates of the mouse when the MouseDown event occurs.

The MouseUp **event**   When you release on any mouse button, this event occurs. A typical event-handling procedure for the MouseUp event is shown here:

```
object_MouseUp(Button As Integer, Shift As Integer, X As Single, Y As Single)
```

The parameters of the MouseUp events are identical to those of the Mouse-Down event.

The MouseMove **event**   This event occurs when you move the mouse. Here is a typical event-handling procedure for the MouseMove event:

*object*_MouseMove (Button As Integer, Shift As Integer, X As Single,Y As Single)

The parameters of the MouseMove events are identical to those of the MouseDown event.

The line-drawing program

Let's look at some examples which explore the mouse events that I presented in this section. The first example explores the MouseDown, MouseUp, and MouseMove events, making use of only the parameters X and Y. The program uses these events to draw black solid lines using the "rubber band" visual effect. This effect enables you to see the constantly-updated line being drawn as you drag the mouse on the form. The next program, MOUSEV1, draws lines differently from the SHAPES program that I presented in the last chapter. The MOUSEV1 requires you to press down a mouse button to start drawing a line. The line is drawn as you drag the mouse. When you release the mouse button, the new line is defined. While you drag the mouse, the line connecting the start point and the current point is constantly redrawn. I will explain how to implement this effect later in this section.

Figures 13-1 to 13-4 show the specifications for the MOUSEV1.MAK project file and the MOUSEV1.FRM form. The program's form contains one control, namely, a text box that displays the current mouse coordinates. Figure 13-5 shows a sample session with the MOUSEV1 program.

Application name: Line-Drawing Demo
Application code name: MOUSEV1
Version: 1.0   Date created: July 16, 1991
Programmer(s): Namir Clement Shammas
List of filenames
Storage path: \VB\EASYVB
Project SHAPES.MAK
Global GLOBAL.BAS
Form 1 MOUSEV1.FRM

13-1   The basic specifications for the MOUSEV1.MAK project file.

Form #1   Form filename: MOUSEV1.FRM
Version: 1.0   Date: July 10, 1991

Control object type   **Default CtlName**   **Purpose**
Text Box   Text1   Displays the current coordinates of
                                                         the mouse

13-2   List of control objects for the MOUSEV1.FRM form.

Listing 13-1 (starting on p. 263) shows the code attached to the MOUSEV1.FRM form. The general declarations section contains the declarations of two constants and a number of arrays and variables.

Application (code) name: MOUSEV1
Form #1
Version: 1.0   Date: July 10, 1991

Original control name	Property	New setting
Form	Caption	Mouse Events (part 1)
Text1	CtlName	MouseCoordBox
	Text	(empty string)

13-3 The updated settings of MOUSEV1.FRM form.

Form #1   Form filename: MOUSEV1.FRM
Version: 1.0   Date: July 16, 1991

Caption	Property	Setting	Purpose
&Quit	CtlName	QuitCom	Exits application
&Clear	CtlName	ClearCom	Clear line(s) menu
Last Line	CtlName	LastLineCm	Clears the last line drawn
	Accelerator	CTRL+L	
	indented	once	
Screen	CtlName	ScreenCom	Clears the form
	Accelerator	CTRL+S	
	indented	once	

13-4 The controls and structure for the menu of form MOUSEV1.FRM.

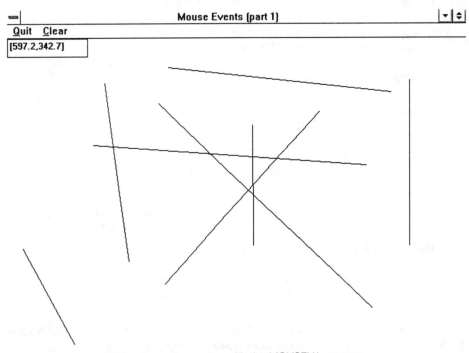

13-5 A sample session with the MOUSEV1 program.

Listing 13-1 The code attached to the MOUSEV1.FRM form.

```
Const MAX_LINES = 100
Const Frmt = "##0.0'"
Dim FirstX As Single, FirstY As Single
Dim LastX As Single, LastY As Single
Dim X1(1 To MAX_LINES) As Single
Dim X2(1 To MAX_LINES) As Single
Dim Y1(1 To MAX_LINES) As Single
Dim Y2(1 To MAX_LINES) As Single
Dim N As Integer ' number of lines
Dim Xstr As String, Ystr As String
Dim MouseIsDown As Integer ' Boolean

Sub QuitCom_Click ( )
  End
End Sub

Sub ScreenCom_Click ( )
  Cls
  N = 0
End Sub

Sub LastLineCom_Click ( )
  Dim I As Integer
  If N > 0 Then
    ' erase the last line
    Line (X1(N), Y1(N)) – (X2(N), Y2(N)), BackColor
    N = N – 1 ' decrease the number of lines
    ' redraw the other lines
    For I = 1 To N
      Line (X1(I), Y1(I)) – (X2(I), Y2(I))
    Next End If
  End Sub

Sub Form_Load ( )
  N = 0
  IsFirst = True
  WindowState = 2
  MousePointer = 2
  BackColor = WHITE
  ForeColor = BLACK
  Scale (0, 0) – (1000, 1000)
End Sub

Sub Form_MouseDown (Button As Integer, Shift As Integer, X As Single, Y As Single)
  If N = MAX_LINES Then Exit Sub
  MouseIsDown = True
  ' store coordinates of start point
  FirstX = X
```

Listing 13-1 Continued.

```
     FirstY = Y
     ' initialize coordinates of end point
     ' with those of the start point
     LastX = X
     LastY = Y
End Sub

Sub Form_MouseUp (Button As Integer, Shift As Integer, X As Single, Y As Single)
     Dim I As Integer
     If N = MAX_LINES Then Exit Sub
     MouseIsDown = False
     ' update lines
     For I = 1 To N
        Line (X1(I), Y1(I)) – (X2(I), Y2(I))
     Next I
     If Not ((LastX = FirstX) And (LastY = FirstY)) Then
        N = N + 1
        X1(N) = FirstX
        Y1(N) = FirstY
        X2(N) = LastX
        Y2(N) = LastY
     End If
End Sub

Sub Form_MouseMove (Button As Integer, Shift As Integer, X As Single, Y As Single)
     Xstr = Format$(X, Frmt)
     Ystr = Format$(Y, Frmt)
     MouseCoordBox.Text = "[" + Xstr + "," + Ystr + "]"
     If MouseIsDown Then
        Line (LastX, LastY) – (FirstX, FirstY), BackColor
        Line (X, Y) – (FirstX, FirstY), ForeColor
        LastX = X
        LastY = Y
     End If
End Sub
```

The MAX_LINES constant specifies the maximum number of lines you draw. The coordinates of these lines are stored in the array X1, Y1, X2, and Y2. The current number of lines is stored in variable N. The reason for using arrays to store the coordinates of the lines you draw will be explained when I discuss the MouseMove event.

The relevant event-handling procedures are:

The Form_Load **procedure** This procedure initializes the application as follows:

- Initializes the variable N to zero.
- Initializes the variable IsFirst to True.
- Sets the WindowState property to maximize the application window.
- Sets the MousePointer property to 2, causing the mouse cursor to appear as a cross hair.
- Selects a black foreground on white background.
- Defines a custom scale, such that the upper left corner is (0, 0) and the lower right corner is (1000, 1000).

The Form_MouseDown **procedure**   Line drawing is started if N is not equal to MAX_LINES. The procedure performs the following tasks:

- Assigns the constant True to the MouseIsDown variable.
- Assigns the current mouse coordinates to the FirstX and FirstY variables. These variables store the start point of a line.
- Assigns the current mouse coordinates to the LastX and LastY variables. These variables contain the current end point of the line. When you begin to draw a line, the start and end points are the same.

The Form_MouseMove **procedure**   With this procedure the line is drawn and updated. The procedure performs the following tasks:

- Displays the current mouse coordinates in the text box.
- If the MouseIsDown variable is True, the procedure erases the last image of the line being drawn and draws an updated one. Erasing a line is actually performed by drawing the line with the background color as the line color.
- Assigns the current mouse coordinates to the variables LastX and LastY.

When you draw the first line, there is nothing unusual about it. But when you draw the other lines, you will see that, as the line you are drawing is dragged across the previous lines, these lines begin to fade. The reason is the side effect of erasing the current line. To correct this side effect, I use arrays to store the coordinates of the previously drawn lines. Once you finish drawing a new line, the other lines are automatically redrawn to eliminate the side effect.

The Form_MouseUp **procedure**   This finishes drawing the new line and redraws the previous lines. The procedure performs the following tasks:

- Exits if the number of current lines is equal to the maximum lines allowed.
- Sets the MouseIsDown variable to False.
- Redraws the previous lines.

- If the start and end points are not the same (that is you did not simply click the mouse), the procedure updates the arrays X1, Y1, X2, and Y2 with the coordinates of the new line.

The ScreenCom_Click **procedure**   The form is cleared and the number of lines is set to 0 by this procedure.

The LastLineCom_Click **procedure**   This procedure erases the last line you drew. It acts as an "undo" command and performs the following tasks:

- If the number of lines is greater than zero, performs the next steps.
- Erases the last line you drew.
- Decreases the current number of lines.
- Redraws the other lines. This is done in case the last line had erased parts of the remaining lines.

Run the program and experiment with drawing various lines. Drag some of these lines around to cross over the other existing lines to watch the side effect of erasing the current line (in procedure Form_MouseMove). When you release the mouse button the other lines are restored.

The Box-Drawing Program

MOUSEV2, the second program in this section, expands on the techniques shown in program MOUSEV1. The MOUSEV2 program draws either empty or filled boxes. The rubber band visual effect is also implemented. This dictates that coordinates of the previously drawn lines be stored in arrays.

The MOUSEV2 program illustrates the following features:

Using the left and right mouse buttons for different purposes   The left mouse button draws empty boxes, while the right one draws filled boxes.

Using the Ctrl, Shift, and Alt keys with the mouse events.   The Ctrl key enables you to erase the topmost box at the current mouse coordinates. The Alt key allows you to make the topmost box the new last box. Using Alt key does not affect the appearance of the boxes, only the order of storing their coordinates in array X1, Y1, X2, Y2, and FillBox. The Shift key allows you to move the topmost box on the form — the order of box is not changed as a result of relocating a box.

The boxes you draw do not lie on the same level. Instead, each box is placed on a new level in the sequence in which it is created. These levels have nothing to do with the visual appearance of the boxes. For example, you can have two nonoverlapping boxes on a form, and yet each is at a different level. These levels are important in using the Ctrl, Alt, and Shift keys.

Figures 13-6 to 13-9 show the specifications for the MOUSEV2.MAK project file and the MOUSEV2.FRM form. The program's form contains

Application name: Box-Drawing Demo
Application code name: MOUSEV2
Version: 1.0   Date created: July 16, 1991
Programmer(s): Namir Clement Shammas

List of filenames

Storage path: \VB\EASYVB
Project SHAPES.MAK
Global GLOBAL.BAS
Form 1 MOUSEV2.FRM

13-6 The basic specifications for the MOUSEV2.MAK project file.

Form #1   Form filename: MOUSEV2.FRM
Version: 1.0   Date: July 10, 1991

Control object type	Default CtlName	Purpose
Text Box	Text1	Displays the current coordinates of the mouse

13-7 List of control objects for the MOUSEV2.FRM form.

Application (code) name: MOUSEV2
Form #1
Version: 1.0   Date: July 10, 1991

Original control name	Property	New setting
Form	Caption	Mouse Events (part 2)
Text1	CtlName	MouseCoordBox
	Text	(empty string)

13-8 The updated settings of MOUSEV2.FRM form.

Form #1   Form filename: MOUSEV2.FRM
Version: 1.0   Date: July 16, 1991

Caption	Property	Setting	Purpose
&Quit	CtlName	QuitCom	Exits application
&Clear	CtlName	ClearCom	Clear line(s) menu
Last box	CtlName	LastBoxCom	Clears the last line drawn
	Accelerator	CTRL+L	
	indented	once	
Screen	CtlName	ScreenCom	Clears the form
	Accelerator	CTRL+S	
	indented	once	

13-9 The controls and structure for the menu of form MOUSEV2.FRM.

one control, namely, a text box that displays the current mouse coordinates. Figure 13-10 shows a sample session with the MOUSEV2 program.

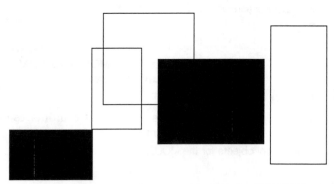

13-10   A sample session with the MOUSEV2 program.

Listing 13-2 (starting on p. XXX) contains the code attached to the MOUSEV2.FRM form. The code contains three groups of statements: the general declaration section, the auxiliary procedures, and the event-handling procedures.

Listing 13-2   The code attached to the MOUSEV2.FRM form.

```
Const MAX_BOXES = 100
Const Frmt = "##0.0"
' declare scalar variables
Dim FirstX As Single, FirstY As Single
Dim LastX As Single, LastY As Single
Dim ShiftX As Single, ShiftY As Single
' declare the arrays of data for the boxes
Dim X1(1 To MAX_BOXES) As Single
Dim X2(1 To MAX_BOXES) As Single
Dim Y1(1 To MAX_BOXES) As Single
Dim Y2(1 To MAX_BOXES) As Single
Dim FillBox(1 To MAX_BOXES) As Integer
Dim N As Integer ' number of lines
Dim DBI As Integer ' DBI is short for DraggedBoxIndex
Dim Xstr As String, Ystr As String
' —————————— Boolean Variables ——————————
Dim MouseIsDown As Integer
Dim PressedSHIFT As Integer
Dim IsFillBox As Integer
```

Listing 13-2 Continued.

```
Sub QuitCom_Click ( )
  End
End Sub

Sub ScreenCom_Click ( )
  Cls
  N = 0
End Sub

Sub Form_Load ( )
  N = 0
  IsFirst = True
  WindowState = 2
  MousePointer = 2
  BackColor = WHITE
  ForeColor = Red
  Scale (0, 0) – (1000, 1000)
End Sub

Sub Form_MouseDown (Button As Integer, Shift As Integer, X As Single, Y As Single)
  ' initialize Boolean flags
  MouseIsDown = False
  PressedSHIFT = False
  If Shift And 1 Then ' SHIFT key pressed ?
    DBI = FindBox(X, Y)
    If DBI > 0 Then
      MouseIsDown = True
      PressedSHIFT = True
    End If
  ElseIf Shift And 2 Then ' CTRL key pressed?
    RemoveBox X, Y
  ElseIf Shift And 4 Then ' ALT key pressed
    AlterBoxOrder X, Y
  Else
    ' attained the maximum number of boxes?
    IF N = MAX_BOXES Then Exit Sub
    MouseIsDown = True
    ' store coordinates of start point
    FirstX = X
    FirstY = Y
    ' initialize coordinates of end point
    ' with those of the start point
    LastX = X
    LastY = Y
    If Button = RIGHT_BUTTON Then
      IsFillBox = True
    Else
      IsFillBox = False
```

Listing 13-2 Continued.

```
      End If
    End If
End Sub

Sub Form_MouseUp (Button As Integer, Shift As Integer, X As Single, Y As Single)
    Dim I As Integer
    If Not MouseIsDown Then Exit Sub
    MouseIsDown = False
    If PressedSHIFT Then ' updated box move
        Cls
        UpdateBoxes
        Exit Sub
    End If
    UpdateBoxes
    ' add a new box?
    If (N < MAX_BOXES) And (LastX < > FirstX) And (LastY < > FirstY) Then
        N = N + 1
        X1(N) = FirstX
        Y1(N) = FirstY
        X2(N) = LastX
        Y2(N) = LastY
        FillBox(N) = IsFillBox
    End If
End Sub

Sub Form_MouseMove (Button As Integer, Shift As Integer, X As Single, Y As Single)
    Xstr = Format$(X, Frmt)
    Ystr = Format$(Y, Frmt)
    MouseCoordBox.Text = "[" + Xstr + "," + Ystr + "]"
    ' dragging a box?
    If MouseIsDown And PressedSHIFT Then
        ' calculate shift in coordinates
        ShiftX = X − (X1(DBI) + X2(DBI)) / 2
        ShiftY = Y − (Y1(DBI) + Y2(DBI)) / 2
        If FillBox(DBI) Then
            Line (X1(DBI), Y1(DBI)) − (X2(DBI), Y2(DBI)), BackColor, BF
            X1(DBI) = X1(DBI) + ShiftX
            Y1(DBI) = Y1(DBI) + ShiftY
            X2(DBI) = X2(DBI) + ShiftX
            Y2(DBI) = Y2(DBI) + ShiftY
            Line (X1(DBI), Y1(DBI)) − (X2(DBI), Y2(DBI)), ForeColor, BF
        Else
            Line (X1(DBI), Y1(DBI)) − (X2(DBI), Y2(DBI)), BackColor, B
            X1(DBI) = X1(DBI) + ShiftX
            Y1(DBI) = Y1(DBI) + ShiftY
            X2(DBI) = X2(DBI) + ShiftX
            Y2(DBI) = Y2(DBI) + ShiftY
            Line (X1(DBI), Y1(DBI)) − (X2(DBI), Y2(DBI)), ForeColor, B
```

Listing 13-2   Continued.

```
        End If
      ' drawing a box?
      ElseIf MouseIsDown Then
        If IsFillBox Then
            Line (LastX, LastY) – (FirstX, FirstY), BackColor, BF
            Line (X, Y) – (FirstX, FirstY), ForeColor, BF
        Else
            Line (LastX, LastY) – (FirstX, FirstY), BackColor, B
            Line (X, Y) – (FirstX, FirstY), ForeColor, B
        End If
        LastX = X
        LastY = Y
      End If
End Sub


Function FindBox (X As Single, Y As Single) As Integer
' find the "topmost" box which contains the coordinates
' (X, Y) the function returns the index of the matching
' box, or 0 if no box is found
    Dim I As Integer
    Dim DiffX As Single, DiffY As Single
    I = N
    Do While I > 0
        DiffX = (X – X1(I)) * (X – X2(I))
        DiffY = (Y – Y1(I)) * (Y – Y2(I))
        ' is (X, Y) between (X1(I),Y1(I)) and (X2(I),Y2(I)) ?
        If (DiffX < = 0) And (DiffY < = 0) Then ' yes? then exit
            Exit Do
        End If
        I = I – 1
    Loop
    FindBox = I ' return the function result
End Function


Sub UpdateBoxes ( )
    Dim I As Integer
    For I = 1 To N
        If FillBox(I) Then
            Line (X1(I), Y1(I)) – (X2(I), Y2(I)), , BF
        Else
            Line (X1(I), Y1(I)) – (X2(I), Y2(I)), , B
        End If
    Next I
End Sub


Sub RemoveBox (X As Single, Y As Single)
' remove the topmost box at the (X, Y) coordinates.
    Dim M As Integer, I As Integer, J As Integer
```

Listing 13-2 Continued.

```
      M = FindBox(X, Y) ' find matching box
      If M > 0 Then ' found one?
        If M < N Then ' not the last box?
          ' erase the box
          Line (X1(M), Y1(M)) – (X2(M), Y2(M)), BackColor, BF
          ' shift the data for the other boxes
          For I = M To N – 1
            J = I + 1
            X1(I) = X1(J)
            Y1(I) = Y1(J)
            X2(I) = X2(J)
            Y2(I) = Y2(J)
            FillBox(I) = FillBox(J)
          Next I
          N = N – 1
          UpdateBoxes
        Else
          LastLineCom_Click ' delete the last box
        End If
      End If
    End Sub

    Sub AlterBoxOrder (X As Single, Y As Single)
    ' make the topmost box at the (X, Y) location the
    ' topmost box in the set of boxes
      Dim I As Integer, J As Integer, M As Integer
      Dim XX1 As Single, YY1 As Single
      Dim XX2 As Single, YY2 As Single
      Dim TheFillBox As Integer
      M = FindBox(X, Y) ' find the box
      ' if found a box that is not already the topmost
      If (M > 0) And (M < N) Then
        ' store data of selected box
        XX1 = X1(M)
        YY1 = Y1(M)
        XX2 = X2(M)
        YY2 = Y2(M)
        TheFillBox = FillBox(M)
        ' shift the data for the other boxes
        For I = M To N – 1
          J = I + 1
          X1(I) = X1(J)
          Y1(I) = Y1(J)
          X2(I) = X2(J)
          Y2(I) = Y2(J)
          FillBox(I) = FillBox(J)
        Next I
        ' update the data of the topmost box
```

Listing 13-2 Continued.

```
    X1(N) = XX1
    Y1(N) = YY1
    X2(N) = XX2
    Y2(N) = YY2
    FillBox(N) = TheFileBox
  End If
End Sub

Sub LastBoxCom_Click ( )
' delete the topmost box
  Dim I As Integer
  If N > 0 Then
    Line (X1(N), Y1(N)) – (X2(N), Y2(N)), BackColor, BF
    N = N – 1
    UpdateBoxes
  End If
End Sub
```

The general declarations section contains the declarations for the following kinds of identifiers:

The constants MAX_BOXES **and** Frmt   The MAX_BOXES constant specifies the maximum number of boxes that you can draw. The Frmt constant is used to display the current mouse coordinates in the text box.

The scalar variables   These variables store the various coordinates. The FirstX and FirstY variables store the start point of a box, while the LastX and LastY variables hold the end point of a box. The ShiftX and ShiftY variables store the data used in moving a box.

The family of arrays X1, Y1, X2, Y2, **and** FillBox   The first four arrays store the coordinates of the boxes. The FillBox is an array of Boolean values that indicate whether a box is empty or filled.

The Boolean variables MouseIsDown, PressedSHIFT, **and** IsFillBox.   These variables flag the state of various aspects of drawing and the state of the Shift key.

The miscellaneous variables   These include N (the number of boxes), DBI (the dragged box index), Xstr (the string image of the X mouse coordinate), and Ystr (the string image of the Y mouse coordinate).

The family of auxiliary procedures includes the following:

The UpdateBoxes() **procedure**   The boxes are redrawn by this procedure. The data in the FillBox array determines whether to draw an empty box or a filled one.

The FindBox(X As Single, Y As Single) **function**   FindBox locates the topmost box at the given (X, Y) coordinates and returns the index of that box. If there is no box at the specified coordinates, the function returns a 0. The function examines the boxes starting with the topmost boxes. To detect if a box contains the (X, Y) coordinates, the function performs the following:

- Calculates the product of the differences between X and X1(I), and between X and X2(I). The result is assigned to the local variable DiffX.
- Calculates the product of the differences between Y and Y1(I), and between Y and Y2(I). The result is assigned to the local variable DiffY.
- The point (X, Y) lies inside a box if the values for both DiffX and DiffY are either negative or zero.

The RemoveBox(X As Single, Y As Single) **procedure** This removes the topmost box located at the (X, Y) coordinates. The procedure performs the following tasks:

- Locates the topmost box by invoking the FindBox function. The function result is assigned to the local variable M.
- If the value of M is positive, the target box has been located. If that box is not the topmost box, the RemoveBox procedure erases it; shifts the values of the X1, Y1, X2, Y2, and FillBox arrays; decreases the number of boxes; and then redraws the remaining boxes by calling the UpdateBoxes procedure. If the target box is the topmost box, the procedure calls the LastBoxCom_Click procedure to remove that box and redraw the other boxes.

The AlterBox(X As Single, Y As Single) This procedure alters the level of the topmost box located at the (X, Y) coordinates. The procedure performs the following tasks:

- Locates the topmost box by invoking the FindBox function. The function result is assigned to the local variable M.
- If the value of variable M is greater than zero (that is, function FindBox found a box) and is less than N (that is, the matching box is not already the topmost box) then continues with the next tasks.
- Stores the data of the selected box in local variables.
- Shifts the data stored in the arrays X1, Y1, X2, Y2, and FillBox.
- Assigns the data of the temporary variables to the N'th members of the arrays X1, Y1, X2, Y2, and FillBox.

The group of relevant event-handling procedures consists of the following:

The Form_Load **procedure** The procedure is identical to the Form_Load procedure of program MOUSEV1.

The Form_MouseDown **procedure** This manages the various options associated with the MouseDown event. These options include drawing, altering the order of, deleting, or moving a box. The procedure performs the following tasks:

- Assigns False to the Boolean variables MouseIsDown and PressedSHIFT.
- Tests if the Shift argument has its least significant bit (that is, bit number 0) on by Anding the argument with 1 (the on value of bit 0). If the test is positive, the procedure invokes function FindBox to locate the box to move. The function result is assigned to the variable DBI. If the value of DBI is greater than zero, a box is found, and both of the variables MouseIsDown and PressedSHIFT are assigned the True constant.
- Tests if the Shift argument has bit number 1 on by Anding the argument with 2 (the on value of bit 1). If the test is positive, the procedure invokes RemoveBox with the arguments X and Y.
- Tests if the Shift argument has bit number 2 on by Anding the argument with 4 (the on value of bit 2). If the test is positive, the procedure invokes AlterBoxOrder with the arguments X and Y.

When all of the above tests fail, the procedure executes the statements of the Else clause. These statements set the MouseIsDown variable to True, store the coordinates of the start point in variable FirstX and FirstY, save the initial value of the end point coordinates in variables LastX and LastY, and test if the value of the Button argument is the constant RIGHT_BUTTON. If the test is true, the IsFillBox variable is assigned True; otherwise, the variable is assigned False.

☞ The tests that examine the value of the Shift argument use the logical And operator. This operator can be replaced by the logical = comparative operator. What is the difference in program operations? When you run the program in its current form, you can move a box by pressing the Shift key and dragging the mouse — the Ctrl and/or Alt keys can be pressed without influencing the effect of the first If statement. The reason is that the And operator is able to detect if a specific bit (or set of bits) is on, regardless of the state of other bits in the variable Shift. By contrast, the = operator tests whether or not all of the bits of the Shift argument make up a tested number. This test is more rigid and causes the Alt and/or Ctrl keys to interfere in the first If statement (when the And operator is replaced with the = operator). Keep in mind the sequence of the tested conditions in Listing 13-2 that involve the Shift argument. If you hold down the Ctrl and Alt keys and press the mouse button, the condition of the first If statement is false, because bit 0 of the Shift argument is off. The second If statement is true, since bit 1 of Shift is on. Changing the sequence of the tested conditions changes the program's response to pressing the Shift, Alt, and Ctrl keys. By contrast, if you replace the And with an = operator, the sequence of testing the Shift value has no effect on the program's behavior.

The Form_MouseMove **procedure** This procedure manages the drawing or moving of boxes. The procedure carries out the following tasks:

- Updates the current mouse coordinates displayed in the text box.
- Tests if the MouseIsDown and PressedSHIFT variables are both True. If the above condition is true, the procedure executes statements that move a box selected by the DBI index. The shift is X and Y coordinates are calculated and stored in the ShiftX and ShiftY variables. The current box is erased and its corner coordinates X1(DBI), Y1(DBI) and (X2(DBI), Y2(DBI) are recalculated using the ShiftX and ShiftY variables. The new box is then redrawn. The Boolean value of FillBox(DBI) element determines whether the box is empty or filled.
- Tests if the MouseIsDown variable is True. If so, the procedure executes statements that erase the last instance of a new box, and redraw the other instances. The IsFillBox variable determines whether the box is empty or filled.

The Form_MouseUp **procedure** Form_MouseUp finalizes drawing or moving a box. The procedure performs the following tasks:

- Exits if the MouseIsDown is false. This condition is induced by the MouseDown procedure when the number of current boxes has reached the maximum limit.
- Sets the MouseIsDown variable to False. This means that subsequent MouseMove events neither draw nor move a box before another MouseDown event occurs.
- Tests if the variable PressedSHIFT is true. Accordingly, the procedure clears the form, redraws the boxes using the UpdateBoxes procedure, and then exits.
- Redraws the boxes by invoking the UpdateBoxes procedure.
- If there is room for storing more boxes and the start point is not the same as the end point, the procedure updates the variable N and arrays X1, Y1, X2, Y2, and FillBox.

The LastBoxCom_Click **procedure** The topmost box is erased and the remaining boxes are redrawn by this procedure.

Dragging and dropping controls

One of the features of graphical user interface (GUI) environments is the ability to drag icons and other controls. In Visual Basic you can drag a control over on a form or on other controls. The dragging ends when you release the mouse button and effectively drop the control on another control or on the form. Visual Basic calls the control being dragged the *source*. In addition, the control or the form over which a source control is dropped is called the *target*.

Visual Basic offers the following two properties that are related to dragging controls:

The DragMode **property** DragMode sets the manual or automatic mode for a drag-and-drop operation. This property is available for a wide variety of controls. The general syntax for the DragMode property is:

[*form.*]*control*.DragMode [=mode%]

The DragMode property can be set at design time or at run time. The property can accept one of two values, 0 or 1. Assigning 0 to the DragMode property sets the manual drag mode. This is the default property setting. A control with a DragMode of setting 0 can be dragged by using the Drag method. Assigning 1 to the DragMode property sets the automatic mode. In this mode, the control is dragged when you click the mouse over it.

When the DragMode is set to 1, the control does not respond to the mouse events in the usual way, that is, the control does not recognize the KeyDown, KeyUp, KeyPress, MouseDown, MouseMove, or MouseUp events. What good is that control you may ask? The control can respond to events triggered by the code or by a DDE link, which will be covered in a later chapter.

The DragIcon **property** This property sets or determines the icon displayed as the pointer in a drag-and-drop process. This property can be set and queried during run time, but only set at design time. The general syntax for the DragIcon property is:

[*form.*]*control*.DragIcon [=*icon*]

The drag icon can be either loaded using the LoadPicture function or assigned from another icon loaded either at design time or earlier at run time. The drag icon enhances the visual appearance of the drag-and-drop operation.

Visual Basic offers the Drag method to manage when the dragging of a control starts and stops, and when it is cancelled. Using the Drag command offers better control than manipulating the DragMode property. The general syntax for the Drag method is:

[*control.*]Drag [action%]

The values of action% range from 0 to 2. When action% is 0, the drag operation is canceled. When action% is 1, dragging a control begins. Dragging stops when action% is 2 and the control is dropped (causing a DragDrop event to occur).

Visual Basic offers the following two events that are related to the drag-and-drop operations:

The DragOver event occurs when the control is being dragged over a target (either a form or another control). The general syntax for the DragOver event-handling procedure has two forms:

Sub Form_DragOver(*Source* As Control, *X* As Single, *Y* As Single, *State* As Integer)
Sub *control*_DragOver([*Index* As Integer,] *Source* As Control, *X* As Single, *Y* As Single, *State* As Integer)

The Source parameter represents the control being dragged over the target (a form or the control to which the event-handler is attached). Using the Source argument, you can alter the properties of the dragged control. For example, you can make it invisible by setting its Visible property to False. The X and Y parameters specify the current mouse coordinates. The values of these coordinates are based on the target's coordinate system, as defined by the ScaleHeight, ScaleWidth, ScaleLeft, and ScaleTop properties.

The State parameter offers important information regarding the transition of the source over the target. A value of 0 (represented by the ENTER global constants in GLOBAL.BAS) indicates that the source control is dragged within range of the target. A value of 1 (represented by the LEAVE global constant) indicates that the source control is dragged out of range of the target. A value of 2 (represented by the OVER global constant) signals that the source has moved within the target.

The Index parameter is relevant to a source control that is a member of a control array. The Index parameter enables you to select the proper source control.

The DragDrop event occurs when the source control is dropped over a target either by releasing the mouse button or by a Drag 2 statement. The general syntax for the DragDrop event-handling procedure has two forms:

```
Sub Form_DragDrop(Source As Control, X As Single, Y As Single, State As Integer)
Sub control_DragDrop([Index As Integer,] Source As Control, X As Single, Y As Single, State As Integer)
```

The Source parameter represents the control being dragged over the target (a form or the control to which the event-handler is attached).

The X and Y parameters specify the current mouse coordinates. The values of these coordinates are based on the target's coordinate system, as defined by the ScaleHeight, ScaleWidth, ScaleLeft, and ScaleTop properties.

The Index parameter is relevant to a source control that is a member of a control array. The Index parameter enables you to select the proper source control.

☞ The source controls are moved using the Move method. These methods are usually placed in a DragDrop event handler (typically, the Form_DragDrop procedure). Otherwise, the source controls remain where they were when you started dragging them.

Let's look at a program that illustrates a simple dragging of controls. The next program, MOUSEV3, illustrates how to drag a command button and a text button and then drop them in a trash-box picture box. The program, shown in FIG. 13-11, contains three controlling command buttons. The button labeled Quit exits the application. The button labeled Drag "Button" triggers the dragging of a button marked "Button." The button labeled Drag "Text" triggers the dragging of the text box containing "Text." At the lower right corner is a picture box that displays trash can icons at run

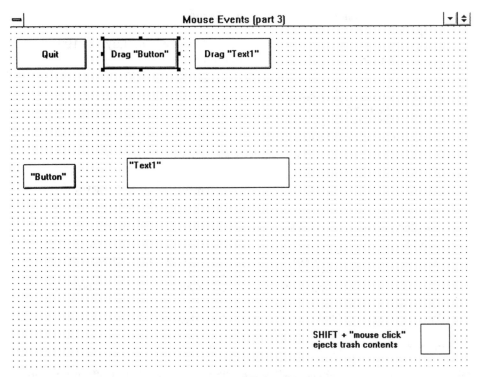

Quit   Drag "Button"   Drag "Text1"

"Button"   "Text1"

SHIFT + "mouse click"
ejects trash contents

13-11   The MOUSEV3.FRM at design time.

time. Initially, the icon is that of an empty trash can. Once you drop either
the "Button" command button or the text box, these controls disappear and
the icon changes into that of a nonempty trash can. If you click the mouse
on the picture box while pressing the Shift key, the invisible controls
(presumed to be in the trash can) reappear and the trash can icon
changes back to image of an empty can. When you drop a source control
in the trash box, its drag-enabling command button is disabled. When
you empty the trash, these drag-enabling command buttons are enabled.

The "Button" command button and the text box can only be moved
after you click on their respective drag-enabling command buttons. You
can drop the source controls on the form. Once you drop these controls on
the form, they cannot be dragged without clicking again on the drag-enabling buttons. I programmed the "Button" command button to respond with
a message box when clicked upon. I also programmed the text box to
maintain the "Text" (with the quotes). While not being dragged these controls respond to the mouse and keyboard events as programmed.

Figures 13-12 to 13-14 contain the specifications for the MOU-
SEV3.MAK project file and the MOUSEV3.FRM for file.

Application name: Control Dragging Demo
Application code name: MOUSEV3
Version: 1.0   Date created: July 16, 1991
Programmer(s): Namir Clement Shammas

List of filenames

Storage path: \VB\EASYVB
Project MOUSEV3.MAK
Global GLOBAL.BAS
Form 1 MOUSEV3.FRM

13-12 The general specifications for the MOUSEV3.MAK project.

Form #1   Form filename: MOUSEV3.FRM
Version: 1.0   Date: July 16, 1991

Control object type	Default CtlName	Purpose
Command Button	Command1	Exits the demo program
	Command2	Triggers dragging Command4
	Command3	Triggers dragging Text1
	Command4	The dragged command button
Text Box	Text1	The dragged text box
Picture Box	Picture1	The trash box
Label	Label1	Trash box label that offers help on ejecting the trash

13-13 The list of control objects for the MOUSEV3.FRM form.

Application (code) name: MOUSEV3
Form #1
Version: 1.0   Date: July 16, 1991

Original control name	Property	New setting
Form	Caption	Mouse Events (part 3)
Command1	CtlName	QuitBtn
	Caption	Quit
	Cancel	True
Command2	CtlName	DragButtonBtn
	Caption	Drag "Button"
	Default	True
Command3	CtlName	DragTextBtn
	Caption	Drag "Text"
Command4	CtlName	ButtonBtn
	Caption	"Button"

13-14 The update setting for the MOUSEV3.FRM form.

Original control name	Property	New setting
Text1	CtlName	TextBox
	Text	"Text"
Label1	CtlName	TrashLbl
	Caption	SHIFT + "mouse click" to eject trash
Picture1	CtlName	TrashboxPct

13-14 Continued.

Listing 13-3 shows the code attached to the MOUSEV3.FRM form. The relevant procedures are:

The Form_Load **procedure**   This procedure sets the window state and loads the icon of an empty trash can (TRASH04B.ICO) into the picture box.

The TrashboxPct_DragDrop **procedure**   This procedure performs the following tasks:

- Hides the Source control by setting its Visible property to False.
- Disables the associated drag-enabling command button. An If-Then-ElseIf statement uses the TypeOf-Is operator to detect the control type of the Source argument.
- Loads the icon of a nonempty trash can (TRASH04A.ICO).

Listing 13-3   The code attached to the MOUSEV3.FRM form.

```
Sub QuitButton_Click ( )
  End
End Sub

Sub Form_Load ( )
  WindowState = 2
  TrashboxPct.Picture = LoadPicture(" \ vb \ icons \ computer \ trash04b.ico")
End Sub

Sub TrashboxPctDragDrop (Source As Control, X As Single, Y As Single)
  Source.Visible = False
  If TypeOf Source Is TextBox Then
    DragTextBtn.Enabled = False
  ElseIf TypeOf Source Is CommandButton Then
    DragButtonBtn.Enabled = False
  End If
  TrashboxPct.Picture = LoadPicture(" \ vb \ icons \ computer \ trash04a.ico")
End Sub

Sub Form_DragDrop (Source As Control, X As Single, Y As Single)
```

Listing 13-3 Continued.

```
   Source.Move (X − Source.Width / 2), (Y − Source.Height / 2)
End Sub

Sub DragButtonBtn_Click ( )
   ButtonBtn.Drag 1
End Sub

Sub ButtonBtn_Click ( )
   MsgBox "I am a dud!", 0, "For Your Precious Information"
End Sub

Sub TextBox_DragOver (Source As Control, X As Single, Y As Single, State As Integer)
   Dim TColor As Long
   If (State = ENTER) Or (State = LEAVE) Then
      TColor = TextBox.BackColor
      TextBox.BackColor = TextBox.ForeColor
      TextBox.ForeColor = TColor
   End If
End Sub

Sub DragTextBtn_Click ( )
   TextBox.Drag 1
End Sub

Sub TrashboxPct_MouseDown (Button As Integer, Shift As Integer, X As Single, Y As Sin-
gle)
   If Shift And 1 Then
      TrashboxPct.Picture = LoadPicture(" \ vb \ icons \ computer \ trash04b.ico")
      TextBox.Visible = True
      ButtonBtn.Visible = True
      DragTextBtn.Enabled = True
      DragButtonBtn.Enabled = True
   End If
End Sub

Sub TextBox_KeyPress (KeyAscii As Integer)
   KeyAscii = 0
End Sub

Sub TextBox_Change ( )
   TextBox.Text = Chr$(34) + "Text" + Chr$(34)
End Sub
```

☞ **The** Form_DragDrop **procedure** Form_DragDrop is responsible for actually moving the source control. The Source.Move method enables this
procedure to relocate either the command button or the text box. Without

the Move method, the source controls remain in their original places after they are dropped.

The DragButtonBtn_Click **procedure**   This enables you to drag the "Button" command button by using the ButtonBtn.Drag method with an argument of 1.

The ButtonBtn_Click **procedure**   ButtonBtn_Click displays a message box when you click on the ''Button'' command button.

The TextBox_DragOver **procedure**   This procedure specifies what happens to the text box itself when a source control is dragged. The If statement examines whether the State argument is either ENTER or LEAVE. In these cases, the foreground and background colors of the text box are swapped. The effect of the If statement is that the text box regains its original colors when the source control leaves the text box.

The DragTextBtn_Click **procedure**   This enables you to drag the text box by issuing a TextBox.Drag 1 statement.

The TrashboxPct_MouseDown **procedure**   This procedure permits you to restore the source controls that were dropped into it. The source controls become visible and their drag-enabling command buttons are enabled.

The TextBox_KeyPress **procedure**   This serves to prevent you from typing anything in the text box.

The TextBox_Change **procedure**   TextBox_Change makes sure that the Text setting is "Text."

Run the MOUSEV3 program and drag the "Button" command button and the text box around. Drop them in the trash can picture box and notice the change in icons. Click on the picture box while pressing the Shift key and watch the source controls that you dropped earlier reappear. In fact, they appear in the last location before they were dropped in the picture box, because the picture box never moved them—it only made them invisible.

14
Interactive Visual Basic programs

This chapter looks at writing Visual Basic programs that are more interactive, including the ability of Visual Basic programs to exchange data among themselves and with other Windows applications using the Clipboard. Another aspect of creating interactive Visual Basic programs deals with using timer controls to periodically trigger timer events. In addition, this chapter looks at how you can detect any key on your keyboard, including functions keys and cursor control keys. You will learn about the following topics:

- Using the Windows Clipboard from within Visual Basic programs.
- Working with the Visual Basic timer controls.
- Writing and using idle loops.
- Developing low-level keyboard handlers.

Using the Clipboard

In chapter 7 I discussed the features of text boxes. Part of the discussion focused on working with selected text using the SelText, SelStart, and Sel-Length properties. The SelText property can be used to transfer data between a Visual Basic program and the Clipboard, a special object. The Clipboard is a temporary data storage area where information is sent and received by one or more Windows applications. For example, you can transfer a picture from a graphics paint program to a Windows-based word processor. This is accomplished by loading the graphics paint program, copying the picture, loading the word processor, and then pasting the picture that you cut earlier. The Clipboard serves as the holding place where text and graphics are stored when they are copied or cut. Pasting is an operation that retrieves the contents of the Clipboard into the current Windows application.

The Visual Basic Clipboard object is a special object that is void of properties and events—it has only a few methods for manipulating its contents. The Visual Basic Clipboard object taps into the Windows Clipboard using the following methods:

The SetText **method**   This method copies text onto the Clipboard, overwriting the previous contents of the Clipboard. The general syntax for the SetText method is:

Clipboard.SetText *stringExpression$ [, format%]*

where stringExpression$ is the new content of the Clipboard. The format% parameter is a numeric code that refers to the format of the data and is equal to 1 for text, by default. The GLOBAL.BAS contains the CF_TEXT global constant that is assigned the value of 1. Use this global constant to enhance the readability of your program.

Text can be copied onto the Clipboard from any string or selected text using the SetText method. Several examples are shown below:

```
Clipboard.SetText "Hello There!" ' string constant
Clipboard.SetText aTextLine$ ' string variable
Clipboard.SetText TextBox.Text ' a Text property
Clipboard.SetText TextBox.SelText ' copy selected text
```

The GetText **method**   This retrieves the text stored in the Clipboard. The general syntax for the GetText method is:

targetString$ = Clipboard.GetText()

Here are some examples of using the GetText method:

```
aTextLine$ = Clipboard.GetText() ' to a string variable
TextBox.Text = Clipboard.GetText() ' to a Text property
TextBox.SelText = Clipboard.GetText() ' copy to selected text
```

Using the SetText and GetText methods you can write event-handling procedures that work with Copy, Cut, and Paste menu options that you might include in your Visual Basic applications. Typical code that transfers the text between the text box TextBox and the Clipboard is shown below:

```
Sub CopyCom_Click ()
   Clipboard.SetText TextBox.SelText
End Sub

Sub CutCom_Click ()
   Clipboard.SetText TextBox.SelText
   TextBox.SelText = ""
End Sub
```

```
Sub PasteCom_Click ()
   TextBox.SelText = Clipboard.GetText()
End Sub
```

The above sample code shows the interaction between the Clipboard and a single text box. The SelText property plays a pivotal role in indicating the text that is cut, copied, or pasted.

☞ Visual Basic allows you to make better use of the Clipboard object by allowing it to interact with any text box, as long as that text box has the focus. The ActiveControl property of the Screen object enables you to access the focused text box. The following set of procedures shows how a more general set of procedures is written to support the Copy, Cut, and Paste menu options:

```
Sub CopyCom_Click ()
   Clipboard.SetText Screen.ActiveControl.SelText
End Sub

Sub CutCom_Click ()
   Clipboard.SetText Screen.ActiveControl.SelText
   Screen.ActiveControl.SelText = ""
End Sub

Sub PasteCom_Click ()
   Screen.ActiveControl.SelText = Clipboard.GetText()
End Sub
```

The SetData **method**   SetData places a picture in the Clipboard using a specified format. The general syntax for the SetData method is:

```
Clipboard.SetData data% [, format%]
```

The data% parameter is an Image or Picture property for the picture copied onto the Clipboard. The format% parameter specifies the picture format. Table 14-1 shows the values for the format% parameter. If the format% argument is omitted, a value of 2 (*CF_BITMAP*) is assumed.

Table 14-1   The values for the format% parameter.

Format value	GLOBAL.BAS constant	Meaning
2	CF_BITMAP	Bit-mapped format
3	CF_METAFILE	Meta-file format
8	CF_DIB	DIB format

Some examples of using the SetData method are shown here:

```
Clipboard.SetData PicturePct.Picture, CF_BITMAP
Clipboard.SetData MyPicturePct.Picture
Clipboard.SetData TrashCanPct.Picture, CF_METAFILE
```

The GetData **method** With this method, a picture is retrieved from the Clipboard. The general syntax for the GetData method is:

```
[form.]pictureBox.Picture = Clipboard.GetData([format%])
```

The format% parameter is the same as the one in the SetData method. If the format% argument is omitted, a value of 2 (CF_BITMAP) is assumed. Examples of using the GetData method are:

```
PicturePct.Picture = Clipboard.GetData()
MyPicture.Picture = Clipboard.GetData(CF_METAFILE)
```

The GetFormat **method** This method is a Boolean function that returns an integer, −1 or 0, indicating whether or not the clipboard contains an item that matches the specified format. The general syntax for the GetFormat method is:

```
[booleanVar% = ] Clipboard.GetFormat(format%)
```

The values for the format% parameter include 1 (CF_TEXT), the list of numbers shown in TABLE 14-1, and &HBF00 (CF_LINK). An example of using the GetFormat method is shown next:

```
If Clipboard.GetFormat(CF_BITMAP) Then
    PicturePct.Picture = Clipboard.GetData(CF_BITMAP)
End If
```

The Clear **method** This method clears the contents of the Clipboard. The general syntax for using the Clear method is:

```
Clipboard.Clear
```

Let's look at a program that uses the GetText and SetText methods to manipulate the clipboard. The WINEDIT1 program implements a simple Windows text editor. This menu-driven program is derived from the FVIEW2C.MAK project and includes the ability to write text to a file.

The program features that are related to the Clipboard include the following menu selections:

The Edit menu selection The Cut, Copy, and Paste options are offered in this selection. These options enable you to cut and copy text from the currently selected text box into the Clipboard. The Paste option permits you to paste text from the Clipboard into the currently selected text box.

The Clipboard menu selection This menu selection contains the options to view and clear the Clipboard, as well as to append the selected text to the Clipboard. When you view the Clipboard you actually copy its contents into the edit text box—the original text lines of the edit text box are stored in a variable. Placing the contents of the Clipboard into the edit text box allows you to edit the clipboard. While you are viewing the Clipboard the Clear and Append menu options are disabled, and the View Clipboard caption is replaced with the caption View File. In addition, the filename text box shows the name Clipboard, instead of the name of the edited file.

I have also included the following changes and additions to enhance the text editor over its parent text file viewer program:

- The Read option is renamed Load.
- The Save option is added. The name of the file in the Filename text box is used to save the edited text lines. By changing the filename in the text box you save the text lines into a new file; there is no need for a Save As menu option.
- The Read-Only option is added to the File menu. This option prevents you from writing the edited text lines to a file. Initially, this option is triggered by the Load_Form procedure to prevent you from accidentally overwriting a text file with a null string.
- The Add File and Delete File options have the Ctrl-A and Ctrl-D accelerator keys, respectively.
- The Search menu selection has a new option, Find Selected Text. This option automatically copies the selected text of the edit text box into the Find text box, and then initiates the text search. The accelerator key for this new search option is Ctrl-S.
- The Case Sensitive check box is a new control that enables you to specify whether or not to use case-sensitive text search.

```
═┃                          Window Editor (Ver. 1)                    │▼│▲│
 File   Edit   Clipboard   Search   Command

                                  DOS/Win Input  [                              ]

   Filename Input                            ⊠ Case Sensitive

   \autoexec.bat                   Find Input  subst

  ┌──────────────────────────────────────────────────────────────────┐▲
  │@echo off                                                           │█
  │break on                                                            │
  │verify on                                                           │
  │c:                                                                  │
  │cd\                                                                 │
  │C:\DOS\subst n: \util\norton                                        │
  │C:\DOS\subst p: \util\pcmag                                         │
  │C:\DOS\subst q: \qedit                                              │
  │C:\DOS\subst x: \tp60\bin                                           │
  │n:\sa bright white on blue                                          │
  │p > NUL                                                             │
  │\utility\superpck /s:384 /h-                                        │
  │p u > NUL                                                           │
  │: \edos\dosedit > NUL                                               │
  │C:\DOS\doskey                                                       │
  │\edos\dimmer/5                                                      │
  │p u > NUL                                                           │
  │cd\keys                                                             │
  │key dos.k/ml > NUL                                                  │
  │cd\                                                                 │
  │cls                                                                 │
  │prompt $g$p  $t$h$h$h$h$h$h $d$_Yes, Namir?                         │▼
  ┌◄│────────────────────────────────────────────────────────────────►┘
```

14-1 A sample session with the WINEDIT1 program.

I suggest that you run the WINEDIT1 program first to get a feel for its features. I also recommend that you make a few copies of text files and experiment with editing these copies, since the WINEDIT1 program does not automatically create backup files. Use the options of the Edit and Clipboard menu selections to manipulate blocks of text. In fact, you can run multiple copies of the WINEDIT1.EXE program and transfer text between each running copy by using the options of the Edit menu. A sample session with the WINEDIT1 program is shown in FIG. 14-1 (on previous page).

Figures 14-2 to 14-5 contain the specifications of the WINEDIT1.MAK project file, the WINEDIT1.FRM form, and the menu structure.

Application name: Menu-Driven Text File Editor
Application code name: WINEDIT1
Version: 1.0   Date created: July 17, 1991
Programmer(s): Namir Clement Shammas

List of filenames

Storage path: C:\VB\EASYVB
Project WINEDIT1.MAK
Global GLOBAL.BAS
Form 1 WINEDIT1.FRM

14-2   General project specifications for the WINEDIT1 project.

Form #1   Form filename: WINEDIT1.FRM
Version: 1.0   Date: July 17, 1991

Control object type	Default CtlName	Purpose
Text Box	Text1	Contains the filename to read
	Text2	Contains the text search string
	Text3	Contains the DOS/Windows command line
	Text4	Displays the text lines of a file
Label	Label1	Label of Text1
	Label2	Label of Text2
	Label3	Label of Text3
Check Box	Check1	Specifies case-sensitive search

14-3   List of control objects for the WINEDIT1 project.

Appication (code) name: WINEDIT1
Form #1
Version: 1.0   Date: July 17, 1991

Original control name	Property	New setting
Form	Caption	File Viewer (ver. 2A)
Text1	CtlName	FilenameBox
	Text	(empty string)
Text2	CtlName	FindBox
	Text	(empty string)
Text3	CtlName	DosBox
	Text	(empty string)
Text4	CtlName	TextBox
	Text	(empty string)
	MultiLine	True
	ScrollBars	3 - both
Label1	CtlName	FilenameLbl
	Caption	Filename Input
Label2	CtlName	FindLbl
	Caption	Find Input
Label3	CtlName	DosLbl
	Caption	DOS/Win Input
Check1	CtlName	CaseSenseChk
	Caption	Case Sensitive

14-4 The modified control settings for the WINEDIT1 project.

Form #1   Form filename: WINDEDIT1.FRM
Version: 1.0   Date: July 17, 1991

Caption	Property	Setting	Purpose
&File	CtlName	FileCom	
Load	CtlName	LoadCom	Reads a file in Text1
	Accelerator	F3	
	indented	once	
Save	CtlName	SaveCom	Saves the text lines
	Accelerator	F2	
	indented	once	

14-5 The menu structure for the WINDEDIT1 project.

Caption	Property	Setting	Purpose
Toggle Read	CtlName	ToggleReadCom	Toggles Read menu
	indented	once	option
Read-Only	CtlName	ReadOnlyCom	Sets file to read-onlyql.
	indented	once	
Find File	CtlName	FindFileCom	Finds a file
	Accelerator	CTRL-F	
	indented	once	
–	CtlName	Sep1	
	indented	once	
Add File	CtlName	AddFileCom	Adds a filename
	Accelerator	CTRL-A	
	indented	once	
Delete File	CtlName	DeleteFileCom	Deletes a filename
	Accelerator	CTRL-D	
	indented	once	
–	CtlName	Sep2	
	indented	once	
(noname)	CtlName	QuickFilename	
	Index	0	
	Visible	off	
	indented	once	
–	CtlName	Sep3	
	indented	once	
Quit	CtlName	QuitCom	Exits the application
	Accelerator	CTRL-Q	
	indented	once	
&Edit	CtlName	EditCom	Copy, cut, and paste menu
Cut	CtlName	CutCom	Cuts the selected text
	Accelerator	CTRL-X	
	indented	once	
Copy	CtlName	CopyCom	Copies the selected text into the Clipboard
	Accelerator	CTRL-C	
	indented	once	
Paste	CtlName	PasteCom	Pastes the text from the Clipboard
	Accelerator	CTRL-V	
	indented	once	
&Clipboard	CtlName	ClipboardCom	Clipboard menu
View Clipboard	CtlName	ViewCom	Views the Clipboard
	indented	once	
Clear	CtlName	ClearCom	Clears the Clipboard
	indented	once	
Append	CtlName	AppendCom	Appends selected text to the Clipboard
	indented	once	

14-5 Continued.

Caption	Property	Setting	Purpose
&Search	CtlName	SearchCom	
Find	CtlName	FindCom	Finds text in Text1
	Accelerator	CTRL-I	
	indented	once	
Find Selected	CtlName	FindSelTextCom	Finds selected text
	Accelerator	CTRL-S	
Text	indented	once	
&Command	CtlName	CommandCom	
DOS Command	CtlName	DosCom	Executes a DOS
	Accelerator	CTRL-O	command
	indented	once	
Windows Command	CtlName	WinCom	Runs a Windows
	Accelerator	CTRL-W	application
	indented	once	
Toggle OS	CtlName	ToggleOsCom	Shows/hides command
	indented	once	options.

14-5 Continued.

Listing 14-1 shows the code attached to the WINEDIT1.FRM form. Here are the procedures relevant to the features that program WINEDIT1 added to FVIEW2C program:

The FindCom_Click **procedure** FindCom_Click uses the following If-Then-Else to perform both case-sensitive and -insensitive text searches:

```
If CaseSenseChk.Value = 1 Then
    CurIndex = InStr(CurIndex + 1, TextBox.Text, Find)
Else
    CurIndex = InStr(CurIndex + 1, UCase$(TextBox.Text), UCase$(Find))
End If
```

The tested condition compares the CaseSenseChk.Value property with 1. If this condition is true, the case-sensitive search is conducted by using the TextBox.Text and Find strings. Otherwise, the UCASE$ function is applied to both these strings in order to carry out a case-insensitive search.

The FindSelTextCom_Click **procedure** This procedure copies the selected text of the edit text box and initiates a text search. If the selected text in the edit text box is not an empty string, the Text property of FindBox is assigned the selected text. The procedure then calls the FindCom_Click procedure to conduct the text search.

The Form_Load **procedure** This procedure initializes the application. This includes setting the window state to maximum, selecting the Courier 9.75-point font, and invoking the ReadOnlyCom_Click procedure to set the editor into read-only mode.

The SaveCom_Click **procedure** SaveCom_Click saves the text lines of the edit text box into the specified filename. The procedure exits if the edit text box or the filename are empty strings. The statements in the procedure open the specified file for output, and perform the file I/O error-trapping if you specify an invalid filename.

The CutCom_Click **procedure** This procedure deletes the selected text in the text box that has the focus. This feature is implemented using the Screen.ActiveControl mentioned earlier.

The CopyCom_Click **procedure** This copies a nonempty selected text from the focused text box into the Clipboard.

The AppendCom_Click **procedure** AppendCom_Click appends the selected text of the edit text box to the Clipboard. A pair of new line and carriage return characters are inserted before the appended text.

The PasteCom_Click **procedure** This pastes text from the Clipboard to the currently selected text box. The Cut, Copy, and Paste menu options enable you to exchange text among the various text boxes of the program.

The ClearCom_Click **procedure** This procedure clears the Clipboard using the Clear method.

The ViewCom_Click **procedure** ViewCom_Click enables you to view and edit the contents of the Clipboard. The edited text lines and the filename are stored in static local variables. The procedure toggles between viewing the text lines and the Clipboard. The Clipboard menu options are also affected. The procedure disables the Clear and Append options when the ClipBoard is being viewed. In addition, the ViewCom.Caption property is set to View Clipboard.

When the edited text lines are restored the Clipboard menu options are also returned to their original condition.

The ReadOnlyCom_Click **procedure** This disables the Save menu options and places a check mark to the left of the Read-Only menu option.

Listing 14-1   The code attached to the WINEDIT1.FRM form.

```
Dim NumFiles As Integer

Sub QuitCom_Click ( )
  End
End Sub

Sub DosCom_Click ( )
  Dim Dummy As Integer
  ' invoke the DOSBAT batch file
  Dummy = Shell("dosbat.bat " + DosBox.Text, 1)
End Sub
```

Listing 14-1 Continued.

```
Sub FindCom_Click ( )
   Static CurIndex As Long
   Dim Find As String
   ' update the index to the current character
   CurIndex = TextBox.SelStart + 1
   ' store the text of the Find box in the variable Find
   Find = FindBox.Text
   ' is variable Find empty?
   If Find = " " Then Exit Sub ' nothing to find
   ' locate the index of the next substring Find in the
   ' text box
   If CaseSenseChk.Value = 1 Then
      CurIndex = InStr(CurIndex + 1, TextBox.Text, Find)
   Else
      CurIndex = InStr(CurIndex + 1, UCase$(TextBox.Text), UCase$(Find))
   End If
   ' found a match?
   If CurIndex > 0 Then
      ' Yes! Display the matching text as selected text
      TextBox.SelStart = CurIndex - 1
      TextBox.SelLength = Len(Find)
      TextBox.SetFocus
      FindCom.Checked = True
   Else
      ' No! Clear any selected text
      TextBox.SelStart = 0
      TextBox.SelLength = 0
      FindCom.Checked = False
   End If
End Sub


Sub FindFileCom_Click ( )
   Dim Dummy As Integer
   ' invoke the DOS dir command with the /s
   ' subdirectory option and the /p paginated
   ' output option
   Dummy = Shell("dosbat.bat dir " + FilenameBox.Text + " /s/p", 1)
End Sub


Sub WinCom_Click ( )
   Dim Dummy As Integer
   ' invoke a Windows application
   Dummy = Shell(DosBox.Text, 1)
End Sub


Sub ToggleOSCom_Click ( )
   ' toggle the Visible property of the DosBox text box,
   ' the DosBtn button, the WinBtn button, and the DosLbl
```

Listing 14-1 Continued.

```
  ' label
  DosBox.Visible = Not DosBox.Visible
  DosCom.Visible = Not DosCom.Visible
  WinCom.Visible = Not WinCom.Visible
  DosLbl.Visible = Not DosLbl.Visible
End Sub

Sub FindLbl_Change ( )
  FindCom.Checked = False
End Sub

Sub FindBox_Change ( )
  FindCom.Checked = 0
End Sub

Sub AddFileCom_Click ( )
  Dim theFilename As String
  theFilename = InputBox$("Enter full file name: ")
  NumFiles = NumFiles + 1 ' increment the menu count
  Load QuickFilename(NumFiles) ' load a new menu command
  QuickFilename(NumFiles).Caption = theFilename
  QuickFilename(NumFiles).Visible = True
End Sub

Sub QuickFilename_Click (Index As Integer)
  FilenameBox.Text = QuickFilename(Index).Caption
  LoadComClick
End Sub

Sub DeleteFileCom_Click ( )
  Dim N As Integer, I As Integer
  N = Val(InputBox$("Enter number to delete: "))
  If (N > 0) And (N > = NumFiles) Then
    For I = N To NumFiles - 1
      QuickFilename(I).Caption = QuickFilename(I + 1).Caption
    Next I
    Unload QuickFilename(NumFiles)
    NumFiles = NumFiles - 1
  Else
    MsgBox "The number is out-of-range", 0, "Input Error"
  End If
End Sub

Sub Form_Load ( )
  NumFiles = 0
  WindowState = 2
  TextBox.FontName = "Courier"
  TextBox.FontSize = 9.75
```

Listing 14-1 Continued.

```
    ReadOnlyCom_Click
End Sub

Sub LoadCom_Click ( )
    Dim F As String
    Dim L As String
    Dim NL As String * 2
    ' obtain filename from the filename text box
    F = FilenameBox.Text
    ' if filename is an empty string, exit
    If F = " " Then Exit Sub
    NL = Chr$(13) + Chr$(10)
    ' set error-handler
    On Error GoTo BadFile
    ' open the file
    Open F For Input As 1
    F = " " ' clear variable to reuse it
    ' loop to read the text lines from the ASCII file
    Do While Not EOF(1)
        Line Input #1, L
        F = F + L + NL ' append a new line
    Loop
    TextBox.Text = F ' copy F into text box
    ' close the file
    Close #1
    ' exit procedure
    Exit Sub
' ********** Error-handler **********
BadFile:
    Beep
    MsgBox "Cannot open file " + F, 0, "File I/O Error"
    On Error GoTo 0
    Resume EndOfSub
EndOfSub:
End Sub

Sub SaveCom_Click ( )
    If (FilenameBox.Text <> " ") And (TextBox.Text <> " ") Then
        On Error GoTo BadSaveFilename
        Open FilenameBox.Text For Output As #1
        On Error GoTo 0
        Print #1, TextBox.Text
        Close #1
    End If
    Exit Sub

' **************** Error-Handler ****************
BadSaveFilename:
```

Listing 14-1 Continued.

```
   On Error GoTo 0
   MsgBox "Cannot write to file " + FilenameBox.Text, 0, "File I/O Error"
   Resume ExitSaveFile
ExitSaveFile:
End Sub

Sub CutCom_Click ( )
   Clipboard.SetText Screen.ActiveControl.SelText
   Screen.ActiveControl.SelText = " "
End Sub

Sub CopyCom_Click ( )
   If Screen.ActiveControl.SelText = " " Then
       Clipboard.SetText Screen.ActiveControl.SelText, CFTEXT
   End If
End Sub

Sub AppendCom_Click ( )
   Dim S As String
   If TextBox.SelText = " " Then Exit Sub
   S = Clipboard.GetText( )
   S = S + Chr$(13) + Chr$(10) + TextBox.SelText
   Clipboard.SetText S, CF_TEXT
End Sub

Sub PasteCom_Click ( )
   Screen.ActiveControl.SelText = Clipboard.GetText( )
End Sub

Sub ToggleLoadCom_Click ( )
   LoadCom.Enabled = Not LoadCom.Enabled
   ToggleLoadCom.Checked = Not LoadCom.Enabled
End Sub

Sub ClearCom_Click ( )
   Clipboard.Clear
End Sub

Sub ViewCom_Click ( )
   Static ViewClipboard As Integer
   Static theFilename As String
   Static theFileText As String
   If ViewClipboard Then
       ViewClipboard = False
       ViewCom.Caption = "View Clipboard"
       ClearCom.Enabled = True
       AppendCom.Enabled = True
       FilenameBox.Text = theFilename
```

Listing 14-1 Continued.

```
    Clipboard.SetText TextBox.Text, CF_TEXT
    TextBox.Text = theFileText
    theFileText = " "
Else
    ViewClipboard = True
    ViewCom.Caption = "View File"
    ClearCom.Enabled = False
    AppendCom.Enabled = False
    theFilename = FilenameBox.Text
    theFileText = TextBox.Text
    FilenameBox.Text = "Clipboard"
    TextBox.Text = Clipboard.GetText( )
    End If
End Sub

Sub ReadOnlyCom_Click ( )
    SaveCom.Enabled = Not SaveCom.Enabled
    ReadOnlyCom.Checked = Not SaveCom.Enabled
End Sub

Sub FindSelTextCom_Click ( )
    If TextBox.SelText < > " " Then
        FindBox.Text = TextBox.SelText
    End If
    FindCom_Click
End Sub
```

The timer control

Visual Basic offers the Timer control. This is a special control in that it is always invisible at run time. The Timer control is either disabled or enabled. When it is enabled, this control generates a Timer event at set time intervals.

Timer controls have a few properties, such as CtlName, Enabled, and Index, that are common with other controls. The Interval property is peculiar to the Timer control. It can be set either at design time or at run time. The general syntax for the Interval property is:

    [*form.*]timer.*Interval* [*=milliSeconds&*]

The valid range of values for the Interval property is 0 to 65,535 milliseconds. When the setting is 0, the timer is disabled. The value of 60,000 represents one minute. Therefore, the maximum timer interval is just greater than one minute.

The Timer control generates a Timer event every Interval milliseconds. The Timer event invokes the event-handling procedure of the associated timer control to perform the tasks you specify.

The following two steps are involved in using a timer control:

- Setting the Enabled property of the timer control to −1 (True).
- Assigning a value to the Interval setting of the timer control.

To stop a timer control, set its Enabled property to 0 (False). That's all there is to it.

Let's see how the timer control is put to work. The next program uses two timer controls, one as a timer and one to display a clock. Figure 14-6 shows the TIMER1.FRM form containing the various controls. The timer

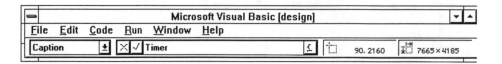

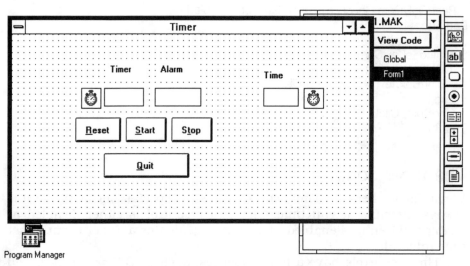

14-6 The TIMER1.FRM during design time.

control is triggered by clicking on the Start button. The timer stops in one of three cases:

- You click on the Stop command button. This button simply stops the timer, but does not reset the display of the Timer text box.
- You click on the Reset command button. The Timer text box is reset to 00:00.
- The contents of the Timer box match those of the Alarm text box.

You can type the number of minutes and seconds (in a mm:ss format) in the alarm text box to specify when the timer stops and displays a message box. You supply the text of the message box when you exit the alarm box (and the box is not empty)—a dialog box requests that you enter the message associated with the alarm. When the alarm is due (that is, when the text appearing in both the timer and alarm boxes is the same), the program pops a message box with the message you timed in earlier. This feature works even if you run the compiled program in minimized mode.

The program also has a text box that displays the current time. The Time box is updated once a minute, regardless of whether or not you are running the timer.

Figures 14-7 to 14-9 contain the specifications for the TIMER1.MAK project file and the TIMER1.FRM file.

Application name: Timers Demo
Application code name: TIMER1
Version: 1.0   Date created: July 17, 1991
Programmer(s): Namir Clement Shammas

List of filenames

Storage path: \VB\EASYVB
Project TIMER1.MAK
Global GLOBAL.BAS
Form 1 TIMER1.FRM

14-7 General project specifications for the TIMER1 project.

Form #1   Form filename: TIMER1.FRM
Version: 1.0   Date: July 17, 1991

Control object type	Default CtlName	Purpose
Timer	Timer1	Implements a timer
	Timer2	Displays a hh:mm clock
Command Box	Command1	Exits the demo program
	Command2	Resets the timer
	Command3	Starts the timer
	Command4	Stops the timer
Text Box	Text1	Timer box
	Text2	Alarm box
	Text3	Clock box
Label	Label1	Timer label
	Label2	Alarm label
	Label3	Clock label

14-8 List of control objects for the TIMER1 project.

Application (code) name: TIMER1
Form #1
Version: 1.0   Date: July 17, 1991

Original control name	Property	New setting
Form	Caption	Timer
Timer1	CtlName	TimerClk
Timer2	CtlName	TimeClk
Command1	CtlName	QuitBtn
	Caption	&Quit
Command2	CtlName	ResetBtn
	Caption	&Reset
Command3	CtlName	StartBtn
	Caption	&Start
Command4	CtlName	StopBtn
	Caption	S&top
Text1	CtlName	TimerBox
	Text	(empty string)
Text2	CtlName	AlarmBox
	Text	(empty string)
Text3	CtlName	TimeBox
	Text	(empty string)
Label1	CtlName	TimerLbl
	Caption	Timer
Label2	CtlName	AlarmLbl
	Caption	Alarm
Label3	CtlName	TimeLbl
	Caption	Time

14-9 The modified control settings for the TIMER1 project.

Listing 14-2 contains the code attached to the TIMER1.FRM form. The following procedures are relevant to the timer controls:

The Form_Load **procedure** This procedure performs the following tasks:

- Sets the NumSec variable, which holds the number of seconds, to 0.
- Enables the TimeClk timer control and sets its Interval property to 60000 (one minute).

- Displays the current time in the Time box.
- Resets the Timer box.

The ResetBtn_Click **procedure** in this procedure, the timer is reset by setting the Enabled property of the TimerClk control to False. The procedure also sets the variable NumSec to zero and places 00:00 in the Timer text box.

The StartBtn_Click **procedure** This triggers the timer by setting the TimerClk.Enabled property to True. The procedure also assigns 987 milliseconds to the TimerClk.Interval property. This value is a bit less than 1000, presumably the correct value to trigger the Timer event once every second. The difference is made up by the approximate time for code execution. You might need to fine-tune this number further to accommodate the speed of execution on your system.

The StopBtn_Click **procedure** The timer is disabled by assigning False to the TimerClk.Enabled property.

The TimerClk_Timer **procedure** This procedure displays the timer and performs the following tasks:

- Increments the NumSec variable that stores the time in seconds.
- Calculates the number of seconds and the number of minutes.
- Displays the mm:ss time in the Timer text box.
- Compares the Text properties in the Time and Alarm text boxes. If these properties are equal, the timer stops and the alarm message is displayed. Two beeps are sounded before displaying the message box.

The TimeClk_Timer **procedure** This displays the current time using the hh:mm format.

The AlarmBox_LostFocus **procedure** With this procedure you can type in the alarm message when you exit the Alarm text box. If the Alarm text box is empty, no action is taken.

Listing 14-2 The code attached to the TIMER1.FRM form.

```
Dim NumSec As Long
Dim AlarmMessage As String

Sub QuitBtn_Click ( )
  End
End Sub

Sub Form_Load ( )
  NumSec = 0
  AlarmMessage = "Testing!"
  TimeClk.Enabled = True
  TimeClk.Interval = 60000 ' once a minute
```

Listing 14-2 Continued.

```
    TimeBox.Text = Mid$(Time$, 1, 5)
    ResetBtn_Click
End Sub

Sub ResetBtn_Click ( )
    NumSec = 0
    TimerBox.Text = "00:00"
    TimerClk.Enabled = False
End Sub

Sub StartBtn_Click ( )
    TimerClk.Enabled = True
    TimerClk.Interval = 987
End Sub

Sub StopBtn_Click ( )
    TimerClk.Enabled = False
End Sub

Sub TimerClk_Timer ( )
    Dim Secs As Integer, Min As Integer
    NumSec = NumSec + 1
    Secs = NumSec Mod 60
    Min = NumSec \ 60
    TimerBox.Text = Format$(Min, "00") + ":" + Format$(Secs, "00")
    If AlarmBox.Text = TimerBox.Text Then
        TimerClk.Enabled = False
        Beep: Beep
        MsgBox AlarmMessage, 0, "Alarm!"
    End If
End Sub

Sub TimeClk_Timer ( )
    TimeBox.Text = Mid$(Time$, 1, 5)
End Sub

Sub AlarmBox_LostFocus ( )
    Dim S As String
    If AlarmBox.Text = " " Then Exit Sub
    S = InputBox$("Enter alarm message", "Input", AlarmMessage)
    If S < > " " Then AlarmMessage = S
End Sub

Sub TimerBox_KeyPress (KeyAscii As Integer)
    KeyAscii = 0
End Sub
```

Listing 14-2 Continued.

```
Sub TimeBox_KeyPress (KeyAscii As Integer)
    KeyAscii = 0
End Sub
```

Writing idle loops

Visual Basic applications are event-driven programs. In such programs, code is executed in response to an event. There are applications that perform specific tasks, such as various types of updates, only when the program is idle. Visual Basic enables you to write idle loops that perform a task when there are no events being handled. The following steps must be followed:

1. Create a module that contains the Sub procedure Main.
2. Include the following Do-While idle loop:

```
Do While DoEvents()
    ' statements for idle loop
Loop
```

The DoEvents function returns the number of forms in the application that are loaded. If no form is loaded, the DoEvents function exits the loop. In addition, when an End statement is executed anywhere in a procedure, all of the application's forms are unloaded and the DoEvents function returns 0, causing the idle loop to terminate.

The DoEvents function turns the control over to the operating system. The function regains control as soon as all of the other Windows programs have had a chance to respond to their pending events.

3. Select the module containing the procedure Main as the start-up module. Consequently, you need to include a Load or Show statement to load or show the application forms, respectively.

Let me give you an example of an idle loop by modifying the TIMER1 program. The new version updates the time text box using the idle loop shown in LISTING 14-3. The new program is made up of the TIMER2.MAK project file, the TIMER2.FRM form file, and the TIMER2MD.BAS module. The TIMER2 program is very similar to TIMER1. The differences are:

- The TimeClk timer control is deleted.
- The code that was attached to TimeClk is also removed.
- The TIMER2MD.BAS is added. It contains the code shown in LISTING 14-3.

Listing 14-3 The Main procedure located in the TIMER2MD.BAS module.

```
Sub Main ( )
  Form1.Show
  Do While DoEvents( )
    Form1.TimeBox.Text = Mid$(Time$, 1, 5)
  Loop
End Sub
```

Run the TIMER2 program. It produces the same operations of program TIMER1. The difference is that the time text box is updated whenever there are no events to handle.

Developing low-level keyboard handlers

Visual Basic offers the KeyDown and KeyUp events to allow you to detect the exact keys pressed. In an earlier chapter I presented the KeyPress event, which enabled you to process the ASCII characters being typed. By comparison, the KeyUp and KeyDown events provide you with information that is related to the *key* being pressed or released, not the ASCII code of the character it generates. The KeyUp and KeyDown events allow you to detect whether the following keys were pressed:

- The Shift, Ctrl, and/or Alt keys were pressed.
- Arrow keys and other cursor control keys.
- The numeric keypad digits vs. the typewriter digits.

The KeyUp and KeyDown events enable you to perform a variety of tasks. You can provide on-line help, for example by pressing the F1 function. You can also perform additional processing on the Text property of a text box. For example, you may specify that a function key converts the characters in a text box into upper case or lower case. Using such a function key is an option that you can offer in your programs.

KeyUp and KeyDown can also serve to display preset text in a text box by pressing one or more function keys, and to store selected text or the contents of a text box in special strings.

The general form for the KeyUp and KeyDown event-handling procedure is shown next:

```
object_KeyUp (KeyCode As Integer, Shift As Integer)
object_KeyDown (KeyCode As Integer, Shift As Integer)
```

The KeyCode parameter refers to the physical key that is pressed or released. Keep in mind that most keys produce multiple characters. For example, the typewriter key 5 also produces the % character when pressed with the Shift key. The KeyCode for the key producing the 5 and the % is the same!

The GLOBAL.BAS file contains a set of KEY_XXXX global constants that code the various keys. Using these constants is definitely easier than trying to remember the hexadecimal keys codes.

The Shift parameter plays the same role with the KeyUp and KeyDown events as it did with the MouseUp, MouseDown, and MouseMove events in chapter 13.

Let me illustrate using the KeyDown event to improve the WINEDIT1 program. The new program version, WINEDIT2, is identical to WIN-EDIT1, except for the following special features:

1. Pressing the Shift key with any of the function keys (F1 to F10) stores the selected text of the Edit text box in an element of a special array of strings.
2. Pressing the Ctrl key with any of the function keys (F1 to F10) recalls the characters previously saved in the array of strings.

Listing 14-4 shows the additional code that I inserted in WINEDIT1 in order to produce program WINEDIT2. The general declarations section contains the declaration of a 10-member string array. This array stores various instances of the selected text. You could say that the array elements store snapshots of the selected text.

Listing 14-4 The additional code of WINDEDIT2.FRM.

```
' declare the strings that store the ten text blocks
Dim KeyStr(1 To 10) As String

Sub TextBox_KeyDown (KeyCode As Integer, Shift As Integer)
    If Shift = SHIFT_MASK Then
       Select Case KeyCode
          Case KEY_F1: KeyStr(1) = TextBox.SelText
          Case KEY_F2: KeyStr(2) = TextBox.SelText
          Case KEY_F3: KeyStr(3) = TextBox.SelText
          Case KEY_F4: KeyStr(4) = TextBox.SelText
          Case KEY_F5: KeyStr(5) = TextBox.SelText
          Case KEY_F6: KeyStr(6) = TextBox.SelText
          Case KEY_F7: KeyStr(7) = TextBox.SelText
          Case KEY_F8: KeyStr(8) = TextBox.SelText
          Case KEY_F9: KeyStr(9) = TextBox.SelText
          Case KEY_F10: KeyStr(10) = TextBox.SelText
       End Select
    ElseIf Shift = CTRLMASK Then
       Select Case KeyCode
          Case KEY_F1: TextBox.SelText = KeyStr(1)
          Case KEY_F2: TextBox.SelText = KeyStr(2)
          Case KEY_F3: TextBox.SelText = KeyStr(3)
          Case KEY_F4: TextBox.SelText = KeyStr(4)
          Case KEY_F5: TextBox.SelText = KeyStr(5)
```

Listing 14-4 Continued.

```
        Case KEY_F6: TextBox.SelText = KeyStr(6)
        Case KEY_F7: TextBox.SelText = KeyStr(7)
        Case KEY_F8: TextBox.SelText = KeyStr(8)
        Case KEY_F9: TextBox.SelText = KeyStr(9)
        Case KEY_F10: TextBox.SelText = KeyStr(10)
      End Select
    End If
End Sub
```

The TextBox_KeyDown procedure handles storing and recalling the characters. The If-Then-ElseIf statement detects pressing the Ctrl and the Shift keys along with a function key. The first tested condition compares the Shift argument with the global constant SHIFT_MASK. This condition is true when the Shift key is pressed along with a function key. If the condition is true, a Select-Case statement is used to store the selected text in the proper element of array KeyStr.

The ElseIf clause compares the Shift argument with the global constant CTRL_MASK. This condition is true when the Ctrl key is pressed simultaneously with a function key. If the condition is true, a Select-Case statement is used to recall the characters from the proper element of array KeyStr.

Run the WINEDIT2 program and use this new feature. Now you can emulate text macros with the text editor.

15
Run time errors

The ideal program is one that does not encounter any errors. The reality of programming practices, however, involves dealing with various levels of errors. First, there is the *syntax error* that is generated by typing errors and the wrong use of procedures or functions. Such errors are caught by the syntax checker or the compiler. The second level of errors is the *logical program error*, where the program does what you are telling it to do and not what you really want it to do. Such errors are detected by testing the operations of the program. These two types of errors are related to the design time. A third kind of error creeps in at run time when invalid arguments are supplied in a statement. This chapter briefly looks at the error-handling techniques offered by Visual Basic. Before you read further, I want to point out that the error-handling facilities of Visual Basic are practically identical to those of Quick Basic. If you are a practicing Quick Basic programmer, you may want to skim through this chapter or skip it altogether.

In this chapter you will learn about:

- Defensive programming techniques.
- Visual Basic error-handlers.
- The various types of errors that can be dealt with in Visual Basic.
- Local versus central error-handling.

Run time errors can appear in just about every aspect of your program. Every task executed by even one block of statements can go wrong (Murphy's law). Therefore, I will only present examples for run time errors.

Defensive programming techniques

There is a car commercial on TV that says, "The best way to survive a collision is to avoid having one." This is the basic philosophy of defensive programming techniques—avoid the occurrence of a run time error. Defensive programming employs code that checks for possible error generating conditions to avoid the occurrence. This preemptive approach to run time error handling (or error avoiding, if you prefer) is optional in Visual Basic and other Microsoft Basic implementations. It is interesting to point out that prominent languages like Pascal, C, and Modula-2 rely on defensive programming techniques to avoid run time errors!

An example of defensive programming is shown in the next Function procedure that returns a −1 if the file argument exists, and 0 when otherwise. Attempting to open a nonexistent file for input generates a run time error. A function like FileExists enables you to avoid that type of run time error. The function is shown below:

```
Sub Function FileExists (Filename As String) As Integer
    If Dir$(Filename) = "" Then
        FileExists = 0 ' False
    Else
        FileExists = −1 ' True
    End If
End If
```

The FileExists function employs the predefined Dir$() function to return the first name of the file that matches the wildcard filename argument; in the case of the FileExists function, the filename itself is used as the search wildcard filename. If the Dir$ function returns an empty string no matching file is found, because the specified file does not exist. Otherwise, Dir$ returns a nonempty string, because the sought file does exist.

The FileExists function accomplishes its task without using the technique of attempting to open the sought file for input to see whether it exists.

Visual Basic error handling

Visual Basic offers the On Error and Resume statements to trap and handle run time errors. The general syntax for the On Error statement is:

```
On [Local] Error { GoTo { line ¦ label } ¦ Resume Next ¦ GoTo 0 }
```

The Local keyword is permitted in procedure-level error handling for the sake of compatibility with other Microsoft Basic implementation. The Goto { line ¦ label } clause directs program execution to the line containing the specified line number of label. The line or label must reside in the same procedure; otherwise, Visual Basic emits an error message. The Resume Next clause indicates that the program should resume at the next statement; the error is practically ignored. The GoTo 0 clause disables any active error handling.

When the program execution is directed to the error-handling statements, you typically use the Resume statement to determine how to resume the program. The general syntax for the Resume statement is:

Resume { [0] ¦ Next ¦ *line* }

The Resume 0 statement causes the program execution to continue with the offending statement, or the most recently executed call out of the procedure that contains the error handler.

The Resume Next statement results in resuming the program execution with the statement that directly follows the offending statement, or with the statement that follows the most recently executed call out of the procedure that contains the error handler.

The Resume *line* statement directs program execution to a specific local label.

:skull: Visual Basic reports additional error when misapplying the Resume statement in the following cases:

- A Resume statement is encountered when there is no error condition to handle. In other words, you must not allow program execution to run into a Resume statement when no error is raised.
- The Resume line statement points to a label outside the current procedure.
- Executing an End, End Sub, or End Function before a Resume statement is encountered, when an error is raised by the run time system. This means that you cannot sweep a run time error under the rug, so to speak.

Visual Basic offers the following functions that enable you to examine the type of the error that occurred:

The Err function   This function returns an integer which represents the run time error code for the error that just occurred.

The Errl function   This returns an integer that indicates the line number of the offending statement, or the closest line number before that statement.

The Error$ function   With this function, a message is returned that describes the most recent error or the error of a given code. The general syntax of the Error$ function is:

[*stringExpression$* =] Error$([*errorCode%*)]

When the errorCode% argument is omitted, the Error$ function describes the most recent error. This is the same message you obtain from the expression Error$(Err).

Visual Basic also offers the Error statement to simulate a run time error. The general syntax for the Error statement is:

    Error errorCode%

The range of values for the errorCode% argument is 1 to 32767. When the errorCode% matches a Visual Basic error code, that error is simulated. To use your own error code, Microsoft recommends that you start with 32767 and work your way down. This strategy ensures that you have enough numbers to simulate your own errors and not overlap with the numbers reserved by Visual Basic. The Error$ function returns the string User-defined error for error codes that are not used by Visual Basic.

Visual Basic allows you to turn off an error handler by executing an On Error GoTo 0 statement.

The types of run time errors

In this section I discuss various ways of handling run time errors. This list is by no means comprehensive, but rather includes the most frequent error handling strategies.

The fatal error type This is the type of error that cannot be recovered without at least rebooting (or even changing machines!). In this case an On Error Goto Resume directs the program execution to the error-handling section that displays a message and then ends the program. A general form of a procedure that handles fatal errors is shown below:

```
Sub CriticalProcedure ()
    ' statements that do not generate error
    On Error Resume FatalError
    . . .
    ' error generating statement(s)
    . . .
Exit Sub
FatalError:
    MsgBox FatalErrorMessage$, 0, "Fatal Error!"
        End
End Sub
```

The abandon-error type This is the kind of error that causes you to exit the host procedure. I have used this type of error handler with procedures that perform file I/O. Frequently, file I/O errors are caused by a bad filename. The strategy used directs the program execution to the error-handling statements, as shown next:

```
Sub DoFileIO (Filename As String)
    ' statements that do not generate error
    On Error GoTo FileIOError
    . . .
```

```
Open Filename For Input As #1
      . . .
   Exit Sub
FilelOError:
   MsgBox ErrorMessage$, 0, "File I/O Error"
   Resume ExitDoFileIO
ExitDoFileIO:
End Sub
```

The error-handling statements display an error message and then resume to a label placed just before the End Sub.

The abandon-error type can also be used to implement a version of
the FileExists function, as shown below:

```
Function FileExists (Filename As String) As Integer
   On Error GoTo FileNotFound
   Open Filename For Input As #1
   Close #1
   FileExists = −1 ' True
   Exit Function
FileNotFound:
   Resume NextLine
NextLine:
   FileExists = 0 ' False
End Function
```

The ignore-error type   This error-handling strategy assumes that you can
resume executing the next statement. For example, you need to rename a
file with the .BAK extension name. However, you need to first make sure
that any possible .BAK file with the same name is erased. The Resume Next
clause, shown below, permits you to delete the older .BAK first:

```
On Error Resume Next
Kill filename$ + ".BAK"
On Error GoTo 0
```

If the older .BAK file does not exist, the error trap enables you to simply
resume program execution at the next statement.

The retry type   This kind of error is typically associated with trying to read
a file from a disk whose door is open. The error-handling statements
display a message asking you to make sure that the disk drive door is
closed before you try reading the file again. The general form of a procedure containing this kind of error-handling scheme is shown next:

```
Sub DoFileIO (Filename As String)
   ' statements that do not generate error
   On Error GoTo FilelOError
      . . .
```

```
    Open Filename For Input As #1
    . . .
    Exit Sub
FileIOError:
  If Err = Err_DiskNotReady Then
    MsgBox "Disk drive door is open, please close it", 0, "Error"
    Resume 0
  Else
    MsgBox ErrorMessage$, 0, "File I/O Error"
    Resume ExitDoFileIO
  End If
ExitDoFileIO:
End Sub
```

The Else clause of the If statement in the error-handling section deals with other file I/O errors.

The limited-retry method   This scheme is a modified version of the last one. The basic philosophy is that there should be a limit to certain types of errors. A maximum limit is specified using either a local or global constant along with an error occurrence counter variable. The general form is shown here:

```
Sub DoFileIO (Filename As String)
    Const MAX_ERRORS = 3
    Dim ErrorCount
    ErrorCount = 0
    ' statements that do not generate error
    On Error GoTo FileIOError

    . . .
    Open Filename For Input As #1

    . . .
    Exit Sub
FileIOError:
  If Err = Err_DiskNotReady Then
    ErrorCount = ErrorCount + 1
    If ErrorCount < MAX_ERRORS Then
      MsgBox )Disk drive door is open, please close it", 0, "Error"
      Resume 0
    Else
      MsgBox "Drive is considered invalid", 0, "Bad Error!"
      Resume ExitDoFileIO
    Else
    MsgBox ErrorMessage$, 0, "File I/O Error"
    Resume ExitDoFileIO
  End If
ExitDoFileIO:
End Sub
```

The Then clause of the first If statement increments the ErrorCount variable and compares its value with MAX_ERRORS. While the number of error occurrences is below the limit tolerated, the code uses a Resume 0 to retry executing the offending statement. Beyond that limit, the code performs a Resume ExitDoFileIO to exit the procedure.

The retry-with-new-data type   This error-handling approach looks for alternate information that will not raise the error condition when the offending statement is executed again. The new data is obtained either by prompting the user (typically using the InputBox$ function) or by retrieving data from an array or a control. The following general form shows the user input case:

```
Sub DoFileIO (Filename As String)
    Dim S As String
    ' statements that do not generate error
    On Error GoTo FileIOError
    . . .

    Open Filename For Input As #1
    . . .
    Exit Sub
FileIOError:
    S = InputBox$(ErrorMessage$, "File I/O Error", Filename)
    If S <> ""Then ' user pressed the OK button
        Filename = S ' update filename
        Resume 0 ' retry file I/O statement
    Else ' user pressed the Cancel button
        Resume ExitDoFileIO ' exit
    End If
ExitDoFileIO:
End Sub
```

When you use the InputBox$, you should take into consideration that the user might press the Cancel button. This action is interpreted as meaning the user does not wish to supply new data (for whatever reason). Consequently, the procedure is exited.

The delayed-error-handling type   This approach stores the error code in a variable in order to deal with the error later. Unless this approach makes better sense or is far more suitable than the previous ones, I do not recommend it.

16
Working with the file system controls

Windows applications, including Visual Basic, typically employ filename dialog boxes when you want to load a file or save a file under a new name. We have grown accustomed to this kind of dialog box in a Windows application, because it enables us to navigate through any drive and any directory. The Visual Basic designers have elected to include control objects that permit Visual Basic applications to offer the same type of filename dialog boxes. These controls are the Drive list box, the Directory list box, and the File list box. In this chapter you will learn about the following:

- The relevant properties and events of the Drive list box, the Directory list box, and the File list box.
- Using the above controls to implement a directory tree browser, and a general purpose filename dialog box.

The drive list box

The Drive list box is a drop down combo list box that returns the current drive and switches between the disk drives at run time. The properties relevant to selecting a current drive are discussed next.

The Drive **property**   This returns and assigns the selected drive at run time. It is not available at design time. The general syntax for the Drive property is:

> [*form.*]driveListBox.Drive [=*driveName$*]

The valid range of values for the Drive setting includes all the drives that are on-line (physical or logical). By default, the Drive setting is assigned the current drive. The Drive property returns the drive information using one of the following formats:

- a:, b:, etc. for floppy drives.
- c:[volume id] for hard disks.
- x:\\server\share for networks.

When you write to a new drive you should observe the following rules:

- The first character of the driveName$ string is the only significant part of the assigned string. The assignment is not case-sensitive.
- When the Drive property is changed, a Change event occurs.
- Assigning a new Drive setting causes the regeneration of the drive list.
- Assigning a nonexistent drive results in a run time error.

The ListCount, List, **and** ListIndex **properties**   These properties are similar to the ones in the list box and combo list box controls that I presented earlier in this book. The difference between the Drive list box and the other list box controls is that the drive's properties are read-only. The ListCount property specifies the number data items in the drive list box. The ListIndex points to the currently selected data item. The values of the ListIndex range from 0 to ListCount − 1. The List(I%) property enables you to select the I%th list item.

The Change event is relevant to changing the current drive. This event can be used to update the directory list box. This will be discussed later in this chapter.

The Directory list box

The Directory list box shows the directories and the current path at run time; it also displays the ancestor directories and subdirectories of the current directory. When you select the root directory, the control shows all of the immediate subdirectories in the current drive. The properties discussed in the following paragraphs are relevant to selecting a current directory.

The Path **property**   This property returns and assigns the selected directory at run time. This property is not available at design time. The general syntax for the Path property is:

[*form.*]*fileListBox*.Path [=*pathName$*]

The default Path setting is the current directory. The Path property retrieves the current directory. Assigning a new setting to the Path property selects a new directory. This has the same effect as the ChDir statement. The assigned directory can be a partial path or even a drive name (without the colon). In the latter case, the Path setting changes the current drive and simultaneously selects the current directory of that drive.

Assign a new Path setting results in the occurrence of a Change event for the directory list box and a PathChange event for the accompanying file list boxes.

The ListCount, List, **and** ListIndex **properties**   These properties are similar to the ones in the Drive list box.

The Change event is used to change the current directory. This event can be used to update the File list box, as I will describe later in this chapter.

The File list box

The File list box is a drop down combo list box that selects a file to be opened, saved, deleted, copied, renamed, or processed in other ways. The file list box properties that are relevant to selecting a file are:

The Pattern **property**   This defines which filenames are displayed in the File list box. The general syntax for the Pattern property is:

> [*form.*]*fileListBox.Pattern* [*=filenameWildcard$*]

The default Pattern setting is *.* that shows all of the files. The Pattern property returns the current filename pattern. To change the list of files, assign a new setting to the Pattern property. Typical pattern settings include wildcards, such as *.*, *.BAS, *.EXE, and *.TXT, to name just a few. When you change the Pattern setting a PatternChange event occurs.

The file attribute properties   These Boolean properties, which can be set or queried, specify files that appear in the list box based on the matching file attributes. These properties are the Archive, Hidden, Normal, ReadOnly, and System properties. The general syntax for these properties is shown below:

> [*form.*]*fileListBox.*Archive [*=Boolean%*]
> [*form.*]*fileListBox.*Hidden [*=Boolean%*]
> [*form.*]*fileListBox.*Normal [*=Boolean%*]
> [*form.*]*fileListBox.*ReadOnly [*=Boolean%*]
> [*form.*]*fileListBox.*System [*=Boolean%*]

The default setting for the Archive, Normal, and ReadOnly properties is −1 (True). The default setting for the other properties is 0 (False).

☞ The file list box displays a file that meets the following conditions:

- The file fits the filename Pattern setting, such as *.*, *.EXE, or *.TXT.
- All of the file attributes correspond to file attribute settings that are equal to −1 (True).

The file attribute properties act as an additional file display filter together with the Pattern property.

The ListCount, List, **and** ListIndex **properties**   These properties are similar to the ones in the drive list box. The selected file is given by the expression *fileListBox*.List(*fileListBox*.ListIndex).

The Filename **property**   This property returns the file selected in the File list box. It also allows you to assign a new drive, path, and/or pattern. The general syntax for the Filename property is:

>   [*form*.]*fileListBox.Filename* [=*filename$*]

When the program starts running, the Filename setting is an empty string, because there is no file selected. Using the Filename property is the shortcut for using the List and ListIndex properties.

When you assign a new Filename setting you should take note of the following rules:

- If the new setting contains a drive, path, or pattern, the Drive property (of a drive list box), Path property (of a directory list box), and Pattern property are automatically updated.
- If the new Filename setting specifies the name of an existing file, that file is displayed and also selected.
- The new setting may generate PathChange, PatternChange, and DblClick (when you select an existing file).

☞   The unique aspect of the Drive and Directory list boxes is that all of the instances of their controls tap into the same information. In other words, there is only one currently selected drive and one currently selected directory. Regardless of how many Drive or Directory list boxes you have, you will get the same information. The file list box is different. You can have multiple file list boxes, each with different Pattern and file attribute properties, that display different files.

Next, I present two programs that show how the various properties of the Drive, Directory, and File list boxes work together.

The directory tree viewer

The first demonstration program is a simple utility that displays the files in the current directory. The Pattern and file attribute properties specify the files that appear in the file list box. In addition, I implemented a secondary feature that automatically selects a predefined file.

Figures 16-1 to 16-3 contain the specifications for the TREEVU1.MAK project file and the TREEVU1.FRM form file. Figure 16-4 shows a sample session with the directory tree viewer.

Application name: Directory Tree Viewer
Application code name: TREEVU1
Version: 1.0   Date created: July 19, 1991
Programmer(s): Namir Clement Shammas

List of filenames

Storage path: \VB\EASYVB
Project TREEVU1.MAK
Global GLOBAL.BAS
Form 1 TREEVU1.FRM

16-1 The basic specifications for the TREEVU1.MAK project file.

Form #1   Form filename: TREEVU1.FRM
Version: 1.0   Date: July 19, 1991

Control object type	Default CtlName	Purpose
Drive List Box	Drive1	Shows and selects the current drive
Directory List	Dir1	Shows, selects the current directory
File List Box	File1	Shows a group of files
Frame	Frame1	Contains the file attribute check boxes
Check Box	Check1	Toggles the Archive property
	Check2	Toggles the Hidden property
	Check3	Toggles the ReadOnly property
	Check4	Toggles the Normal property
	Check5	Toggles the System property
Text Box	Text1	Specifies the filename pattern
	Text2	Specifies the selected file
Command Box	Command1	Exits the program
	Command2	Find a matching file
Label	Label1	Label for filename pattern
	Label2	Label for selected file
	Label3	Label for drive list box
	Label4	Label for directory list box
	Label5	Label for file list box

16-2 The list of controls in the TREEVU1.FRM form.

Application (code) name: TREEVU1
Form #1
Version: 1.0   Date: July 19, 1991

Original control name	Property	New setting
Form	Caption	Directory Tree Viewer
Drive1	CtlName	DiskDrv

16-3 The customized settings of the TREEVU1.FRM form.

Original control name	Property	New setting
Dir1	CtlName	TreeDir
File1	CtlName	FileFlb
Frame1	CtlName	FileAttrFrm
	Caption	"File Attributes" (no quotes)
Check1	CtlName	ArchiveChk
	Caption	Archive
Check2	CtlName	HiddenChk
	Caption	Hidden
Check3	CtlName	ReadOnlyChk
	Caption	Read-Only
Check4	CtlName	NormalChk
	Caption	Normal
Check5	CtlName	SystemChk
	Caption	System
Text1	CtlName	PatternBox
	Text	(empty string)
Text2	CtlName	FindFileBox
	Text	(empty string)
Command1	CtlName	QuitBtn
	Caption	&Quit
	Cancel	True
Command2	CtlName	FindFileBtn
	Caption	&Find File
Label1	CtlName	PatternLbl
	Caption	Filename:
Label2	CtlName	FindFileLbl
	Caption	Find Filename:
Label3	CtlName	DriveLbl
	Caption	Drive:
Label4	CtlName	DirectoryLbl
	Caption	Directory:
Label5	CtlName	FilesLbl
	Caption	Files:

16-3 Continued.

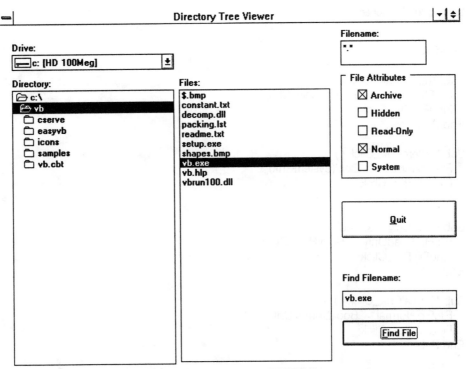

16-4 A sample session with the TREEVU1 program.

Listing 16-1 contains the code attached to the TREEVU1.FRM form. Several procedures should be noted.

Listing 16-1 The code attached to the TREEVU1.FRM form.

```
Sub Form_Load ( )
    WindowState = 2
    PatternBox.Text = "*.*"
    FileFlb.Archive = True
    ArchiveChk.Value = 1
    FileFlb.Hidden = False
    FileFlb.Normal = True
    NormalChk.Value = 1
    FileFlb.ReadOnly = False
    FileFlb.System = False
End Sub

Sub DiskDrv_Change ( )
    ' update file tree path when the disk is changed
    TreeDir.Path = DiskDrv.Drive
End Sub

Sub QuitBtn_Click ( )
```

Listing 16-1 Continued.

```
  End
End Sub

Sub ArchiveChk_Click ( )
  FileFlb.Archive = Bool(ArchiveChk)
  FindFileBtn_Click
End Sub

Sub SystemChk_Click ( )
  FileFlb.System = Bool(SystemChk)
  FindFileBtn_Click
End Sub

Sub ReadOnlyChk_Click ( )
  FileFlb.ReadOnly = Bool(ReadOnlyChk)
  FindFileBtn_Click
End Sub

Sub NormalChk_Click ( )
  FileFlb.Normal = Bool(NormalChk)
  FindFileBtn_Click
End Sub

Sub HiddenChk_Click ( )
  FileFlb.Hidden = Bool(HiddenChk)
  FindFileBtn_Click
End Sub

Sub TreeDir_Change ( )
  FileFlb.Path = TreeDir.Path
  FindFileBtn_Click
End Sub

Sub PatternBox_KeyPress (KeyAscii As Integer)
  KeyAscii = Asc(LCase$(Chr$(KeyAscii)))
End Sub

Sub PatternBox_LostFocus ( )
  Dim I As Integer
  If PatternBox.Text = " " Then PatternBox.Text = "*.*"
  I = InStr(PatternBox.Text, " ") ' find first space
  If I > 0 Then
    PatternBox.Text = Mid$(PatternBox.Text, 1, I − 1)
  End If
  FileFlb.Filename = PatternBox.Text
  FindFileBtn_Click
End Sub
```

Listing 16-1 Continued.

```
Sub FindFileBox_KeyPress (KeyAscii As Integer)
   KeyAscii = Asc(LCase$(Chr$(KeyAscii)))
End Sub

Sub FindFileBtn_Click ( )
   Dim I As Integer
   Dim S As String
   If FindFileBox.Text = " " Then Exit Sub
   S = FindFileBox.Text
   I = BinSearch(S, FileFlb)
   If I > −1 Then
      FileFlb.ListIndex = I
   End If
End Sub

Function BinSearch (Filename As String, Flb As Control) As Integer
   ' perform binary search on the file list box entries
   Dim Lo As Integer, Hi As Integer, Median As Integer
   If TypeOf Flb Is FileListBox Then
   Else
      BinSearch = −1
      Exit Function
   End If
   Lo = 0
   Hi = Flb.ListCount − 1
   Do
      Median = (Lo + Hi) \ 2
      If Filename < Flb.List(Median) Then
         Hi = Median − 1
      Else
         Lo = Median + 1
      End If
   Loop Until (Filename = Flb.List(Median)) Or (Lo > Hi)
   If Filename = Flb.List(Median) Then
      BinSearch = Median
   Else
      BinSearch = −1
   End If
End Function

Sub FileFlb_PatternChange ( )
   FindFileBtn_Click
End Sub

Function Bool (C As Control) As Integer
   Bool = −1 * C.Value
End Function
```

The Form_Load procedure This procedure initializes the form and its controls when loaded. Of interest are the following initialization tasks:

- Assigns *.* to the Text property of the pattern text box.
- Assigns the global constant True to the Archive and Normal properties of the FileFlb file list box.
- Sets the Value property of the Archive and Normal check boxes to 1. These controls appear checked when the program starts running.
- Assigns the global constant False to the Hidden, ReadOnly, and System properties of the FileFlb file list box.

The DiskDrv_Change procedure The Path setting of the Directory list box is updated by this procedure with the new Drive setting of the Drive list box. This synchronizes the Directory list box with the Drive list box.

The TreeDir_Change procedure TreeDir_Change updates the Path setting of the File list box with the new Path setting of the Directory list box. The procedure also invokes the FindFileBtn_Click procedure to search for the target file in the updated File list box.

The FileFlb_PatternChange procedure This procedure calls the FindFileBtn_Click procedure when the pattern is updated.

The Bool function Bool returns True if the Value setting of its control-typed parameter is 1. If the setting is 0, the function returns False.

The Family of event-handling procedures This group of procedures handles the Click events for the check boxes. These procedures set the file attribute properties based on the Value setting of the corresponding check box. The Bool function obtains a True or False value from the check box argument.

The PatternBox_LostFocus procedure This essentially updates the Filename property of the File list box. This procedure performs the following tasks:

- Assigns *.* to the Text setting if the pattern text box is empty.
- Scans for the occurrence of the first space within the characters of the text box. If a space is found, the characters from the space to the end are deleted. This action ensures the elimination of multiple wildcards.
- Assigns the Text property of the pattern text box to the Filename property. You can replace the Filename property with the Pattern property. The program works fine until you specify a pattern that includes a drive; then, Visual Basic generates a run time error.

- Invokes the FindFileBtn_Click procedure to search for a matching file that is specified in the Find Filename text box.

The FindFileBtn_Click **procedure**   This procedure searches for the file list box member that matches the filename in the Find Filename text box. If the latter text box is empty, the search is aborted. The BinSearch function is invoked to obtain the index of the matching item in the File list box. If no match is found the BinSearch function returns −1. When a match is found the ListIndex of the file list box is set to the index of the matching item. This causes that item to be selected.

The BinSearch **function**   BinSearch searches for the Filename argument in the Flb file list box argument. I wrote this function as a general purpose routine. The function uses the efficient binary search method algorithm that is applied to the ordered members of the file list box. The function returns the index of the matching list item, or −1 when no match is found.

Run the directory tree viewer program and experiment with selecting different drives, directories, filename patterns, and file attributes. Once you get a feel for the basic program features, type in a filename in the Find Filename text box. I suggest that you select the name of a file that is present in more than one directory. Click on the Find File button. If the sought file is in the current directory, the program selects it. Now move to other directories that contain a file that matches the file specified in the Find Filename text box. As soon as the file list appears, the program zooms in on the matching file and selects it.

The text editor

In chapter 14 I presented two versions of a simple menu-driven text editor. The Load and Add menu options prompted you for the name of a file using a simple dialog box. These programs lack the ability to show you a file dialog box that enables you to choose the file you want without guessing its correct name and/or path. In this section, I present a new version of the text editor that uses a dialog box with the Drive, Directory, and File list boxes. The program uses two forms. The first form shows the same interface of the WINEDIT1 and WINEDIT2 programs. The second form is shown in FIG. 16-5. That form contains the dialog box controls.

The new version of the text editor, WINEDIT3, uses the modal file dialog box when you invoke the Load and Add options of the File menu.

Figure 16-6 contains the specifications for the WINEDIT3.MAK project file. The specifications for the WINEDIT3.FRM form file and its menu structure is the same as those shown in FIG. 14-3 to 14-5. Figures 16-7 and 16-8 contain the specifications for the FILEDLG.FRM form file.

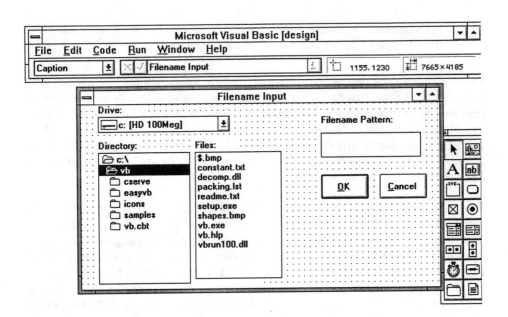

Program Manager

16-5 The FILEDLG.FRM interface.

Application name: Window Text Editor (version 3)
Application code name: WINEDIT3
Version: 1.0   Date created: July 19, 1991
Programmer(s): Namir Clement Shammas

List of filenames
Storage path: \VB\EASYVB
Project WINEDIT3.MAK
Global GLOBAL2.BAS
Form 1 WINEDIT3.FRM
Form 2 FILEDLG.FRM

16-6 The general specifications for the WINEDIT3.MAK project file.

Form #2   Form filename: FILEDLG.FRM
Version: 1.0   Date: July 19, 1991

Control object type	Default CtlName	Purpose
Drive List Box	Drive1	Shows and selects the current drive
Directory List	Dir1	Shows and selects the current directory
File List Box	File1	Shows a group of files

16-7 The list of controls of the FILEDLG.FRM form.

Control object type	Default CtlName	Purpose
Text Box	Text1	Specifies the filename pattern
Command Box	Command1	Accepts the selected file and exits the dialog box
	Command2	Rejects the file selection and exits the dialog box
Label	Label1	Label for filename pattern
	Label2	Label for drive list box
	Label3	Label for directory list box
	Label4	Label for file list box

16-7 Continued.

Application (code) name: WINEDIT3
Form #2
Version: 1.0   Date: July 19, 1991

Original control name	Property	New setting
Form	Caption	FileDialog Box
	FormName	FileDialogBox
Drive1	CtlName	DiskDrv
Dir1	CtlName	TreeDir
File1	CtlName	FileFlb
Text1	CtlName	FilenameBox
	Text	(empty string)
Command1	CtlName	OKBtn
	Caption	&OK
Command2	CtlName	CancelBtn
	Caption	&Cancel
	Cancel	True
Label1	CtlName	FilenameLbl
	Caption	Filename:
Label2	CtlName	DriveLbl
	Caption	Drive:
Label3	CtlName	DirectoryLbl
	Caption	Directory:
Label4	CtlName	FilesLbl
	Caption	Files:

16-8 The customized settings of form FILEDLG.FRM.

The program uses the global file GLOBAL2.BAS. This file is similar to the GLOBAL.BAS file that I have been using so far. The only difference is the following declaration that is placed at the beginning of file GLOBAL2.BAS:

```
Global GlobalFilename As String
```

This global variable enables the file dialog box to return the name of the selected file. I will describe the role of that variable in more detail when I present the updated procedure of the text editor.

Listing 16-2 contains the code attached to the WINEDIT3.FRM form. The updated code portions for this new version are discussed next.

Listing 16-2 The code attached to the WINEDIT3.FRM form.

```
Dim NumFiles As Integer
Dim UseFileDialogBox As Integer
' declare the strings that store the ten text blocks
Dim KeyStr(1 To 10) As String

Sub QuitCom_Click ( )
  End
End Sub

Sub DosCom_Click ( )
  Dim Dummy As Integer
  ' invoke the DOSBAT batch file
  Dummy = Shell("dosbat.bat " + DosBox.Text, 1)
End Sub

Sub FindCom_Click ( )
  Static CurIndex As Long
  Dim Find As String
  ' update the index to the current character
  CurIndex = TextBox.SelStart + 1
  ' store the text of the Find box in the variable Find
  Find = FindBox.Text
  ' is variable Find empty?
  If Find = " " Then Exit Sub ' nothing to find
  ' locate the index of the next substring Find in the
  ' text box
  If CaseSenseChk.Value = 1 Then
    CurIndex = InStr(CurIndex + 1, TextBox.Text, Find)
  Else
    CurIndex = InStr(CurIndex + 1, UCase$(TextBox.Text), UCase$(Find))
  End If
  ' found a match?
  If CurIndex > 0 Then
    ' Yes! Display the matching text as selected text
    TextBox.SelStart = CurIndex - 1
```

Listing 16-2   Continued.

```
      TextBox.SelLength = Len(Find)
      TextBox.SetFocus
      FindCom.Checked = True
    Else
      ' No! Clear any selected text
      TextBox.SelStart = 0
      TextBox.SelLength = 0
      FindCom.Checked = False
    End If
End Sub


Sub FindFileCom_Click ( )
   Dim Dummy As Integer
   ' invoke the DOS dir command with the /s
   ' subdirectory option and the /p paginated
   ' output option
   Dummy = Shell("dosbat.bat dir " + FilenameBox.Text + " /s/p", 1)
End Sub


Sub WinCom_Click ( )
   Dim Dummy As Integer
   ' invoke a Windows application
   Dummy = Shell(DosBox.Text, 1)
End Sub


Sub ToggleOSCom_Click ( )
   ' toggle the Visible property of the DosBox text box,
   ' the DosBtn button, the WinBtn button, and the DosLbl
   ' label
   DosBox.Visible = Not DosBox.Visible
   DosCom.Visible = Not DosCom.Visible
   WinCom.Visible = Not WinCom.Visible
   DosLbl.Visible = Not DosLbl.Visible
End Sub


Sub FindLbl_Change ( )
   FindCom.Checked = False
End Sub


Sub FindBox_Change ( )
   FindCom.Checked = 0
End Sub


Sub AddFileCom_Click ( )
   FileDialogBox.Show 1
   If GlobalFilename < > " " Then
      NumFiles = NumFiles + 1 ' increment the menu count
      Load QuickFilename(NumFiles) ' load a new menu command
```

Listing 16-2 Continued.

```
        QuickFilename(NumFiles).Caption = GlobalFilename
        QuickFilename(NumFiles).Visible = True
      End If
  End Sub

  Sub QuickFilename_Click (Index As Integer)
    FilenameBox.Text = QuickFilename(Index).Caption
    UseFileDialogBox = False
    LoadCom_Click
    UseFileDialogBox = True
  End Sub

  Sub DeleteFileCom_Click ( )
    Dim N As Integer, I As Integer
    N = Val(InputBox$("Enter number to delete: "))
    If (N > 0) And (N < = NumFiles) Then
      For I = N To NumFiles − 1
        QuickFilename(I).Caption = QuickFilename(I + 1).Caption
      Next I
      Unload QuickFilename(NumFiles)
      NumFiles = NumFiles − 1
    Else
      MsgBox "The number is out-of-range", 0, "Input Error"
    End If
  End Sub

  Sub Form_Load ( )
    NumFiles = 0
    WindowState = 2
    TextBox.FontName = "System"
    TextBox.FontSize = 10
    UseFileDialogBox = True
    ReadOnlyCom_Click
  End Sub

  Sub LoadCom_Click ( )
    Dim F As String
    Dim L As String
    Dim NL As String * 2
    If UseFileDialogBox Then
      FileDialogBox.Show 1
      If GlobalFilename < > " " Then
        FilenameBox.Text = GlobalFilename
      Else
        Exit Sub
      End If
    End If
    ' obtain filename from the filename text box
```

Listing 16-2 Continued.

```
   F = FilenameBox.Text
   ' if filename is an empty string, exit
   If F = " " Then Exit Sub
   NL = Chr$(13) + Chr$(10)
   ' set error-handler
   On Error GoTo BadFile
   ' open the file
   Open F For Input As 1
   F = " " ' clear variable to reuse it
   ' loop to read the text lines from the ASCII file
   Do While Not EOF(1)
      Line Input #1, L
      F = F + L + NL ' append a new line
   Loop
   TextBox.Text = F ' copy F into text box
   ' close the file
   Close #1
   ' exit procedure
   Exit Sub
' ********** Error-handler **********
BadFile:
   Beep
   MsgBox "Cannot open file " + F, 0, "File I/O Error"
   On Error GoTo 0
   Resume EndOfSub
EndOfSub:
End Sub

Sub SaveCom_Click ( )
   If (FilenameBox.Text < > " ") And (TextBox.Text < > " ") Then
      On Error GoTo BadSaveFilename
      Open FilenameBox.Text For Output As #1
      On Error GoTo 0
      Print #1, TextBox.Text
      Close #1
   End If
   Exit Sub


' *************** Error-Handler **************
BadSaveFilename:
   On Error GoTo 0
   MsgBox "Cannot write to file " + FilenameBox.Text, 0, "File I/O Error"
   Resume ExitSaveFile
ExitSaveFile:
End Sub

Sub CutCom_Click ( )
   Clipboard.SetText Screen.ActiveControl.SelText
```

Listing 16-2 Continued.

```
    Screen.ActiveControl.SelText = " "
End Sub

Sub CopyCom_Click ( )
  If Screen.ActiveControl.SelText < > " " Then
    Clipboard.SetText Screen.ActiveControl.SelText, CF_TEXT
  End If
End Sub

Sub AppendCom_Click ( )
  Dim S As String
  If TextBox.SelText = " " Then Exit Sub
  S = Clipboard.GetText( )
  S = S + Chr$(13) + Chr$(10) + TextBox.SelText
  Clipboard.SetText S, CF_TEXT
End Sub

Sub PasteCom_Click ( )
  Screen.ActiveControl.SelText = Clipboard.GetText( )
End Sub

Sub ToggleLoadCom_Click ( )
  LoadCom.Enabled = Not LoadCom.Enabled
  ToggleLoadCom.Checked = Not LoadCom.Enabled
End Sub

Sub ClearCom_Click ( )
  Clipboard.Clear
End Sub

Sub ViewCom_Click ( )
  Static ViewClipboard As Integer
  Static theFilename As String
  Static theFileText As String
  If ViewClipboard Then
    ViewClipboard = False
    ViewCom.Caption = "View Clipboard"
    ClearCom.Enabled = True
    AppendCom.Enabled = True
    FilenameBox.Text = theFilename
    Clipboard.SetText TextBox.Text, CF_TEXT
    TextBox.Text = theFileText
    theFileText = " "
  Else
    ViewClipboard = True
    ViewCom.Caption = "View File"
    ClearCom.Enabled = False
    AppendCom.Enabled = False
```

Listing 16-2 Continued.

```
      theFilename = FilenameBox.Text
      theFileText = TextBox.Text
      FilenameBox.Text = "Clipboard"
      TextBox.Text = Clipboard.GetText( )
   End If
End Sub

Sub ReadOnlyCom_Click ( )
   SaveCom.Enabled = Not SaveCom.Enabled
   ReadOnlyCom.Checked = Not SaveCom.Enabled
End Sub

Sub FindSelTextCom_Click ( )
   If TextBox.SelText < > " " Then
      FindBox.Text = TextBox.SelText
   End If
   FindCom_Click
End Sub

Sub TextBox_KeyDown (KeyCode As Integer, Shift As Integer)
   If Shift = SHIFT_MASK Then
      Select Case KeyCode
         Case KEY_F1: KeyStr(1) = TextBox.SelText
         Case KEY_F2: KeyStr(2) = TextBox.SelText
         Case KEY_F3: KeyStr(3) = TextBox.SelText
         Case KEY_F4: KeyStr(4) = TextBox.SelText
         Case KEY_F5: KeyStr(5) = TextBox.SelText
         Case KEY_F6: KeyStr(6) = TextBox.SelText
         Case KEY_F7: KeyStr(7) = TextBox.SelText
         Case KEY_F8: KeyStr(8) = TextBox.SelText
         Case KEY_F9: KeyStr(9) = TextBox.SelText
         Case KEY_F10: KeyStr(10) = TextBox.SelText
      End Select
   Elself Shift = CTRL_MASK Then
      Select Case KeyCode
         Case KEY_F1: TextBox.SelText = KeyStr(1)
         Case KEY_F2: TextBox.SelText = KeyStr(2)
         Case KEY_F3: TextBox.SelText = KeyStr(3)
         Case KEY_F4: TextBox.SelText = KeyStr(4)
         Case KEY_F5: TextBox.SelText = KeyStr(5)
         Case KEY_F6: TextBox.SelText = KeyStr(6)
         Case KEY_F7: TextBox.SelText = KeyStr(7)
         Case KEY_F8: TextBox.SelText = KeyStr(8)
         Case KEY_F9: TextBox.SelText = KeyStr(9)
         Case KEY_F10: TextBox.SelText = KeyStr(10)
      End Select
   End If
End Sub
```

The UseFileDialogBox **variable**   This variable is a Boolean flag used to decide whether or not to invoke the file dialog box.

The Form_Load **procedure**   This initializes the UseFileDialogBox variable with the global constant True.

The LoadCom_Click **procedure**   This procedure now includes the following If-Then statement that decides whether or not to load and invoke the file dialog box form:

```
If UseFileDialogBox Then
   FileDialogBox.Show 1
   If GlobalFilename <> "" Then
      FilenameBox.Text = GlobalFilename
   Else
      ExitSub
   End If
End If
```

A nested If statement decides whether or not the global variable Global-Filename is assigned to the filename text box. This enables you to preserve the name of the currently viewed file. The Else clause of the nested If statement causes program execution to exit the LoadCom_Click procedure.

The AddFileCom_Click **procedure**   In this procedure, the file dialog box is invoked to obtain the name of the quickly-loaded file to add in the File menu. The AddFileCom_Click procedure is shown here:

```
Sub AddFileCom_Click ()
   FileDialogBox.Show 1
   If GlobalFilename <> "" Then
      NumFiles = NumFiles + 1 ' increment the menu count
      Load QuickFilename(NumFiles) ' load a new menu command
      QuickFilename(NumFiles).Caption = GlobalFilename
      QuickFilename(NumFiles).Visible = True
   End If
End Sub
```

Notice that an If statement tests if the global variable GlobalFilename is not a null string (the result of pressing the Cancel button). If the condition is true, the selected filename is added to the list of QuickFilename controls.

The QuickFilenameCom_Click **procedure**   This procedure assigns the False constant to the variable UseFileDialogBox before calling LoadCom_Click. The procedure assigns the constant True to the variable UseFileDialogBox after calling LoadCom_Click, restoring the normal value of that variable. If the first assignment to the variable UseFileDialogBox is omitted, the procedure ends up invoking the file dialog box. This task defeats the purpose of having the quickly-loaded files in the first place.

Listing 16-3 shows the code attached to the FILEDLG.FRM form. The procedures in that form are described in the next several paragraphs.

Listing 16-3 The code attached to the FILEDLG.FRM form.

```
Sub CancelBtn_Click ( )
  GlobalFilename = " "
  Unload FileDialogBox
End Sub

Sub DiskDrv_Change ( )
  TreeDir.Path = DiskDrv.Drive
End Sub

Sub TreeDir_Change ( )
  FileFlb.Filename = TreeDir.Path
End Sub

Sub FilenameBox_LostFocus ( )
  If FilenameBox.Text = " " Then Exit Sub
  FileFlb.Filename = FilenameBox.Text
End Sub

Sub OKBtn_Click ( )
  If Right$(TreeDir.Path, 1) < > " \ " Then
    GlobalFilename = TreeDir.Path + " \ " + FileFlb.Filename
  Else
    GlobalFilename = TreeDir.Path + FileFlb.Filename
  End If
  Unload FileDialogBox
End Sub

Sub Form_Load ( )
  FileFlb.Archive = True
  FileFlb.Normal = True
  FileFlb.ReadOnly = False
  FileFlb.Hidden = False
  FileFlb.System = False
  FileFlb.Pattern = " *.* "
  FilenameBox.Text = " *.* "
End Sub

Sub FileFlb_DblClick ( )
  OKBtn_Click
End Sub
```

The Form_Load **procedure** This procedure initializes the file attribute properties, setting the Archive and Normal properties to True, and all of the other file attribute properties to False. The string *.* is assigned to both the Pattern property of the File list box and the Text property of the Filename text box.

The CancelBtn_Click **procedure** This implements a cancel request by assigning a null string to the global variable GlobalFilename. The procedure unloads the file dialog form and returns the control to the main form.

The OKBtn_Click **procedure** OKBtn_Click accepts the selected file and assigns it, along with the file's path, to the global variable GlobalFilename. The procedure then unloads the file dialog form and returns the control to the main form.

The FileFlb_DblClick **procedure** This procedure implements a shortcut for accepting the selected file. The procedure invokes OKBtn_Click, which does the rest of the work.

The DiskDrv_Change **procedure** This updates the Path setting of the Directory list box with the Drive setting of the Drive list box.

The TreeDir_Change **procedure** This procedure revises the Filename setting of the File list box with the Path setting of the Directory list box.

The FilenameBox_LostFocus **procedure** This updates the Filename setting of the File list box with the Text setting of the Filename text box.

I made the file dialog box form unload itself when finished. This measure preserves the memory used by secondary forms that act as dialog boxes. The price to pay for this feature is the use of the global variable GlobalFilename. You can modify the file dialog box form so that it hides itself when finished. This enables you to store the selected file in an invisible text box that you must also add (call it SelectedFileBox). The primary form is able to obtain the name of the selected file by using the expression FormDialogBox.SelectedFileBox.Text.

17
File I/O

The file I/O system of Visual Basic greatly resembles that of Quick Basic versions 4 and 4.5. If you are quite familiar with the file I/O of these implementations you can focus on the examples of this chapter. File I/O is vital in processing information located on disks. In this chapter you will learn about the following:

- Sequential file I/O.
- Random-access file I/O.
- Binary file I/O.

The discussions in this chapter assume that you are at least a little familiar with file I/O in GW-BASIC, BASICA, or Quick Basic. Therefore, the information that I present here serves to update you on the Visual Basic file I/O. This assumption also allows me to present the topics of file I/O in a special order. The chapter also contains a number of examples that can also serve as utilities, including a Visual Basic listing sort utility, a contacts database application, and a text file sorter.

Common file I/O

Before I discuss the various types of file I/O, I next present a number of functions and statements that work with either type.

The FreeFile **function**   FreeFile automatically returns the next available file handle number. The general syntax for the FreeFile function is:

    FileNumber% = FreeFile

The FreeFile function takes the guesswork out of keeping up with the file handles you have used so far.

The Eof **function**   This is a Boolean function that returns −1 (True) when you have reached the end of the file. The general syntax for the Eof function is:

    Eof(*fileNumber%*)

The Eof function enables the program to detect the end of the file when reading a sequence of text lines, records, or single bytes. The Eof function is typically used in a Do-While loop, as shown below:

```
' open the file for input
fileNumber% = FreeFile
Open Filename$ For Input As #fileNumber%
Do While Eof(fileNumber%)
    ' read and process data
Loop
```

The Lof **function**   Lof returns the byte size of an opened file. The general syntax for the Lof function is:

    Lof(*fileNumber%*)

I recommend assigning the result of the Lof function to a long integer, since file sizes can very well be larger than 32767 bytes (the upper limit of the integer type).

The Close **statement**   This statement closes one or more files and restores their buffers. The general syntax for the Close statement is:

    Close [*#fileNumber1%* [,*#fileNumber2* [, . . .]]]

You can specify the files to close in a comma-delimited list of file handle numbers. If you want to close all of the files, simply omit the file handle number arguments. This feature also takes the guesswork out of which files to close. Failing to close a file in the output mode may result in the loss of output data (that is, information that is transient in the output buffer).

The Kill **statement**   Kill allows you to delete a file. The file need not be opened. The general syntax for the Kill statement is:

    Kill *filename$*

The filename$ is a string expression that may include the drive name, the path, and the wildcard characters ? and *. The latter characters allow you to delete multiple files that fit the specified filename pattern.

The Name **statement**   This statement permits you to rename a file and even move a file to a different existing directory. The general syntax for the Name statement is:

    Name *oldFileName$* As *newFileName$*

The oldFileName$ and newFileName$ are string expressions that specify the old and new filenames. These expressions may contain the path of the file. If they specify a different path, the file is moved to the directory specified in the newFileName$ expression. In fact, you can move a file to another directory and maintain the same name — just change the path in the two string expressions. Visual Basic generates errors for the following conditions:

- The file or path specified by oldFileName$ does not exist.
- The paths specified by these string expressions are not on the same disk.
- The path specified in newFileName$ does not exist.
- The file specified by newFileName$ already exists.

☞ **The** Dir$ **function** $Dir returns the filename that meets the supplied filename pattern. The general syntax for the Dir$ function is:

Dir$ [(filePattern$)]

The argument filePattern$ usually contains the ? and * wildcard characters to return the names of the matching files. The Dir$ function performs this task sequentially, returning one filename per function call. The rules for using the Dir$ are as follows:

- The first time you call the Dir$ function, supply it with the filePattern$ argument. The function returns the name of the first matching file, or an empty string if no match was found.
- When Dir$ returns the first matching file, you can obtain the next matching file by calling the Dir$ function without an argument. Again, Dir$ returns the name of the next matching file, or an empty string if no match was found.

The Dir$ function is typically used in a Do-While loop, like the one shown below:

```
theFile$ = Dir$ filePattern$
Do While theFile$ <> "
    ' process theFile$
    theFile$ = Dir$ ' obtain the next matching file
Loop
```

The above loop enables you to obtain the names of the files matching the specified pattern and process them one at a time. Once the Dir$ function returns an empty string, you should use the filename pattern argument with the next call to Dir$; otherwise, Visual Basic generates an error condition.

Sequential file I/O

Sequential file I/O primarily serves to read and write text files. If you have ever employed file I/O in your BASIC programs, it is this type that you most likely used. Using sequential file I/O is compared with reading a scroll—to get to a specific data, you have to read all the information that comes before it. The various BASIC implementations support sequential file I/O to read and write text lines. Each text line is terminated by a pair of carriage return (ASCII 13) and line feed (ASCII 10) characters. These text lines are considered to be variable-length records. The advantages of variable-length records is that they require no extra bytes of storage. Their disadvantage is that you cannot immediately tell where the records are located in the file.

Visual Basic offers the following statements to open, close, read, and write from a sequential file:

The Open **statement**   This statement opens a file for input or output. In the case of a sequential file, the general syntax for the Open statement is:

Open *filename$* For {Input ¦ Output ¦ Append} As *[#]fileNumber%*

The filename$ is a string expression that specifies the filename. You can include the drive and path to access files that are not in the current directory. If the filename$ refers to a nonexistent file, Visual Basic raises an error.

The For clause allows you to specify the file mode. The Input mode opens an existing file to input. If the file does not exist, Visual Basic raises an error. The Output and Append modes are used to write and append data to a file. If the file is nonexistent, a new file is created. In this case, the Append mode works just like the Output mode.

The As clause specifies the file handle number used as an index for performing file input and output.

The Print# **statement**   Print# writes data to a sequential file. The general syntax for the Print# statement is:

Print *#fileNumber%, expressionList* [{; ¦ ,}]

where the fileNumber% parameter is the file handle number. The expression-List contains a comma-delimited list of constants, variables, and expressions that are written to the data file. The expressionList may be followed by a comma or semicolon. The Print# statement writes to a file in a manner similar to the way the Print statement writes to a form or picture box, and is also the same as the Print statement in the other Microsoft BASIC implementations. When the expression list is followed by a comma, the next Print# output to the same file is tabbed on the same line. When the expression list is followed by a semicolon, the next Print# output to the same file appears after the last previous output character.

The Write# **statement**   Write# is similar to the Print# statement, except that it separates the members of the expression list with commas. The general syntax for the Write# statement is:

Write *#fileNumber%, expressionList*

The Input# **statement** This statement reads data from a sequential file and stores the data in variables. The general syntax for the Input# statement is:

Input #fileNumber%, variableList

The type of data read must match the type of variable in the comma-delimited variableList. Leading spaces are ignored. In the case of numeric variables, the first nonspace character that is encountered is used as the start of a number. Reading this number ends when a space, a comma, or the end of the line is encountered. In the case of strings, leading spaces are also ignored. The first nonspace character is interpreted as the first string character. The input string ends when either a comma or the end of the line is encountered. A blank line yields a 0 when reading a numerical variable, and returns an empty string when reading a string variable.

The Line Input# **statement** This statement reads an entire line of text. The general syntax for the Line Input# statement is:

Line Input #fileNumber%, stringVariable$

The Line Input reads all of the characters up to the carriage return and line feed. Typically, the entire lines of a text file are read using the following kind of Do-While loop:

```
fileNumber% = FreeFile
Open Filename$ For Input As #fileNumber%
Do While Not Eof(fileNumber%)
    Line Input #fileNumber%, TextLine$
    ' process TextLine$
Loop
Close #fileNumber%
```

The Input$ **function** Input$ returns a specified number of characters from a file. The general syntax for the Input$ function is:

[stringVariable$ =] Input$ (n%, [#]fileNumber%)

In the case of sequential files, the Input$ function reads the next n% characters from the file whose handle is fileNumber%. These characters include carriage returns, line feeds, and leading spaces; that is, Input$ reads every subsequent n% characters. The value of n% ranges from 1 to 32767 for sequential files.

Listing sort utility

Let's look at a Visual Basic program that illustrates sequential file I/O in a way that is relevant to Visual Basic. Visual Basic offers the Save Text option in the Code menu to save the code attached to a form or a module in a text file (the default file extension is .TXT). However, the procedures in the output text files appear in the order in which you typed them, instead of being listed alphabetically. This disorder makes it more difficult to locate a particular procedure when you have a long listing with many procedures. The next program solves this problem. It reads the text file produced by Visual Basic and rewrites it such that the procedures are listed alphabetically. The original text file is renamed with a .BAK file extension.

The visual interface of the program contains various types of list boxes, command buttons, and a text box. These controls include the Drive, Directory, and Files list boxes that enable you to locate and select the file you want to process. The command buttons allow you to exit the program, sort the listing file, view a text file, and print a text file. The multiline scrollable text box facilitates viewing text files. I have included the viewing and printing options for the sake of convenience.

When you click on the Sort listing file button, the current selection in the files list box is processed. The program performs the following tasks:

- Reads through the source listing file mainly to count the number of procedures. The heading of the procedures are displayed in the text box in the order in which they appear in the source listing file.
- Reads the source listing file a second time to write into temporary files the lines that are associated with the general declarations section and with each procedure.
- Sorts the data related to procedures, using the procedure name as the sort key.
- Builds the target text file by copying the text lines from the temporary files, starting with the temporary file that contains the general declarations section. The other temporary files are copied in the order of the procedure names. I will discuss the details of these operations when I present the code attached to the program's form.

Figures 17-1 to 17-3 contain the specifications for the CATALOG.MAK project file and the CATALOG.FRM form file. Figure 17-4 shows a sample session with the program. Listing 17-1 shows the code attached to the CATALOG.FRM form. I would like to point out that LISTING 17-1 was obtained by using the Listing Sort Utility program itself. The procedures and functions that are used in sorting the Visual Basic procedures are described in the next few paragraphs.

The Form_Load **procedure**   This procedure sets the following:

- The WindowState property to 2 (maximized).
- The file pattern to *.TXT.
- The Archive and Normal file attribute properties to True. The rest of the file attribute properties are set to False.

Application name: Listing Sort Utility
Application code name: CATALOG
Version: 1.0   Date created: July 23, 1991
Programmer(s): Namir Clement Shammas

List of filenames

Storage path: \VB\EASYVB
Project CATALOG.MAK
Global GLOBAL.BAS
Form 1 CATALOG.FRM

17-1 The basic specifications for the CATALOG.MAK project file.

Form #1   Form filename: CATALOG.FRM
Version: 1.0   Date: July 23, 1991

Control object type	Default CtlName	Purpose
Drive List Box	Drive1	Shows and selects the current drive
Directory List	Dir1	Shows and selects the current directory
File List Box	File1	Shows a group of files
Text Box	Text1	Specifies the filename pattern
	Text2	Views and edits a text file
Command Box	Command1	Exits the program
	Command2	Sorts the procedures of a listing file
	Command3	Loads a text file
	Command4	Saves a text file
	Command5	Prints a text file
Label	Label1	Label for filename pattern
	Label2	Label for drive list box
	Label3	Label for directory list box
	Label4	Label for file list box

17-2 The list of controls in the CATALOG.FRM form file.

The GetFileExt **function** This extracts the file extension from the Filename argument. If the file has a null extension, an empty string is returned. The returned string does not include the dot that separates the primary filename from the file extension.

The GetFilename **function** GetFilename returns the primary filename, including the names of the drive and path if supplied by the Filename argument.

☞ **The** GetFunctionName **function** This function extracts the name of the function from a text line. The GetFunctionName function assumes that

Application (code) name: CATALOG
Form #1
Version: 1.0   Date:

Original control name	Property	New setting
Form	Caption	Program to Sort VB .TXT files
Drive1	CtlName	DiskDrv
Drl1	CtlName	TreeDir
File1	CtlName	FileFlb
Text1	CtlName	PatternBox
	Text	(empty string)
Text2	CtlName	TextBox
	Text	(empty string)
	MultiLine	True
	ScrollBars	3 - Both
Command1	CtlName	QuitBtn
	Caption	&Quit
	Cancel	True
Command2	CtlName	SortVBfileBtn
	Caption	&Sort VB .TXT file
Command3	CtlName	LoadBtn
	Caption	&Load File
Command4	CtlName	SaveBtn
	Caption	&Save File
Command5	CtlName	PrintBtn
	Caption	&Print File
Label1	CtlName	PatternLbl
	Caption	Filename:
Label2	CtlName	DriveLbl
	Caption	Drive:
Label3	CtlName	DirectoryLbl
	Caption	Directory:
Label4	CtlName	FilesLbl
	Caption	Files:

17-3 The customized settings for the CATALOG.FRM form.

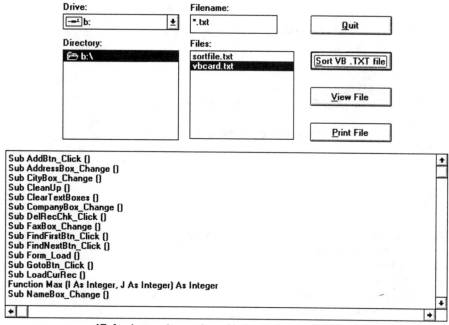

Drive:

b:

Filename:

*.txt

Directory:

b:\

Files:

sortfile.txt
vbcard.txt

Quit

Sort VB .TXT file

View File

Print File

```
Sub AddBtn_Click ()
Sub AddressBox_Change ()
Sub CityBox_Change ()
Sub CleanUp ()
Sub ClearTextBoxes ()
Sub CompanyBox_Change ()
Sub DelRecChk_Click ()
Sub FaxBox_Change ()
Sub FindFirstBtn_Click ()
Sub FindNextBtn_Click ()
Sub Form_Load ()
Sub GotoBtn_Click ()
Sub LoadCurRec ()
Function Max (I As Integer, J As Integer) As Integer
Sub NameBox_Change ()
```

17-4   A sample session with the Listing Sort Utility.

Listing 17-1   The code attached to the CATALOG.FRM form.

```
Sub DiskDrv_Change ( )
    ' update file tree path when the disk is changed
    TreeDir.Path = DiskDrv.Drive
End Sub

Sub Form_Load ( )
    WindowState = 2
    PatternBox.Text = "*.txt"
    FileFlb.Filename = "*.txt"
    ' set Archive and Normal attributes to True and all
    ' of the other file attributes to False
    FileFlb.Archive = True
    FileFlb.Normal = True
    FileFlb.Hidden = False
    FileFlb.ReadOnly = False
    FileFlb.System = False
End Sub

Function GetFileExt (Filename As String) As String
' get the file extension name
```

Listing 17-1 Continued.

```
  Dim I As Integer
  If Filename <> " " Then
    ' locate the "." in the filename
    I = InStr(Filename, ".")
    ' found the "." ?
    If I > 0 Then
      ' get the file extension name
      GetFileExt = Mid$(Filename, I + 1, Len(Filename) − I)
    Else
      GetFileExt = " " ' file extension name is a null string
    End If
  Else
    GetFileExt = " "
  End If
End Function

Function GetFilename (Filename As String) As String
' get the file name (without the dot delimiter)
  Dim I As Integer
  If Filename <> " " Then
    ' locate the "." in the filename
    I = InStr(Filename, ".")
    ' found the "." ?
    If I > 0 Then
      ' extract the filename without the dot delimiter
      GetFilename = Left$(Filename, I − 1)
    Else
      GetFilename = Filename ' filename has no dot delimitor
    End If
  Else
    GetFilename = " "
  End If
End Function

Function GetFunctionName (TextLine As String) As String
' get the name of the declared Function
  Dim I As Integer, L As Integer
  ' locate the open parenthesis
  I = InStr(TextLine, " (") − 1
  L = Len("Function ")
  ' extract the name of the function
  GetFunctionName = UCase$(Mid$(TextLine, L + 1, I − L))
End Function

Function GetSubName (TextLine As String) As String
' get the name of the procedure
  Dim I As Integer, L As Integer
  ' locate the open parenthesis
```

Listing 17-1 Continued.

```
    I = InStr(TextLine, " (") − 1
    L = Len("Sub ")
    ' extract the file name
    GetSubName = UCase$(Mid$(TextLine, L + 1, I − L))
    End Function

Function GetTempFilename (N As Integer) As String
' return the name of the temporary file #N (as $<N>.$$$)
    GetTempFilename = "$" + Format$(N) + ".$$$"
End Function

Function Max (I As Integer, J As Integer) As Integer
' return the larger value of I or J
    If I > J Then
        Max = I
    Else
        Max = J
    End If
End Function

Sub PatternBox_KeyPress (KeyAScii As Integer)
    KeyAScii = Asc(LCase$(Chr$(KeyAScii)))
End Sub

Sub PatternBox_LostFocus ( )
    Dim I As Integer
    If PatternBox.Text = " " Then PatternBox.Text = "*.*"
    ' locate and remove multiple wildcards
    I = InStr(PatternBox.Text, " ") ' find first space
    If I > 0 Then
        PatternBox.Text = Mid$(PatternBox.Text, 1, I − 1)
    End If
    FileFlb.Filename = PatternBox.Text
End Sub

Sub PrintFileCom_Click ( )
' performs a simple print task
    Dim F As String, TextLine As String
    Dim FileNum As Integer
    If FileFlb.Filename <> " " Then
        Form1.MousePointer = 11 ' hourglass
        FileNum = FreeFile ' get the next file buffer
        ' obtain the full filename
        F = TreeDir.Path
        If Right$(F, 1) <> "\" Then F = F + "\"
        F = F + FileFlb.Filename
        Open F For Input As #FileNum ' open file
        ' read each line and print it
```

Listing 17-1 Continued.

```
    Do While Not EOF(FileNum)
        Line Input #FileNum, TextLine
        Printer.Print TextLine
    Loop
    Printer.EndDoc ' close printer buffer
    Close #FileNum ' close file buffer
    Form1.MousePointer = 0 ' restore mouse pointer
  End If
End Sub

Sub QuitBtn_Click ( )
  End
End Sub

Sub SortProcedureData (ProcName$( ), FileNum%( ), N%)
' perform a Comb-sort on the arrays ProcName and FileNum.
' The arrays are sorted by using the data in ProcName.
  Dim Skip As Integer, InOrder As Integer
  Dim I As Integer, J As Integer
  Skip = N%
  Do
    Skip = Max(Int(Skip / 1.3), 1)
  InOrder = True
  For I = 1 To N% – Skip
      J = I + Skip
    If ProcName$(I) > ProcName$(J) Then
        ' swap array members
        InOrder = False
        ProcName$(0) = ProcName$(I)
        ProcName$(I) = ProcName$(J)
        ProcName$(J) = ProcName$(0)
        FileNum%(0) = FileNum%(I)
        FileNum%(I) = FileNum%(J)
        FileNum%(J) = FileNum%(0)
      End If
    Next I
  Loop Until InOrder And (Skip = 1)
End Sub

Sub SortVBfileBtn_Click ( )
  Dim NL As String * 2
  Dim F As String
  Dim TextLine As String
  Dim MainFilename As String ' main filename
  Dim ExtFilename As String ' extension name
  ' declare file I/O channel variables
  Dim InputFileNum As Integer
  Dim OutputFileNum As Integer
```

Listing 17-1 Continued.

```
' declare procedure counters
Dim CountProc As Integer, MaxProc As Integer
' declare dynamic arrays for procedure names
Dim ProcName( ) As String ' name
Dim FileNum( ) As Integer ' file number
'_____
If FileFlb.Filename = " " Then Exit Sub
NL = Chr$(13) + Chr$(10)
Form1.MousePointer = 11 ' hourglass
' obtain the full filename
F = TreeDir.Path
If Right$(F, 1) < > " \ " Then F = F + " \ "
F = F + FileFlb.Filename
MainFilename = GetFilename(F) ' extract main filename, including the path
ExtFilename = GetFileExt(F) ' extract the file extension name
' delete previous ".BAK" file
On Error Resume Next
Kill MainFilename + ".BAK"
On Error GoTo 0 ' turn off error-handler
' rename file as .BAK
Name F As MainFilename + ".BAK"
' first pass simply counts the number of
' procedures in the file
InputFileNum = FreeFile ' get the next file buffer
CountProc = 0 ' initialize procedure counter
TextBox.Text = " " ' clear text box
Open MainFilename + ".BAK" For Input As #InputFileNum
' loop to read examine each line
Do While Not EOF(InputFileNum)
   Line Input #InputFileNum, TextLine
   If (InStr(TextLine, "Sub ") = 1) Or (InStr(TextLine, "Function ") = 1)
      Then CountProc = CountProc + 1
      ' insert procedure heading in the text box
      TextBox.Text = TextBox.Text + TextLine + NL
   End If
Loop
Close #InputFileNum ' close file buffer
If CountProc = 0 Then ' found no procedures
   ' rename file back to original
   Name MainFilename + ".BAK" As F
   MsgBox "No Sub or Function were found", 0, "Information"
   Form1.MousePointer = 0 ' restore mouse pointer
   Exit Sub
End If
' redimension the arrays
ReDim ProcName(0 To CountProc), FileNum(0 To CountProc)
' start pass 2
MaxProc = CountProc
```

Listing 17-1 Continued.

```
CountProc = 0
InputFileNum = FreeFile ' get the next file buffer
Open MainFilename + ".BAK" For Input As #InputFileNum
OutputFileNum = FreeFile ' get the next file buffer
' open the temporary file $0.$$$ that stores the general
' declarations section
Open GetTempFilename(CountProc) For Output As #OutputFileNum
' loop to locate the Sub and Function declarations
Do While Not EOF(InputFileNum)
  Line Input #InputFileNum, TextLine ' read the next line
  ' does the line contain a Sub procedure?
  If InStr(TextLine, "Sub ") = 1 Then
    CountProc = CountProc + 1
    ProcName(CountProc) = GetSubName(TextLine) ' get procedure name
    FileNum(CountProc) = CountProc ' get the name of the next $n.$$$ file
    Close #OutputFileNum ' close current file
    OutputFileNum = FreeFile ' get the next file buffer
    ' open file $n.$$$, where n = CountProc
    Open GetTempFilename(CountProc) For Output As OutputFileNum
  ElseIf InStr(TextLine, "Function ") = 1 Then
    CountProc = CountProc + 1
    ProcName(CountProc) = GetFunctionName(TextLine) ' get function name
    FileNum(CountProc) = CountProc ' get the name of the next $n.$$$ file
    Close #OutputFileNum ' close current file
    OutputFileNum = FreeFile ' get the next file buffer
    ' open file $n.$$$, where n = CountProc
    Open GetTempFilename(CountProc) For Output As OutputFileNum
  End If
  Print #OutputFileNum, TextLine ' write text line to $n.$$$ file
Loop
' close file buffers
Close #InputFileNum
Close #OutputFileNum
' sort the arrays of procedures
SortProcedureData ProcName( ), FileNum( ), MaxProc
OutputFileNum = FreeFile ' get the next file buffer
' open the target file
Open F For Output As #OutputFileNum
InputFileNum = FreeFile ' get the next file buffer
F = GetTempFilename(0) ' get $0.$$$
Open F For Input As #InputFileNum
' copy the lines of the general declarations
Do While Not EOF(InputFileNum)
  Line Input #InputFileNum, TextLine
  Print #OutputFileNum, TextLine
Loop
Close #InputFileNum
Kill F ' delete $0.$$$
```

Listing 17-1 Continued.

```
' get the other $n.$$$ files
For CountProc = 1 To MaxProc
    InputFileNum = FreeFile ' get the next file buffer
    F = GetTempFilename(FileNum(CountProc)) ' get the $n.$$$ file name
    Open F For Input As #InputFileNum
    ' copy the lines of file $n.$$$ into the target file
    Do While Not EOF(InputFileNum)
        Line Input #InputFileNum, TextLine
        Print #OutputFileNum, TextLine
    Loop
    Close #InputFileNum ' close input buffer
    Kill F ' remove $n.$$$ file
Next CountProc
Close #OutputFileNum ' close output buffer
Form1.MousePointer = 0 ' restore mouse cursor
End Sub

Sub TextBox_KeyPress (KeyAScii As Integer)
    KeyAScii = 0
End Sub

Sub TreeDir_Change ()
    FileFlb.Path = TreeDir.Path
End Sub

Sub ViewFileBtn_Click ()
' view the target file in TextBox
    Dim F As String, TextLine As String
    Dim FileNum As Integer
    Dim NL As String * 2
    If FileFlb.Filename < > " " Then
        NL = Chr$(13) + Chr$(10)
        FileNum = FreeFile ' get the next file buffer
        F = TreeDir.Path
        If Right$(F, 1) < > " \ " Then F = F + " \ "
        F = F + FileFlb.Filename
        Open F For Input As #FileNum
        F = " "
        Do While Not EOF(FileNum)
            Line Input #FileNum, TextLine
            F = F + TextLine + NL
        Loop
        Close #FileNum
        TextBox.Text = F
    End If
End Sub
```

the function declarations appear in the following general format. Note: leading spaces or tab characters are not allowed.

    Function *functionName* (. . .

The dots indicate that what comes after the open parenthesis is not relevant to the GetFunctionName function. The above format is generated by Visual Basic. The Listing Sort Utility assumes that you do not change that format. The Function keyword must appear in that form and there must be single space before and after the function name.

The GetSubName **function** This extracts the name of the Sub procedure from a text line. The GetSubName procedure assumes that the procedure declaration appears in the following general format. Note: leading spaces or tab characters are not allowed.

    Sub *procedureName* (. . .

Again, the dots mean that what comes after the open parenthesis is not relevant to the GetSubName procedure. The above format is generated by Visual Basic. The Listing Sort Utility assumes that you do not change that format. The Sub keyword must appear in that form, and there must be a single space before and after the procedure name.

The GetTempFilename **function** This function returns the name of the temporary file using the $<N>.$$$ filename pattern. The general declarations section is stored in file $0.$$$, the lines of the first procedure is stored in file $1.$$$, and so on.

The Max **function** Max returns the larger value of either argument, I or J.

The SortProcedureData **procedure** This procedure sorts the arrays that store the names of the procedures and their sequence in the original text file. The SortProcedureData uses the new Combsort method developed by Richard Box and Stephen Lacey (see their article in the April 1991 issue of *BYTE* magazine). The algorithm of this method resembles that of the Shell-Metzner sort. However, the Combsort method is 2.5 to 3 times faster than the Shell-Metzner method if the original array is not sorted. By contrast, if the original array is in reverse order, the Combsort is hardly faster.

The SortVBfileBtn_Click **procedure** Here is the main workhorse for the program. The procedure performs the tasks described in the next several paragraphs.

First, the procedure declares a variety of variables. I would like to point out that the arrays ProcName and FileNum are declared as dynamic. The ProcName array stores the name of the procedures, whereas the FileNum array stores the sequence in which the procedures appear in the source listing file. The value of this sequence is used in creating the $<N>.$$$ temporary files that I mentioned earlier (where N is the sequence of a procedure).

Next, the mouse cursor is changed to the hour glass while the file processing is in order. The procedure then obtains the full name of the listing file being processed and stores it in the variable F. It also extracts the primary and extension filenames of the input file, and stores them in the variables MainFilename and ExtFilename, respectively.

At this point, the backup file is deleted using the Kill Statement. This file has the same primary filename as the input file and the .BAK extension name. Since this file may not exist, use the On Error Resume Next statement to trap the run time error resulting from trying to delete a nonexistent file. The On Error statement basically tells the program to keep going if the Kill statement raises a run time error. The error trapping is turned off right after the Kill statement.

The procedure renames the file extension of the source file listing using the Name statement. This step creates a .BAK backup file out of the original listing file. Also, the source file (which was just renamed as a .BAK file) is opened for input. The procedure then reads the text lines of the source listing file and counts the number of lines that contain the declarations of a Sub or Function procedure. The procedure headings are also posted in the text box. Then the source listing file is closed.

Next, the procedure examines the value of the CountProc variable. If it is zero, the source file has no procedures. Consequently, the original name of the source listing file is restored, using the Name statement. A message box appears to let you know that the file has no procedures. Finally, the mouse cursor is restored before exiting the procedure. If procedures are found, the arrays ProcName and FileNum are redimensioned using 0 and the variable CountProc as the lower and upper limits, respectively. The 0 elements of both arrays are used for special purposes. The ProcName(0) and FileNum(0) elements are used in swapping other array elements. In addition, the FileNum(0) element is later assigned 0, the number associated with the file $0.$$$ that stores the general declarations section.

Next, the procedure prepares to read the source listing file a second time. This time, the text lines for the procedures are written to temporary files. The procedure opens the source listing and the first temporary file, $0.$$$. The text lines of the general declarations section are written to the $0.$$$ file.

The procedure then reads, scans, and writes the text lines using a Do-While loop. The lines of the source listing file are read in each loop iteration. When the string Sub appears at the beginning of the line, the current temporary file is closed and a new one is opened. The name of the new file is obtained by calling the GetTempFilename with the CountProc variable as the argument. The array elements ProcName(CountProc) and FileNum(CountProc) keep track of the name of the scanned procedure and its sequence, which is also its file number. When the loop detects the declaration of a function, it performs steps that are similar to those of a Sub procedure.

The last statement in the Do-While loop writes the currently read text line into the currently opened temporary file.

After the Do-While loop is exited, the procedure closes the source listing file and the currently opened temporary file. It sorts the arrays ProcName and FileNum by calling procedure SortProcedureData. The elements of ProcName are used in ordering both arrays. Then the target listing file is opened for output.

The procedure uses a For-Next loop to copy the lines from the temporary files into the target listing file. The FileNum array supplies the arguments for the GetTempFilename function. These arguments specify the name of the temporary files to process in each loop iteration. The For-Next loop opens, copies, closes, and then deletes the temporary files.

Finally, the procedure closes the target listing file and restores the mouse cursor to its default setting.

Listing 17-2 shows the skeleton code that represents the contents of the original source listing file for LISTING 17-1. I have omitted the lines of code from the procedures that have more than two lines. Listing 17-2 shows the order of the procedures as written by Visual Basic. You can use the Load Text option in the Code menu to read the ordered listing text file. This action results in overwriting the previous sequence of procedures with the new ordered sequence.

Listing 17-2 The skeleton code that represents the contents of the original source listing file for Listing 17-1.

```
Sub Form_Load ( )
  WindowState = 2
  ...
End Sub

Sub DiskDrv_Change ( )
  ' update file tree path when the disk is changed
  TreeDir.Path = DiskDrv.Drive
End Sub

Sub QuitBtn_Click ( )
  End
End Sub

Sub TreeDir_Change ( )
  FileFlb.Path = TreeDir.Path
End Sub

Sub PatternBox_KeyPress (KeyAScii As Integer)
  KeyAScii = Asc(LCase$(Chr$(KeyAScii)))
End Sub

Sub PatternBox_LostFocus ( )
  Dim I As Integer
```

Listing 17-2 Continued.

```
  ...
End Sub

Function GetFilename (Filename As String) As String
' get the file name (without the dot delimiter)
  ...
End Function

Function GetFileExt (Filename As String) As String
' get the file extension name
  ...
End Function

Sub SortVBfileBtn_Click ( )
   Dim NL As String * 2
  ...
End Sub

Function GetSubName (TextLine As String) As String
' get the name of the procedure
  ...
End Function

Function GetFunctionName (TextLine As String) As String
' get the name of the declared Function
  ...
End Function

Function GetTempFilename (N As Integer) As String
' return the name of the temporary file #N (as $<N>.$$$)
   GetTempFilename = "$" + Format$(N) + ".$$$"
End Function

Sub SortProcedureData (ProcName$( ), FileNum%( ), N%)
' perform a Comb-sort on the arrays ProcName and FileNum.
  ...
End Sub

Sub ViewFileBtn_Click ( )
' view the target file in TextBox
  ...
End Sub

Sub TextBox_KeyPress (KeyAScii As Integer)
   KeyAScii = 0
End Sub

Sub PrintFileCom_Click ( )
' performs a simple print task
```

Listing 17-2 Continued.

...

End Sub
Function Max (I As Integer, J As Integer) As Integer
' return the larger value of I or J

...

End Function

Random-access file I/O

The data in sequential files are regarded as stored in variable-length records. By contrast, random-access files use fixed-length records to read and write their data. This storage scheme is compared to reading a book —you can open it up to a particular page without scrolling through the previous pages. In fact, you can open random-access files for input, output, or both. The latter mode is very convenient when you need to read, update, and store data in the file. Using fixed-length records you can zoom in on the record you want to read or write, and not be concerned about the other records. Updating random-access files is faster than updating sequential files. The difference in speed increases as the sizes of the two file types increase.

Visual Basic provides the following statements to support random-access file I/O:

The Open **statement** This statement opens the file for random access using the following general syntax:

Open *fileName$* For Random As *[#]fileNumber% [Len = recLen%]*

The filename$ expression specifies the name of the file to open for random-access. The For clause specifies one file mode for random-access file, which allows you to read and write records. The fileNumber% parameter specifies the file handle number, while the Len clause specifies the length of the each record in the file. The default and maximum record lengths are 128 and 32767 bytes, respectively. I strongly recommend that you include the Len clause when you open a random-access file to read or write data.

The Get **statement** Get enables you to retrieve a record from a random-access file. The general syntax for the Get statement is:

Get [#] *fileNumber%, [recordNumber&], recordVariable*

The fileNumber% specifies the file handle number. The recordNumber& variable indicates which record you want to read. When this parameter is omitted, the next record is read and the file pointer is advanced by one record. The first record in the file is record 1. The valid arguments for recordNumber& are 1 to the number of actual records in the file. The run time system calculates the actual byte position by multiplying the record-

Number& by the record length, recLen%, declared in the Open statement. The largest record number is 2,147,483,647 (equal to 2^31 - 1).

The Put **statement**   This statement allows you to store a record in a random-access file. The general syntax for the Put statement is:

Put [#] fileNumber%, [recordNumber&], recordVariable

The fileNumber% specifies the file handle number. The recordNumber& variable indicates which record you want to write to. When this parameter is omitted, the next recordVariable is written to the next record and the file pointer is advanced by one record. The first record in the file is record 1. The valid arguments for recordNumber& are from 1 to the number of actual records in the file plus 1. Writing to the latter limit enables you to expand the random-access file.

The Seek **statement**   Seek allows you to position the file pointer to a specific record for the next read or write operation. The Seek statement performs no file I/O. Its general syntax is:

Seek [#]fileNumber%, position&

The fileNumber% specifies the file handle number. The position& parameter designates the record number. Seeking one record beyond the current number of records expands the random-access file.

The Seek **function**   This function returns a long integer that represents the file pointer of the current record number. The general syntax for the Seek function is:

Seek(fileNumber%)

The fileNumber% specifies the file handle number.

The contacts database application

Random-access files are typically used to maintain the records of a database. The ability to read, write, and update a particular record makes random-access very suitable for the task of maintaining records. The next program implements a database for your contacts. The database stores the person's name, company name, address, city, state, zip code, phone number, and fax number. Figure 17-5 shows the program's form at design time. The figure shows the text boxes and labels that store the above fields for each record. The figure also shows a number of picture boxes, command buttons, and other controls that perform the task described here:

- The picture boxes with the left-arrow and right-arrow icons allow you to scroll through your database. When you reach either end of the database, you view the record at the other end. Thus, the picture boxes provide you with a circular-list effect.

- The Quit button closes the random-access file and exits the application.
- The Add button inserts a new record into your database.
- The Sort button sorts the records of the database by zip code.
- The Find First button allows you to search for the first record that contains a specified name. You specify the name in an input dialog box.
- The Find Next button allows you to search for the next record that contains a name that you specified earlier.
- The Goto button permits you to move to a specific record by number. Keep in mind that sorting the records changes the record numbers.
- The Delete Record check box enables you to mark and unmark the record for deletion. The records marked for deletion are removed from the database when you click the Quit button.

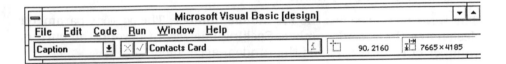

17-5 The controls of the VBCARD.FRM at design time.

Figures 17-6 to 17-8 show the specifications for the VBCARD.MAK project file and the VBCARD.FRM form file.

Application name: Contacts Database Application
Application code name: VBCARD
Version: 1.0   Date created: July 23, 1991
Programmer(s): Namir Clement Shammas

List of filenames

Storage path: \VB\EASYVB
Project VBCARD.MAK
Global RANDOM.BAS
Form 1 VBCARD.FRM

17-6 The basic specifications for the VBCARD.MAK project file.

Form #1   Form filename: VBCARD.FRM
Version: 1.0   Date: July 23, 1991

Control object type	Default CtlName	Purpose
Text Box	Text1	Stores the person's name
	Text2	Stores the company name
	Text3	Stores the address
	Text4	Stores the city
	Text5	Stores the state
	Text6	Stores the zip code
	Text7	Stores the phone number
	Text8	Stores the fax number
	Text9	Displays the current record number and the total number of records
Label	Label1	Label for the person's name
	Label2	Label for the company name
	Label3	Label for the address
	Label4	Label for the city
	Label5	Label for the state
	Label6	Label for the zip code
	Label7	Label for the phone number
	Label8	Label for the fax number
	Label9	Label for current record number
	Label10	Label for the Command
Command Button	Command1	Exits the application
	Command2	Adds a new record
	Command3	Sorts the database
	Command4	Find the first name
	Command5	Finds the next name
	Command6	Goes to a record number
Picture Box	Picture1	Moves to the previous record
	Picture2	Moves to the next record
Check Box	Check1	Toggles the delete status of a record

17-7 The list of controls in the VBCARD.FRM form file.

The contacts database application   361

Application (code) name: VBCARD
Form #1
Version: 1.0   Date:

Original control name	Property	New setting
Form	Caption	Contacts Card
Text1	CtlName Text	NameBox (empty string)
Text2	CtlName Text	CompanyBox (empty string)
Text3	CtlName Text	AddressBox (empty string)
Text4	CtlName Text	CityBox (empty string)
Text5	CtlName Text	StateBox (empty string)
Text6	CtlName Text	ZipBox (empty string)
Text7	CtlName Text	PhoneBox (empty string)
Text8	CtlName Text	FaxBox (empty string)
Text9	CtlName Text	CurRecBox (empty string)
Label1	CtlName Caption	NameLbl Name:
Label2	CtlName Caption	CompanyLbl Company:
Label3	CtlName Caption	AddressLbl Address:
Label4	CtlName Caption	CityLbl City:
Label5	CtlName Caption	StateLbl State:

17-8 The customized settings for the VBCARD.FRM form.

Original control name	Property	New setting
Label6	CtlName	ZipLbl
	Caption	Zip:
Label7	CtlName	PhoneLbl
	Caption	Phone
Label8	CtlName	FaxLbl
	Caption	Fax:
Label9	CtlName	RecNumLbl
	Caption	Record #
Label10	CtlName	FindLbl
	Caption	Find Name
Command1	CtlName	QuitBtn
	Caption	&Quit
Command2	CtlName	AddBtn
	Caption	&Add
Command3	CtlName	SortBtn
	Caption	&Sort
Command4	CtlName	FindFirstBtn
	Caption	Find &First
Command5	CtlName	FindNextBtn
	Caption	Find &Next
Command6	CtlName	GotoBtn
	Caption	&Goto
Picture1	CtlName	PrevPct
	Picture	\vb\icons\arrow\arw04lt.ico
Check1	CtlName	DelRecChk
	Caption	Delete Record

17-8 Continued.

Listing 17-3 contains the declarations of the global module RAN-DOM.BAS. In addition to the TRUE and FALSE constants, this global module declares a family of constants that specify the maximum string sizes for the fields of the CardType data type. In addition, these same constants are used to set the limit of how much you can type in the various text boxes.

Listing 17-3 The declarations of the RANDOM.BAS global module.

```
Global Const TRUE = -1
Global Const FALSE = 0
Global Const NAME_LEN = 30
Global Const COMPANY_LEN = 40
Global Const ADDRESS_LEN = 40
Global Const CITY_LEN = 15
Global Const STATE_LEN = 2
Global Const ZIP_LEN = 10
Global Const PHONE_LEN = 14

Type CardType
   fName As String * NAME_LEN
   fCompany As String * COMPANY_LEN
   fAddress As String * ADDRESS_LEN
   fCity As String * CITY_LEN
   fState As String * STATE_LEN
   fZip As String * ZIP_LEN
   fPhone As String * PHONE_LEN
   fFax As String * PHONE_LEN
   IsDel As String * 1
End Type
```

The CardType declares the fields for the various parts of the contacts record. In addition, a single-character string field IsDel keeps track of whether or not the record is marked for deletion.

Listing 17-4 shows the code attached to the VBCARD.FRM form, which includes the procedures discussed in the next few paragraphs.

Listing 17-4 The code attached to the VBCARD.FRM form.

```
Dim CurIndex As Long
Dim CurRec As CardType
Dim NumRecs As Integer
Dim NumDelRecs As Integer ' number of deleted records
Dim RecLen As Integer
Dim FileNum As Integer
Dim RecNotSaved As Integer ' Boolean
Dim FindStr As String
Dim FoundStr As Integer

Sub AddBtn_Click ()
   SaveThisRec
   NumRecs = NumRecs + 1
   CurIndex = NumRecs
   ClearTextBoxes
   CurRecBox.Text = Str$(CurIndex) + " of " + Str$(NumRecs)
   'RecNotSaved = True
End Sub
```

Listing 17-4 Continued.

```
Sub AddressBox_Change ( )
  If Len(AddressBox.Text) > ADDRESS_LEN Then
    Beep
    AddressBox.Text = Left$(AddressBox.Text, Len(AddressBox.Text) − 1)
    AddressBox.SelStart = Len(AddressBox.Text)
  End If
  RecNotSaved = True
End Sub

Sub CityBox_Change ( )
  If Len(CityBox.Text) > CITY_LEN Then
    Beep
    CityBox.Text = Left$(CityBox.Text, Len(CityBox.Text) − 1)
    CityBox.SelStart = Len(CityBox.Text)
  End If
  RecNotSaved = True
End Sub

Sub CleanUp ( )
  Dim FileNum2 As Integer
  Dim I As Integer
  Close
  If NumDelRecs > 0 Then
    On Error Resume Next
    Kill "VBCARD.BAK"
    On Error GoTo 0
    Name "VBCARD.DAT" As "VBCARD.BAK"
    FileNum = FreeFile
    Open "VBCARD.BAK" For Random As FileNum Len = Len(CurRec)
    FileNum2 = FreeFile
    Open "VBCARD.DAT" For Random As FileNum2 Len = Len(CurRec)
    For I = 1 To NumRecs
      Get #FileNum, , CurRec
      If CurRec.IsDel = " " Then
        Put #FileNum2, , CurRec
      End If
    Next I
    Close ' close all buffers
  End If
  End
End Sub

Sub ClearTextBoxes ( )
  NameBox.Text = " "
  CompanyBox.Text = " "
  AddressBox.Text = " "
  CityBox.Text = " "
  StateBox.Text = " "
```

Listing 17-4 Continued.

```
    ZipBox.Text = " "
    PhoneBox.Text = "() – "
    FaxBox.Text = "() – "
    DelRecChk.Value = 0
End Sub

Sub CompanyBox_Change ( )
    If Len(CompanyBox.Text) > COMPANY_LEN Then
        Beep
        CompanyBox.Text = Left$(CompanyBox.Text, Len(CompanyBox.Text) – 1)
        CompanyBox.SelStart = Len(CompanyBox.Text)
    End If
    RecNotSaved = True
End Sub

Sub DelRecChk_Click ( )
    If DelRecChk.Value = 1 Then
        NumDelRecs = NumDelRecs + 1
    Else
        NumDelRecs = NumDelRecs – 1
    End If
End Sub

Sub FaxBox_Change ( )
    If Len(FaxBox.Text) > PHONE_LEN Then
        Beep
        FaxBox.Text = Left$(FaxBox.Text, Len(FaxBox.Text) – 1)
        FaxBox.SelStart = Len(FaxBox.Text)
    End If
    RecNotSaved = True
End Sub

Sub FindFirstBtn_Click ( )
    Dim OrigCurIndex As Long
    Dim I As Integer
    SaveThisRec
    FindStr = InputBox$("Partial name to find", "Name Search")
    If FindStr < > " " Then
        Form1.MousePointer = 11
        OrigCurIndex = CurIndex
        FoundStr = False
        For CurIndex = 1 To NumRecs
            ReadCurRec
            I = InStr(CurRec.fName, FindStr)
            If I > 0 Then
                FoundStr = True
                Exit For
            End If
```

Listing 17-4   Continued.

```
      Next CurIndex
      If FoundStr Then
        LoadCurRec
        NameBox.SelStart = I − 1
        NameBox.SelLength = Len(FindStr)
        NameBox.SetFocus
      Else
        CurIndex = OrigCurIndex
        ReadCurRec
        LoadCurRec
        MsgBox "Search found no match", 0, "Information"
      End If
      Form1.MousePointer = 0
    End If
End Sub

Sub FindNextBtn_Click ( )
  Dim OrigCurIndex As Long
  Dim I As Integer
  SaveThisRec
  If FindStr < > " " Then
    Form1.MousePointer = 11
    OrigCurIndex = CurIndex
    FoundStr = False
    For CurIndex = OrigCurIndex + 1 To NumRecs
      ReadCurRec
      I = InStr(CurRec.fName, FindStr)
      If I > 0 Then
        FoundStr = True
        Exit For
      End If
    Next CurIndex
    If FoundStr Then
      LoadCurRec
      NameBox.SelStart = I − 1
      NameBox.SelLength = Len(FindStr)
      NameBox.SetFocus
    Else
      CurIndex = OrigCurIndex
      ReadCurRec
      LoadCurRec
      MsgBox "Search found no match", 0, "Information"
    End If
    Form1.MousePointer = 0
  End If
End Sub

Sub Form_Load ( )
```

Listing 17-4 Continued.

```
      CurIndex = 0
      RecLen = Len(CurRec)
      FileNum = FreeFile
      Open "VBCARD.DAT" For Random As #FileNum Len = RecLen
      NumRecs = LOF(FileNum) / RecLen
      If NumRecs > 0 Then
        CurIndex = 1
        Get #FileNum, CurIndex, CurRec
        LoadCurRec
        RecNotSaved = False
      Else
        AddBtn_Click
      End If
  End Sub

Sub GotoBtn_Click ( )
' go to a user-specified page
  Dim S As String
  Dim N As Long
  SaveThisRec ' save a new or updated record?
  ' prompt for record number
  S = InputBox$("Go to record number", "Go To Record", "1")
  If S < > " " Then
    N = Val(S)
    If (N > 0) And (N < = NumRecs) Then
      CurIndex = N
      ReadCurRec
      LoadCurRec
    Else
      MsgBox "Record number is out-of-range", 0, "Error!"
    End If
  End If
End Sub

Sub LoadCurRec ( )
  NameBox.Text = RTrim$(CurRec.fName)
  CompanyBox.Text = RTrim$(CurRec.fCompany)
  AddressBox.Text = RTrim$(CurRec.fAddress)
  CityBox.Text = RTrim$(CurRec.fCity)
  StateBox.Text = RTrim$(CurRec.fState)
  ZipBox.Text = RTrim$(CurRec.fZip)
  PhoneBox.Text = RTrim$(CurRec.fPhone)
  FaxBox.Text = RTrim$(CurRec.fFax)
  If CurRec.IsDel < > " " Then
    DelRecChk.Value = 1
  Else
    DelRecChk.Value = 0
  End If
```

Listing 17-4 Continued.

```
   CurRecBox.Text = Str$(CurIndex) + " of " + Str$(NumRecs)
End Sub

Function Max (I As Integer, J As Integer) As Integer
  If I > J Then
    Max = I
  Else
    Max = J
  End If
End Function

Sub NameBox_Change ( )
  If Len(NameBox.Text) > NAME_LEN Then
    Beep
    NameBox.Text = Left$(NameBox.Text, Len(NameBox.Text) − 1)
    NameBox.SelStart = Len(NameBox.Text)
  End If
  RecNotSaved = True
End Sub

Sub NextPct_Click ( )
  If NumRecs = 0 Then Exit Sub
  SaveThisRec ' save pending record
  CurIndex = CurIndex Mod NumRecs + 1
  ReadCurRec
  LoadCurRec
End Sub

Sub PhoneBox_Change ( )
  If Len(PhoneBox.Text) > PHONE_LEN Then
    Beep
    PhoneBox.Text = Left$(PhoneBox.Text, Len(PhoneBox.Text) − 1)
    PhoneBox.SelStart = Len(PhoneBox.Text)
  End If
  RecNotSaved = True
End Sub

Sub PrevPct_Click ( )
  If NumRecs = 0 Then Exit Sub
  SaveThisRec ' save pending record
  If CurIndex > 1 Then
    CurIndex = CurIndex − 1
  Else
    CurIndex = NumRecs
  End If
  ReadCurRec
  LoadCurRec
End Sub
```

Listing 17-4   Continued.

```
Sub QuitBtn_Click ( )
  SaveThisRec
  CleanUp
End Sub

Sub ReadCurRec ( )
  Get #FileNum, CurIndex, CurRec
End Sub

Sub SaveCurRec ( )
  CurRec.fName = NameBox.Text
  CurRec.fCompany = CompanyBox.Text
  CurRec.fAddress = AddressBox.Text
  CurRec.fCity = CityBox.Text
  CurRec.fState = StateBox.Text
  CurRec.fZip = ZipBox.Text
  CurRec.fPhone = PhoneBox.Text
  CurRec.fFax = FaxBox.Text
  If DelRecChk.Value = 1 Then
    CurRec.IsDel = "X"
  Else
    CurRec.IsDel = " "
  End If
End Sub

Sub SaveThisRec ( )
  If RecNotSaved Then
    SaveCurRec
    WriteCurRec
    RecNotSaved = False
  End If
End Sub

Sub SortBtn_Click ( )
' sort by Zip
  Dim Skip As Integer, I As Integer, J As Integer
  Dim InOrder As Integer
  Dim RecJ As CardType, RecI As CardType
  Form1.MousePointer = 11 ' set mouse to hourglass
  SaveThisRec ' save pending record
  Skip = NumFiles
  Do
    Skip = Max(Int(Skip) / 1.3, 1)
    InOrder = True
    For I = 1 To NumRecs - Skip
      J = I + Skip
      Get #FileNum, I, RecI
      Get #FileNum, J, RecJ
```

Listing 17-4 Continued.

```
        If RecI.fZip > RecJ.fZip Then
            ' swap records
            InOrder = False
            Put #FileNum, J, RecI
            Put #FileNum, I, RecJ
        End If
    Next I
    Loop Until InOrder And (Skip = 1)
    Form1.MousePointer = 0 ' rstore default mouse
    ' show the first record
    CurIndex = 1
    ReadCurRec
    LoadCurRec
End Sub

Sub StateBox_Change ( )
    If Len(StateBox.Text) > STATE_LEN Then
        Beep
        StateBox.Text = Left$(StateBox.Text, Len(StateBox.Text) - 1)
        StateBox.SelStart = Len(StateBox.Text)
    End If
    RecNotSaved = True
End Sub

Sub WriteCurRec ( )
    Put #FileNum, CurIndex, CurRec
End Sub

Sub ZipBox_Change ( )
    If Len(ZipBox.Text) > ZIP_LEN Then
        Beep
        ZipBox.Text = Left$(ZipBox.Text, Len(ZipBox.Text) - 1)
        ZipBox.SelStart = Len(ZipBox.Text)
    End If
    RecNotSaved = True
End Sub
```

The WriteCurRec **procedure** This procedure writes the current record (stored in the CurRec variable) to the current record index (stored in the variable CurIndex). The procedure uses a Put statement to write the record at the intended record number.

The ReadCurRec **procedure** This reads the record indicated by the CurIndex variable into the current record variable, CurRec. The procedure uses a single Get statement to seek and read the target record.

The SaveCurRec **procedure**   In this procedure the Text property of the various text boxes is saved into the corresponding fields of the current record variable, CurRec. The single character string field, IsDel, stores an X if the delete record check box is checked; otherwise, the IsDel field stores a space character.

The LoadCurRec **procedure**   Here the data is copied from the CurRec fields into their respective text boxes. The RTrim$ function is used to remove the trailing spaces that exist in the fields of CurRec. The value of the IsDel field is translated into the proper DelRecChk.Value setting.

The Form_Load **procedure**   Form_Load performs the required initialization when you start the VBCARD program. This includes the following tasks:

- Assigns the size of the CardType record to the variable RecLen.
- Opens the VBCARD.DAT for random-access with the Len parameter set to the value of the variable RecLen.
- Calculates the number of records in the database and assign the result to the variable NumRecs.
- If the database is not empty (it is not newly created), Form_Load reads and shows the first record, and sets the Boolean variable RecNotSaved to false, since the record has been read from the file. By contrast, if the number of records is zero, invokes the procedure the AddBtn_Click procedure to add a new record—the most logical step.

The SaveThisRec **procedure**   This ensures that a new or modified record is saved in the database before retrieving another record. The procedure examines the Boolean value of variable RecNotSaved. If that value is −1 (True), the current record is written into the database. This is a two-step process that involves copying the data from the text boxes into the fields of CurRec and then writing the CurRec variable to the file. The RecNotSaved variable is set to 0 (False).

The AddBtn_Click **procedure**   This procedure adds a new record using the following steps:

- Calls the SaveThisRec procedure to make sure that the current record is stored in the file if it is a new record or was modified.
- Increments the total number of records stored in the variable NumRecs.
- Makes the new record the current one.
- Clears the contents of the text boxes by invoking the ClearTextBoxes procedure.
- Updates the record counter text box.

The ClearTextBoxes **procedure**   In this procedure, the text boxes that store the contacts data are reset as follows:

- The name, company, address, city, state, and zip text boxes are cleared.
- The phone and fax text boxes are assigned the template string (—) -, for the area code and telephone exchange separators.
- The Delete Record check box is cleared.

The family of <text>Box_Change **procedures** These procedures ensure that their respective text boxes do not contain more characters than are allowed. The extra characters are deleted. These procedures use the XXXX_ LEN global constants to control the maximum string size for each text box. In addition, each procedure sets the Boolean variable RecNotSaved to True, signaling that the record has been modified. A typical example is the CompanyBox_Change procedure, shown here:

```
Sub CompanyBox_Change ()
    If Len(CompanyBox.Text) > COMPANY_LEN Then
        Beep
        CompanyBox.Text = Left$(CompanyBox.Text, Len(CompanyBox.Text) — 1)
        CompanyBox.SelStart = Len(CompanyBox.Text)
    End If
    RecNotSaved = True
End Sub
```

The DelRecChk_Click **procedure** This procedure toggles the Value setting of the delete record check box and keeps track of the number of deleted records. When the X appears in the control, the NumDelRecs variable is increased by one. When the X disappears from the control, the NumDelRecs variable is decreased by one. This value change enables the program to keep track of the exact number of deleted records.

The SortBtn_Click **procedure** Here, the records of the database are sorted by zip code. The procedure applies the Combsort algorithm to the records of the database. This means that the number of disk accesses increases as the number of records increase—the VBCARD program is not a speed demon when it comes to sorting. The Get and Put statements are used to read and write records.

The FindFirstBtn_Click **procedure** This procedure finds the First Name text box that contains the name you specify. This search feature allows you to search when you know either the first name, the last name, or even part of the last name. The procedure performs the following tasks:

- Saves the current record, if needed.
- Prompts you for the search name using an input dialog box.
- Starts searching the database from the first record. The program loads the first record that contains the name you specified. If no match is found, a message box appears to inform you of the failed search, and the original record you were viewing is restored.

The FindNextBtn_Click **procedure** This attempts to find the next record that contains the name you specified. The code for this procedure is similar to that of FindFirstBtn_Click. The search begins with the record that comes right after the last matching record.

The GotoBtn_Click **procedure** With this procedure, you are able to view a record by specifying its number. The procedure prompts you for the record number. If your input corresponds to an existing record, that record is loaded in the text boxes. Otherwise, a message box appears to inform you that the value you keyed in is out of range.

The PrevPct_Click **and** NextPct_Click **procedures** These allow you to move to the previous and next records, respectively. When the current record index reaches either end of the database, the index is assigned the value of the other end. This assignment implements a wrap around (or circular-list) feature.

The Clean_Up **procedure** Clean_Up performs an important shut down process that involves removing the records that are marked for deletion. The problem with the random-access files is that you can expand them, but you cannot truncate them. This means that once a record is inserted it maintains its location in the file. There are various schemes for handling deleted records. I chose the following scheme for the contacts database program:

- A record can be marked for deletion. This does not cause the record to be deleted right away.
- A record marked for deletion can be unmarked, restoring its status as a normal record.
- A record that is marked for deletion is treated like a normal record.
- When you exit the application, the marked records are removed. This is performed by copying the unmarked records of the original database file into another file. The original file is renamed as VBCARD.BAK, while the new file becomes VBCARD.DAT.

The CleanUp procedure implements the last feature and performs a number of tasks.

It closes the database file, determines if there are one or more records to delete, and deletes any existing VBCARD.BAK. This step involves error trapping, in case there is no VBCARD.BAK file.

Then the procedure renames the VBCARD.DAT database file as VBCARD.BAK, and opens both VBCARD.BAK and the new database file VBCARD.DAT as random-access file. A For-Next loop is then used to read the records from VBCARD.BAK and write only the unmarked records in VBCARD.DAT. After this, the procedure closes both files.

The QuitBtn_Click **procedure** This exits the application. The procedure first writes the current record (if that record is new or modified), then invokes the CleanUp procedure to perform the proper shut down.

Run the VBCARD program and experiment with adding, searching, sorting, deleting, and viewing various records. You can use this utility to keep track of your daily contacts. Figure 17-9 shows a sample session.

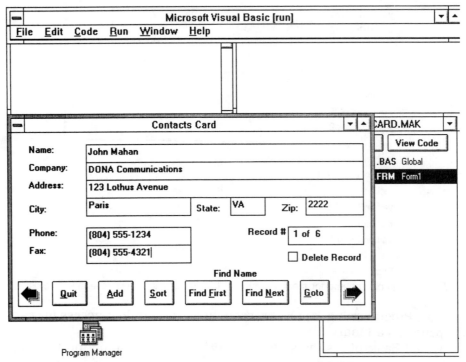

17-9 A sample session with program VBCARD.

Binary file I/O

Binary files may be regarded as a special case of random-access files, where the record length is one byte. Binary files delegate the privilege of organizing the data to the programmer. This privilege means that the programmer must be more careful in reading and writing to the file. On the other hand, the programmer has the advantage of maintaining complex storage schemes. For example, you can have a binary file store different groups of fixed-length records followed by a single group of variable-length records. Figure 17-10 shows a sample scheme for storing data in such a file.

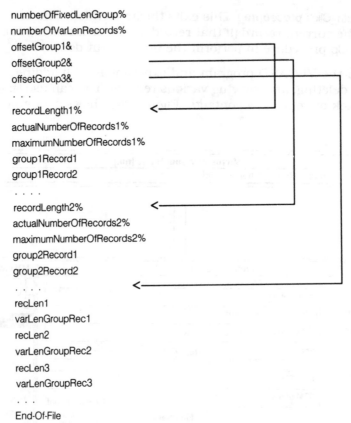

numberOfFixedLenGroup%
numberOfVarLenRecords%
offsetGroup1&
offsetGroup2&
offsetGroup3&
. . .
recordLength1%
actualNumberOfRecords1%
maximumNumberOfRecords1%
group1Record1
group1Record2
. . . .
recordLength2%
actualNumberOfRecords2%
maximumNumberOfRecords2%
group2Record1
group2Record2
. . . .
recLen1
varLenGroupRec1
recLen2
varLenGroupRec2
recLen3
varLenGroupRec3
. . .
End-Of-File

17-10 A sample scheme for storing groups of fixed-length and variable-length records.

☞ Programming Tip: Every sequential and random-access file can be opened as a binary file.

Visual Basic offers the statements discussed now to perform binary file I/O.

The Open **statement**   This statement opens a file for binary file I/O using the following general form:

Open *fileName$* For Binary As [*#*]*FileNumber%*

The fileName$ is a string expression that specifies the name of the opened file. The For Binary clause set the file mode as binary. The As clause designates the file handle number.

The Get **statement**   Get enables you to retrieve one or more bytes from the binary file. The general syntax for the Get statement is:

Get [*#*] *fileNumber%, [byteNumber&], variable*

The fileNumber% specifies the file handle number. The byteNumber& variable indicates which byte you want to read. When this parameter is omitted, the next Len(variable) bytes are read. The first byte in the file is byte 1. The valid arguments for byteNumber& are 1 to the number of actual bytes in the file. The largest byte number is 2,147,483,647 (equal to 2^31 − 1).

When a variable-length string variable is used with the Get statement, the number of bytes read from the binary file equals the current length of the string. This input feature allows you to specify the exact number of bytes to read by using the Space$ function. This function is used to create a string with a size equal to the number of bytes to read, as shown below:

InputString$ = Space$(*numberOfBytes%*)
Get #*fileNumber%*,,*InputString$*

The Put **statement**   This allows you to store one or more bytes in a binary file. The general syntax for the Put statement is:

Put [#] *fileNumber%*, *[byteNumber&]*, *variable*

The fileNumber% specifies the file handle number. The byteNumber& variable indicates where want to write the first byte. When this parameter is omitted, the next Len(variable) bytes are written. The first byte in the file is byte 1. When the Put statement writes beyond the current end-of-file, the file is expanded.

The Seek **statement**   This statement allows you to position the file pointer to a specific byte for the next read or write operation. It performs no file I/O. The general syntax for the Seek statement is:

Seek [#]*fileNumber%*, *bytePosition&*

The fileNumber% specifies the file handle number. The bytePosition& parameter designates the byte number. Seeking one byte beyond the current number of bytes expands the binary file.

The Seek **function**   This function returns a long integer that represents the file pointer of the current byte number. The general syntax for the Seek function is:

Seek(*fileNumber%*)

The fileNumber% specifies the file handle number.

The text sorting utility

The problem with text files is that they contain variable-length records. The most common text file processing techniques involve sequential input or output. These techniques fail to read a text line more than once without first rereading the text lines before it. The good news is that binary files can be used with the help of indexing arrays to implement pseudo-random-access text files.

The next program uses this technique to implement a utility that sorts the lines of a text file. The basic scheme is as follows:

- Read the text file sequentially, keeping track of the original line index (that is, the sequence of reading it), its byte position, and length (including the carriage return and line feed characters).
- Sort the array of line indices. This process involves reading the text lines and comparing their contents. Any swapping is applied only to the array of line indices. The text lines remain in their original locations. They are only read to perform this step.
- Once the array of line indices is ordered, the text lines in the original file are read as pseudo-random-access records into written sequentially in the target file. The text lines of the original file are selected using the sorted line indices.

The next program has an interface that is derived from that of program CATALOG, which I presented earlier in this chapter. The only differences are that the program form has the caption Program to Sort Text Files, and the sort button has the caption Sort Text File and has the control name of SortFileBtn.

The code attached to the SORTFILE.FRM is shown in LISTING 17-5. Most of the procedures in that listing are similar to those in LISTING 17-1. The only different procedure is SortFileBtn_Click. This procedure sorts the selected text file using the process described here.

Listing 17-5 The Code attached to the SORTFILE.FRM form.

```
Sub Form_Load ( )
  WindowState = 2
  PatternBox.Text = "*.txt"
  FileFlb.Filename = "*.txt"
  FileFlb.Archive = True
  FileFlb.Normal = True
  FileFlb.Hidden = False
  FileFlb.ReadOnly = False
  FileFlb.System = False
End Sub

Sub DiskDrv_Change ( )
  ' update file tree path when the disk is changed
  TreeDir.Path = DiskDrv.Drive
End Sub

Sub QuitBtn_Click ( )
  End
End Sub

Sub TreeDir_Change ( )
```

Listing 17-5 Continued.

```
   FileFlb.Path = TreeDir.Path
End Sub

Sub PatternBox_KeyPress (KeyAScii As Integer)
   KeyAScii = Asc(LCase$(Chr$(KeyAScii)))
End Sub

Sub PatternBox_LostFocus ( )
   Dim I As Integer
   If PatternBox.Text = " " Then PatternBox.Text = "*.*"
   I = InStr(PatternBox.Text, " ") ' find first space
   If I > 0 Then
      PatternBox.Text = Mid$(PatternBox.Text, 1, I – 1)
   End If
   FileFlb.Filename = PatternBox.Text
End Sub

Function GetFilename (Filename As String) As String
   Dim I As Integer
   If Filename <> " " Then
      I = InStr(Filename, ".")
      If I > 0 Then
         GetFilename = Left$(Filename, I – 1)
      Else
         GetFilename = Filename
      End If
   Else
      GetFilename = " "
   End If
End Function

Function GetFileExt (Filename As String) As String
   Dim I As Integer
   If Filename <> " " Then
      I = InStr(Filename, ".")
      If I > 0 Then
         GetFileExt = Mid$(Filename, I + 1, Len(Filename) – I)
      Else
         GetFileExt = " "
      End If
   Else
      GetFileExt = " "
   End If
End Function

Sub ViewFileBtn_Click ( )
   Dim F As String, TextLine As String
   Dim FileNum As Integer
```

Listing 17-5 Continued.

```
   Dim NL As String * 2
   If FileFlb.Filename < > " " Then
      NL = Chr$(13) + Chr$(10)
      FileNum = FreeFile
      F = TreeDir.Path
      If Right$(F, 1) < > "\" Then F = F + "\"
      F = F + FileFlb.Filename
      Open F For Input As #FileNum
      F = " "
      Do While Not EOF(FileNum)
         Line Input #FileNum, TextLine
         F = F + TextLine + NL
      Loop
      Close #FileNum
      TextBox.Text = F
   End If
End Sub

Sub TextBox_KeyPress (KeyAScii As Integer)
   KeyAScii = 0
End Sub

Sub PrintFileCom_Click ( )
   Dim F As String, TextLine As String
   Dim FileNum As Integer
   If FileFlb.Filename < > " " Then
      Form1.MousePointer = 11 ' hourglass
      FileNum = FreeFile
      F = TreeDir.Path
      If Right$(F, 1) < > "\" Then F = F + "\"
      F = F + FileFlb.Filename
      Open F For Input As #FileNum
      Do While Not EOF(FileNum)
         Line Input #FileNum, TextLine
         Printer.Print TextLine
      Loop
      Printer.EndDoc
      Close #FileNum
      Form1.MousePointer = 0
   End If
End Sub

Function Max (I As Integer, J As Integer) As Integer
   If I > J Then
      Max = I
   Else
      Max = J
```

Listing 17-5 Continued.

```
     End If
End Function

Sub SortFileBtn_Click ( )
     Dim LineIndex( ) As Integer ' index of lines
     Dim LinePos( ) As Long ' byte index for line
     Dim LineLen( ) As Integer ' size of line
     Dim NumLines As Integer ' number of text lines in file
     Dim I As Integer, J As Integer ' indices
     Dim II As Integer, JJ As Integer ' indices
     Dim Skip As Integer ' used in sorting
     Dim InOrder As Integer ' in-order flag
     Dim LineI As String, LineJ As String ' lines of text
     Dim F As String ' full filename
     Dim MainFilename As String ' main filename
     Dim ExtFilename As String ' extension name
     ' declare variables for file I/O channels
     Dim BinFileNum As Integer
     Dim InputFileNum As Integer
     Dim OutputFileNum As Integer
     '_____
     If FileFlb.Filename = " " Then Exit Sub
     Form1.MousePointer = 11 ' hourglass
     F = TreeDir.Path
     If Right$(F, 1) < > " \ " Then F = F + " \ "
     F = F + FileFlb.Filename
     MainFilename = GetFilename(F)
     ExtFilename = GetFileExt(F)
     ' delete previous ".BAK" file
     On Error Resume Next
     Kill MainFilename + ".BAK"
     On Error GoTo 0 ' turn off error-handler
     ' rename file as .BAK
     Name F As MainFilename + ".BAK"
     ' first pass simply counts the number of lines
     InputFileNum = FreeFile
     NumLines = 0
     Open MainFilename + ".BAK" For Input As #InputFileNum
     Do While Not EOF(InputFileNum)
        Line Input #InputFileNum, LineI
        NumLines = NumLines + 1
     Loop
     Close #InputFileNum
     If NumLines = 0 Then ' file is empty
        ' rename file back to original
        Name MainFilename + ".BAK" As F
        MsgBox "The text file is empty!", 0, "Information"
```

Listing 17-5 Continued.

```
  Form1.MousePointer = 0
  Exit Sub
End If
' redimension the arrays
' LineIndex(0) is used in swapping the other elements of LineIndex
ReDim LineIndex(0 To NumLines)
ReDim LinePos(1 To NumLines + 1)
ReDim LineLen(1 To NumLines)
'start pass 2
LinePos(1) = 1 ' position of first byte
InputFileNum = FreeFile
Open MainFilename + ".BAK" For Input As #InputFileNum
LenBigTextLine = 0
For I = 1 To NumLines
  Line Input #InputFileNum, LineI ' read text line
  LineIndex(I) = I ' set index of line
  LineLen(I) = Len(LineI) ' store length of line
  ' calculate the byte position of the next line
  ' the 2 represent the Chr$(13)+Chr$(10) characters
  ' that delimit the text lines
  LinePos(I + 1) = LinePos(I) + LineLen(I) + 2
Next I
' close file buffers
Close #InputFileNum
' sort the text lines
BinFileNum = FreeFile
Open MainFilename + ".BAK" For Binary As #BinFileNum
' start the Comb-sort algorithm
Skip = NumLines
Do
  Skip = Max(Int(Skip / 1.3), 1)
  InOrder = True
  For I = 1 To NumLines - Skip
    J = I + Skip
    ' get indirect indices
    II = LineIndex(I)
    JJ = LineIndex(J)
    ' get line I
    LineI = Space$(LineLen(II))
    Get #BinFileNum, LinePos(II), LineI
    ' get line J
    LineJ = Space$(LineLen(JJ))
    Get #BinFileNum, LinePos(JJ), LineJ
    If LineI > LineJ Then
      InOrder = False
      ' swap LineIndex elements
      ' the element LineIndex(0) is used as a
      ' temporary swap buffer
```

Listing 17-5 Continued.

```
        LineIndex(0) = LineIndex(I)
        LineIndex(I) = LineIndex(J)
        LineIndex(J) = LineIndex(0)
      End If
    Next I
  Loop Until InOrder And (Skip = 1)
  ' now copy lines from .BAK file into the text file
  OutputFileNum = FreeFile
  Open F For Binary As #OutputFileNum ' open as binary
  For I = 1 To NumLines
    II = LineIndex(I) ' get the I'th line
    ' size string LineI to read the I'th text line
    LineI = Space$(LineLen(II) + 2)
    ' use Get and Put to copy lines
    Get #BinFileNum, LinePos(II), LineI
    Put #OutputFileNum, , LineI
  Next I
  Close ' close all buffers
  Form1.MousePointer = 0
End Sub
```

First, the procedure changes the shape of the cursor into the hour-glass, obtains the full name of the selected text file, and obtains the main and extension names of the selected file. It then erases any previous .BAK file that has the same primary filename as the selected text file, and renames the selected file using the .BAK file extension.

At this point, the procedure opens the selected file as a sequential file, reads the text line in sequence to count the number of lines, and then closes the selected file. If the file is empty, the procedure restores the original filename, displays a message that the file is empty, and exits. If the file is not empty, the procedure dimensions the size of the LineIndex (line index), LinePos (byte position), and LineLen (length of line) arrays using the number of lines, and opens the file for a second sequential pass. Next, the file lines are read using a For-Next loop to obtain the values for the LineIndex, LinePos, and LineLen arrays. The file is then closed.

Now, the procedure reopens the selected file as a binary file, and applies the Combsort algorithm to sort the LineIndex array. The Get statements read the various text lines into the variables LineI and LineJ. These string variables are compared to determine whether or not the array LineIndex is ordered. Only the elements of LineIndex are swapped. Notice that the function calls Space$(LineLen(II)) and Space$(LineLen(JJ)) are used to create string LineI and LineJ with the exact size for the subsequent Get statements.

At this point, the procedure opens the output file using the original name of the selected file. The output file is opened as a binary file. The text lines are then copied using a For-Next loop. The Ith line is specified by the element LineIndex(I). The text lines are sequentially written to the output file. Finally, the file buffers are closed, and the mouse cursor is restored to the default shape.

Run the program and sort a short text file. This should give you an indication that the program is very slow with large text files. However, the program does illustrate the use of binary files to implement the read-only pseudo-random access of text files.

18
Providing on-line help

In chapter 2 I discussed the Visual Basic on-line help system. In general, providing on-help is becoming more desirable and somewhat expected, especially for nontrivial applications. In this chapter I will discuss a method for incorporating on-line help in your own Visual Basic applications. You will learn about the following topics:

- Building and using a compiler for the help source text.
- Building and using a simple context-sensitive on-line help.

The process of providing on-line help in your Visual Basic applications involves two steps. The first step uses a help compiler that takes a text file and produces special help files. The second step consists of adding a help form that uses the help files to provide the required on-line help.

The help compiler

The first step in providing on-line help begins with preparing a text file that specifies the help topics and their accompanying text. The accompanying text may include hypertext links; however, this is beyond the scope of this book. A help compiler transforms the source file into one or more files that organize the help topics and text into a more suitable form.

The help compiler that I will present in this chapter is a simple one. It has the following main features and requirements:

- The source file is an ASCII text file.

- The help topics are declared on separate lines (one topic per line) using topic directives that have the following format:

  .Topic *topicName*

  The line must begin with the topic directive, .Topic. This directive is not case-sensitive, but the topicName is. This means that the current compiler version allows you to create different topic names that use the same name but have different letter cases. I recommend that you explore this feature with great care. Remember to make the first line a topic directive.
- The lines that are not topic directives make up the text for the associated topic.

The secondary features of the help compiler are loading, editing, and storing a text file; and printing a text file. These features are implemented without "bells and whistles." Feel free to use other utilities to edit and print your text files.

The help compiler uses the constants and user-type shown in LISTING 18-1. These are identifiers declared in the file HELP.GLB which is a variant of GLOBAL.BAS. Listing 18-1 shows only the first few file lines that relate to the help system that I present.

Listing 18-1 The first few lines in the file HELP.GLB that contains global declarations.

```
Global Const TOPIC_SIZE = 40
Global Const KEY_FILENAME = ".key"
Global Const HELP_FILENAME = ".hlp"

Global HelpTopic As String
Global KeyFilename As String
Global HelpFilename As String

Type HelpRec
   Topic As String * TOPIC_SIZE
   Offset As Long
   TextLen As Integer
End Type
```

The HelpRec user-type declares three fields, namely, Topic, Offset, and TextLen. The Topic field stores the topic name in a fixed string whose length is specified by TOPIC_SIZE. If you plan to change the value of TOPIC_SIZE, do so *before* you use the help compiler to generate help files.

The help compiler produces two files. The first file, a .key file, is a random-access file that stores the HelpRec type. The second file is a .hlp file that stores the text for the topic in a binary file. The Offset field of the HelpRec indicates the location of the first byte for the text associated with the topic stored in the Topic field. The TextLen field specifies the length of the text, including the carriage return and line field characters.

The variables HelpTopic, KeyFilename, and HelpFilename are used to transfer data between the application and the form that provides on-line help. I will discuss these variables in more detail in the next section.

Figures 18-1 to 18-3 show the specifications for the HELPCOMP.MAK project file and the HELPCOMP.FRM form file. Figure 18-4 shows a sample session with the help compiler.

Application name: Help Compiler
Application code name: HELPCOMP
Version: 1.0   Date created: July 24, 1991
Programmer(s): Namir Clement Shammas

List of filenames

Storage path: \VB\EASYVB
Project HELPCOMP.MAK
Global HELP.GLB
Form 1 HELPCOMP.FRM

18-1   The basic specifications for the HELPCOMP.MAK project file.

Form #1   Form filename: HELPCOMP.FRM
Version: 1.0   Date: July 24, 1991

Control object type	Default CtlName	Purpose
Drive List Box	Drive1	Shows and selects the current drive
Directory List	Dir1	Shows and selects the current directory
File List Box	File1	Shows a group of files
Text Box	Text1	Specifies the filename pattern
	Text2	Views and edits a text file
Command Box	Command1	Exits the program
	Command2	Compiles a text file
	Command3	Loads a text file
	Command4	Saves a text file
	Command5	Prints a text file
Label	Label1	Label for filename pattern
	Label2	Label for drive list box
	Label3	Label for directory list box
	Label4	Label for file list box

18-2   The list of controls in the HELPCOMP.FRM form file.

Application (code) name: HELPCOMP
Form #1
Version: 1.0   Date:

Original control name	Property	New setting
Form	Caption	Help Compiler
Drive1	CtlName	DiskDrv
Dir1	CtlName	TreeDir
File1	CtlName	FileFlb
Text1	CtlName	PatternBox
	Text	(empty string)
Text2	CtlName	TextBox
	Text	(empty string)
	MultiLine	True
	Scroll Bars	3 - Both
Command1	CtlName	QuitBtn
	Caption	&Quit
	Cancel	True
Command2	CtlName	CompileBtn
	Caption	&Compile Help File
Command3	CtlName	LoadBtn
	Caption	&Load File
Command4	CtlName	SaveBtn
	Caption	&Save File
Command5	CtlName	PrintBtn
	Caption	&Print File
Label1	CtlName	PatternLbl
	Caption	Filename:
Label2	CtlName	DriveLbl
	Caption	Drive:
Label3	CtlName	DirectoryLbl
	Caption	Directory:
Label4	CtlName	FilesLbl
	Caption	Files:

18-3 The customized settings for the HELPCOMP.FRM form.

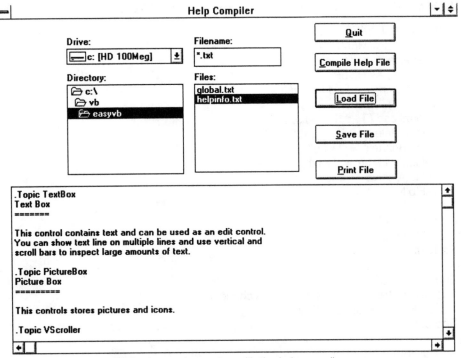

18-4 A sample session with the help compiler.

Listing 18-2 shows the code attached to the HELPCOMP.FRM form. The general declarations section declares the following constants and variables:

- The MAX_TOPICS constant that specifies the initial upper bound of the array Topics.
- The SIZE_INCREMENT constant that defines the increase in the size of array Topics.
- The HelpRec-typed array Topics. This is a dynamic array whose actual size is declared in the CompileBtn_Click procedure and expanded in the procedure ExpandTopicsArray.
- The variable F stores the name of the help source file. I use a short name to reduce the size of the Visual Basic code lines.

The relevant procedures in the HELPCOMP.FRM form are discussed in the next few paragraphs.

The CompileBtn_Click **procedure**   This contains the code that compiles help files. It ensures that you have selected a file from the files list box. (If no selection is made, the procedure does not perform any action.) The cursor shape is changed to the hour-glass while the procedure is compiling a source help file. The cursor is restored at the end of the procedure, which then obtains the source filename and opens it as a sequential for input.

Listing 18-2 The source code attached to the HELPCOPM.FRM form.

```
Const MAX_TOPICS = 50
Const SIZE_INCREMENT = 10
' declare the array of topic records
Dim Topics( ) As HelpRec
Dim F As String ' edited filename

Sub FormLoad ( )
   WindowState = 2
   PatternBox.Text = "*.txt"
   FileFlb.Filename = "*.txt"
   FileFlb.Archive = True
   FileFlb.Normal = True
   FileFlb.Hidden = False
   FileFlb.ReadOnly = False
   FileFlb.System = False
End Sub

Sub DiskDrv_Change ( )
' update file tree path when the disk is changed
   TreeDir.Path = DiskDrv.Drive
End Sub

Sub QuitBtn_Click ( )
   End
End Sub

Sub TreeDir_Change ( )
   FileFlb.Path = TreeDir.Path
End Sub

Sub PatternBox_KeyPress (KeyAScii As Integer)
   KeyAScii = Asc(LCase$(Chr$(KeyAScii)))
End Sub

Sub PatternBox_LostFocus ( )
   Dim I As Integer
   If PatternBox.Text = " " Then PatternBox.Text = "*.*"
   I = InStr(PatternBox.Text, " ") ' find first space
   If I > 0 Then
      PatternBox.Text = Mid$(PatternBox.Text, 1, I – 1)
   End If
   FileFlb.Filename = PatternBox.Text
End Sub

Function GetFilename (Filename As String) As String
' get the primary filename, including the drive and path
   Dim I As Integer
   If Filename <> " " Then
```

Listing 18-2 Continued.

```
      I = InStr(Filename, ".")
      If I > 0 Then
         GetFilename = Left$(Filename, I – 1)
      Else
         GetFilename = Filename
      End If
   Else
      GetFilename = " "
   End If
End Function

Sub PrintFileCom_Click ( )
' simple file printer
   Dim F As String, TextLine As String
   Dim FileNum As Integer
   If FileFlb.Filename < > " " Then
      Form1.MousePointer = 11 ' hourglass
      FileNum = FreeFile
      F = TreeDir.Path
      If Right$(F, 1) < > " \ " Then F = F + " \ "
      F = F + FileFlb.Filename
      Open F For Input As #FileNum
      Do While Not EOF(FileNum)
         Line Input #FileNum, TextLine
         Printer.Print TextLine
      Loop
      Printer.EndDoc
      Close #FileNum
      Form1.MousePointer = 0
   End If
End Sub

Function Max (I As Integer, J As Integer) As Integer
' Get the maximum value of either I or J
   If I > J Then
      Max = I
   Else
      Max = J
   End If
End Function

Sub LoadFileBtn_Click ( )
' load text file into the TextBox for viewing and editing
   Dim TextLine As String
   Dim FileNum As Integer
   Dim Lines As String
   Dim NL As String * 2
      '_____
```

Listing 18-2 Continued.

```
  If FileFlb.Filename < > " " Then
    NL = Chr$(13) + Chr$(10)
    FileNum = FreeFile
    F = TreeDir.Path
    If Right$(F, 1) < > " \ " Then F = F + " \ "
    F = F + FileFlb.Filename
    Open F For Input As #FileNum
    Lines = " "
    Do While Not EOF(FileNum)
      Line Input #FileNum, TextLine
      Lines = Lines + TextLine + NL
    Loop
    Close #FileNum
    TextBox.Text = Lines
  End If
End Sub

Sub SaveFileBtn_Click ( )
' save TextBox in file F
  Dim FileNum As Integer
  If (F < > " ") And (TextBox.Text < > " ") Then
    FileNum = FreeFile
    Open F For Output As #FileNum
    Print #FileNum, TextBox.Text
    Close #FileNum
  End If
End Sub

Sub CompileBtn_Click ( )
' compile file in the text box
  Dim TextLine As String
  Dim Lines As String
  Dim HelpFilename As String
  Dim KeyFilename As String
  ' declare variables for file handles
  Dim InputFileNum As Integer
  Dim KeyFileNum As Integer
  Dim HelpFileNum As Integer
  ' declare other variables
  Dim N As Integer, I As Integer
  Dim CurrMaxSize As Integer
  Dim NL As String * 2
  '_____

  If FileFlb.Filename < > " " Then
    Form1.MousePointer = 11 ' hour-glass
    NL = Chr$(13) + Chr$(10)
    ' initialize the current maximum array size
    ' with the constant MAX_TOPICS
```

Listing 18-2 Continued.

```
CurrMaxSize = MAX_TOPICS
ReDim Topics(0 To CurrMaxSize) ' resize array
' prepare to open source file
InputFileNum = FreeFile
F = TreeDir.Path
If Right$(F, 1) < > " \ " Then F = F + " \ "
F = F + FileFlb.Filename
Open F For Input As #InputFileNum ' open source file
' open help file
HelpFileNum = FreeFile
HelpFilename = GetFilename(F) + HELPFILENAME
Open HelpFilename For Binary Access Write As #HelpFileNum
Lines = " "
N = 0 ' initialize number of topics
' read lines from source file
Do While Not EOF(InputFileNum)
    ' read the next line
    Line Input #InputFileNum, TextLine
    ' doe sit start with .Topic ?
    If InStr(UCase$(TextLine), ".TOPIC ") = 1 Then
        If Lines < > " " Then ' write previous help topic text
            Put #HelpFileNum, , Lines
            Topics(N).TextLen = Len(Lines)
            Lines = " " ' reset variables
        End If
        If N = CurrMaxSize Then
            ' resize the array
            ExpandTopicsArray CurrMaxSize
        End If
        N = N + 1
        ' obtain the name of the topic
        TextLine = Mid$(TextLine, Len(".TOPIC ") + 1)
        TextLine = LTrim$(RTrim$(TextLine))
        Topics(N).Topic = TextLine ' store topic name
        If N > 1 Then
            ' calculate text offset
            Topics(N).Offset = Topics(N - 1).Offset + Topics(N - 1).TextLen
        Else
            Topics(1).Offset = 1
        End If
    Else
        Lines = Lines + TextLine + NL ' accumulates lines
    End If
Loop
' store the text for the last topic
Put #HelpFileNum, , Lines
Topics(N).TextLen = Len(Lines) ' obtain length of text
Close ' close input and .hlp files
```

Listing 18-2 Continued.

```
      ' now sort the keys
      SortKeys Topics( ), N
      ' write the sorted key sto the .KEY file
      KeyFileNum = FreeFile
      KeyFilename = GetFilename(F) + KEY_FILENAME
      I = Len(Topics(1))
      Open KeyFilename For Random Access Write As #KeyFileNum Len = I
      For I = 1 To N
        Put #KeyFileNum, , Topics(I)
      Next I
      Close ' close all file buffers
    Form1.MousePointer = 0
    End If
End Sub

Sub SortKeys (Topics( ) As HelpRec, N As Integer)
' sort the array Topics using the Topic field.
' This procedure uses the new Comb-sort method
    Dim Skip As Integer
    Dim InOrder As Integer
    Dim I As Integer, J As Integer
    Skip = N
    Do
      Skip = Max(Int(Skip / 1.3), 1)
      InOrder = True
      For I = 1 To N − Skip
        J = I + Skip
        If Topics(I).Topic > Topics(J).Topic Then
          InOrder = False
          ' swap the I and J elements of Topics using
          ' the element Topic(0)
          Topics(0) = Topics(I)
          Topics(I) = Topics(J)
          Topics(J) = Topics(0)
        End If
      Next I
    Loop Until InOrder And (Skip = 1)
End Sub

Sub ExpandTopicsArray (CurrSize As Integer)
    ' expand the array Topics
    Dim TopicsCopy( ) As HelpRec
    Dim I As Integer, NewSize As Integer
    '_____
    ReDim TopicsCopy(0 To CurrSize)
    For I = 0 To CurrSize
      TopicsCopy(I) = TopicsCopy(I)
    Next I
```

Listing 18-2 Continued.

```
   NewSize = CurrSize + SIZEINCREMENT
   ReDim Topics(0 To NewSize)
   For I = 0 To CurrSize
     Topics(I) = TopicsCopy(I)
   Next I
   CurrSize = NewSize ' update current size
End Sub
```

The procedure next obtains the name of the compiled help text file. This file has the same primary name as the input file. The global constant HELP_FILENAME specifies the file extension, which is currently set to .hlp. The help file is opened as a binary file for output, and the topic-text variable Lines and the topic counter variable N are initialized.

The procedure next starts a Do-Loop to process the text lines of the input file. Inside the loop, the procedure reads the text lines and detects the topic directive. When a topic directive is found, the procedure extracts its name and stores in the Topics(N).Topic field. The Offset and TextLine fields are also supplied with data. When the procedure is not processing a topic directive, it accumulates the ordinary text line in the Lines variable. The array Topics is dynamically expanded as needed. If the number of topics equals the value stored in the CurrtMaxSize, the ExpandTopicsArray procedure is called to expand the array by SIZE_INCREMENT elements. When the CompileBtn_Click procedure starts execution, the local variable CurrMaxSize is assigned MAX_TOPICS. Therefore, the constant MAX_TOPICS represents only the initial upper limit.

When the Do-While loop terminates, the procedure stores the last set of text lines and closes the file buffers. It sorts the array Topics using the Topic field; the SortKey procedure is invoked for this purpose. Then the ordered keys are written to the key file. This file has the same primary name as the input file. The file extension is given by the global constant KEY_FILENAME, currently set to .key. The key file is then closed and the mouse cursor restored.

The SortKeys **procedure** This procedure sorts the array Topics using the topic name (stored in the field Topic). The Combsort method is used to sort the array.

The ExpandTopicsArray **procedure** This procedure is used to expand the size of the array Topics. Since the Redim statement, used in expanding array Topics, destroys the array's contents, a local array TopicsCopy is used to retain the data of Topics. The first For-Next loop copies the elements of array Topics into array TopicsCopy. The array Topics is then expanded to its new size. A second For-Next loop copies the original data of Topics back into the redimensioned array Topics. The CurrSize argument, which is passed by reference, of the ExpandTopicsArray is increased by SIZE_INCREMENT.

Figure 18-5 shows a sample source help file, HELPINFO.TXT. I will be using this file with the next program in this chapter. Run the help compiler and compile the HELPINFO.TXT file to produce the HELPINFO.KEY and HELPINFO.HLP. If you view the HELPINFO.HLP file you might be surprised to see that it looks like the HELPINFO.TXT file, except the topic directives are missing. In fact, the HELPINFO.HLP file is a text file, but a special one. The position and length of the text for each topic is stored in the HELPINFO.KEY file. While you may edit this special text file with great care (by overwriting characters), I strongly advise against it.

```
.Topic TextBox
Text Box
=======

This control contains text and can be used as an edit control. You can show text line on
multiple lines and use vertical and scroll bars to inspect large amounts of text.

.Topic PictureBox
Picture Box
=========

This control stores pictures and icons.

.Topic VScroller
VerticalScroller
==============
This control allows you to select from a large number of values.

.Topic HScroller
Horizontal Scroller
================

This control allows you to select from a large number of values.

.Topic DriveBox
Drive List Box
===========

This control enables you to select new drives.

.Topic DirBox
Directory List Box
===============

This control enables you to select the current directory.

.Topic FileBox
File List Box
==========
```

18-5   A sample source help file HELPINFO.TXT.

This control allows you to select a file.

.Topic OptionButon
Option button
============

This control is also known as a radio button. The option buttons are mutually exclusive controls, allowing you to select only one option.

.Topic CheckBox
Check Box
========

This is a check box. Check boxes allow you to select combinations of options. The check boxes are not mutually exclusive.

.Topic Command
Command Button
==============

This control is perhaps the most popular. By clicking on a command button you generate the Click event that is usually handled by a procedure that animates the command button to perform a task.

.Topic ComboBox
Combo List Box
=============

This control combines the list box and the text box.

.Topic ListBox
List Box
=======

This control presents a list of items to choose from.

18-5 Continued.

From a programming perspective, the HELPINFO.HLP file is opened for output as a binary file and not as a sequential file. This enables the CompileBtn_Click procedure to write the text lines accumulated in the variable Lines with a single Print statement.

Offering on-line help

Once the compiled help files are available, they are ready to be used in the help system that is integrated in your Visual Basic programs. In this section, I present an example of a simple context-sensitive help system that does an adequate job of providing you with the on-line help you need. The next program is a simple program that shows various mute controls on a form. On-line help is available in one of two ways:

- Focusing on a control and then pressing the F1 function key. As a result, the program uses a help form to offer help information that is related to the focused control. This is the context-sensitive aspect of the help system. Once you are in the help form, you can select other topics to view their help information.
- Selecting the Help menu to open the help form. From there you can select one or more topics to view their help information.

The help form contains four command buttons, a help-information text box, and a help-topic list box. The command buttons allow you to exit the help form, view the previous help topic, view the next help topic, or view the topic selected in the list box. Double clicking on the topic selected in the list box results in viewing the related help text.

Figures 18-6 to 18-11 show the specifications for the HELPDEMO.MAK project file, HELPDEMO.FRM form file, and the HELOFORM.FRM form

Application name: Help Demonstration Program
Application code name: HELPDEMO
Version: 1.0   Date created:
Programmer(s): Namir Clement Shammas

List of filenames

Storage path: \VB\EASYVB
Project HELPDEMO.MAK
Global HELP.GLB
Form 1 HELPDEMO.FRM
Form 2 HELPFORM.FRM

18-6 The basic specifications for the HELPDEMO.MAK project file.

Form #1   Form filename: HELPDEMO.FRM
Version: 1.0   Date:

Control object type	Default CtlName	Purpose
TextBox	Text1	Sample text box
Picture	Picture1	Sample picture box
Vertical Scrollbar	VScroll1	Sample vertical scroll bar
Horizontal Scrollbar	HScroll1	Sample horizontal scroll bar
Drive List Box	Drive1	Sample drive list box
Directory List Box	Dir1	Sample directory list box
Files List Box	File1	Sample file list box

18-7 The list of controls in the HELPDEMO.FRM form file.

Control object type	Default CtlName	Purpose
Option Button	Option1	Sample option button
Check Box	Check1	Sample check box
Command Button	Command1	Sample command box
Combo List Box	Combo1	Sample combo list box
List Box	List1	Sample list box

18-7 Continued.

Application (code) name: HELPDEMO
Form #1
Version: 1.0   Date:

Original control name	Property	New setting
Form	CtlName	Help Demo Program
Picture1	Picture	\vb\icons\computer\disk01.ico

18-8 The customized settings for the HELPDEMO.FRM form.

Form #1   Form filename: HELPDEMO.FRM
Version: 1.0   Date: July 24, 1991

Caption	Property	Setting	Purpose
&Quit	CtlName	QuitCom	Exits the demo program
&Help	CtlName	HelpCom	Shows the help form

18-9 The menu structure for HELPDEMO.FRM.

Form #2   Form filename: HELPFORM.FRM
Version: 1.0   Date: July 24, 1991

Control object type	Default CtlName	Purpose
Command Button	Command1	Exits the help form
	Command2	Selects the previous topic
	Command3	Selects the next topic
	Command4	Views the information on the topic selected in List1
Text Box	Text1	Views the help information
List Box	List1	Lists the available topics

18-10 The list of controls in the HELPFORM.FRM form file.

Application (code) name: HELPDEMO
Form #2
Version: 1.0   Date: July 24, 1991

Form	Caption	Help
Command1	CtlName	ExitBtn
	Caption	&Exit
	Cancel	True
Command2	CtlName	PreviousBtn
	Caption	&Previous
Command3	CtlName	NextBtn
	Caption	&Next
Command4	CtlName	SearchBtn
	Caption	&Search
	Default	True
Text1	CtlName	HelpBox
	Text	(empty string)
	MultiLine	True
	ScrollBars	3 - Both
List1	CtlName	TopicsLst

18-11 The customized settings for the HELPFORM.FRM form.

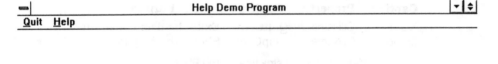

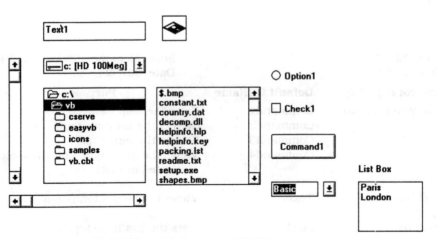

18-12 The controls on the HELPDEMO.FRM form.

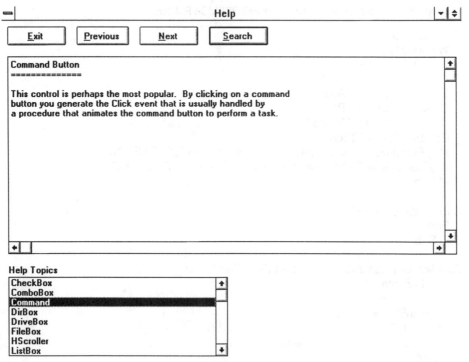

18-13 A sample help session with the HELPFORM.FRM form.

file. Figure 18-12 shows the controls on the HELPDEMO.FRM form, while FIG. 18-13 shows a sample session with the help form.

I created the help form to make it highly independent of the application it serves. This enables you to reuse the help form in your Visual Basic applications with little or no recoding.

Listing 18-3 contains the code attached to the HELPDEMO.FRM form. This form communicates with the help form using the global variables HelpTopic, KeyFilename, and HelpFilename. The HelpTopic variable enables the main form (or any other form) to request specific help topic. The help form examines the HelpTopic variable to decide which topic to display. The HelpFilename and KeyFilename variables tell the help forms which files to read to provide the on-line help.

The relevant procedures in the main form are presented in the next several paragraphs.

The HelpCom_Click **procedure** This procedure assigns an empty string to global variable HelpTopic and shows the help form as a modeless window. Since the variable HelpTopic is an empty string, the help form displays an empty help text box.

Listing 18-3 The code attached to the HELPDEMO.FRM form.

```
Sub Form_Load ()
  WindowState = 2
  List1.AddItem "Paris"
  List1.AddItem "London"
  Combo1.AddItem "Ada"
  Combo1.AddItem "Basic"
  Combo1.AddItem "Pascal"
  Combo1.Text = "Basic"
  HelpFilename = "\vb\easyvb\helpinfo" + HELP_FILENAME
  KeyFilename = "\vb\easyvb\helpinfo" + KEY_FILENAME
End Sub

Sub QuitBtn_Click ()
  End
End Sub

Function GetFilename (Filename As String) As String
  Dim I As Integer
  If Filename <> "" Then
    I = InStr(Filename, ".")
    If I > 0 Then
      GetFilename = Left$(Filename, I − 1)
    Else
      GetFilename = Filename
    End If
  Else
      GetFilename = ""
    End If
End Function

Sub QuitCom_Click ()
  End
End Sub

Sub HelpCom_Click ()
  HelpTopic = "" ' no particular help topic
  HelpForm.Show
End Sub

Sub Text1_KeyDown (KeyCode As Integer, Shift As Integer)
  If KeyCode = KEY_F1 Then
    HelpTopic = "TextBox"
    HelpForm.Show
  End If
End Sub

Sub Picture1_KeyDown (KeyCode As Integer, Shift As Integer)
  If KeyCode = KEY_F1 Then
```

Listing 18-3 Continued.

```
      HelpTopic = "PictureBox"
      HelpForm.Show
   End If
End Sub

Sub VScroll1_KeyDown (KeyCode As Integer, Shift As Integer)
   If KeyCode = KEY_F1 Then
      HelpTopic = "VScroller"
      HelpForm.Show
   End If
End Sub

Sub Combo1_KeyDown (KeyCode As Integer, Shift As Integer)
   If KeyCode = KEY_F1 Then
      HelpTopic = "ComboBox"
      HelpForm.Show
   End If
End Sub

Sub Command1_KeyDown (KeyCode As Integer, Shift As Integer)
   If KeyCode = KEY_F1 Then
      HelpTopic = "Command"
      HelpForm.Show
   End If
End Sub

Sub Dir1_KeyDown (KeyCode As Integer, Shift As Integer)
   If KeyCode = KEY_F1 Then
      HelpTopic = "DirBox"
      HelpForm.Show
   End If
End Sub

Sub Drive1_KeyDown (KeyCode As Integer, Shift As Integer)
   If KeyCode = KEY_F1 Then
      HelpTopic = "DriveBox"
      HelpForm.Show
   End If
End Sub

Sub File1_KeyDown (KeyCode As Integer, Shift As Integer)
   If KeyCode = KEY_F1 Then
      HelpTopic = "FileBox"
      HelpForm.Show
   End If
End Sub

Sub HScroll1_KeyDown (KeyCode As Integer, Shift As Integer)
```

Listing 18-3   Continued.

```
  If KeyCode = KEY_F1 Then
    HelpTopic = "HScroller"
    HelpForm.Show
  End If
End Sub

Sub List1_KeyDown (KeyCode As Integer, Shift As Integer)
  If KeyCode = KEY_F1 Then
    HelpTopic = "ListBox"
    HelpForm.Show
  End If
End Sub

Sub Option1_KeyDown (KeyCode As Integer, Shift As Integer)
  If KeyCode = KEY_F1 Then
    HelpTopic = "OptionButton"
    HelpForm.Show
  End If
End Sub

Sub Check1_KeyDown (KeyCode As Integer, Shift As Integer)
  If KeyCode = KEY_F1 Then
    HelpTopic = "CheckBox"
    HelpForm.Show
  End If
End Sub
```

The XXXX_KeyPress **procedures**   These procedures detect pressing the F1 function key and invoke the help form to display information related to the XXXX control. A sample procedure is shown here:

```
Sub Text1_KeyDown (KeyCode As Integer, Shift As Integer)
  If KeyCode = KEY_F1 Then
    HelpTopic = "TextBox"
    HelpForm.Show
  End If
End Sub
```

The procedure uses an If-Then statement to detect pressing the F1 function key. The Then clause has two statements. The first one assigns the name of the text box topic to the global variable HelpTopic. This topic name must also appear in a topic directive, found in the source help file HELPINFO.TXT. The second statement loads and shows the help form. Since no argument is supplied, the help form is modeless—you can select another window before you are finished with the help form.

The Form_Load **procedure**   This procedure loads a few data items in the combo list box and in the list box. The purpose of this action is to enhance the visual appearance of these boxes when the program starts running. It then assigns the name of the help file to the global variable HelpFilename, and assigns the name of the Key file to the global variable KeyFilename.

Listing 18-4 shows the code attached to the HELPFROM.FRM form. The listing contains the following variables:

- The NumTopics variable stores the number of topics found in the file KeyFilename. This variable is also used to specify the upper limit of the dynamic array Topics.
- The Topics array is declared as a dynamic array.
- The KeyFileNum variable stores the file handle number for the KeyFilename.
- The HelpFileNum variable stores the file handle number for the HelpFilename.
- The TopicIndex keeps track of the index of the current topic.

The relevant procedures of the help form are described in the paragraphs after the listing.

Listing 18-4   The code attached to the HELPFORM.FRM form.

```
Dim NumTopics As Integer
Dim Topics( ) As HelpRec
Dim KeyFileNum As Integer
Dim HelpFileNum As Integer
Dim TopicIndex As Integer

Sub ExitBtn_Click ( )
   Close ' close all of the help file buffers
   Unload HelpForm
End Sub

Sub Form_Load ( )
   Dim Index As Integer
   Dim HelpVar As HelpRec
   '_____
   WindowState = 2
   ' open .key file
   KeyFileNum = FreeFile
   Open KeyFilename For Random Access Read As #KeyFileNum Len = Len(HelpVar)
   ' open .hlp file
   HelpFileNum = FreeFile
   Open HelpFilename For Binary Access Read As #HelpFileNum
   'calculate the number of topics
   NumTopics = LOF(KeyFileNum) / Len(HelpVar)
   ReDim Topics(0 To NumTopics) ' custom-size the array
   ' insert topic names in the topic list
   For Index = 1 To NumTopics
      ' read a topic record
      Get #KeyFileNum, , Topics(Index)
      ' add topic name to the list
      TopicsLst.AddItem RTrim$(Topics(Index).Topic)
```

Listing 18-4 Continued.

```
    Next Index
    ' did the main menu request help on a particular topic?
    If HelpTopic < > " " Then
        Index = BinSearch(HelpTopic) ' get topic index
        If Index > 0 Then LoadTopic (Index) ' load topic
    End If
End Sub

Function BinSearch (Find As String) As Integer
    ' performs a binary search on the topic
    Dim Low As Integer, High As Integer
    Dim Median As Integer
    Dim FindStr As String * TOPIC_SIZE
    FindStr = Find ' make a String * TOPIC_SIZE version
    Low = 1
    High = NumTopics
    Do
        Median = (Low + High) \ 2
    If FindStr < Topics(Median).Topic Then
            High = Median - 1
        Else
            Low = Median + 1
        End If
    Loop Until (FindStr = Topics(Median).Topic) Or (Low > High)
    If FindStr = Topics(Median).Topic Then
        BinSearch = Median
    Else
        BinSearch = 0
    End If
End Function

Sub LoadTopic (ByVal Index As Integer)
    ' load a topic by index
    Dim S As String
    ' is Index within valid range
    If (Index > 0) And (Index < = NumTopics) Then
        ' create string buffer equal to the length of the
        ' related topic text
        S = Space$(Topics(Index).TextLen)
        ' read the topic text
        Get #HelpFileNum, Topics(Index).Offset, S
        HelpBox.Text = S ' assign to help text box
        TopicIndex = Index ' store the topic index
    End If
End Sub
```

Listing 18-4 Continued.

```
Sub HelpBox_KeyPress (KeyAscii As Integer)
    KeyAscii = 0
End Sub

Sub TopicsLst_DblClick ( )
    ' load topic selected in the list box
    HelpTopic = TopicsLst.Text
    LoadTopic (BinSearch(HelpTopic))
End Sub

Sub SearchBtn_Click ( )
    TopicsLst_DblClick
End Sub

Sub PreviousBtn_Click ( )
    ' find the previous topic
    If TopicIndex > 1 Then
        TopicIndex = TopicIndex − 1
    Else
        TopicIndex = NumTopics
    End If
    LoadTopic (TopicIndex)
End Sub

Sub NextBtn_Click ( )
    ' find the next topic
    TopicIndex = TopicIndex Mod NumTopics + 1
    LoadTopic (TopicIndex)
End Sub
```

The ExitBtn_Click **procedure**   This procedure closes all of the file buffers before unloading the help form.

The Form_Load **procedure**   This performs the required initialization when the help form is loaded. To do so, the procedure sets the WindowState property to 2, maximizing the window of the help form, opens the key and help data files, calculates the number of topics, and assigns the result to the variable NumTopics. The array Topics is then redimensioned, using NumTopics to specify the upper limit.

The procedure then reads the key file that contains the HelpRec-typed data and stores the information in the Topics array, and inserts the topic names in the TopicsLst list box. Finally, it tests whether the global variable HelpTopic is not an empty string. If the tested condition is true, then the main form has requested help information on a topic stores in HelpTopic.

The Then clause invokes the BinSearch function to locate the index of the help topic. If the index is greater than zero (this is an extra precaution) then the text for the requested topic is loaded.

The BinSearch **function** This function performs a binary search on the ordered elements of array Topics and returns the index of the matching array element. If no match is found the function returns 0. Notice that the function uses a local fixed-string variable FindStr in searching for the sought element. This search compares FindStr with the fixed-string fields Topic of the various elements of array Topics. If you replace FindStr with Find (the supplied argument), the BinSearch will most likely fail to locate the specific topic because of the spaces that are padded to the Topic field. Using FindStr gives a faster function execution than if the expression RTrim$(Topics (Median).Topic) is used.

The LoadTopic **procedure** This procedure loads the topic specified by the parameter Index. The function checks the validity of the argument for Index before reading the appropriate help text from the help file. The local variable S is used to read the help text in one swoop. Once the text is read the contents of variable S are then assigned to the Text property of the HelpBox text box. The TopicIndex variable is assigned the value of the Index argument.

The TopicsLst_DblClick **procedure** With this procedure, the topic selected in the TopicsLst list box is loaded. The first statement puts the selected topic into the variable HelpTopic. The second statement invokes the BinSearch and the LoadTopic procedures to retrieve the requested help information.

The SearchBtn_Click **procedure** This simply issues a call to TopicsLst_DblClick to load the help information for the topic selected in the TopicsLst list box.

The PreviousBtn_Click **and** NextBtn_Click **procedures** These load the previous and next topics, respectively. Both procedures are coded to wrap around the topic list when you reach either the first or last topic.

Run the help demonstration program. Select a control and press the F1 function key. This takes you to the help form and displays the help information related to the selected control. Click on the Previous and Next buttons to scroll through the various help topics. In addition, select topics at your discretion from the list box and double click to see the related help information. When you are finished experimenting with the help window, click the Exit button. You can select another window when the help window appears. However, you cannot select another help topic from the main form before you close the help form.

19
Extending Visual Basic

The Windows environment makes extensive use of what are called the *Dynamic Link Libraries* (DLL). These are libraries that a Windows program can link to at run time instead of at link time (during the traditional compile-link cycle). In fact, Visual Basic programs use the run time DLL to access many of the predefined Visual Basic routines. In this chapter I discuss using DLLs in your own Visual Basic programs. These DLLs can be in the form of third party add-on products, or they can be calls to low-level Windows functions. You will learn about the following:

- Declaring and calling DLL routines in your Visual Basic program.
- Special considerations when declaring DLL routines.
- Calling DLL routines with particular data types.
- Tapping into the Windows DLL routines.

Declaring and calling DLL routines

Visual Basic provides a simple mechanism to declare and call DLL routines in your own Visual Basic applications. The general syntax for declaring a DLL routine as a Sub procedure is:

Declare Sub *subName* Lib *library$* [Alias *aliasName$*] (*parameterList*)

The subName parameter specifies the name of the DLL routine. The library$ parameter designates the DLL library name. The Alias clause enables you to specify an *alias name*, discussed later in this chapter. The parameterList is the list of parameters, usually passed by value.

Similarly, the general syntax for declaring a DLL routine as a function is:

Declare Function *fnName* Lib *library$* [Alias *aliasName$*] (*parameterList*) As *dataType*

DLL routines should be declared either in the global module, or in the general declarations section of a module or a form. Examples of DLL routines are shown below:

```
Declare Sub ReverseString Lib "bona.dll" (S As String)
' get the time in milliseconds since the system was first booted
Declare Function GetCurrentTime Lib "User" () As Long
' determine if the ASCII code belongs to a lower-case character
Declare Function IsCharLower Lib "User" (ByVal C As Integer) As Integer
```

Once a DLL is declared it can be called just like any other procedure. In the following example, I declare the IsLower function as a "shell" function around the DLL routine IsCharLower. The IsLower function allows you to use a string-typed argument:

```
Function IsLower (S As String) As Integer
  If S <> "" Then
    IsLower = IsCharLower(Asc(Left$(S, 1)))
  Else
    IsLower = 0
  End If
End If
```

Warning! Visual Basic performs no checking on the arguments that are passed to a DLL routine. Passing incorrect values may cause the routines to crash your system.

Special considerations when declaring DLL routines

Visual Basic requires that you properly declare and use DLL routines. This section focuses on various aspects of declaring DLL routines.

Defining the DLL library

The Declare statement contains the Lib clause that specifies the name of the DLL library. The Windows environment uses the User, GDI, and Kernel DLL libraries. In addition, there are a number of device driver DLLs, such as Sound. If you use custom or third-party DLLs, you need to use the DLL filename with the full path. An example is shown here that declares the DLL routine DrawPoly to be in the \dlls\graf.dll file:

```
Declare Sub DrawPoly Lib "\dlls\graf.dll" (ByVal N%, Points%(1))
```

Passing arguments to DLL routines

By default, Visual Basic passes arguments by reference unless they are constants or expressions. On the other hand, the C language (which Microsoft used to build Windows) passes arguments by values. Therefore, you need to include the ByVal clause to when you declare a parameter that must be passed by value. Otherwise, Visual Basic passes it by reference (that is, it passes the 32-bit far pointer to that argument). Passing the wrong type of data to the DLL routines is like playing Russian roulette with a fully loaded six-shooter!

You may ask, "when do I pass a parameter by value or by reference?" The answer lies with the particular DLL routine you are declaring. You need to look at the routines that are documented in SDK manuals or in the *Microsoft Windows Programmer's Reference*. In general C routines pass structures (similar to user-defined types in Visual Basic) and arrays by reference.

Variable-type arguments

The C language allows for general pointers parameters. This means that these parameters accept arguments that vary in data type. Visual Basic allows you to declare DLL routines that accept variable-type arguments, by using the As Any clause. The parameters declared with the As Any clause must be passed by reference, since the DLL routine needs the pointer to the data. An example is shown below:

```
Declare Sub XmsgBox Lib "Xpert" (ByVal Msg$, X As Any, TypeCode%)
```

This procedure displays various types of argument X in a message box. Sample procedure calls are given next:

```
XmsgBox "The name is", winner$, 1
XmsgBox "Sum = ", Average#, 2
XmsgBox "Match found at element ", Index%, 3
```

Notice that the argument for parameter X must always be a variable, to allow the DLL to take the address of the argument.

Conflicting DLL routine names

Normally, you use the name of the DLL routine in the Declare statement. This may not always be possible for two reasons:

- The DLL routine name contains a character that is not part of a valid Visual Basic identifier.
- The DLL routine name is the name of a reserved Visual Basic keyword, such as Next.

In this case, the Alias clause assists in renaming the DLL routine. The clause specifies the original DLL routine name while the Sub or Function clause defines the alias name. For example, the following statement declares a DLL routine named Next as NextElement$:

```
Declare Function NextElement$ Lib "List.DLL" Alias "Next" ()
```

Using the Alias clause is not limited to resolving conflicts in DLL routine names. You can also use it to create an alias name that is shorter, clearer, or more convenient.

Calling DLL routines with particular data types

In this section I discuss calling DLL routines with strings, arrays, user-defined types, and other kinds of data types.

Passing string arguments

The DLL routines that declare string parameters use the standard C strings. These strings end with the ASCII 0 null character (which has earned them the name of ASCIIZ strings). When you declare a string parameter with the ByVal clause, Visual Basic performs the one-way translation from the Visual Basic internal format of the ASCIIZ format. Since the string argument is passed by value, there are no problems in modifying the string. For example, the following DLL routine accepts the argument for a filename and returns a long integer that contains the date and time stamp of the file:

```
Declare Sub GetFileDateTime Lib "MyLib" (ByVal Filename$) As Long
```

You can call this routine later using string constants, variables, and expressions, as shown below:

```
DateTime& = GetFileDateTime("\autoexec.bat")
DateTime& = GetFileDateTime(batFile$)
DateTime& = GetFileDateTime("\autoexec." + FILE_EXT)
```

Passing strings by value is a very safe process. By contrast, passing a string by reference allows the DLL routine to change the string character. Since C and Visual Basic use different string formats, you should observe the following rules regarding what the DLL can do to the passed-by-reference string arguments:

1. The string cannot be increased in length by adding more characters.
2. The string characters can only be overwritten.
3. The string argument should be long enough to anticipate the changes made by the DLL routine.
4. Typically, the operating environment DLL routines do not return strings that are longer than 255 characters.

For example, the following GetPattern routine passes the TextLine$ argument by value and the Pattern$ argument by reference. The Pattern$ passes the sought text pattern argument (which may include ? and * wildcards), and returns the string in TextLine$ that matches the text pattern:

```
Declare Sub GetPattern Lib "Pattern.DLL" (ByVal TextLine$, Pattern$)
```

You can use the predefined String$ function to create a string with an adequate size and fill it with ASCII zeroes. This string is then passed to the DLL routine by reference. Applying this solution to the above DLL routine, you can write:

```
Pattern$ = String$(255, 0)
GetPattern(TextLine$, Pattern$)
```

The number 255 is the one recommended by rule 4 for string arguments. Alternately, you can specify the value of the maximum line length. For example, if you know that the line length does not exceed 80 characters, you can write the following code:

```
Const MAX_LINE = 80
Pattern$ = String$(MAX_LINE, 0)
GetPattern(TextLine$, Pattern$)
```

Another programming method uses fixed-length strings. When you pass a fixed-length string by reference, Visual Basic first converts it into a variable-length string of the same size. Thus you can rewrite the above lines of code as follows, using a fixed-length string:

```
Const MAX_LINE = 80
Dim Pattern$ = String * MAX_LINE
GetPattern(TextLine$, Pattern$)
```

Passing array arguments

Visual Basic allows you to pass individual array elements, just like scalar variables. Passing arrays has a number of rules and restrictions. First, numeric arrays are passed by declaring the first array element by reference (similar to the way arrays are passed in C). This strategy causes no problems, since numeric arrays have fixed-length elements that are stored in a contiguous fashion. In the case of string arrays, the strings are not necessarily stored in a contiguous fashion. As a result, the DLL routines may corrupt the memory area when it attempts to access beyond the end of the first array member.

Passing user-defined types

The variables that are user-defined types must be passed by reference to DLL routines. They cannot be passed by value. Passing user-defined types causes Visual Basic to send the address of the first element to the DLL routine. This address enables the DLL routine to access the rest of the fields in the user-defined type. The following C structures, POINT and RECT, are used in the Windows DLL. The POINT structure stores the pixel location, while the RECT structure stores the coordinates for the upper left and lower right corners of a rectangle. These C structures are declared as follows:

```
typedef struct tagPOINT {
    int X;
    int Y;
} POINT;

typedef struct tagRECT {
    int left;
    int top;
    int right;
    int bottom;
}RECT;
```

The equivalent Visual Basic declarations are:

```
Type PointRec
    X As Integer
    Y As Integer
End Type

Type Rectangle
    Left As Integer
    Top As Integer
    Right As Integer
    Bottom As Integer
End Type
```

You can use different identifiers, but you must use data types that have the same size. The PointType type is declared in file GLOBAL4.BAS that is used with the program that I will present next.

Listing 19-1 contains the code for a demonstration program (stored in project file DLLDEMO.MAK and form file DLLDEMO.FRM) that passes an array of PointRec type to a DLL function Polyline. The Polyline function is declared as follows:

```
Declare Function Polyline Lib "GDI"(ByVal hDC%, P As PointRec, ByVal N%) As Integer
```

The first parameter is a handle for the current object (the form in this case). The second parameter has the user-defined PointerRec type that is passed by reference. This declaration supplies the DLL function with the address of the parameter P, and permits an array of PointRec to be passed.

Listing 19-1 The code attached to the DLLDEMO.FRM form.

```
Declare Function Polyline Lib "GDI" (ByVal hDC%, P As PointRec, ByVal N%) As Integer
Const MAX_POINTS = 5
Dim IsFirst As Integer
```

Listing 19-1   Continued.

```
Sub Form_Load ( )
   IsFirst = True
   WindowState = MAXIMIZED
   BackColor = WHITE
   ForeColor = RED
   Scale (0, 0) – (1000, 1000)
   ScaleMode = PIXELS
   MousePointer = CROSSHAIR
End Sub

Sub QuitCom_Click ( )
   End
End Sub

Sub ClearCom_Click ( )
   Cls
   IsFirst = True
End Sub

Sub Form_MouseDown (Button As Integer, Shift As Integer, X As Single, Y As Single)
   Dim N As Integer
   Static PointArr(1 To MAX_POINTS) As PointRec
   Static X1, Y1, X2, Y2
   If IsFirst Then ' first point?
      X1 = X
      Y1 = Y
   Else
      X2 = X
      Y2 = Y
      ' set the vertices of the rectangle
      PointArr(1).X = X1
      PointArr(1).Y = Y1
      PointArr(2).X = X1
      PointArr(2).Y = Y2
      PointArr(3).X = X2
      PointArr(3).Y = Y2
      PointArr(4).X = X2
      PointArr(4).Y = Y1
      PointArr(5).X = X1
      PointArr(5).Y = Y1
      N = MAX_POINTS
      ' draw polyline
      If Polyline(hDC, PointArr(1), N) = 0 Then
         MsgBox "Error in Polyline function", 0, "Error!"
      End If
   End If
   IsFirst = Not IsFirst ' toggle isFirst flag
End Sub
```

The third parameter is the number of elements in the PointType array. The Polyline function returns 0 if it fails to draw the lines; otherwise, it returns a nonzero value.

The program accompanying LISTING 19-1 is a simple menu-driven application that draws rectangles using the Polyline DLL routine. The program has two menu selections, namely Quit and Clear. The Quit selection exits the application, whereas the Clear selection clears the form. When you run the program, the window is maximized and the cursor shape is changed to the cross hair. You draw a rectangle by clicking twice to define the two opposite corners of the rectangle.

The Form_MouseDown procedure draws the rectangles. The IsFirst variable is used to determine whether you are clicking to define the starting or ending corner. When you define the latter corner, the X and Y fields of the array PointArr store the coordinates that define the rectangle. The variable N is assigned the number of points, 5. Then the procedure draws the rectangle by invoking the DLL routine, as follows:

```
Polyline(hDC, PointArr(1), N)
```

The hDC is the handle for the form's drawing context. The Pointer(1) is the first element of array PointArr and serves as a pointer to the entire array. The variable N is passed by value to indicate the number of lines to draw.

Using DLLs sometimes exacts a toll. For example, if you set the AutoRedraw property to True, no rectangles appear on the form! Moreover, I had to set the ScaleMode to pixels to make the program draw the rectangles where you click the mouse. Otherwise, the program was using twips and Polyline was using pixels. The resulting rectangles were shifted toward the lower right corner.

Passing null pointers

A number of DLL routines expect some of their arguments to be null pointers (they are different from null strings). To accomodate such arguments you need to perform two steps:

1. Declare the parameter for the null-pointer argument using the As Any clause.
2. Pass the 0& argument for the null-pointer argument.

For example, assume that the following GetInfo DLL requires that the argument for the first parameter may be passed as a null-pointer:

```
Declare Sub GetInfo Lib "MyLib" (DataType As Any, Info$)
```

The DataType argument is declared using the As Any clause and passed by reference. The Info$ is a string parameter that is also passed by reference. A sample call using the GetInfo DLL might be:

```
Info$ = String$(255, 0)
GetInfo(0&, Info$)
SystemBox.Text = Info$
```

Passing handles

Handles are unique indices that are used to access various Windows components, such as windows and device contexts. Using handles you can set and query the properties of various Windows components, as well as perform a variety of other tasks. Visual Basic requires that you pass handles by value. The Visual Basic handles are:

- The hWnd handle is a property of the form. This handle enables you to query and manipulate the window's characteristics.
- The hDC handle is a property available for the form and picture box. These handles are related to drawing graphics and displaying text.

The declaration and call for the DLL function Polyline, in LISTING 19-1, includes an hDC handle.

Passing properties

Visual Basic allows you to pass properties by value as arguments to DLL routines. You cannot pass properties by reference. If you need to have the DLL routine assign new values to a property, you must utilize an intermediate variable of the same type. For example, if the GetInfo DLL needs to read and then update the Text property of the SystemBox control, you need to use an intermediate string variable. The code below shows the use of the fixed-string Info for this purpose:

```
Dim Info As String * 255
Info = SystemBox.Text
GetInfo(0&, Info)
SystemBox.Text = RTrim$(Info)
```

The string Info is supplied with the contents of SystemBox.Text. The Info variable is passed by reference to the DLL routine, which overwrites it with new characters. The updated characters are then assigned to SystemBox.Text.

Passing forms and controls

Forms and controls are made up of fairly complex data structures. You can pass forms and controls to DLL routines that are specifically written for Visual Basic. Otherwise, you need to pass the individual properties of the forms and controls to the DLL routines.

Tapping into the Windows DLL routines

After you have read the above sections, you might want to tap more into the Windows DLL routines. You will need a copy of the Microsoft SDK manuals or a copy of the *Microsoft Windows Programmer's Reference*. If you are not familiar with the C language, the contents of these manuals can be very frustrating to read. In this section I will introduce you to the most common and typical data types that are used by the Windows' routines. In addition, I will show you how to translate the C declaration of a DLL routine into a Visual Basic Declare statement.

Translating basic data types

Table 19-1 shows a number of common and typical data types used by the various Windows DLL routines. Notice that the LPSTR is a pointer to a C string. This is translated into passing a String type parameter by reference to supply the address of the string variable. The table also shows the HANDLE, HWND, and HDC handles. They are equivalent to the Visual Basic Integer type. In fact, the Windows DLL uses a variety of identifiers to declare handles for different objects. All of these handles are equivalent to the Visual Basic Integer type.

☞ Table 19-1 shows that the 16-bit signed Integer type in Visual Basic is the corresponding type of 16-bit unsigned integer types in C. This is also true regarding the number of bits. Concerning the values stored in

Table 19-1   The common and typical basic data types used by the Windows DLL routines.

C type	Visual Basic type	Meaning of C type
BOOL	Integer	16-bit Boolean value
BYTE	String	8-bit unsigned integer[1]
char	String	8-bit character[1]
HANDLE	Integer	16-bit unsigned integer that is used as a general handle
HWND	Integer	16-bit integer that is used as a handle to windows
HDC	Integer	16-bit integer that is used as a handle to a GDI's device context table
int	Integer	16-bit signed integer
long	Long	32-bit signed integer
LONG	Long	32-bit signed integer
LPSTR	String (reference)	32-bit pointer to a CHAR type
WORD	Integer	16-bit unsigned integer
DWORD	Long	32-bit signed integer or segment/offset

[1]The BYTE and char C types are equivalent to String * 1 fixed-length strings. The arguments that are used for BYTE and char types must be declared as String * 1 and passed as ByVal String.

both, they have the range of 0 to 32676. Unsigned integer types have values up to 65535. If you need to supply an argument for a 16-bit unsigned integer with a value greater than 32767, you must be aware of the role played by the most significant bit. The rule to follow for converting negative signed integers into unsigned integers is given by the next formula:

unsigned integer = 65536 + negative signed integer

or, the reciprocal formula:

negative signed integer = unsigned integer − 65536

So, for example, if you need to pass an argument of 50000 to an unsigned integer, you need a Visual Basic integer of −15536 (= 50000 − 65536).

Translating C structures

In addition to the basic data types, such as the ones shown in TABLE 19-1, Windows uses various structures. The RECT and POINT structures, which I presented earlier in this chapter, are merely simple examples. Here are a few examples of more complex Windows structures and how to translate them into Visual Basic user-defined types:

The BITMAPCOREHEADER **structure**   This is declared in C as:

```
typedef struct tagBITMAPCOREHEADER {
    DWORD      bcSize;
    WORD       bcWidth;
    WORD       bcHeight;
    WORD       bcPlanes;
    WORD       bcBitCount;
} BITMAPCOREHEADER;
```

where the bcSize specifies the number of bytes required by the BITMAP-COREHEADER structure. The bcWidth and bcHeight fields define the width and height of the bitmap pixels, respectively. The bcPlanes field specifies the number of planes for the target device and must be set to 1. The bcBitCount defines the number of bits per pixel.

The BITMAPCOREHEADER structure can be declared as the following Visual Basic user-defined type:

```
Type BITMAPCOREHEADER
    bcSize As Long
    bcWidth As Integer
    bcHeight As Integer
    bcPlanes As Integer
    bcBitCount As Integer
End Type
```

The MSG structure This structure is declared in C as:

```
typedef struct tagMSG {
    HWND      hwnd;
    WORD      message;
    WORD      wParam;
    LONG      lParam;
    DWORD     time
    POINT     pt;
} MSG;
```

where hwnd identifies the window that receives the message. The message field designates the message number. The wParam and lParam fields specify the additional information about the message. The time field specifies the time of posting the message. The pt parameter designates the position of the cursor when the message was posted.

The C MSG structure can be translated into the following:

```
Type MSG
    hwnd As Integer
    message As Integer
    wParam As Integer
    lParam As Long
    fTime As Long
    pt As PointRec
End Type
```

The declaration of the pt field assumes that the PointRec has been previously defined.

The C OFSTRUCT structure This contains the file information which results from opening a file:

```
typedef struct tagOFSTRUCT {
    BYTE      cBytes;
    BYTE      fFixedDisk;
    WORD      nErrCode;
    BYTE      reserved[4];
    BYTE      szPathName[120];
} OFSTRUCT;
```

The cBytes field specifies the length of the OFSTRUCT structures in bytes. The fFixedDisk field indicates whether or not the file is on a fixed disk. The nErrorCode field indicates the DOS error code if opening the file has failed. The array reserves 4 bytes. The szPathName specifies 120 bytes that store the path of the file.

The above structure can be translated into the following user-defined type in Visual Basic:

```
Type OFSTRUCT
   cByte As String * 1
   fFixed As String * 1
   nErrCode As Integer
   reserved as String * 4
   szPathName As String * 120
End Type
```

Notice that the BYTE type in the C structure is translated into String * 1 field in Visual Basic. The fields that specify arrays of bytes are translated into fixed-strings with lengths equal to the size of the C arrays.

Translating C DLLs

Let's look at sample DLL routines to show how they are translated. The examples I give in this subsection vary in complexity. The routines are:

The GetCurrentTime **function**   This function returns the Windows time. This value represents the number of milliseconds since the system has been booted. This DLL function is valuable in timing loops and other events. The GetCurrentTime function is declared as:

```
DWORD GetCurrentTime( )
```

The above C declaration is translated into the following Visual Basic Declare statement:

```
Declare Function GetCurrentTime Lib "User" ( ) As Long
```

An example of using this DLL function is shown next:

```
Time1& = GetCurrentTime( )
For I% = 1 To 1000
   X# = Sin(1.0)
Next I%
Time2& = CurrentTime( )
TextBox.Text = "Sin(x) : " + Str$(Time2& − Time1&) + " sec"
```

The GetDC **function**   In this function, the handle of a window is translated into a display context handle for the GDI display context. The GetDC function is declared as:

```
HDC GetDC(hWnd)
```

where parameter hWnd has the HWND data type. The above C declaration can be translated into the next Visual Basic Declare statement:

```
Declare Function GetDC Lib "GDI" (ByVal hWnd As Integer) As Integer
```

The GetCursorPos **routine**   This routine returns the

```
void GetCursorPos(lpPoint)
```

where lpPoint is the pointer to POINT structure. The above C declaration can be translated into the next Visual Basic Declare statement:

    Declare Sub GetCursor Lib "User" (lpPoint As PointRec)

Since the C function has a void return type, it returns no value. Consequently, the C function is translated into a Visual Basic Sub procedure. The lpPoint parameter is a reference parameter that has the user-defined PointRec type described earlier.

The IsCharLower **function** This function, presented earlier in this chapter, is declared as follows in C:

    BOOL IsCharLower(cChar)

where cChar has the C char type. The above C declaration can be translated into the following Visual Basic Declare statement:

    Declare Function IsCharLower Lib "User" (ByVal *cChar*%) As Integer

Both the char and BOOL data types are translated into the Visual Basic Integer types. When you pass the argument for cChar% it must be the ASCII code of the tested character.

The OffsetRect **routine** moves a rectangle in both the X and the Y directions. The OffsetRect function is declared as follows:

    void OffsetRect(lpRect, X, Y)

where lpRect is a pointer to the RECT type. The fields X and Y are of type int, and represent the displacement of the rectangular region in the X and Y directions. The above C declaration can be translated into the next Visual Basic Declare statement:

    Declare Sub OffsetRect Lib "GDI" (lpRect As Rectangle,
      ByVal X%, ByVal Y%)

The Polyline **function** This function, which was presented previously in this chapter, has the following C declaration:

    BOOL Polyline(hDC, lpPoints, nCount)

The lpPoints is a pointer to an array of POINT type. The above C declaration can be translated into the next Visual Basic Declare statement:

    Declare Function Polyline Lib "GDI" (ByVal hDC%, P As PointRec, ByVal N%) As
      Integer

The lpPoints parameter is translated into a PointerRec-typed parameter that passes its arguments by reference. The arguments for the P parameter should be the first member of a PointerRec array.

A
Visual Basic language quick reference

This appendix contains a quick reference for the Visual Basic programming language. If you are familiar with Quick Basic, then you are familiar with most of the language syntax of Visual Basic. If you are only familiar with GW-BASIC, BASICA, or other BASIC dialects, then this reference should give you a brief idea of the syntax of Visual Basic. The material here is *not* intended to teach you about the Visual Basic language. Instead, it is meant to offer you a quick reference and to update you on the basic constructs of Visual Basic.

Data types

Visual Basic supports the six data types shown in TABLE A-1. The Currency data type is introduced in Visual Basic to maintain a floating-point that is dedicated for financial calculations.

The type names in TABLE A-1 are reserved keywords used by Visual Basic in declaring variables and user-defined types.

Literal constants

Literal constants present explicit constants in one of the basic data types. Table A-2 offers examples of the literal constants for each basic type.

Visual Basic supports both dynamic (variable-length) and fixed-length strings. Dynamic strings are declared using the String keyword. Fixed-length strings are declared using the following syntax:

String * *size*

The size parameter determines the length of the fixed string. A fixed-length string retains the same size.

Table A-1   The predefined basic data types.

Type name	Description	Type-declaration character	Range
Integer	%	2-byte integer	−32768 to 32767
Long	&	4-byte integer	−2,147,483,648 to 2,147,483,647
Single (default)	!	4-byte floating-point number	−3.37E+38 to 3.37E+38
Double	#	8-byte floating-point number	−1.67D+308 to 1.67D+308
Currency	@	number with fixed decimal point	−9.22E+14 to 9.22E+14
String	$	string	N/A

Table A-2   Example of literal constants.

Type name	Example	Comments
Integer	−12, 344 &011 &HFFFF	Octal number Hexadecimal number
Long	100000, −345245 &0123& &HFFFFF&	Octal number Hexadecimal number
Single (default)	−345.2, 1.2E+11, 2.3E-09	
Double	−345.664, 2.34D+98, 2.3D-09	
Currency	12.33	
String	"Hello there"	

Operators

Visual Basic supports the assignment, math, string, relational, Boolean, and access operators, as shown in TABLE A-3.

Table A-3   The Visual Basic operators.

Operator	Unary?	Class	Purpose	Example
+	Yes	Math	Plus sign	+2
	No	Math	Addition	2 + I%

Operator	Unary?	Class	Purpose	Example
	No	String	Concatenate	FirstName$ + "Shammas"
—	Yes	Math	Negate	− 2∗ Rate!
	No	Math	Subtract	23.4 - Rate!
∗	No	Math	Multiply	Length# ∗ Width#
/	No	Math	Floating-point divide	355.0 / 113.0
\	No	Math	Integer division	355 \ 113
Mod	No	Math	Integer modulo	355 Mod 113
^	No	Math	Exponentiation	10 ^X#
=	No	General	Assignment	X# = 10 ^2.3
	No	Relational	Test if equal to	I% = J%
<	No	Relational	Test if less than	I% < J%
>	No	Relational	Test if greater than	I% > J%
>=	No	Relational	Test if greater than or equal to	I% >= J%
<=	No	Relational	Test if less than or equal to	I% <= J%
And	No	Boolean	Logical/bitwise AND	(I% = O) And (J% = O)
Or	No	Boolean	Logical/bitwise OR	(I% = O) Or (J% = O)
Xor	No	Boolean	Logical/bitwise XOR	(I% = O) Xor (J% = O)
Not	Yes	Boolean	Logical/bitwise NOT	Not ((I%=1) And (J%=1))
Imp	No	Boolean	Implication (first operand is false, or second operand true)	(I%=O) Imp (J%=1)
Eqv	No	Boolean	Logical equivalence	(I%=O) Eqv (J%=O)
TypeOf-Is	No	Boolean	Test type of control	TypeOf Btn Is Option
()	Yes	General	Indexed access	X# = A (I%)
.	No	General	Field access	X# = MyRec.Weight

Identifiers

Identifiers are the names of data types, constants, variables, operators, procedures, and functions. These names are either predefined (also called *reserved words*) by Visual Basic, or are user-defined. An identifier must follow these rules:

- It may be up to 40 characters long.
- It must start with a letter.
- It may include digits and the underscore character.
- It cannot be the same as a reserved keyword. However, these keywords can be imbedded in an identifier.

Examples of identifiers are:

myName

Your_name

Your_Name

R2D2

Day10

Day_10_Rate

Visual Basic identifiers are not case-sensitive. This means that identifiers like MyName, myName, myname, and MYNAME are treated as the same identifier.

Symbolic constants

Symbolic constants are identifiers that are associated with literal constants. Symbolic constants provide a much clearer program readability and empower you to change the constant value in one location. Constants may be either global or local. The general syntax for declaring global and local constants is:

[Global] Const constantName1 = value1 [, constantName2 = value2, . . .]

Some examples of declaring constants are:

Global Const True = −1, False = 0

Const SecPerMinute = 60.0

Const SecPerHour = 3.6D+3

Variables

Variables are identifiers that are able to store data during run time. All variables must have a data type associated with them. This association may be explicit or implicit. Explicit type association occurs when the variable name is appended by one of the type-declaration characters, shown in TABLE A-1.

For example, X# denotes the variable X that stores the double data type. Similarly, MyName$ is a variable that stores a string of characters. By default, a variable has the single data type.

Visual Basic offers the Deftype declaration to permit you to alter the default data types. The rule of using these statements is that you specify the default type of variables by their first letter. The general syntax for using a Deftype declaration is:

Deftype letter1 [—letter2] [,letter3, . . .]

The Deftype declares the default types by using a single character, a range of contiguous characters, or a comma-delimited list that combines the first two kinds. Since the Visual Basic identifiers are case-insensitive, the uppercase and lowercase characters can be interchanged in a DefType without altering the outcome of the declaration. The various Deftype declarations are shown below:

DefInt	Integer
DefLng	Long
Def	Single
DefDbl	Double
DefCur	Currency
DefStr	String

Here are a few examples of the DefType declarations:

DefDbl A-Z
DefInt I-O, X

The first Deftype declares that all of the variables are double type by default. The second DefType declares that the variables beginning with I to O, and with X, are integers by default. The two declarations can occur in the same program. The effect is that the second Deftype overrides the first one. The general rule is that Deftype declarations override the previous one.

Visual Basic also permits you to declare the data types of variables using the entire variable names and not just the first letter. Such declarations includes global, static, and normal (*local volatile*) variables. The general syntax for such declarations is:

[Global ¦ Static ¦ Dim] *variable1 As type1 [, variable2 As type2, . . .]*

Global variables are accessed by all of the parts of the program. Static declarations are used by variables declared inside procedures and functions. Several examples of declaring global and normal variables are shown below:

```
Dim Index As Integer
Dim Z, X, Y As Double
Dim TheFilename As String
Global ProgramParameter As String
Dim ZipCode As String *9
Global I, J, K, L As Integer
```

Notice that you can only declare fixed strings using the As String * size format. Using the $ type-declaration character or the DefStr results in declaring dynamic strings.

Arrays of variables

Arrays are data structures that are popular in the majority of programming languages. An array represents a group of variables that share the same name and data type, and are accessed by an index number. Each array you declare has a lower and an upper index range (and, therefore, a specific size). The Option Base statement sets the default lower index to either 0 or 1. The general syntax for using Option Base is:

```
Option Base {0 ¦ 1}
```

If there is no Option Base statement in the program, the default Option Base 0 is assumed. The general syntax for declaring an array is:

```
{Dim ¦ Global ¦ Static ¦ ReDim} array([low1 To] high1 [,[low2 To] high2]) As type
```

The above general form shows that you can explicitly declare the lower index range of an array. This is the recommended method since it makes the declaration of the array crystal clear. If you omit the lower bound and the To keyword, the default lower range is specified by the Option Base statement.

Visual Basic supports both dynamic (variable-size) and ordinary (fixed-size) arrays. The difference between the two is that dynamic arrays can be resized at run time, while fixed arrays cannot. Therefore, choose the size of your fixed array with care. If it is hard to predict the required size of a fixed array, use a dynamic array.

You should observe the following rules when dealing with fixed arrays:

- Use the Global statement to declare arrays in the global module.
- Use the Dim statement to declare arrays in the forms and modules.
- Use the Static statement to declare arrays in a procedure. You may use the Dim statement if the entire procedure is declared Static.

Here are some examples of declaring arrays in a global module, a form, or a module:

```
' arrays declared in the global module
Option Base 1
Global Names1 (10) As String
Global Names2 (1 To 10) As String
Global Names3$ (1 To 10)
Global Names4$ (10)
```

The four arrays declared here are equivalent in the way their range indices and data types are defined. The array Names1 relies on the Option Base statement to supply its default lower limit. The As String declares the array to have String-typed elements. The array Names2 explicitly defines the lower and upper index ranges. Again, the As String declares the basic array type to be String. The Names3 array declares the index range just like array Names2. However, the $ type-declaration character is used to indicate the basic type of the array element. Finally, the fourth array Name4 declares the array size just like Name1, and the array type just like Name3.

Additional declarations of arrays are shown next:

```
' arrays in a global module
Global TheVars (65 To 90) As Double, X#(-4 To 4)
' arrays in a module
Dim Filename$(1 To 55), IdxArray(1 To 55) As Integer
' arrays in a subroutine
Static SizeArray (1 To MAX_SIZE) Integer ' MAX_SIZE is a constant
```

The () operator is used in accessing the array members. Here is an example of manipulating an array:

```
Static FactorialTable (1 To 20) As Double
Dim I, J As Integer
For I = 1 To 20
  FactorialTable(I) = 1
  For J = 1 To I
    FactorialTable(I) = I * FactorialTable(I)
  Next J
Next I
```

The array FactorialTable stores the factorials of the first 20 integers. The outer For-Next loop is used to select each element of the FactorialTable array. The inner For-Next loop is used to calculate the sought factorials.

Two-dimensional arrays

Visual Basic supports two-dimensional arrays, which are commonly known as *matrices*. The declaration of matrices is merely an extension of the declaration of one-dimensional arrays. Matrices add a second index range. Example of matrices are shown here:

```
' matrices in the global module
Option Base 1
Global MainMatrix, SolutionMatrix ( 10, 1 To 10) As Double

' matrices in a module
Dim Mat1#( 20, 20), Mat2 (3 To 5, 5 To 9) As Integer

' matrices in a procedure
Static Appointments (1 To 7, 9 To 17) As String
Static Apps$ (7, 9 To 17)
```

The () operator is also used to access the elements of a matrix. However, in this case, the () operator takes two integer-typed arguments that are separated by a comma. An example of accessing the elements of a matrix is:

```
Static Mat (1 To MAT_SIZE, 1 To MAT_SIZE) As Double
Dim I, J As Integer
For I = 1 To MAT_SIZE
  For J = 1 To MAT_SIZE
    Mat(I, J) = Sqr(I * J)
  Next J
Next I
```

Multi-dimensional arrays

Visual Basic enables you to declare arrays that have up to 60 dimensions. From a practical point of view, the probability of using multi-dimensional arrays decreases significantly with the number of dimensions. One-dimensional arrays are very common; two-dimensional ones are slightly less common; three-dimensional arrays are rather rare; and four-dimensional arrays and up are very rare. The declaration and access of multi-dimensional arrays are very similar to the one- and two-dimensional arrays. An example for declaring and using a three-dimensional array is shown here:

```
Option Base 1
Static Cube (1 To CUBE_SIZE, 1 To CUBE_SIZE, 4) As Double
Dim I, J, K As Integer
For I = 1 To CUBE_SIZE
  For J = 1 To CUBE_SIZE
    For K = 1 To 4
      Cube(I, J, K) = Sqr(I * J) / K
    Next K
  Next J
Next I
```

Dynamic arrays

Visual Basic also implements dynamic arrays. The advantage of these arrays is that you can alter both their sizes and number of dimensions during run time. As a result, dynamic arrays provide tailor-fitted sizes and take the guesswork out of sizing arrays at design time. The creation of dynamic arrays is a simple process.

First, declare the array with a Dim statement, using an empty dimension list. Use the Global statement if the declaration of the dynamic array occurs in the global module. This step does not allocate any array elements.

Then allocate the array elements using a Redim statement. This statement specifies the exact dimensions of the array. Note that every time you redimension a dynamic array with the Redim statement, the values of the elements created by a previous Redim statements are lost. This is called *destructive redimensioning*.

Dynamic arrays are typically used inside procedures and functions. An example of creating a dynamic array is:

```
Dim Mat () As Double ' declare dynamic matrix
Sub ProcessMatrix ()
    .
    .
    .
    ReDim Mat (1 To 10, 1 To 10)
    .
    .
    .
End Sub
```

Control arrays

Visual Basic supports a new kind of array structure that is applied to controls. While control arrays share a number of properties with both fixed and dynamic standard arrays, they also have their differences.

Control arrays represent a group of controls that offers very similar or closely related operations. For example, consider an array of option boxes used in a text search dialog box. The control array is used to determine the search direction—forward, backward, or global.

Since control arrays contain similar individual controls, they can share the same event-handling procedures. For example, the array of the text-search option buttons can share the same SearchDirBtn_Click procedure, as shown here:

```
Sub SearchDirBtn_Click(Index As Integer)
```

The Index parameter is required to select the proper control element in the array. Inside the event-handling procedure you can access the sought control using the Index parameter. Thus, the controlArrayName(Index) terms accessed the Indexth control for the SearchDirBtn(Index) procedure.

Control arrays have the following features and rules:

- The control array can only be one-dimensional.
- The lowest array index is 0.
- Control arrays do not have preset upper bounds.
- The Visual Basic program can expand the control array at run time. The expansion is *nondestructive*, unlike the ReDim statement used with dynamic arrays.
- Unlike standard arrays, control arrays can be sparse. This means that you can create a control array with an arbitrary sequence of indices. For example, you can have the SearchDirBtn option button array have elements that are indexed by 0, 1, 5, 9, 10, 11, and 21 — the indices need not be in perfect sequence.
- Control arrays are *not* declared in the application code.
- Control arrays are created at design time by using either one of the following methods: in the first method, you assign the same name to the CtlName property of two similar controls. The second method creates a control array by assigning a value to the Index property (which is blank for controls that are members of a control array).
- You can change the setting of the Index property of a control at design time only.
- Control arrays cannot be passed as arguments to a procedure or function. However, you can pass an individual element of the control array as an argument.

User-defined data types

Visual Basic, like Quick Basic, allows you to declare your own data types. Each user-defined data type is made up of one or more elements (or fields). The general syntax for user-defined types is:

```
Type userType
  elementName1 As typeName
  [elementName2 As typeName
    .
    .
    .
  .]
End Type
```

The typeName refers to the basic data types, dynamic strings, and other previously declared user-defined types. User-defined types cannot contain elements that are arrays.

Some examples of user-defined data types are shown here:

```
Type PersonRec
  LastName As String * 10
```

```
        FirstName As String * 6
        SSN As String * 10
    End Type

    Type HealthRec
        Person As PersonRec
        Weight As Single
        Age As Integer
    End Type
```

Once a user-defined data type is defined, you can declare variables that have that type, using the As type form. Examples of declaring variables that have user-defined types are shown next:

```
Dim Me As PersonRec

Static Machismo As HealtRec

Dim Employees(100) As PersonRec
```

The individual fields (or elements) are accessed using the dot access operator. The general syntax for using the access operator is:

user_defined_type_variable.field

Here are some examples of accessing the data fields:

```
Me.LastName = "Shammas"
FullName$ = Me.FirstName + " " + Me.LastName
Employees(3).SSN = "333-33-3333"
Machismo.Age = 32
Machismo.Person.LastName = "Hercules"
```

In this example, the variable Machismo is of type HealtRec. This data type has the Person field that is of type PersonRec. This means that to access the LastName field in the Person field, the dot operator must be used twice, as shown in this example.

Decision-making control structures

Decision-making control structures enable you to examine conditions and take alternate actions. The Visual Basic decision-making structures are:

- The If-Then structure.
- The If-Then-Else structure.
- The Select-Case structure.

The If-Then structure

The If-Then is a single alternative decision-making control structure. There are two general syntaxes for the If-Then structure:

If *condition* Then *statement*

If *condition* Then
  sequence of statements
End If

The If-Then structure examines the condition. If it is true (that is, not equal to 0), the statements in the Then clause are executed.

    Examples of the If-Then structure are:

If ErrorMessageBox.Text = "" Then ResultBox.Text = Str$(NumericResult)

If X# > 0 Then
  Z# = Log(X#)
  ResultBox.Text = Str$(Z#)
End If

The If-Then-Else structure

The basic If-Then-Else is a dual-alternative control structure. The structure allows you to take alternate actions based on the tested condition. The general syntax for the basic If-Then-Else structure is:

If *condition* Then
  sequence of statements
Else
  sequence of statements
End If

If the tested condition is true, the block of statements in the Then clause is executed. Otherwise, the block of statements in the Else clause are executed. An example of the If-Then-Else structure is:

If X# > 0 Then
  Z# = Log(X#)
  ResultBox.Text = Str$(Z#)
Else
  Beep
  ErrorMessageBox.Text = "Invalid argument for function Log"
End If

The If-Then-Else structure can offer multiple-alternative decision making. This is made possible by inserting one or more ElseIf clauses after the first Then clause. The general syntax for the extended If-Then-Else structure is:

If *condition1* Then
  sequence of statements #1
ElseIf condition2 Then
  sequence of statements #2

```
[ElseIf condition3 Then
    sequence of statements #3]
Else
    default sequence of statements
End If
```

The Else clause of the extended If-Then-Else structure serves as a catch-all clause. The structure tests the conditions of the If and ElseIf in the sequence in which they appear in the structure. When any one of these conditions is true, the statements in the corresponding Then clause are executed. Program execution resumes after the End If. If all of the tested conditions are not true, the statements of the Else clause are executed. To make the extended If-The-Else structure run faster, arrange the tested conditions in the order of likelihood of being true. This arrangement generally minimizes the number of conditions that must be evaluated.

An example of using the extended If-Then-Else structure is shown here:

```
X = Val(Operand1Box.Text)
Y = Val(Operand2Box.Text)
Operator$ = OperatorBox.Text
If Operator = "+" Then
    Z = X + Y
ElseIf Operator = "−" Then
    Z = X − Y
ElseIf Operator = "*" Then
    Z = X * Y
ElseIf (Operator = "/") AND (Y <> 0) Then
    Z = X / Y
Else
    Beep
    ErrorMessageBox.Text = "Invalid operator or divide-by-zero error"
End If
```

The If-Then-Else structure examines the value of a series of conditions that compare the string variable, Operator$, with literal strings that represent the basic math operations. If Operator$ contains "−", the condition of the first If is false. This causes the second condition, Operator$ = "−", to be tested. This turns out to be true, and the statement, $Z = X - Y$, is executed. Execution resumes after the End If. Notice that the last tested condition uses the relational AND operator to combine two smaller tests, Operator$ = "/" and Y <> 0. This test prevents the division of X by Y from occurring when the value of Y is zero.

The Select-Case structure

The multi-alternative If-Then-Else structure may be replaced by the Select-Case structure when the tested conditions compare the same expression with different values. The general syntax for the Select-Case structure is:

```
Select Case expression
  Case expressionList1
    sequence of statements #1
  [Case expressionList1
    sequence of statements #2]
  [Case Else
    sequence of statements #n]
End Select
```

The expression examined by the Select-Case statement may be a variable, a function, or a BASIC expression involving constants, variables, and functions. The Case clauses contain a comma-delimited list of values that are compared against the examined expression. This means that the expression and the data in the expression list must have matching, or at least compatible, data types. The types of items that appear in an expression list are:

- A single value.
- A range of values, used for numeric types, that uses the following general syntax:

  small To *big*

- A relational operator with a value. This compares the examined expression with that value, using the relational operator. The general syntax is:

  Is *relational_operator value*

The values mentioned in these basic items may be literal constants, symbolic constants, or variables.

The following simple example of the Select-Case structure is one that modifies the last example of the If-Then-Else structure:

```
X = Val(Operand1Box.Text)
Y = Val(Operand2Box.Text)
Operator$ = OperatorBox.Text
Select Case Operator$
  Case "+"
    Z = X + Y
  Case "−"
    Z = X − Y
  Case "*"
    Z = X * Y
  Case "/"
    If Y <> 0 Then Z = X / Y
```

```
      Else
         Beep
         ErrorMessageBox.Text = "Invalid operator"
      End Select
```

The examined expression in this Select-Case structure is the value of the string variable Operator$. Each Case clause provided a single-item expression list of values to compare with Operator$. If Operator$ contains "−" it will match the expression list of the second Case clause, and the statement Z = X − Y is executed. Execution resumes after the End Select.

The above example can be expanded to include multi-value expression lists. The next example also compares the Operator$ with strings that contain the names of the sought operations, in long and short form. The examined expression is actually a function named UCase$(Operator$). This allows the strings that describe the operations to be in upper case, with the benefit that the Select-Case structure can respond to the name of the sought operator typed in any letter case combination, such as Multiply, multiply, and even mUITiPIY!

```
X = Val(Operand1Box.Text)
Y = Val(Operand2Box.Text)
Operator$ = OperatorBox.Text
Select Case UCase$(Operator$)
   Case "+", "ADD"
      Z = X + Y
   Case "−", "SUBTRACT", "SUB"
      Z = X − Y
   Case "*", "DIVIDE" ,"DIV"
      Z = X * Y
   Case "/", "MULTIPLE", "MUL"
      If Y <> 0 Then Z = X / Y
   Else
      Beep
      ErrorMessageBox.Text = "Invalid operator"
End Select
```

The third example of the Select-Case structure involves a numeric expression. It shows the use of the three basic items of an Case expression list:

```
Select Case DangerLevel%
   Case 0, 4, 6, 10 To WARNING1, Is > CriticalLimit%
      MessageBox.Text = "Case 1"
   Case 1 To 3, 5, 7, WARNING1+1 To WARNING2, CriticalLimit%
      MessageBox.Text = "Case 2"
   Case 8 To 9, WARNING2+1 To CtriticalLimit%−1
      MessageBox.Text = "Case 3"
```

```
        Case Else
          For I% = 1 To 10
            Beep
          Next I%
          MessageBox.Text = "Reactor core melt-down!"
      End Select
```

The WARNING1 and WARNING2 identifiers are symbolic constants (that I wrote in uppercase letters). The CriticalLimit% is an integer variable.

Loop control structures

Loops are structures that are used for iterating (or re-executing) one or more statements. There are three types of loops, all of which are supported by Visual Basic. These are the *fixed-iteration* loop, the *conditional* loop, and the *open* loop. As their names suggest, a fixed-iteration loop iterates for a fixed number of times; a conditional loop iterates while or until a tested condition is true; and an open loop iterates indefinitely. Visual Basic offers the For-Next fixed-iteration loop, the Do-While and Do-Until conditional loops, and the Do-Loop open loop.

The For-Next loop

The For-Next loop is the oldest and most popular loop in any BASIC implementation. The general syntax for the For-Next loop is:

```
For loopCounter = start To finish [Step increment]
    sequence of statements
    [Exit For]
    [sequence of statements]
Next [loopCounter [,loopCounter]]
```

The loopCounter is a variable that is used to keep track of the number of iterations. There are four possible general loop settings:

```
For loopCounter = smallStart To bigFinish
For loopCounter = smallStart To bigFinish Step increment
For loopCounter = bigStart To smallFinish Step −1
For loopCounter = bigStart To smallFinish Step decrement
```

The first two forms of the For-Next loop are upward-counting loops, where smallStart is less than or equal to bigFinish. In the first form, the loop control is incremented by 1, the default value. The second form shows the Step clause with an increment other than 1. (This increment can be greater or less than 1, or you can use Step 1 for clarity.) The number of iterations for the first form of the For-Next loop is equal to bigFinish − smallStart + 1. If this number is negative, the For-Next loop does not iterate (that is, there is no such thing as a negative number of iterations). The number of iterations for the second form is equal to (bigFinish − smallStart + 1) / increment.

The third and fourth forms of the For-Next loops are downward-counting loops, where bigStart is greater or equal to smallFinish. In the third form, the loop control is decremented by 1 (conversely, it can be said that the loop counter is incremented by -1). In the fourth form, the Step has an increment with a negative value other than -1. You could say that the third form is a special case of the fourth form. The number of iterations for the third form of the For-Next loop is equal to bigStart − smallFinish + 1. The number of iterations for the fourth form is equal to (bigStart − smallFinish + 1) / −decrement.

If the value of the Step increment or decrement is 0, the For-Next loop iterates indefinitely.

The Exit For statement allows you to exit the current For-Next loop and resume execution after its Next statement. Exiting loops is discussed in detail in the "Exiting from Loops" section.

The Next statement may be followed by the name of the loop control. In the case of nested loops that logically end at the same location, you can use a single Next statement followed by a list of the loop controls for the nested loops.

Examples for various forms of the For-Next are:

```
For I% = 1 To 100
   A#(I%) = 2 * I%
Next

For I% = 34 To 55 Step 2
   Sum = Sum + Value#(I%)
Next I%
For I% = 23 To 4 Step −1
   A#(I%0 = Sqr(I%)
Next I%

For I% = 23 To 4 Step −2
   A#(I%0 = Sqr(I%)
Next I%
```

The following nested loops are equivalent, even though the second loop uses a single Next statement:

```
For I% = 1 To 10
   For J% = 1 To 10
      DataMatrix#(I%, J%) = 0
   Next J%
Next I%
```

```
For I% = 1 To 10
  For J% = 1 To 10
    DataMatrix#(I%, J%) = 0
Next J%, I%
```

The Do-While loop

The Do-While loop is a conditional loop, which iterates based on a tested condition. Visual Basic implements two forms of the Do-While loop, which I name the *leading* and the *trailing*. The general syntaxes for the two Do-While loops are:

```
' the "leading" Do-While loop
Do While condition
  sequence of statements
  [Exit Do]
  sequence of statements
Loop
```

```
' the "trailing" Do-While loop
Do
  sequence of statements
  [Exit Do]
  sequence of statements
Loop While condition
```

The leading Do-While loop is much more common than the trailing version. The leading Do-While loop is also equivalent to the While-Wend loop that is available in BASICA, GW-BASIC, and Quick Basic. The leading Do-While loop iterates while a condition is true. This means that if the condition is false the first time it is tested, the leading Do-While loop does not iterate. Instead, the program execution resumes after the Loop statement.

The trailing Do-While loop examines the condition at the end of the loop. This guarantees that the loop iterates at least once.

The Exit Do statement enables the program to exit the current loop and resume after the Loop statement.

Examples of using either form of the Do-While loop are:

```
' remove the leading spaces from a string
L% = Len(S$)
Do While (L% > 0) AND (Mid$(S$, 1, 1) = " ")
  S$ = Mid$(S$, 2, L%)
  L% = L% - 1
Loop
```

This code uses a leading Do-While loop to trim the string S$ from leading spaces. The condition tested is made up of two sub-conditions. The first sub-condition tests if L% is positive (that is, the length of the string is not zero). This serves two purposes: it detects if string S$ is either originally empty (i.e., null) or has become empty in the course of the iteration (the original S$ contained nothing but spaces).

The second example is a trailing Do-While loop that obtains the square root of a variable X# by applying Newton's method. The loop iterates while the difference between X# and the square of the variable Guess# (the guess for the square root) exceeds some acceptable small number:

```
' find the square root of X# using Newton's algorithm
Guess# = X# / 2
Do
    If Guess# <= 0 Then Exit Do
    Guess# = 0.5 * (X# / Guess# + Guess#)
Loop While Abs(X# - Guess#^2) > 0.000001
```

The Do-Until loop

The Do-Until loop is another conditional loop, which iterates based on a tested condition. Again, Visual Basic implements two forms of the Do-Until loop, which I refer to as leading and trailing. The general syntaxes for the two Do-Until loops are:

```
' the "leading" Do-Until loop
Do Until condition
    sequence of statements
    [Exit Do]
    sequence of statements
Loop
```

```
' the "trailing" Do-Until loop
Do
    sequence of statements
    [Exit Do]
    sequence of statements
Loop Until condition
```

The trailing Do-Until loop is much more common than the leading version. The leading Do-Until loop iterates until a condition is true. This means that if the condition is true the first time it is tested, the leading Do-Until loop does not iterate. Instead, the program execution resumes after the Loop statement. The trailing Do-Until loop, on the other hand, examines the condition at the end of the loop. This guarantees that the loop iterates at least once.

The Exit Do statement enables the program to exit the current loop and resume after the Loop statement.

Examples of using either form of the Do-Until loop are shown here:

```
' remove the leading spaces from a string
L% = Len(S$)
Do Until (L% = 0) OR (Mid$(S$, 1, 1) <> " ")
    S$ = Mid$(S$, 2, L%)
    L% = L% - 1
Loop
```

The above code uses a leading Do-Until loop to trim the string S$ from leading spaces. The condition tested is made up of two sub-conditions. The first sub-condition tests if L% is zero (that is, the length of the string is zero). This accomplishes two tasks: it detects if string S$ is either originally empty (i.e., null) or has become empty in the course of the iteration (the original S$ contained nothing but spaces).

The second example is a trailing Do-Until loop that obtains the square root of a variable, X#, by applying Newton's method. The loop iterates until the difference between X# and the square of the variable Guess# (the guess for the square root) is less than or equal to some acceptable small number:

```
' find the square root of X# using Newton's algorithm
Guess# = X# / 2
Do
    If Guess# <= 0 Then Exit Do
    Guess# = 0.5 * (X# / Guess# + Guess#)
Loop Until Abs(X# - Guess#^2) <= 0.000001
```

The Do loop

Visual Basic offers the open Do-Loop. In principle, this loop iterates indefinitely. While this aspect sounds like the program is asking for trouble, the Do loop invariably tests for a condition inside the loop body and uses the Exit Do statement to terminate the iteration. The general syntax for the Do loop is:

```
Do
    sequence of statements
    [If exit_condition Then Exit Do]
    sequence of statements
Loop
```

As you can see, if you add a While or Until clause at either end of the open loop, you end up with a Do-While or Do-Until loop.

An example of using a Do-Loop is shown here:

```
Sum# = 0
I% = 1
```

```
Do
   Term# = I%^2 / Factorial(I%)
   If Term# < 0.00001 Then Exit Do
   Sum# = Sum# + Term#
   I% = I% + 1
Loop
```

This loop calculates a summation series. Each term of the series is a function of the variable I%. As more terms are added, the value of each term decreases. The If statement, inside the loop, tests if the calculated term is too small, and accordingly exits the loop. If the value of the term is still significant, the remaining loop statements are executed and the loop reiterates.

Exiting from loops

The description of the normal use of the open Do-Loop earlier in this section included a discussion about using the Exit Do statement. While the Exit Do plays a key role in using the Do loop, it can still be used with the Do-While and Do-Until conditional loops. Similarly, the Exit For statement can be used with the For-Next loops to perform an "early" exit or loop termination. Using Exit Do and Exit For provides Visual Basic programming with powerful constructs that rival more structured languages like Pascal and C.

The following code example is a modified version of the Do loop example. A For-Next loop is used to calculate the summation series. Notice that the loop control, I%, ranges from 1 to 32767 (the upper limit of integers). In reality, the loop will iterate a few times before the tested condition invokes the Exit For:

```
Sum# = 0
For I% = 1 TO 32767
   Term# = I%^2 / Factorial(I%)
   If Term# < 0.00001 Then Exit For
   Sum# = Sum# + Term#
Next I%
```

Nesting control structures

Visual Basic allows you to write code that nests the various control structures. The Exit statements can serve to cleverly exit some or all of these nested control structures. An example of nesting control structures is given below—the code of a rather elaborate matrix initialization:

```
For I% = 1 To MatSize%
   For J% = 1 To MatSize%
      Select Case I%
```

```
      Case 1 To 10
         Mat#(I%, J%) = I% + J%
      Case 11 To 20
         Mat#(I%, J%) = I% * J%
      Case 21, 35, 65
         If J% > 5 Then
            Mat#(I%, J%) = I% + 2 * J%
         Else
            Mat#(I%, J%) = 0
         End If
      Case Else
         Mat#(I%, J%) = Sqr(I% * J%)
   End Select
 Next J%
Next I%
```

Sub and Function procedures

Visual Basic implements three types of routines: event-handling procedures, Sub procedures, and Function procedures. Event-handling procedures are actually special Sub procedures that handle specific events for certain objects. All of these procedures can call each other, as long as they are all located in the same form or module.

The event-handling procedures are Sub procedures that associate an object with an event. The names of these procedures are derived from the names of related the object and events. The general syntax for an event-handling procedure is:

```
SUB objectName_eventName([parameter list])
   sequence of statements
End Sub
```

When the program is running and you generate an event, such as a mouse click, the object where the event has occurred recognizes the event and attempts to respond to it. This attempt is made using the following steps:

1. The program locates the procedure that has the name of the responding object and the occurring event.
2. If the sought procedure exists, it is automatically called. When the event-handling procedure finishes working, the event is considered handled.
3. If the sought procedure does not exist, the event is abandoned.

Event-handling procedures are very similar to ordinary Sub procedures discussed next.

Sub procedures

The general syntax for a Sub procedure is:

```
Sub procedureName([parameter list])
    sequence of statements
End Sub
```

The parameter list contains a comma-delimited list of parameters that determine the amount and type of information that is passed to the Sub procedure. When a Sub procedure is invoked, a set of arguments is supplied to match the parameter list. The general syntax for each parameter is:

```
[By Val] parameterName [()] [As type]
```

The By Val option causes an argument (the value passed to a parameter when the procedure is called) to be passed *by value*. This means that a *copy* of the argument is submitted to the procedure. Consequently, any changes made to that argument inside the procedure do not affect the original argument. By default, arguments are passed *by reference*, unless they are expressions. Passing an argument by reference means that the procedure accesses the address of the argument. Consequently, any changes made to the argument inside the procedure affect that argument outside the procedure. Enclosing a variable in parentheses makes the argument an expression and passes its data by value. Passing arguments by reference offers a two-way communication of data between the procedure and its caller.

The parameter list may include arrays. To indicate that the parameter is an array, include the parentheses after the parameter name.

The data type of the parameters can be specified in one of two ways. The first method uses the type-declaration characters after the parameter name (!, @, #, $, %, or &). This method works only for the predefined data types. The second method uses the As type clause. This method must be used in declaring a parameter that is of a user-defined type. When declaring a parameter to be of a standard type, use one of the following names: Integer, Single, Double, Long, Currency, or String. In addition, Visual Basic allows you to pass special types, namely, Form and Control. These parameters enable you to use the procedure to set and query the properties of the forms and control objects at run time.

Examples of Sub procedures are shown here:

```
Option Base 1
Const True = −1, False = 0

Sub ShellSort(A( ) As String, By Val N As Integer, InOrder As Integer)
' Shell sort methods
Dim Skip, I, J As Integer
Dim Temp As String
```

```
        Skip = N
        Do While Skip > 1
          Skip = Skip \ 2
          InOrder = True
          Do
            For J = LBound(A, 1) To UBound(A,1) + N − 1 − Skip
              I = J + Skip
              If A(J) > A(I) Then
                Temp = A(I)
                A(I) = A(J)
                A(J) = Temp
                InOrder = False
              End If
            Next J
          Loop Until InOrder
        Loop
        End Sub

        Sub BinSearch(By Val Find$, A( ) As String, By Val N%, Index%)
        ' binary search in ordered arrays
        Dim Hi, Lo, Median As Integer
        Lo = LBound(A, 1)
        Hi = LBound(A, 1) + N − 1
        Do
          Median = (Lo + Hi) \ 2
          If Find$ < A(Media) Then
            Hi = Median − 1
          Else
            Lo = Median + 1
          End If
        Loop Until (Find$ = A(Median) Or (Lo > Hi)
        If Find$ = A(Median) Then
          Index% = Median
        Else
          Index% = LBound(A, 1) − 1
        End If
        End Sub

        Sub SearchData(By Val Find$, A( ) As String, By Val N%, InOrder%,
          Index%)
        ' search for Find$ in array A( )
        If Not InOrder% Then
          ShellSort A, N%, InOrder%
        End If
        BinSearch Find$, A, N%, Index%
        End Sub
```

The ShellSort procedure sorts the first N elements of the array, using the Shell-Metzner algorithm. The lower bounds of the array are not restricted to 0 or 1. The BinSearch procedure performs a binary search on the ordered array A. The first N elements are involved in the search. The SearchData procedure is a more general search procedure. It examines the value of the argument for InOrder. If that argument is not false (that is, true), it calls the ShellSort procedure to sort the array. The arguments A and InOrder% are passed by reference, allowing the ShellSort to change their values. By contrast, the argument N% is passed by value (as specified in the declaration of the parameter list). Once the array is sorted, the BinSearch procedure is called. The arguments Find$ and N% are passed by value (as specified in the declaration of the parameter list), while the arguments A and Index% are passed by reference. The Index% argument returns the index of the matching element or LBound(A,1)-1 if no match is found. It is recommended that arrays be passed by reference, to save memory. Passing by value means that the array is copied in memory. Since this process can be repeated in chained procedure calls, you may easily run out of memory when handling large arrays.

Function procedures

The general syntax for Function procedures is:

```
Function functionName([parameter list]) [As type]
    sequence of statements
    functionName = functionResult
    [sequence of statements]
End Function
```

The Function procedures resemble the Sub procedures in many aspects. The main difference is that the Function procedure, as the name might suggest, returns a value. Secondary differences between the Sub and the Function procedures include:

- When the function has no parameters, you must include empty parentheses with each function call.
- The data type of the function result is declared in one of two ways. The first uses the type-declaration character that is appended to the function's name. The second method employs the "As type" clause. The first method works only for the basic data types. The second method must be used with user-defined data types.
- The function result is obtained by assigning an expression to an identifier that matches the function's name.

Some examples of Function procedures are shown next. The functions BinSearch and SearchData are modified versions of the Sub procedures with the same name, shown earlier. Notice that for both functions, the search result is not returned via an argument passed by value. Instead, the sought result is returned using the function's names:

```
Function BinSearch(By Val Find$, A( ) As String, By Val N%) As Integer
' binary search in ordered arrays
Dim Hi, Lo, Median As Integer
Lo = LBound(A, 1)
Hi = LBound(A, 1) + N − 1
Do
    Median = (Lo + Hi) \ 2
    If Find$ < A(Media) Then
        Hi = Median − 1
    Else
      Lo = Median + 1
        End If
Loop Until (Find$ = A(Median) Or (Lo > Hi)
If Find$ = A(Median) Then
    BinSearch = Median
Else
    BinSearch = LBound(A, 1) − 1
End If
End Function

Function SearchData%(By Val Find$, A( ) As String, By Val N%, InOrder%)
' search for Find$ in array A( )
If Not InOrder% Then
    ShellSort A, N%, InOrder%
End If
SearchData% = BinSearch(Find$, A, N%)
  End Function
```

The data type of the result for the BinSearch function is declared using the As clause. By contrast, the data type of the result emitted by function SearchData is declared using the type-declaration character, %. Both functions return an integer result.

Exiting procedures

The Sub and Function procedures can be exited using the Exit Sub and Exit Function statements, respectively. These statements return control to the caller. Examples of using Exit Sub and Exit Function are shown next. The first procedure is a function that calculates factorials. If the value assigned to the parameter N is less than 2, it assigns a 1 to the function result and exits the function. Otherwise, the function calculates the factorial using a For-Next loop, as shown below:

```
Function Factorial (N As Integer) As Double
    Dim Product As Double
```

```
Dim I As Integer
' when N is less than 1, exit function
If N < 2 Then
    Factorial = 1 ' assign function result
    Exit Function ' exit from here
End If
' calculate factorial using a For-Next loop
Product = 1
For I = 1 TO N
    Product = Product * I
Next I
Factorial = Product ' assign function result
End Function
```

The next Sub procedure calculates the statistical mean and standard deviation, given the number of observations Sum#, the sum of observations SumX#, and the sum of the squares of the observations SumXX#. The mean and standard deviation are returned via the parameters Mean# and Sdev#. The procedure verifies whether the value of parameter Sum# is less than 2. If the test is positive, the procedure exits; otherwise, the sought statistics are calculated.

```
Sub CalcMeanSdev(By Val Sum#, By Val SumX#, By Val SumXX#, Mean#, Sdev#)
' calculate the mean and standard deviation
    Mean# = 0
    Sdev# = 0
    If Sum < 2 Then Exit Sub
    Mean# = SumX# / Sum#
    Sdev# = Sqr((SumXX# - SumX#^2 / Sum#) / (Sum# - 1))
End Sub
```

Static local variables

You can declare local variables using the Static statement instead of the Dim statement. The Static declaration results in storing the local variable in a fixed memory location, allowing the variable to retain its data between calls. Normally, local variables are erased once their host procedure returns control to the caller.

An example of using static variables is shown below. The ToggleButton_Click procedure toggles the case of the string in the TextBox text box. The static local variable Is_UCase is declared to keep track of the upper/lowercase state. As a static variable, Is_UCase is able to retain its data between procedure calls and properly toggle the case of the text box. If the IS_UCase variable is instead declared with a Dim statement, the event handler will always change the string in the text box to upper case:

```
Sub ToggleButton_Click ()
    Static Is_UCase As Integer
```

```
        If TextBox.Text = "" Then
            TextBox.Text = "Hello World!"
        Else
          If Is_UCase = 0 Then
            Is_UCase = 1
            TextBox.Text = UCase$(TextBox.Text)
          Else
            Is_UCase = 0
            TextBox.Text = LCase$(TextBox.Text)
          End If
        End If
    End Sub
```

You can declare the local variables of a procedure to be static. This is performed by placing the Static keyword before the Sub keyword. The local variables can then be explicitly declared with Static or Dim statements. The next example is a version of the ToggleButton_Click procedure that declares its local variables Is_UCase and Counter as static.

```
    Static Sub ToggleButton_Click ()
        Dim Is_UCase As Integer
        Dim Counter As Integer
        Counter = Counter + 1
        ' when Counter is 20 display a special string in the text box
        If Counter = 20 Then
            TextBox.Text = "Surprise!"
            Count = 1
            Exit Sub
        End If
        If TextBox.Text = "" Then
            TextBox.Text = "Hello World!"
        Else
          If Is_UCase = 0 Then
            Is_UCase = 1
            TextBox.Text = UCase$(TextBox.Text)
          Else
            Is_UCase = 0
            TextBox.Text = LCase$(TextBox.Text)
          End If
        End If
    End Sub
```

Form arguments

✳ One of the new aspects of the Visual Basic language is the ability to declare Forms and controls as parameters to procedures. The Form and Control keywords represent special data types that can be applied to procedural parameters. For example, the next Sub procedure enables you to set a new caption and display that caption in underlined bold characters:

```
Sub SetFormCaption(AnyForm As Form, NewCaption As String)
    AnyForm.Caption = NewCaption
    AnyForm.FontBold = −1
    AnyForm.FontUnderline = −1
End Sub
```

As the code for this procedure shows, you can assign new values to the properties of the form. Visual Basic does not allow you to assign data to the form itself, as in copying forms. Moreover, Visual Basic does not permit local variables to be declared with the type Form.

An application that contains the SetFormCaption procedure can issue the following calls:

```
SetFormCaption "Testing. . .1, 2, 3"
SetFormCaption "Bonjour!"
```

Control arguments

❋ Visual Basic enables you to declare parameters that have the Control type. This feature is even more powerful than passing Form-typed parameters, because the Control parameter can represent any kind of control. An example of a simple procedure that manipulates control is shown next:

```
Sub ToggleEnableState (AControl As Control)
    AControl.Enabled = Not AControl.Enabled
End Sub
```

The ToggleEnableState procedure toggles the Enabled property of the Control-typed argument. This procedure works with all of the Visual Basic objects except Clipboard, Debug, Printer, and Screen. You can invoke the ToggleEnabledState procedure with various control objects:

```
ToggleEnabledState Text1
ToggleEnabledState Command1
ToggleEnabledState Text2
ToggleEnabledState List1
```

☠ Warning! Since the properties of a control depends on the kind of control, you need to exercise care in coding procedures that have Control parameters. A run time error is generated if such a procedure attempts to change a nonexistent property of a Control-typed argument. Here is an example. Consider the following procedure that alters the caption of a control:

```
Sub SetCaption(AControl As Control, NewCaption As String)
    AControl.Caption = NewCaption
End Sub
```

Issuing SetCaption calls like the ones shown next cause no error, since the controls passed as arguments do have a Caption property:

```
SetCaption Check1 "Check it Out!"
SetCaption Check2 "Alright!"
SetCaption Box1 "FM/AM"
```

By contrast, attempting to alter the caption of controls like text boxes, directory lists boxes, and ordinary list boxes results in a run time error because these controls lack the Caption property:

```
SetCaption Text1 '--------------- Error!
SetCaption List1 '---------------Error!
```

There are two solutions for the above problem. The first one uses error-rapping techniques to handle the error. For example, the SetCaption procedure can be recoded to trap the error and simply exit:

```
Sub SetCaption(AControl As Control, NewCaption As String)
    On Error GoTo NoCaption ' set error trap
    AControl.Caption = NewCaption
    On Error GoTo 0 ' disable error
    Exit Sub ' exit OK
    NoCaption:
        On Error GoTo 0
        Resume ExitSub
    ExitSub:
End Sub
```

The second solution tackles the problem in a more radical manner. This technique uses the special TypeOf-Is Boolean operator to discern the exact type of control. The general syntax for using the TypeOf-Is operator is:

```
{ If ¦ Elseif } TypeOf control Is controlType Then
```

Visual Basic does not allow any other Boolean or relational operator to appear with the TypeOf-Is operator. Visual Basic uses the following keywords for controlType:

CheckBox	Frame	PictureBox
ComboBox	HScrollBar	TextBox
CommandButton	Label	Timer
DirListtBox	ListBox	VScrollBar
DriveListBox	Menu	
FileListBox	OptionButton	

Using the TypeOf-Is operator I can rewrite the SetCaption procedure to work with check and option boxes only. Passing controls of other types results in no action taken and no run time error:

```
Sub SetCaption(AControl As Control, NewCaption As String)
    If TypeOf AControl Is CheckBox Then
        AControl.Caption = NewCaption
    ElseIf TypeOf AControl Is OptionBox Then
        AControl.Caption = NewCaption
    End If
End Sub
```

Modules

Modules are program libraries that export supporting Sub and Function procedures to other modules or to the various Visual Basic forms. A module passes information to the other modules or forms using either global variables or arguments of procedures. Global variables are declared in the global module, making them accessible to all modules and forms. Consequently, they can pass data between modules and forms. Argument lists offer another, more controlled mechanism for passing data.

The global module

✳ The global module is a special module that contains declarations relevant to the forms and modules—especially the various procedures declared inside these forms and modules. Global modules are not allowed to contain any procedures. Instead, they are specialized with declaring the following items:

- Global variables. These will be discussed in the next section.
- Deftype statements. These statements specify the default type-definition characters. The Deftype statements only apply to the variables declared in the global module.
- Global constants.
- User-defined data types. Visual Basic requires that such data types be declared only in global modules. This results in having all user-defined types accessible to all parts of a Visual Basic application.

Use the Global keyword, instead of Dim, when declaring constants and variables in the global module.

Scope of variables

✳ As an implementation of BASIC, Visual Basic has surely come a long way from the earlier implementations of BASIC that were available up to the mid-1980s. These implementations lacked much structure in both code and data. For one, all variables were global. In addition, Sub and Function procedures were not available then, making the use of GOSUBs more prone to side effects, since all of the variables were global). This, among other reasons, made many programmers look down upon BASIC as an inferior and "toy" programming language.

The advent of Quick Basic began to address the deficiencies of the earlier BASIC implementations. Quick Basic introduced more structured code and data types. As the result of implementing Sub and Function procedures, multi-level data scoping was introduced, making certain variables accessible only at specific program parts.

Visual Basic has extended the levels of scoping variables. Figure A-1 shows the various levels of accessing variables. These levels are described in the following paragraphs.

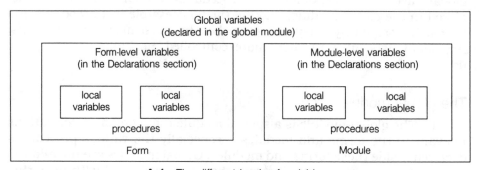

A-1 The different levels of variables.

Global variables   All of the variables declared in the global module of a Visual Basic application are recognized and accessed by all the program components. Global variables must be declared with the Global statement, as shown in the following example:

    Global StatusCode As Integer, StatusMessage As String

It is recommended that global variables be kept to a minimum. Usually, global variables are used to exchange information that is required by various procedures in different forms and modules.

Form and module variables   The variables declared in the general declarations section of a form is accessible by all of the procedures in that form. This enables these forms to share common information. Form-level variables are declared using the Dim statement, as shown in the example below:

    Dim TheFormState As Integer, InternalMessage As String

The variables appearing in the declarations section of a module are also visible to all of the procedures in that module. Form-level and module-level variables are very similar. They share similar purposes and data exchange mechanisms, and are declared in the same way.

Procedure (local) variables All variables declared inside an event-handling, normal Sub, or Function procedure are recognized only inside that procedure. You can declare local variables explicitly by using a Dim statement, or implicitly by simply using them. The latter is discouraged because you might be using the name of another variable that is declared in a higher level. If so, you will most likely change the data in the higher-level variable. Using the Dim statement ensures that the variable you declare overrides any higher-level variable with the same name.

An example of local variables is shown in the event handler Reverse-Button_Click, listed below:

```
Sub ReverseButton_Click ()
    Dim S As String
    Dim I, L As Integer
    If TextBox.Text = "" Then
        TextBox.Text = "Hello World!"
    Else
        L = Len(TextBox.Text)
        S = ""
        For I = 1 To L
            S = S + Mid$(TextBox.Text, L + 1 − I, 1)
        Next I
        TextBox.Text = S
    End If
End Sub
```

The variables S, I, and L are declared local to the procedure. These variables are recognized only in the ReverseButton_Click procedure and override any variables with the same names that are declared in the global or form levels.

The general rule for resolving the access of different variables with the same name, declared at different levels, is this: the variable with the lowest-level is the most accessible. Thus, for example, local variables override variables with the same names, declared in the host form, host module, or global module.

B
The companion disk

This book has a companion disk that contains the .MAK, .FRM, .BAS, and other files that are mentioned in this book. These files are located in the self-extracting archive file EASYVB.EXE. To install and unpack these files perform the following steps:

1. Select the \VB directory where your copy of Visual Basic is located. If you use a different name or different directory to store Visual Basic, then select that directory.
2. Create the subdirectory EASYVB by executing the following DOS command:

   C> MD EASYVB

3. Select the EASYVB subdirectory by executing the following DOS command:

   C> CD EASYVB

4. Insert the companion disk in drive A:.

5. Unpack the self-extracting archive file by executing the following command from DOS:

   C> A:EASYVB

   This command should unpack the archive file and install the files in directory \VB\EASYVB.

The Companion disk contains bonus utilities. Read the README.DOC file to learn more about these bonus programs.

Index

global declarations, HELP.GLB, 386
hlp file, 386-387
key file, 386
operation of program, 389, 395-396
SortKeys procedure, 395
source file sample, HELPIN-FO.TXT, 396
specifications, 387
conditional loops, 438
constants
 global, 426
 literal, 423-424
 local, 426
 symbolic, 426
Contacts Database program, VBCARD.FRM, 359-375
 AddBtn_Click, 372
 Clean_Up, 374
 ClearTextBoxes, 372-373
 coding, 364-371
 controls and buttons, 359-360
 controls list, 361
 custom settings, 362-363
 DelRecChk_Click, 373
 FindFirstBtn_Click, 373
 FindNextBtn_Click, 374
 Form_Load, 372
 global module, RANDOM.BAS, 363-364
 GotoBtn_Click, 374
 LoadCurRec, 372
 NextPct_Click, 374
 operation of program, 371-375
 PrevPct_Click, 374
 QuitBtn_Click, 375
 ReadCurRec, 371
 SaveCurRec, 372
 SaveThisRec, 372
 SortBtn_Click, 373
 specifications, 361
 text box procedures, 373
 WriteCurRec, 371
context-sensitivity of help system, 10-13
Control arguments, procedures use, 451-453
control arrays, 118-127, 431-432
 add new options, AddFileCom-_Click, 122
 delete options, DeleteFileCom-_Click, 125
 features, 118-120
 load file, QuickFilename_Click, 125
 menu use, 120-121
 option buttons grouping, 150-

151
 rules of use, 118-120
 Text File Viewer program use, 121-127
control objects
 aligning, 43-44
 altering properties, 22-23, 27-28, 47-57
 attaching code, 66-72
 coding, 59-73
 command buttons, 31
 current setting, changing, 52-53
 default settings, 47-51
 deleting, 42-43
 documentation of custom settings, 54-55
 drawing, 20-21, 39-40
 mouse management, 276-283
 moving, 41-42
 naming, 22-23, 27
 passing controls to DLL routines, 417
 Properties Bar, 47, 51-53
 property values, 47-51
 resizing, 40-41
 Scientific Calculator, changing settings/properties, 55-57
 source controls, mouse management, 278
 Text File Viewer program, 79
 viewing properties and settings, 51-52
Control Panel for Visual Basic, 3-4
 Code window, 4, 62-66
 Form window, 4
 Palette window, 4
 Project window, 4
 Properties bar, 3-4, 47, 51-53
 Toolbox, 4
control structures
 decision-making, 433-438
 loops, 438-444
 nested, 443-444
Conversions Program, multiple forms example, 132-141
coordinates, graphics, ScaleLeft and ScaleRight, 216
Countdown Timer program, 27-29
CurrentX and CurrentY properties, 196, 222

D

data exchange, 3
data types, 423-424
 Boolean, 66
 logical (see Boolean data

types)
 user-defined, 432-433
 user-defined, passing to DLL routines, 413
 variables declaration/definition (Deftype), 427
 Windows DLL routines, 418-419
databases (see Contacts Database program, VBCARD.FRM)
Date and Time program, 19-27
debugging, 3
decision-making control structures, 433-438
 If-Then, 433-434
 If-Then-Else, 434-435
 Select-Case, 5, 435-438
Default property, command buttons, 78
default$, 7, 168
defensive programming, run-time errors, 310
definition links, hypertext, help-system use, 10
Deftype, 427
delayed-error-handling errors, 315
destructive redimensioning, dynamic arrays, 431
dialog boxes
 buttons, number and type, type% parameter, 169-170
 default contents, default$ parameter, 168
 demonstration program, INPUTBOX.FRM, 170-173
 InputBox$, 168-173
 message position, msg$ parameter, 169
 MsgBox, 168-173
 multiple forms, 129-130
 prompt$ parameter, 168
 title$ parameter, 168
 upper right corner, xpos% and ypos%, 169
Dim, 431
Dir$ function, file I/O, 341
directories
 Directory list box, 36, 318-319, 320
 Directory Tree Viewer program, TREEVU1.FRM, 320-327
 DOSBAT.BAT batch file, 82
 paths, Path property, 318-319
Directory list box, 36, 318-319, 320
 Path property, 318-319
Directory Tree Viewer program,

Other Bestsellers of Related Interest

SQL: Structured Query Language
—2nd Edition—Dr. Carolyn J. Hursch and Dr. Jack L. Hursch

Carolyn J. Hursch and Jack L. Hursch present a complete overview of SQL, tracing its mathematical structure from its basis in first-order logic to its present-day role and the efforts of the American National Standards Institute (ANSI) to develop a standard SQL language. They cover all the components of conventional SQL language; SQL commands, keywords, and data types; and value expressions supported by SQL. 216 pages, illustrated. Book No. 3803, $21.95 paperback, $32.95 hardcover.

HOW TO GET MORE MILES PER GALLON IN THE 1990s—Robert Sikorsky

This new edition of a best-seller features a wealth of commonsense tips and techniques for improving gas mileage by as much as 100 percent. Sikorsky details specific gas-saving strategies that will greatly reduce aerodynamic drag and increase engine efficiency. New to this edition is coverage of the latest fuel-conserving automotive equipment, fuel additives, engine treatments, lubricants, and maintenance procedures that can help save energy. 184 pages, 39 illustrations. Book No. 3793, $7.95 paperback, $16.95 hardcover.

AutoCAD® PROGRAMMING—2nd Edition —Dennis N. Jump

Now, Dennis Jump has updated *AutoCAD Programming* to reflect changes and show you more ways to write accurate and efficient C code and customize the program to meet your individual needs. This edition covers changes to the DXF and DXB file formats, the addition of Binary DXF, new programming hooks, and techniques that take advantage of the Auto-CAD Device Interface. Jump also furnishes source code information that you can use as is or modify. 304 pages, 489 illustrations. Book No. 3779, $29.95 paperback, $39.95 hardcover.

ORACLE® DISTRIBUTED SYSTEMS: A C Programmer's Development Guide
—Kenneth Webb and Lori Lafreniere

Using the simple game of tic-tac-toe as an example, this book explains and demonstrates distributed applications, which run on a PC but maintain their data on a remote central computer. Key concepts developed include: modular C programming, the data communications components needed to support a distributed architecture; relational databases, with the focus on Oracle; graphic user interfaces on PCs; and machine learning. 352 pages, 270 illustrations. Book No. 3774, $24.95 paperback, $34.95 hardcover.

ADVANCED MS-DOS® BATCH FILE PROGRAMMING—2nd Edition—Dan Gookin

Here's a thorough introduction to advanced batch file programming that shows you how to customize your system and simplify many of your everyday computing tasks. Featuring more than 50 new batch files and utilities, this book goes beyond the introductory programs offered in other texts and gives you insight into the operation of your computer, including explanations of the newest release of DOS. 528 pages, 107 illustrations. Book No. 3745, $24.95 paperback, $36.95 hardcover.

OPTIMIZING MICROSOFT™ C LIBRARIES—Len Dorfman

Designed for novices as well as experienced programmers, this book outlines the newest features of the Microsoft C 6.0 compiler—the C compiler that also supports Windows 3.0. It shows you how to make the most of the program's optimizing features while planning and building a multi-model, optimized C library. All library functions are completely explained and documented with demonstration programs. Code and examples that you can use on your own system are included. 352 pages, 138 illustrations. Book No. 3735, $24.95 paperback, $34.95 hardcover.

BUILDING TURBO PASCAL® LIBRARIES:
Data Entry Tools—Jeremy G. Soybel

Create specialized function libraries in the Turbo Pascal environment using this three-in-one guide. Through a series of step-by-step tutorials, you'll develop consistent, easy-to-use interfaces for data management applications. This book presents a basic review of Turbo Pascal and the Environment Menu and specific solutions to everyday data entry and validation problems. 448 pages, 186 illustrations. Book No. 3734, $24.95 paperback only.

WORKING WITH ORACLE® DEVELOPMENT TOOLS
—Graham H. Seibert

Speed up online inquiries and simplify updates. Make data input and manipulation, menu access, form design, and report formatting and layout easier than ever. Discover new approaches to everything from relational data linking to laser printouts. Do all of this and more with the help of this new reference. It contains instructions for using Oracle's SQL*-Forms, SQL*ReportWriter, and SQL*Menu to solve a variety of database management problems. 536 pages, 172 illustrations. Book No. 3714, $24.95 paperback, $36.95 hardcover.

HANDBOOK OF DATA COMMUNICATIONS AND COMPUTER NETWORKS
—2nd Edition—Dimitris N. Chorafas

Completely revised and updated, this results-oriented reference—with over 125 illustrations—progresses smoothly as theory is combined with concrete examples to show you how to successfully manage a dynamic information system. You'll find applications-oriented material on networks, technological advances, telecommunications technology, protocols, network design, messages and transactions, software's role, and network maintenance. 448 pages, 129 illustrations. Book No. 3690, $44.95 hardcover only.

ASSEMBLY LANGUAGE SUBROUTINES FOR MS-DOS® —2nd Edition
—Leo J. Scanlon

Use this collection of practical subroutines to do high-precision math, convert code, manipulate strings and lists, sort data, display prompts and responses, read user commands and responses, work with disks and files, and more. Scanlon gives you instant access to over 125 commonly needed subroutines. Never again will you waste valuable time wading through manuals or tutorials. 384 pages, 211 illustrations. Book No. 3649, $24.95 paperback only.

ENHANCED MS-DOS® BATCH FILE PROGRAMMING—Dan Gookin

This new guide leads you through the development of batch files that incorporate the features of the latest DOS versions, commercial batch file extenders, and utilities written in high-level languages such as Pascal and C. The companion diskettes packaged with the book include the programs described—plus the utilities and source codes. 360 pages, 71 illustrations. Book No. 3641, $24.95 paperback, $34.95 hardcover.

COMPUTER MUSIC IN C
—Phil Winsor and Gene DeLisa

Whether you're a C programmer interested in music or a composer hoping to expand your musical horizon, you'll find dozens of useful pointers in this practical library of algorithms and related C programming functions. Specially designed and tested to ease the transition into computer-assisted composition, the book documents the mechanics of series and motif operations, probability distribution functions, sorting and searching algorithms, sound/text processing algorithms, general composition algorithms, and music graphics functions. 400 pages, 102 illustrations. Book No. 3637, $24.95 paperback only.

OBJECT-ORIENTED ASSEMBLY LANGUAGE—Len Dorfman

Simulate object-oriented program design features with macros! Spelling out instruction for programmers who want to go beyond the specialized syntax of C and Pascal, Dorfman provides you with the necessary theory and source code to simulate object-oriented design in Microsoft MASM and Borland Turbo Assembler. He shows you how to restructure a simple assembly program, section by section, using object-oriented design principles. 376 pages, 170 illustrations. Book No. 3620, $24.95 paperback only.

MASTERING PC TOOLS™ DELUXE —Paul Dlug

Master all the invaluable features of this program—including version 6.0 enhancements—from finding, previewing, and loading a file to using time- and effort-saving macros, and lots more! Each utility is explained in detail, with working examples and screen shots to illustrate specific features. Dlug covers data recovery, desktop tools, telecommunications, caching, DOS Shells, and hard disk backup. Arranged by utility, it makes a great reference, too! 272 pages, 279 illustrations. Book No. 3578, $16.95 paperback only.

Prices Subject to Change Without Notice.

Look for These and Other TAB Books at Your Local Bookstore

To Order Call Toll Free 1-800-822-8158
(in PA, AK, and Canada call 717-794-2191)

or write to TAB Books, Blue Ridge Summit, PA 17294-0840.

Title	Product No.	Quantity	Price

☐ Check or money order made payable to TAB Books

Charge my ☐ VISA ☐ MasterCard ☐ American Express

Acct. No. _____ Exp. _____

Signature: _____

Name: _____

Address: _____

City: _____

_____ Zip: _____

Subtotal $ _____

Postage and Handling
($3.00 in U.S., $5.00 outside U.S.) $ _____

Add applicable state and local
sales tax $ _____

TOTAL $ _____

TAB Books catalog free with purchase; otherwise send $1.00 in check or money order and receive $1.00 credit on your next purchase.

Orders outside U.S. must pay with international money order in U.S. dollars.

TAB Guarantee: If for any reason you are not satisfied with the book(s) you order, simply return it (them) within 15 days and receive a full refund.
BC